The Name of War

The Name of War

KING PHILIP'S WAR AND

THE ORIGINS OF AMERICAN

IDENTITY · JILL LEPORE

ALFRED A. KNOPF *New York* 1999

THIS IS A BORZOI BOOK
PUBLISHED BY ALFRED A. KNOPF, INC.

Copyright © 1998 by Jill Lepore
Map copyright © 1998 by Claudia Carlson

All rights reserved under International and Pan-American Copyright Conventions. Published in the United States by Alfred A. Knopf, Inc., New York, and simultaneously in Canada by Random House of Canada Limited, Toronto. Distributed by Random House, Inc., New York.

www.randomhouse.com

Portions of Chapter 1 are reprinted from "Dead Men Tell No Tales: John Sassamon and the Fatal Consequences of Literacy" (*American Quarterly* 46, December 1994), by permission of The Johns Hopkins University Press.

Library of Congress Cataloging-in-Publication Data
Lepore, Jill, [date]
    The name of war : King Philip's War and the origins of American identity / by Jill Lepore. — 1st ed.
        p.   cm.
    Includes bibliographical references and index.
    ISBN 0-679-44686-9 (hc)
    1. King Philip's War, 1675–1676.   2. Indians of North America—Wars—1600–1750.   3. Great Britain—Colonies—America.
    4. United States—Politics and government—To 1775.   I. Title.
    E87.876.L46   1998
    973.2'4—dc21   97–2820
                                                                    CIP

Manufactured in the United States of America
Published February 3, 1998
Reprinted Three Times
Fifth Printing, February 1999

To my parents

MARJORIE AND FRANK LEPORE

Contents

What's in a Name?

Words like devastation, rape, slaughter, carnage, starvation are lock and key words to keep the pain at bay. Words about war that are easy on the eye.
I'm telling you stories. Trust me.
—JEANETTE WINTERSON,
The Passion

This is a study of war, and of how people write about it. Writing about war can be almost as difficult as waging it and, often enough, is essential to winning it. The words used to describe war have a great deal of work to do: they must communicate war's intensity, its traumas, fears, and glories; they must make clear who is right and who is wrong, rally support, and recruit allies; and they must document the pain of war, and in so doing, help to alleviate it. Not all words about war do all these things, but most of them do some. The words used to describe and define war are among the tiredest in any language. "Bloody," "brutal," "cruel," "savage," "atrocious"—all are overused and imprecise. And yet they remain shocking, perhaps because of their very vagueness. How does someone far from the scene of battle imagine "savage cruelty" except by thinking the worst?

Words about war are often lies. False reports, rumors, deceptions. One nation's propaganda may be its enemy's profanity: truth in war is relative (which is not to say that some kinds of killing aren't worse than others). "Each man calls barbarism whatever is not his own practice," Montaigne observed. Or, to paraphrase Hobbes, one man calls cruelty what another calls justice.[1]

Such words about war, truths, lies, or fine distinctions, constitute what political scientist Michael Walzer has called a "moral vocabulary of warfare," the
language by which combatants justify their own actions while vilifying their
opponents.[2] I call your attack a massacre, you call my resistance treachery. One
of us may be lying, but one of us may lie dying. If I die, your word, "treachery," is almost as important as my wound, since you alone survive to make
meaning of my death. War is a contest of injuries and of interpretation. As the
literary critic Elaine Scarry has argued, war "differs from all other contests in
that its outcome carries the power of its own enforcement."[3] My death gives
you the power to claim the victory. And, even if I survive, you can force me to
confess to "treachery."

Words about war are slippery, and "war" itself may be the slipperiest of all.
War is hell, we say, and war's a game. War is a contagion, the universal perversion. War is politics by other means, at best barbarism, a mean, contemptible
thing. We say many things about war, not all of them profound, and few as
pithy as these.[4] Eminently quotable remarks aside, war is perhaps best understood as a violent contest for territory, resources, and political allegiances, and,
no less fiercely, a contest for meaning. At first, the pain and violence of war are
so extraordinary that language fails us: we cannot name our suffering and,
without words to describe it, reality itself becomes confused, even unreal.[5] But
we do not remain at a loss for words for long. Out of the chaos we soon make
new meanings of our world, finding words to make reality real again, usually
words like "atrocity" and "betrayal." War twice cultivates language: it requires
justification, it demands description.

To say that war cultivates language is not to ignore what else war does: war
kills. Indeed, it is the central claim of this book that wounds and words—the
injuries and their interpretation—cannot be separated, that acts of war gener-
ate acts of narration, and that both types of acts are often joined in a common
purpose: defining the geographical, political, cultural, and sometimes racial
and national boundaries between peoples. If you kill me and call my resistance
"treachery," you have succeeded not only in killing me (and in so doing, ensuring that I will not be able to call your attack a "massacre"), but you have also
succeeded in calling me and my kind a treacherous people. In attacking me,
you have kept me out of your territory; in calling my resistance "treachery,"
you make clear that I was not worthy to be your neighbor. Your success, however, may be short-lived. Future generations and future historians, certainly
my descendants and perhaps even yours, may tell the story of our battle differently. They may even declare it a "massacre." How wars are remembered can
be just as important as how they were fought and first described. If future generations call your attack a "massacre," new ideas about themselves, rather than

any new evidence about you or me, may propel them to do it. Waging, writing, and remembering a war all shape its legacy, all draw boundaries.

How this all works, of course, is rather more complicated than this crude example suggests. War is rarely so straightforward, and most wars require more than a bit of unraveling. Today, one way we unravel wars is with pictures. Since words about war can be easily exhausted of meaning and their truth easily questioned, pictures can sometimes mean more to us. When we hear "atrocity," it is almost impossible not to see stock images: smoking furnaces at Auschwitz, the bloody killing fields of Cambodia, lifeless Bosnian bodies lining a Sarajevo street. Newsreels, photographs, satellite videos. The pictures haunt us. Yet such images were not always so abundant, not because there were fewer atrocities but because they could not be so skillfully captured. Except with words.

This, then, is a study of a war before television, before film, before photography. It is a study of a war in an age and in a place where even crude wood engravings were rare and printed books an uncommon commodity. When the English and Algonquian peoples of seventeenth-century New England went to war in 1675, they devastated one another. In proportion to population, their short, vicious war inflicted greater casualties than any other war in American history.[6] Yet just a single image of the fighting survives: half a dozen tiny, crouching figures shooting at one another along the creases of John Seller's map of New England printed in an English atlas in 1675. It tells us precious little.

The fighting shown on Seller's map began in June 1675, when three men were hanged by the neck not far from Plymouth Rock. They had been convicted of murdering a man named John Sassamon, who, weeks before his death, had warned the governor of Plymouth Colony that Philip, a Wampanoag Indian leader, was planning to wage war against the English settlers. The three convicted men, all Wampanoags loyal to Philip, were suspected of killing Sassamon, a Christian Indian minister, as punishment for his betrayal. On the gallows, two died the slow, jerky death of strangulation; the third was saved when his rope frayed as he dangled and, finally, dropped him to the ground. But two deaths were more than enough to start a war. Whatever his original intentions, Philip began attacking English towns on June 24, just days after his men were hanged. Over the next fourteen months, one English town after another was laid waste. In July, Middleborough, Dartmouth, Plymouth, and Mendon were attacked. Brookfield in August. Springfield, Hatfield, and Northampton in October. Then, in the winter, Pawtuxet, Lancaster, Medfield, Groton, Longmeadow, Marlborough, Simsbury, and Providence. Still more the following summer. It seemed to the colonists as if the Indians had

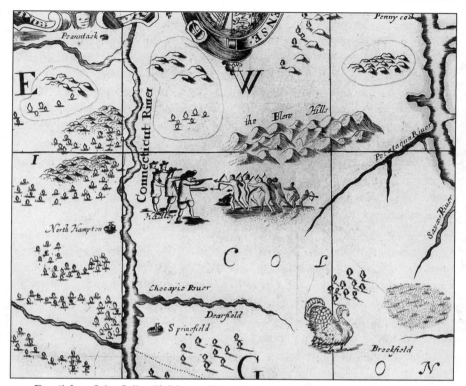

Detail from John Seller, "A Mapp of New England, 1675." *Courtesy of the John Carter Brown Library at Brown University*

"risen almost round the countrey."[7] And indeed, as the war progressed, other northeastern Algonquians—Nipmucks and Pocumtucks in central and western Massachusetts, Narragansetts in Rhode Island, and Abenakis in Maine—joined Philip's campaign or fought the English for reasons of their own.[8] By August 1676, when Philip was shot to death near his home in Mount Hope, twenty-five English towns, more than half of all the colonists' settlements in New England, had been ruined and the line of English habitation had been pushed back almost to the coast. The struggling colonists had nearly been forced to abandon New England entirely, and their losses left them desperately dependent on England for support.[9]

Yet Indian losses were far, far greater. Colonial armies, with their Pequot and Mohegan allies, pursued enemy Indians from Narragansett Bay to the Connecticut River Valley, killing warriors in the field and families in their homes. Those Algonquians who fought the English saw their communities decimated: thousands were killed in the fighting while thousands more died of disease or starvation or were shipped out of the colonies as slaves. Those who retreated beyond the Connecticut River found themselves fighting on two fronts: with their traditional Iroquois enemies, the Mohawks, to the west, and with the English to the east. Closer to the Atlantic, not even Christian Indians loyal to the English were spared; in the fall of 1675 most were removed from their towns and imprisoned on barren islands, where many died of cold or hunger during the long winter. Always brutal and everywhere fierce, King Philip's War, as it came to be called, proved to be not only the most fatal war in all of American history but also one of the most merciless.

However remarkable for the magnitude of its destruction and the depth of its cruelties, King Philip's War is almost as remarkable for how much the colonists wrote about it: more than four hundred letters written during the war survive in New England archives alone, along with more than thirty editions of twenty different printed accounts. In letters, diaries, and chronicles, Englishmen and -women in New England expressed their agonies, mourned their losses, and, most of all, defended their conduct.[10] Not all colonists agreed about the causes of the war, or about how it should be waged, but most agreed about what was at stake: their lives, their land, and their sense of themselves. And, in the end, their writings proved to be pivotal to their victory, a victory that drew new, firmer boundaries between English and Indian people, between English and Indian land, and between what it meant to be "English" and what it mean to be "Indian."[11]

Yet those boundaries were never stable, either before or after the war. Seventeenth-century New England was, after all, a frontier, at once a dividing line and a middle ground between at least two cultures.[12] Boundary setting, as frontier historians have pointed out, is "the very essence of frontier life."[13] And it has been the fate of the American frontier to endlessly repeat itself. (And, perhaps, to echo across the continent: not long after King Philip's War ended, unrelated hostilities erupted in New Mexico when Pueblo Indians revolted to free themselves of Spanish rule.[14]) The same cultural anxieties and land conflicts that drove Indians and colonists to war in 1675 would continue to haunt them after the war had ended. Not only that, but their descendants, and their distant relatives, peoples from other parts of Europe and from more western parts of America, would fight uncannily similar wars over and over again.[15] King Philip's War was not, as some historians have suggested, the foundational American frontier experience or even the archetypal Indian war.[16] Wars like it had been fought before, and every war brings its own stories, its own miseries. Yet there remains something about King Philip's War that hints of allegory. In a sense, King Philip's War never ended. In other times, in other places, its painful wounds would be reopened, its vicious words spoken again.

War cultivates language, but frontier wars cultivate language in a very particular way. As Patricia Nelson Limerick has written, "the process of invasion, conquest, and colonization was the kind of activity that provoked shiftiness in verbal behavior."[17] Much of that shiftiness has its roots in European ideas about nature, God, and man, ideas that can be traced to the earliest New World encounters and to questions about the humanity of the indigenous peoples of America. And words are at the center of the encounter between the Old World and the New, between the European "self" and the native American "other."[18] As the bishop of Avila famously remarked when presenting Queen Isabella with the first Spanish grammar book in 1492, "Language is the perfect instrument of empire."[19] Yet seventeenth-century English colonists in New England were plagued with anxieties of identity, not of self and other but of a more complicated, triangulated self, other, and another.[20] At least as far back as the Reformation, the English had measured themselves—their civility, their piety, their humanity—against other Europeans, especially the Spanish, whom they condemned for their cruelty to Protestants during the Spanish Inquisition. And, after the first European ventures to the New World, the English continued to measure themselves against the Spanish, whom they again condemned for cruelty, now against Indians during the conquest of Mexico.[21] If papistry was a defining element of infidelity, cruelty was a defining element of savagery. Yet a cruel European, from the perspective of the English, was still better than a savage, just as a papist was clearly more pious than a pagan.

Distinctions such as these lay behind much of the Puritans' moral posturing in their writing about King Philip's War. As Stephen Greenblatt has written, "Language is, after all, one of the crucial ways of distinguishing between men and beasts," and, as I argue, the language of cruelty and savagery was the vocabulary Puritans adapted to this end.[22] English colonists in New England defined themselves against both the Indians' savagery and the Spaniards' cruelty: between these two similar yet distinct "others," one considered inhuman and one human, the English in New England attempted to carve out for themselves a narrow path of virtue, piety, and mercy. Out of the chaos of war, English colonists constructed a language that proclaimed themselves to be neither cruel colonizers like the Spaniards nor savage natives like the Indians. Later on, after nearly a century of repetition on successive American frontiers, this triangulated conception of identity would form the basis of American nationalism as it emerged in the late eighteenth and early nineteenth centuries. But by that time, the British had come to replace the Spanish as the third element of the triangle.[23] Meanwhile, Algonquians in New England, who, in the seventeenth century, had defined themselves in opposition to their English and Iroquois neighbors, created a new ethnic identity two centuries later. And, in the twentieth century, they would come to define their own, Indian, nationalism.

WORDS ABOUT WAR—even the names of wars—can be contentious indeed. Historians, admittedly a contentious lot, have failed even to agree on what to *call* King Philip's War. Its very name, each word in its title—"King," "Philip's," "War"—has been passionately disputed. Philip is said to have been neither a "king" nor, truly, "Philip," and not only historians but contemporaries, too, have insisted that what took place in New England in 1675 and 1676 was simply too nasty to "deserve the Name of a War."[24]

Can what happened in New England in 1675 and 1676 rightly be called "King Philip's War"? Alas, three impassioned arguments say no. The first condemns the colonists' aggression and suggests that the conflict be called a "Puritan Conquest." The second celebrates Indian resistance and proposes "Metacom's Rebellion," insisting that Philip is more accurately referred to by his Algonquian name, Metacom (sometimes rendered as "Metacomet" or "Pometacom"), and that calling him a "king" is derisive. A third argument takes the view that the fighting is better understood as an Indian civil war, since many Mohegans and Pequots, as well as Christian Indians, fought alongside the English against the Wampanoags, Pocumtucks, Nipmucks, and Narragansetts.[25] But what really happened? Did the Puritans conquer? Did Metacom rebel? Did one Indian brother fight another? Did King Philip wage a war? Yes, yes, yes, and yes again.

All wars have at least two names. In Vietnam, the conflict Americans call the "Vietnam War" is called the "American War." What most Americans now call the "Civil War" has been called (by Northerners) the "War of the Rebellion" and (by Southerners) the "War of Northern Aggression." Names of wars are always biased; they always privilege one perspective over another. This is no less true of "Metacom's Rebellion" than it is of "King Philip's War." And, though names of wars may tell us a good deal, they rarely tell us everything. Calling what happened between 1739 and 1742 the "War of Jenkins' Ear" tells us about the sad fate of a British sea captain's auditory apparatus, but not that the war was fought between England and Spain. Still, it is a telling name, since Captain Robert Jenkins' ear, cut off by the Spanish as punishment for smuggling, became a symbol of the conflict (especially after Jenkins presented it to Parliament). "King Philip's War" is telling in this same way. Philip was not, literally, a king; his own people may have called him by a name other than "Philip"; and, at the time, they probably called the fighting something other than "King Philip's War." Nevertheless, Philip did begin a war in which his people's sovereignty (their "kingdom") was lost, and his death did become a symbol of the English victory. (His decapitated head was staked on a pole for public viewing in Plymouth.) Meanwhile, the colonists did call what happened "King Philip's War," and the very fact that what their enemies called it has not survived ("Metacom's Rebellion" is mere conjecture) is part of what the fighting was about in the first place: it was a contest for meaning—and the colonists won.

"King Philip's War" is not unbiased, but its biases are telling. (And some of its biases are less biased than historians have assumed.) Perhaps it will be best to consider each of the contested terms in "King Philip's War" in turn. To begin with, calling an Indian leader a "king," though it eventually became mocking, began as a simple (though inaccurate) translation of *sachem.* The English called many prominent Indian leaders "kings," partly in recognition of the sachems' very real political authority and partly as a result of the colonists' overestimation of that authority. Most sachemships were hereditary, and English colonists saw them as roughly analogous to European monarchies, however much smaller in scale; "king" might have seemed a fitting, if not entirely satisfactory, translation of "sachem." "Philip," too, was an English creation; it was the name given to Metacom when he and his brother Wamsutta appeared before the Plymouth Court in 1660 as a gesture of friendship and fidelity.[26] In 1677 one colonist, with the benefit of hindsight, suggested that Metacom, "for his ambitious and haughty Spirit," had been originally "nick-named King Philip."[27] But, in 1660, naming Metacom and Wamsutta "Philip" and "Alexander" after the ancient leaders of Macedonia was most likely a reference (oblique to us but obvious to them) to the seal of the Massachusetts Bay Colony, an engraving of an Indian mouthing the words, "Come Over and Help Us," and itself an echo of Acts 16:9, in which the Apostle Paul sees a vision of a Macedonian begging him, "Come over into Macedonia, and help us."[28] Plymouth authorities, like their Massachusetts counterparts, saw Indians as pagan Macedonians who, at heart, were desperate for the light of the gospel. "Philip" was no compliment, but that doesn't make it a joke.

"War" is, of course, the slipperiest, most disputed word in "King Philip's War," but the recently proposed alternatives are poor substitutes. "Conquest" implies that the outcome of the hostilities was predetermined, while "rebellion" suggests that Philip was a treasonous subject of King Charles. Neither is quite true (much as the colonists would have liked to believe both). "Indian Civil War" rings false, too, since, although the colonists were quick to call upon Indian allies, the majority on both sides perceived the war as an English-on-Indian conflict. In the end, "war" may be the word that takes the conflict most seriously, but, tellingly, even at the time of the fighting, the word "war"

Seal of the Massachusetts Bay Colony.
Courtesy of the Massachusetts Archives

sparked controversy. In the fall of 1676, soon after Philip's death, Increase Mather, the Puritan minister of Boston, published *A Brief History of the Warr with the Indians in New-England.* A few months later, William Hubbard, minister of nearby Ipswich, took exception to the title of Mather's book. In the preface to his own *Narrative of the Troubles with the Indians in New-England,* Hubbard distinguished his book from Mather's by explaining that he had titled his work a "narrative" because "the Matter of Fact therein related (being rather Massacres, barbarous inhumane Outrages, than Acts of Hostility or valiant Atchievements) no more deserve the Name of a War than the Report of them the Title of an History."[29] Here was no "history" of a "war"; this was a "narrative" of some "troubles." In Hubbard's mind, to call the conflict a "war" and the account of it a "history" gave it a dignity it did not deserve, not to mention giving Mather stature he did not merit. Hubbard no doubt bridled that, in his own preface, Mather had boasted, "I have performed the part of an *Historian.*"[30] Did Mather pretend to be Thucydides? Did he suggest that what happened in New England in 1675 and 1676 could be likened to the Peloponnesian War? Perhaps it is only fair to observe that Increase Mather was a bombastic bully, but ultimately the two ministers' petty squabbling is beside the point. When Hubbard declared that the Indians' fighting—"Massacres, barbarous inhumane Outrages"—simply did not "deserve the Name of a War," he made Mather seem somewhat pretentious; more importantly, he made New England's Algonquians seem entirely inhuman.

The Reverends Hubbard and Mather, much as they bickered, had a great deal in common. Most importantly, they shared what the seventeenth-century English scholar Samuel Purchas called the "literall advantage": they could write, and most Indians could not. "Want of Letters," Purchas argued, left Indians in awe of Europeans' astounding abilities and led them "to thinke the Letter it selfe could speake." Compared to men who could read and write, Indians were no more than "speaking Apes." For Purchas, the "literall advantage" truly separated men from beasts—"amongst Men, some are accounted Civill, and more both Sociable and Religious, by the Use of letters and Writing, which others wanting are esteemed Brutish, Savage, Barbarous."[31] With this, both William Hubbard and Increase Mather would have agreed. Like all literate Europeans in the New World, Hubbard and Mather had a veritable monopoly on making meaning, or at least on translating and *recording* the meaning of what they saw and did, and even of what they supposed the Indians to have seen, done, and said. And herein lies the circularity of the "literall advantage": "speaking Apes" cannot respond in writing to the writers who label them inhuman.

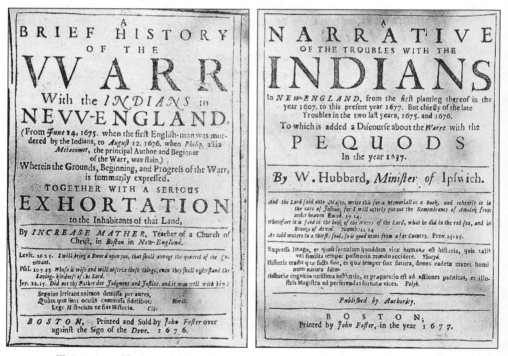

Title pages of Increase Mather, *Brief History*, LEFT, and William Hubbard, *Narrative*, RIGHT. *Both courtesy of the American Antiquarian Society*

LEFT: *Reverend Increase Mather,* London, 1688, by Jan Van der Spriett. *Courtesy of the Massachusetts Historical Society.* RIGHT: *Ninigret, Sachem of the Niantics,* c. 1681, unidentified artist. *Courtesy of the Museum of Art, Rhode Island School of Design. Gift of Mr. Robert Winthrop*

Nowhere are differences like the "literall advantage" better illustrated than in the contrast between two portraits from the 1680s, one of Mather himself, and one of Ninigret, a Narragansett sachem.[32] Mather sits in his library, studying his books and manuscripts; Ninigret stands in the woods, armed with a knife and club. To the Europeans who painted these portraits, Mather was clothed in the fine fabrics of arts and letters (his collar even seems to be made of the pages of an open book), while Ninigret was naked in body, mind, and soul.

If, in the seventeenth century, the "literall advantage" proved decisive, recent challenges to the name "King Philip's War" have attempted to even the odds, to take away the colonists' monopoly on making meaning of the war by asking, What would the Indians have called it? Most historians who have asked this question have begun with the assumption that no Algonquian would have called the conflict "King Philip's War." But those who spoke English might have. At least one Nipmuck, in a note tacked to a tree outside a burning English town, called the fighting a "war," and Metacom at least occasionally called himself "King Philip."[33] (A rebellious letter written from Mount Hope to the governor of Plymouth and transcribed by Philip's inter-

[handwritten signature: Philip alias metacom his P marke]

Mark of Philip, alias Metacom

preter, Tom Sancsuik, begins, "King Philip desire to let you understand that he could not come to the Court."[34]) Moreover, Philip, who probably knew the alphabet, signed documents with a "P," not an "M"—only his scribes occasionally added "alias Metacom" to his mark, probably to accommodate the colonists, who were meticulous record-keepers.[35]

It is possible that Philip called himself "Philip" when addressing the English and "Metacom" when talking with Indians. But it seems more likely that he simply abandoned the name Metacom after 1660. After all, Philip was raised in a culture in which people commonly adopted new names, leaving old names behind. Edward Winslow had observed in 1624, "All their names are significant and variable, for when they come to the state of men and women, they alter them according to their deeds or dispositions."[36] For just this reason, it is possible that Philip renamed himself during the war, to mark a new stage in his life, but surely he would not have returned to Metacom, the name of his youth. That no record of Philip's new name survives should come as no surprise. Those who knew Philip by the name he went by at the time of his death, in August 1676, would not have uttered it: a strict naming taboo prohibited it. As Roger Williams had reported, "the naming of their dead *Sachims,* is one ground of their warres"; in 1665 Philip himself had traveled to Nantucket to kill an Indian who had spoken the name of his deceased father, Massasoit.[37] If Philip took another name during the war, it has not survived. (Although one small, uncorroborated bit of evidence suggests that he may have been renamed "Wewesawamit."[38]) And, since he seems to have initially taken "Philip" in earnest, calling him "Metacom" today is no truer to his memory, especially because "Metacom" became a popular substitute for "Philip" only in the early nineteenth century, when white playwrights, poets, and novelists sought to make the war sound more authentically, and romantically, Indian.[39]

Unfortunately, as relates to seventeenth-century evidence, there are few clues about what Algonquians might have called the war, with the important exceptions of Philip's inky "P" and rare notes left by retreating Indians. Nearly all of what we know about the fighting—whether "brief histories" or "narratives of troubles"—comes from the colonists themselves, and, as the Massachusetts seal ("Come Over and Help Us") so poignantly illustrates, more than a bit of skepticism must be brought to words the colonists quite literally put into the mouths of their Algonquian neighbors. Yet those neighbors were neither as silent as the colonists hoped nor as "inarticulate" as most historians have assumed. Still, perhaps the question of what Algonquians might have called King Philip's War is ultimately futile. Or perhaps it is simply the wrong question. In either case, the question this study asks is slightly different: If war is, at least in part, a contest for meaning, can it ever be a fair fight when only one side has access to those perfect instruments of empire, pens, paper, and printing presses?

THIS STUDY ASKS other questions, too, of course, questions about cruelty, language, memory, and, most of all, identity. I argued earlier that war cultivates language, but in writing this book it has at times seemed to me that war cultivates questions, many of them disturbing and all too few of them answerable. Scholars of the generation whose work has most inspired me were themselves compelled to write about war because of their experiences as witnesses of Vietnam, a war best remembered for the debate over whether it ought to have been waged at all. In his tellingly titled *Just and Unjust Wars*, for instance, Michael Walzer explained, "I did not begin by thinking about war in general, but about particular wars, above all the American intervention in Vietnam."[40] Nor did I, nearly two decades after Walzer, begin by thinking about war in general, but about a particular conflict, the Persian Gulf War. That war, noted for its excess of video images through extensive television coverage, led me to wonder how war could be represented without pictures. In an age when there were few technologies for visual representation, how effective were words in describing and justifying war? That question, in turn, led me to consider how cultures lacking not only television but also literacy come to terms with war. And, like Walzer, while I began by thinking about a particular war, I soon found myself facing some rather grand philosophical questions. To me, the most pressing of these is, How do people reconcile themselves to war's worst cruelties? Or, as Elaine Scarry put it, "By what perceptual process does it come about that one human being can stand beside another human being in agonizing pain and not know it, not know it to the point where he himself inflicts it?"[41] Between each line and on the words on every page, this question drives my investigation. Yet nowhere do I answer it, nor did I ever expect to. It has seemed to me the most unanswerable of all.

As distressing as it can be to study cruelty, King Philip's War, like most bulky chunks of the past, is filled with fascinating characters, bizarre happenings, and strange tales. Not surprisingly, I have found myself caught up in these stories, with the result that the questions that brought me to this topic, however urgent, are sometimes seduced into slumber by the cunning charms of a pressing plot. Analysis, however, is a light sleeper. Just when it seems that plot might take over entirely, rest assured that analysis will soon be awake, as cranky and demanding as ever. In the end, this book is just another story about just another war, but happily, along the way it is also a murder mystery, an adventure story, and a tale of peril on the high seas.

The structure of this book is shaped both by the action of the war and by my own ideas about its importance. Bookended by the Prologue and the Epilogue, the four parts of this study—Language, War, Bondage, and Memory—describe and define four elements of the conflict and also four themes of my analysis. Part One examines why so many colonists wrote so much about King Philip's War while New England's Algonquians wrote so little, investigating, along the way, how war alters an individual's relationship to language. Next, Part Two traces how boundaries were drawn during King Philip's War, both on the physical landscape and on the landscape of the human body, and how the war's cruelties were explained and justified by both sides, especially in religious terms. Part Three contrasts New Englanders' differing experiences of bondage during the war: captivity, confinement, slavery. Last, Part Four analyzes how subsequent generations of Americans have remembered King Philip's War, most notably through *Metamora; or, the Last of the Wampanoags,* a wildly popular play that was performed in theaters across America in the 1830s and 1840s.

Meanwhile, to preserve the flavor of the stories of King Philip's War, and most especially to help readers appreciate the differences in the spoken and written language among colonists and Indians, I have preserved the original spelling, punctuation, and capitalization in all seventeenth- and eighteenth-century sources with the following important exceptions: superscribed characters have been brought down; abbreviations have been spelled out; fanciful or conventional italics have been removed, unless they were clearly intended for emphasis; mistaken homonyms ("there" used for "their") have been corrected if their usage might confuse the reader, but not otherwise; and, when relevant, the following letters have been changed: "u" to "v," "v" to "u," "j" to "i," "y" to "th," and "t" to "c."[42] (Remember that what we see as poor spelling does not always imply poor education; seventeenth-century spelling is entirely idiosyncratic.) Additionally, all "old style" dates have been modernized—that is, dates between January 1 and March 25 have been changed to the modern calendar and are considered part of the new year (thus, what in seventeenth-century notation is "February 10, 1675/6" is here rendered as "February 10, 1676"). And, in rendering Algonquian personal names, whose spellings often vary tremendously, I have in each case chosen the least quirky and simplest spelling for use in the text; variant spellings are recorded in the notes.

Finally, a word about the title of this study. In 1677, when William Hubbard explained why he had called his account of King Philip's War a "narrative," he uttered the mouthful that bears repeating: "The Matter of Fact therein related (being rather Massacres, barbarous inhumane Outrages, than Acts of Hostility or valiant Atchievements) no more deserve the Name of a War than the Report of them the Title of an History."[43] A better illustration of the importance of language I could not have asked for, and so, with a nod to Reverend Hubbard, I borrow the title for this, my own set of words about war.

A Brief Chronology of King Philip's War

1675

JANUARY

29   John Sassamon dies at Assawampsett Pond.

JUNE

8   Sassamon's alleged murderers are executed at Plymouth.

11   Wampanoags are reported in arms near Swansea.

14–25 Rhode Island, Plymouth, and Massachusetts authorities attempt negotiation with Philip and seek guarantees of fidelity from Nipmucks and Narragansetts.

24   Wampanoags begin attacking Swansea.

26   Massachusetts troops march to Swansea to join Plymouth troops.

26–29 Wampanoags attack Rehoboth and Taunton, elude colonial troops, and leave Mount Hope for Pocasset. Mohegans travel to Boston and offer to fight on the English side.

JULY

8–9 Wampanoags attack Middleborough and Dartmouth.

14   Nipmucks attack Mendon.

15   Narragansetts sign a peace treaty with Connecticut.

16–24 Massachusetts envoy attempts to negotiate with the Nipmucks.

19   Philip and his troops escape an English siege and flee Pocasset for Nipmuck territory.

August

2–4   Nipmucks attack Massachusetts troops and besiege Brookfield.

13   Massachusetts Council orders Christian Indians confined to praying towns.

22   A group of unidentified Indians kill seven colonists at Lancaster.

30   Captain Samuel Moseley arrests fifteen Hassanemesit Indians near Marlborough for the Lancaster assault and marches them to Boston.

September

1–2   Wampanoags and Nipmucks attack Deerfield. Massachusetts forces led by Moseley attack the town of Pennacook.

12   Colonists abandon Deerfield, Squakeag, and Brookfield.

18   Narragansetts sign a treaty with the English in Boston. Massachusetts troops are ambushed near Northampton.

October

5   Pocumtucks attack and destroy Springfield.

13   Massachusetts Council orders Christian Indians removed to Deer Island.

19   English repel Indians from Hatfield.

November

c. 1   Nipmucks take captive Christian Indians at Magunkaquog, Chabanakongkomun, and Hassanemesit, including James Printer.

2–12   Commissioners of the United Colonies order a united army to attack the Narragansetts.

DECEMBER

7   Massachusetts Council prints a broadside explaining the case against the Narragansetts.

19 United colonial forces attack Narragansetts at the Great Swamp.

1676

JANUARY

Philip travels westward to Mohawk territory, seeking, but failing to secure, an alliance.

14 Joshua Tift is captured by the English.

27 Narragansetts attack Pawtuxet.

FEBRUARY

10 Nipmucks attack Lancaster; Mary Rowlandson is taken captive.

14 Philip and Wampanoags attack Northampton. Massachusetts Council debates erecting a wall around Boston.

21 Nipmucks attack Medfield.

23 Massachusetts General Court debates the fate of Christian Indians.

Indians assault sites within ten miles of Boston.

MARCH

13 Nipmucks attack Groton.

26 Longmeadow, Marlborough, and Simsbury are attacked.

27 Nipmucks attack English forces near Sudbury.

28 Indians attack Rehoboth.

29 Providence is destroyed.

APRIL

21   Indians attack Sudbury.

MAY

2–3   Mary Rowlandson is released and returns to Boston.
18   English forces attack sleeping Indians near Deerfield.
30   Indians attack Hatfield.
c. 31 Christian Indians are moved from Deer Island to Cambridge.

JUNE

12   Indians attack Hadley but are repelled by Connecticut soldiers.
19   Massachusetts issues a declaration of amnesty for Indians who surrender.
22   Captain Tom is executed in Boston.

JULY

2   Major John Talcott and his troops begin sweeping Connecticut and Rhode Island, capturing large numbers of Algonquians who are transported out of the colonies as slaves throughout the summer.
      James Printer surrenders in Cambridge.
4   Captain Benjamin Church and his soldiers begin sweeping Plymouth for Wampanoags.
11   Indians attack Taunton but are repelled.
27   Nearly two hundred Nipmucks surrender in Boston.

AUGUST

2   Benjamin Church captures Philip's wife and son.
12   Alderman, an Indian soldier under Church, kills Philip.

The Name of War

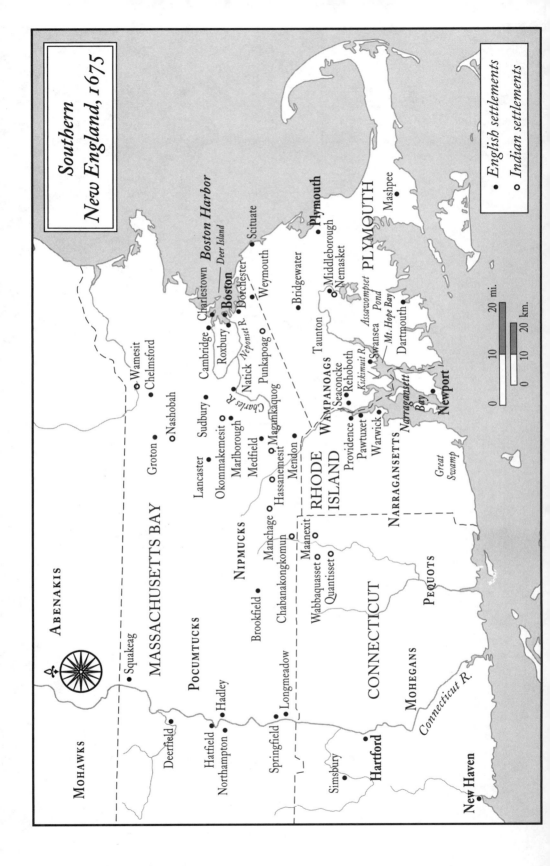

Southern
New England, 1675

• English settlements
○ Indian settlements

MOHAWKS

ABENAKIS

• Squakeag

MASSACHUSETTS BAY

• Wamesit
• Chelmsford
○ Nashobah

POCUMTUCKS

• Deerfield
• Hatfield
• Northampton

• Groton

• Lancaster
○ Okommakemesit
• Marlborough
• Medfield

• Cambridge Charlestown *Boston Harbor*
• Roxbury   **Boston** — *Deer Island*
        Neponset R. • Dorchester
• Natick ○ Punkapoag • Weymouth
○ Magunkaquog
○ Hassanemesit
• Mendon

Charles R.

• Sudbury

NIPMUCKS

• Manchage
○ Chabanakongkomun

• Springfield
• Longmeadow

• Brookfield

○ Maanexit
○ Wabbaquasset
○ Quantisset

○ Maanexit

CONNECTICUT

• Simsbury

MOHEGANS

Connecticut R.

Hartford

PEQUOTS

New Haven

• Scituate

• Bridgewater

Plymouth

PLYMOUTH

• Middleborough
• Nemasket
Assawompset Pond
Mt. Hope Bay
Swansea
• Dartmouth

• Mashpee

WAMPANOAGS

• Taunton
○ Seaconcke
• Rehoboth
Kickimuit R.
• Providence
• Pawtuxet
• Warwick

RHODE
ISLAND

NARRAGANSETTS

Narragansett Bay

Newport

Great Swamp

0   10   20 mi.

0   10   20 km.

THE CIRCLE

They first cut one of his Fingers round in the Joynt, at the Trunck of his Hand, with a sharp Knife, and then brake it off, as Men used to do with a slaughtered Beast, before they uncase him; then they cut off another and another, till they had dismembered one Hand of all its Digits, the Blood sometimes spirting out in Streams a Yard from his Hand . . . yet did not the Sufferer ever relent, or shew any Signs of Anguish. . . . In this Frame he continued, till his Executioners had dealt with the Toes of his Feet, as they had done with the Fingers of his Hands; all the while making him Dance round the Circle, and Sing, till he had wearied both himself and them. At last they brake the Bones of his Legs, after which he was forced to sit down, which 'tis said he silently did, till they had knocked out his Brains.[1]

*J*uly 1676. King Philip's War is almost over. Houses have been burned, children murdered, men beheaded. Hatred has accumulated. And here, it seems, is a typical account of a typical torture—the inexorable slowness of it, the mocking. The torturers are Mohegan Indians. "Making a great Circle, they placed him in the Middle, that all their Eyes might at the same Time, be pleased with the utmost Revenge upon him." The typical spectacle, the typical torments; we can almost see the writhing English colonist, surrounded by men he considers barbarians, suffering stoically. But our imagination, swelled by too many Saturdays spent watching Westerns, has carried us away. The man in the middle is not an Englishman. The account itself might have tipped us off: "*'Tis said*" that the finger-less, toeless man sat down silently while his torturers knocked his brains out. Said by whom? The Englishman whose words we read writes in the third person; he is not that fingerless, toeless, ultimately brainless man. Nor is he a captive forced to watch a gruesome preview of the fate that awaits him, only to be rescued at the last minute. He has only heard this story, second-hand, from someone who witnessed the scene and lived to tell the tale. Who, then, is the man in the middle, and where is the Englishman who watched him die?

The fingerless, toeless man is also nameless. He is called only "a young sprightly Fellow, seized by the Mohegins," though his sprightliness will soon fade. He is no Englishman; the English despise him. He is a formidable foe. "Of all the Enemies" of the war, "this Villain did most deserve to become an Object of Justice and Severity." He is, at first, boastful, too, and brags of shooting nineteen Englishmen dead and then, "unwilling to lose a fair Shot," killing a Mohegan to make an even twenty. "With which, having made up his Number, he told them he was fully satisfied." The Mohegans, after all, are allies of the English, and he who would kill one would as easily kill the other. The man in the middle of the circle could, perhaps, be a Frenchman, enemy to both. But instead he is a "cruel Monster" who has fought to oust the settlers from New England. The picture becomes clearer. The man in the middle, it turns out, is an Indian, a Narragansett.

But if both the sufferer and his tormentors are Indians, where, in this scene, are the English? They are watching, and paying close attention. Aided by the Mohegans, the English have just captured more than three hundred enemy Indians and now they must "gratify" their allies, who ask that this Narragansett man "be delivered into their Hands, that they might put him to Death" and thereby "sacrifice him to their cruel Genius of Revenge." The English quickly consent, "lest by a Denial they might disoblige their Indian Friends," and also, they admit, because they are curious for "an occular Demonstration of the Salvage, barbarous Cruelty of these Heathen." The English, then, have made this torture possible, and now they form part of the "great Circle" of onlookers to the event.

Truly the English are in a difficult position. Being the man in the middle, however horrifying, makes more sense to them, to their sense of themselves, than forming the circle. If they are to think of themselves as different from "these Heathen" whom they condemn for their "barbarous Cruelty," how can they consent to it? How can they stand shoulder to shoulder with Indians and watch as a man is tortured to death, knowing, as they do, that watching is the chief sport of it? Although they insist that the Narragansett man is tortured simply to humor the Mohegans, his suffering seems sublimely satisfying to the English as well. They never look away; this is the "occular Demonstration" they've been waiting for. In many ways, theirs is a safe pleasure. Their enemy is killed, yet they do not have to kill him. They are allowed to witness torture, yet they need not inflict it. Nor are they themselves physically threatened—it is not their legs that are being broken.

Still, there is danger here. "It is a signe of a barbarous and cruell man," according to an influential English Puritan theologian, "if any one bee given to warre simply desiring it and delighting in it."[2] Or, as Thomas Aquinas had written, "brutality or savagery applies to those who in inflicting punishment have not in view a default of the person punished, but merely the pleasure they derive from a man's torture."[3] To the extent that the English soldiers enjoy witnessing this scene of torture, they are relishing "savage" pleasures and thereby jeopardizing their identity as "civilized" men. And protecting that identity—as Christians and, most fundamentally, as Englishmen—is why they are fighting the war in the first place. From the time of their first arrival, in the 1620s and 1630s, the settlers had worried about losing their Englishness. However much they wanted to escape England and its corruptions, they still clung to their English ways—ways of walking, talking, dressing, thinking, eating, and drinking.[4] Being away from England meant religious freedom, but it also meant cultural isolation. Even while in Holland they had complained that it was "grievous to live from under the protection of the State of *England*," likely "to lose our language, and our name of English."[5] If living among the Dutch in a European city threatened English identity, how much more threatening was living among the Indians in the New World. Strange languages, strange people, strange land. Building a "city on a hill" in the American wilderness provided a powerful religious rationale, but on certain days, in many ways, it must have fallen short of making perfect sense. When the corn didn't grow, when the weather turned wild, when the wolves howled, when the Indians laughed at God, these are the times when the colonists might have wondered, What are we doing here? Discouraged and afraid, thousands of colonists simply left—as many as one in six sailed home to England in the 1630s and 1640s, eager to return to a world they knew and understood.[6]

But those who stayed eventually learned to grow corn, predict the weather, shoot wolves, and ignore Indian blasphemies. And then they might have wondered, Who have we become?

The colonists' doubts about their own identity were magnified both by their distance from England and by their nearness to the Indians. Most especially, they worried about the Indians' origins and the reason for their barbarity. Either the Indians were native to America (and more like an elm tree than an Englishman), or else they were migrants from Europe or Asia (and then very much like the English, who were simply more recent migrants). If native, the Indians were one with the wilderness and had always been as savage as their surroundings. As Roger Williams reported, "They say themselves, that they have sprung and growne up in that very place, like the very trees of the Wildernesse."[7] But if the Indians were migrants from Europe or Asia, then they had changed since coming to America and had been contaminated by its savage environment. If this were the case, as many believed, then the English could expect to degenerate, too. Urging the conversion of the Indians to Christianity, Daniel Gookin had warned, "Here we may see, as in a mirror, or looking glass, the woful, miserable, and deplorable estate, that sin hath reduced mankind unto naturally."[8] Instead of being the stage for the perfection of piety, the woods of New England might in truth be a forest of depravity. Instead of becoming "visible saints" for all of Europe to see, the English might expect to become more savage with each passing year, not only less religious but also less and less like Englishmen. And more and more like Indians.[9]

By the 1670s, in the years before King Philip's War broke out, there were many signs that the English had degenerated. Church membership and church attendance had declined. People were settling farther and farther from the coast, nearer to the Indians, and farther from the civilizing influence of English neighbors. Trade and contact with the Indians were increasing, though little of this contact involved sharing the good news of the gospel. In 1674, just a year before the war began, the Puritan minister Increase Mather published a sermon called *The Day of Trouble is Near*, in which he bemoaned the profligacy of his parishioners and the "great decay as to the power of godliness amongst us." It had become almost impossible, he complained, to tell the difference between church members and other men.[10]

Mather's themes of decay and confusion were common concerns. At the farthest extreme, New Englanders worried that they might degenerate so much as to become indistinguishable from beasts. The same year that Mather published his *Day of Trouble*, Samuel Danforth printed a sermon on bestiality (occasioned by a young boy's confession of copulating with a mare, a cow, two goats, five sheep, two calves, and a turkey) in which he condemned the practice as a "monstrous and horrible Confusion" that "turneth man into a bruit Beast."[11] Somewhere between these two fears—of mistaking godly men for ungodly men, or men for beasts—lay the colonists' principal fear: of mistaking Englishmen for Indians. Earlier English colonizers in Ireland had shared the same concerns, worrying, as Edmund Spenser did, that the English there might follow the fate of the original Norman invaders who "degenerated and growen allmoste meare Irishe yea and more malitious to the Englishe than the verye Irishe themselves."[12] In both New England and Ireland, not a few colonists, after all, had run off to live with the natives, abandoning English society altogether.[13] (Nearby, in New France, Frenchmen seemingly "became Savage simply because they lived with them."[14]) Perhaps, the English New Englanders worried, they themselves were becoming Indianized, contaminated by the influence of America's wilderness and its wild people.[15]

Meanwhile, many Algonquians had come to suspect the reverse, worrying that they themselves had become too much like their new European neighbors. Not only had the English taken Indian lands and disrupted traditional systems of trade and agriculture, but they also had corrupted the power of native rulers, or sachems, and attempted to eradicate the influence of powwaws, native religious leaders. When coastal populations became decimated by European diseases, many Indians had even decided to convert to Christianity and to live among the English. Those who resisted the influence of the English commonly attributed all of their people's problems "to the Departure of some of them from their own heathenish Ways and Customs."[16] Philip himself believed that too many Indians had been Anglicized and Christianized, praying to an English God and even learning to read and write. During negotiations with several colonists from Rhode Island, Philip and his counselors claimed "that thay had a great fear to have ani of their indians should be Caled or forsed to be Christian indians. Thay saied that such wer in everi thing more mischivous, only disemblers, and then the English made them not subject to their kings, and by ther lying to rong their kings."[17] Clearly, the boundaries between the two peoples had become blurred.

A day of trouble was indeed near, as Increase Mather had warned. "Ye shall hear of wars, and rumours of wars," he preached, quoting from Matthew 24:6. Calamities showing God's judgment were almost always at hand in Mather's mind, but this time, in 1674, he had a point. It is not entirely clear just exactly how or why the war started when it did, in June 1675, but from the firing of the first shots, both sides pursued the war with viciousness, and almost without mercy. "Christians in this Land have become too like unto the Indians," Increase Mather would later write, "and then we need not wonder if the Lord hath afflicted us by them."[18] The Indians, Wampanoags, Narragansetts, and Nipmucks, as well as Pocomtucks and Abenakis, attacked dozens of English towns, burning as many houses and killing as many inhabitants as they could. And the English, with occasional help from Mohegan, Pequot, Mohawk, and Christian Indians, burned wigwams, killed women and children, and sold prisoners into slavery. Both sides practiced torture and mutilation of the dead.

New England's Algonquians waged war against the English settlers in response to incursions on their cultural, political, and economic autonomy and, at least in part, they fought to maintain their Indianness. Meanwhile, New England colonists waged war to gain Indian lands, to erase Indians from the landscape, and to free themselves of doubts about their own Englishness.[19] For many colonists this was a struggle ordained by God, in which He "in wisdom most devine" would "purg ther dros from purer Coyne."[20] But if the English hoped to do away with enemy Indians by torturing some, killing most, and selling the rest as slaves, there was a catch: that was what the Spanish had done. And to behave as the Spanish had would again jeopardize the colonists' identity as Englishmen.

Frontispiece of Bartolomé de Las Casas, *The Tears of the Indians*, trans. J. P. (London, 1656). *Courtesy of the Huntington Library, San Marino, California*

Spain's brutal conquest of Mexico was widely known in both Old and New England, largely through a work titled *The Tears of the Indians* and commonly referred to as "Spanish Cruelties," but actually a translation of the Spanish friar Bartolomé de Las Casas' sixteenth-century treatise "In Defense of the Indians." Las Casas had spared no details in documenting the atrocities perpetrated by the conquistadors, and "Spanish Cruelties" invited English readers to define their colonial ventures in opposition to that model. In the seventeenth century, the widespread printing and distribution of works such as "Spanish Cruelties" fueled the growth of nationalism in Europe, a development that was predicated on the invention of the printing press.[21] As one New England colonist wrote in 1676, "all men (of reading) condemne the Spaniard for cruelty . . . in destroying men & depopulating the land."[22] Translations of Las Casas were, in fact, part of a propaganda war among the competing imperial powers, Spain, Holland, England, and France, much of which, from the English perspective, centered on proving who was most Christian, and most civilized, in their interactions with America's native inhabitants.[23] When Richard Hakluyt listed for Queen Elizabeth the reasons for planting American colonies, he suggested that the English might easily win the favor of Indians desperate for liberation from Spain's cruelties:

> The Spaniards governe in the Indies with all pride and tyranie; and like as when people of contrarie nature at the sea enter into Gallies, where men are tied as slaves, all yell and crye with one voice *Liberta, liberta,* as desirous of libertie or freedome, so no doubt whensoever the Queene of England . . . shall seate upon that firme of America, and shalbe reported throughout all that tracte to use the naturall people there with all humanitie, curtesie, and freedome, they will yelde themselves to her government and revolte cleane from the Spaniarde.[24]

Sir Walter Ralegh even planned to bring Las Casas' "booke of the Spanish crueltyes with fayr pictures" on his voyage to Guiana in the 1590s, hoping to show it to the natives and impress them with the wisdom of welcoming the kinder, gentler English.[25]

Part of the mission of New England's "city on a hill," then, was to advertise the civility of the English colonists and to hold it in stark contrast with the barbarous cruelty of Spain's conquistadors and the false and blasphemous impiety of France's Jesuit missionaries. Books not only about the Spanish conquest but also about the Spanish Inquisition, both of which illustrated the depravity and cruelty of Spaniards, and of papists in general, were printed and made widely available to English readers ("Spanish Cruelties" was even subtitled "Inquisition for Blood," to make the connection more explicit).

The French, on the other hand, were derided not so much for cruelty as for hypocrisy and sacrilege in their meaningless baptisms of Indians ignorant of the gospel. A popular English joke told of a Jesuit missionary who, having lived in New France for a quarter century, wrote to a friend in Europe to ask him "to send him a Book called the Bible, for he heard there was such a Book in Europe; which might be of some use to him."[26]

Countering these visions of colonial failures, early published accounts of the English colonists' adventures in New England stressed the pleasantness of their interactions with Indians; the fairness of their treaties; and, especially after 1640, the success of their efforts to convert the Indians to Christianity by teaching them to read the Bible.[27] New Englanders' fame as missionaries to the Indians was so well publicized that by 1654 Roger Williams was able to dissuade his fellow colonists from waging war against the Narragansetts by pointing out that their reputation was at stake:

> it Can not be hid, how all England & other Nations ring with the glorious Conversion of the Indians of New England. You know how many bookes are dispersed throughout the Nation of that Subject . . . : how have all the Pulpits in England bene Commanded to Sound of this Glorious Worcke. . . . I beseech you consider how the name of the most holy & jealous God may be preserved betweene the clashings of these Two: Viz: The Glorious Conversion of the Indians in New England & the Unnecessary Warrs & cruell Destructions of the Indians in New England.[28]

Fearful of "Unnecessary Warrs & cruell Destructions," those New England colonists who had read or heard of Las Casas' "Spanish Cruelties" had a vivid idea of what not to do in the New World. In a prefatory address "To all true English-men," the translator of a 1656 English edition of "Spanish Cruelties" asked his readers to imagine watching the horrors of the conquest, to imagine, in a sense, standing in a circle of spectators to that event:

> had you been Eye-witnesses to the transcending Massacres here related; had you been one of those that lately saw a pleasant Country, now swarming with multitudes of People, but immediately depopulated, and drown'd in a Deluge of Bloud: had you been one of those that saw great Cities of Nations and Countries in this moment flourishing with Inhabitants, but in the next, totally ruin'd with such a General Desolation, as left neither Person living nor House remaining: had you seen the poor innocent Heathens shaming and upbraiding, with the ghastliness of their Wounds, the devilish Cruelties of those that called themselves Christians: had you seen the poor creatures torn from the peace and quiet of their own Habitations, where God had planted them, to labour in a Tormenting Captivity . . . your Compassion

must of necessity have turn'd into Astonishment: the tears of Men can hardly suffice. . . .[29]

Compassion, astonishment, and tears. In 1656, when this "Spanish Cruelties" was printed, these were the only proper responses of "true English-men" to the torture and slaughter of Indians.

Twenty years later, those "true English-men" who lived in New England found themselves in a very tricky spot. Barbarism threatened them from every direction: if they continued to live peaceably with the Indians, they were bound to degenerate into savages, but if they waged war, they were bound to fight like savages.[30] Their dilemma was further complicated because, along with the lessons of "Spanish Cruelties," New Englanders were also influenced, however indirectly, by the representation of German, Irish, and Catholic cruelties in English books and stories. In the 1640s England had itself experienced and inflicted some of the worst atrocities of warfare during its civil wars. Meanwhile, Germany's own religious violence warned that England might meet a similar fate and descend into grotesque and enduring civil strife. At the same time, England's experience in Ireland, especially during the Irish Rebellion of 1641, contributed to the powerful tradition of Protestant martyrdom by emphasizing English Protestants' sufferings at the hands of the "wild" and "heathen" Irish and also established a precedent allowing Christian Englishmen to ignore the laws of war when fighting against people England considered "barbarians."[31] Several of these traditions, of course, contradicted one another. The lesson of "Spanish Cruelties" commanded New Englanders to shun cruelty against the Indians, while the English suppression of the Irish Rebellion suggested that cruelty against barbarians might not really be cruelty at all. Yet what linked Spanish, German, and Irish cruelties was that they were all written about at great length, and put into print. This was the lesson New England's colonists would take to heart: as the Boston poet Benjamin Tompson would write in 1676, "All cruelties which paper stained before / Are acted to the life here o'er and o'er."[32]

Here, then, was the solution to the colonists' dilemma between peacefully degenerating into barbarians or fighting like savages: wage the war, and win it, by whatever means necessary, and then write about it, to win it again. The first would be a victory of wounds, the second a victory of words. Even if they inflicted on the Indians as much cruelty as the Spanish had, New Englanders could distance themselves from that cruelty in the words they used to write about it, the same way the English had when writing about the Irish. They could save themselves from both Indian and Spanish barbarity; they could reclaim their Englishness.

Recall now the scene with which we began. It is July 1676; King Philip's War is almost over. Houses have been burned, children murdered, men beheaded. The Indian population has been decimated. It could be said that many have been "torn from the peace and quiet of their own Habitations" and that many now "labour in a Tormenting Captivity." Here, English soldiers and their Mohegan allies stand in a circle while a Narragansett Indian has his fingers and toes chopped off, his legs broken, his brains dashed to the ground. No longer do the English have to imagine watching these "Spanish Cruelties." They are there; these cruelties are their own. But even here, the only proper response is the response of "true English-men": compassion, astonishment, and tears.

The way the story is told, we know that the English are disgusted by the cruelty they witness, and as both anthropologists and historians have pointed out, disgust is one way that one culture differentiates itself from another. The story's expression of disgust goes a long way toward preserving the Englishness of the soldiers present. But the other side of disgust is desire, and, despite their protestations to the contrary, clearly the English feel that, too.[33] Their disgust takes the form of revulsion, their desire fascination. While they may find it painful to watch as a young man has his fingers sawed off, they also find it pleasurable. But for an English soldier to confess his fascination, to admit his pleasure, is to become indistinguishable from the Indian beside him.

Now contrast this scene with another, the torture of several Englishmen by Wampanoag Indians in April 1676:

> They took five or six of the English and carried them away alive, but that night killed them in such a manner as none but Salvages would have done. For they stripped them naked, and caused them to run the Gauntlet, whipping them after a cruel and bloudy manner, and then threw hot ashes upon them, cut out the flesh of their leges, and put fire into their wounds, delighting to see the miserable torments of wretched creatures. Thus are they the perfect children of the Devill.[34]

In this scene, where the English are the sufferers rather than the spectators, who is "savage" and who is "civilized" is much clearer. The torture is what "none but Salvages would have done." And the smug conclusion, "Thus are they the perfect children of the Devill," implies its own antithesis: "Thus are we the perfect children of God."

Yet the key to both of these scenes is not who is being tortured but who is being pleased. When the Englishmen run the gauntlet, the Wampanoags are said to be "delighting to see the miserable torments of wretched creatures."

And when the Narragansett man is butchered, the Mohegans "delight" in this "brutish and devilish Passion." "Delight" is in fact their chief sin—any good Puritan would have been familiar with Psalms 68:30: "Scatter thou the people that delight in war." Although the English soldiers watch, they make it clear that they themselves are "not delighted in Blood." This, in fact, is the only way to excuse their presence: We may be watching, they say, but that doesn't mean we like it; in fact, it makes us sick. What pleases Indian eyes pains English ones. The Mohegans encircle the tormented man so that all eyes might "be pleased" with a good view, but the English admit to no such pleasure; they can only weep at the grisly sight, "it forcing Tears from their Eyes." (These are the very same tears that, had they imagined themselves witnesses to the Spanish conquest, they would have shed in abundance.)

Instead of admitting their pleasure, the English displace it onto the Mohegans standing next to them. Again and again they point out that it is the Indians who are "delighted," not the English. But even that move is not enough. The line between Englishman and Indian is still too thin. To thicken it, the pain of the event must be displaced, too. The Indian in the middle of the circle does not himself "shew any Signs of Anguish." Instead, the English do. He bleeds but they cry. The scene is so painful to the English that it is *torture* just to watch it. By feeling the pain of the fingerless, toeless man, feeling it even more than he does, the English onlookers put themselves in his place. Desperate to distinguish themselves from the "heathen" Mohegans, they figuratively hurl themselves back into the center of the circle, where their identity as the tormented victims of barbarous savages is reestablished. Their Englishness has been preserved.

WHAT THE ENGLISH representation of this scene utterly fails to understand, of course, is the elaborate meanings of the Indians' behavior. Yet, if the Indians' perspective on this scene goes unstated or uncomprehended in the English account, it need not remain unstated or unexamined here. Interpreted in the context of Algonquian ritual, the Mohegans, whom the English condemn for their "delight," are not enjoying the victim's agonies as much as they are admiring his stoicism, his failure to "shew any Signs of Anguish," and the circle they form has social and spiritual significance, uniting the group in collective catharsis. Since captives may have symbolically replaced a recently deceased lost tribe member, torture, for the tormentors, was both an expression of dominance and a release of mourners' emotions. And, for the sufferer who endured it, torture was a ritual of initiation, a test of perseverance, and a spiritual journey. His singing and dancing were expressions of defiance that brought worldly respect and otherworldly rewards both to himself and to the tribe member whom he had symbolically replaced. For the Indians, then, this event was an elaborately ordered ceremony.[35]

Nor should we allow the Narragansett man in the middle of the circle to remain nameless and speechless simply because he is so rendered in the English account. Although his identity cannot be reliably determined, some evidence suggests that he may have been Stonewall John, a Narragansett Indian named for masonry skills he acquired while living among the English. At the start of the war, Stonewall John abandoned the English, joined enemy Indians, and participated in several attacks on English towns. Most notoriously, he was thought to have coordinated the construction of an Indian fort at the Great Swamp.[36] And when Roger Williams attempted to negotiate with Stonewall John and other Indians during an attack on Providence in March 1676, they told him, "You have driven us out of our own Countrie and then pursued us to our Great Miserie, and Your own, and we are Forced to live upon you."[37]

ULTIMATELY, it is not at all surprising that the English have failed to record evidence that might explain the reasons why this man, a "cruel Monster," fought against the English during the war, or to recognize the layers of meaning that might make his torturers' "delight" something other than "savage." The English account, after all, is concerned only with explaining English meanings. In that regard, its strained and twisting moral posturing is not unusual; indeed, it is typical of writing about war. A great deal is at stake when people are trying to kill one another, and the language used to write about it can be very complicated indeed. So much was at stake for the English colonists, in fact, that they had to tell stories like this over and over again. This scene, they say, is an example of "unheard of Cruelty," but it does not go unheard of for long. "'Tis said" that the young Narragansett man sat down silently while his torturers knocked his brains out. Said by whom? Said, no doubt, by many. Clearly, this story made the rounds. People were eager to hear it, and the soldiers were eager to tell it. Often, those who related this torture scene, or the story of the expedition of which it was a part, went out of their way to exonerate the English soldiers. The Rhode Islander William Harris claimed that the English had been "provoked by the barbarous inhumanety they have heard of: & Seen hath bin done to the English whose dead bodyes they founde in the woods." Fearful that the actions of the English soldiers "Should be thought too great Severity," Harris went on to provide a detailed description of "the cruelty of the Indeans" that had so provoked them.[38]

The account of the torture of a captured Narragansett man with which we began is that of William Hubbard, who included it in his *Narrative of the Troubles with the Indians in New-England*, printed in Boston in 1677, and in London, under a slightly different title, that same year. Hubbard was a Puritan minister, but (much as he criticized Mather for hubris) he also called himself a historian. Being a historian, in Hubbard's mind, required only two things: diligence in collecting materials and faithfulness in presenting them. Most of his materials, he claimed, were "either gathered out of the Letters, or taken from the Mouths of such as were eye or ear Witnesses of the things themselves."[39] Hubbard probably obtained an account of the July 1676 torture scene from Major John Talcott, who led the expedition against the Narragansetts, during which, over a single two-day period, his soldiers killed 52 Indian men and 114 women and children, and took 72 captive (of such a disproportionate number of women and children, Hubbard wrote that "being all young Serpents of the same Brood, the subduing or taking so many, ought to be acknowledged as another signal Victory, and Pledg of Divine Favour to the English").[40] When one of those captured Narragansett men was tortured to death, Talcott himself may have stood in that "great Circle," entranced, tearful, repulsed.

But if Talcott stood in that circle, so did Hubbard. And so, too, in a way, did all of Hubbard's readers, Englishmen and -women on both sides of the Atlantic. Hubbard's book was widely read, especially in England, where it probably found an audience among the readers of England's popular literature of gore—tales of executions, murders, and massacres. People who read Hubbard's account might well have experienced the same set of feelings as Talcott—shameful pleasure in being witness to torture; sympathy for the suffering victim; and, most of all, condemnation of the cruel, vicious Mohegans. Compassion, astonishment, and tears. Watching this scene is different from reading about it; readers would probably have felt these things less intensely than Talcott, and certainly they would have felt safer than he. Still, the power of the event resides in its being a spectacle, and readers and spectators have a great deal in common.

Hubbard claimed to be "faithful" in presenting his materials. If an event was "variously reported by the Actors, or Spectators," he would only include those details "which seemed most probable." And yet Hubbard, we can be sure, embellished Talcott's story. First of all, as a clergyman, he felt compelled to contribute a religious interpretation: "Instances of this Nature," he advised, "should be Incentive unto us, to bless the Father of Lights, who hath called us out of the dark Places of the Earth, full of the Habitations of Cruelty." More importantly, perhaps, Hubbard worried that readers in Old and New England might identify too much with the suffering Indian in the middle of the circle. Hubbard's telling of the story encouraged readers to affirm their English-ness by finding the Mohegan tortures appalling and by sensing the Narra-gansett man's pain, but Hubbard never wanted his readers to sympathize with the tormented man too strongly, or for too long. By the time Hubbard wrote his account, near the end of the war, the kind of compassion for Indian vic-tims of cruelty that had been encouraged by "Spanish Cruelties" had been replaced by contempt. Now, the near destruction of an entire population of Indians inspired only further destruction. In August 1676, the Connecticut Council wrote of the Indians that "their wicked contriveances will doubtless incite & animate all *true Englishmen* to endeavoure the confusion of such bloodsuckers, as are now, thorow God's mercy to us, totally routed in theses partes & gathered into a nett . . . ; they being but the gleanings of sundry nations that were great numbers ere while."[41]

To a considerable degree, the response of all "true English-men" to the Spanish conquest—compassion, astonishment, and tears—was predicated on acknowledging the Indians as human. According to a contemporary military manual, it was only because all men are "of one Nature, and deriving their originals both from one Roote," that soldiers "should behold neither mortall wounds, nor the living miseries of their subdued enemies, but with compas-sion."[42] Since the question of whether colonists and Indians were "from one Roote" was at the heart of what caused King Philip's War in the first place, compassion for Indians, as for the tortured Narragansett man, could be, at best, only partial.[43] He was, Hubbard points out, a "Villain," treated as one might treat "a slaughtered Beast." When the Mohegans asked the tortured Narragansett "How he liked the War?" he answered, "He liked it very well, and found it as sweet, as English Men did their Sugar." For this, Hubbard called him an "unsensible and hard-hearted Monster." After all,

> He might have replyed, as the Scotch Gentlemen did after the Loss of a Bat-tel, that being asked how he liked the Match (sc. with our Prince of Wales, (which then was the Occasion of the Quarrel) made Answer, he liked the Match well enough, but no whit liked the Manner of the Wooing written by such Lines of Blood.[44]

This awkward, awful attempt at humor reveals Hubbard's incredible discom-fort with the scene. Unaware of the significance of the Narragansett man's own biting reply, demonstrating his stoicism while mocking English depen-dence on imported goods (a dependence Stonewall John would have observed while living among the English), Hubbard compared it with a Scot's double entendre, as if to say that the Indians, even in death, lack the Saxons' witticism. They, he insisted, are not like us. Whether Indians were fully human is a question writers about the war would take up again and again but would ultimately leave unanswered.

For all its awkwardness, Hubbard's account of the scene of the torture of a Narragansett man in July 1676 is both complicated and, in a sense, sophisticated. In the century and a half since the Spanish conquest, the proliferation of printing, the expansion of literacy, and the growth of nationalism combined to make for just this kind of sophistication. How these themes express themselves in all of the writing and reading about the war is the subject of future chapters. For now it's worth noting that the scene as Hubbard wrote it could only have been written when it was, in the immediate aftermath of the war. Forty years later, another English colonist, Benjamin Church, related his recollections of the war, which included a scene that seems, at least initially, very similar to the one in Hubbard's *Narrative.* Church's scene is set in March 1676, and its backdrop is almost identical to Hubbard's: with their Mohegan allies, the English have just captured an enemy Indian (this time a Nipmuck). In Church's version, however, it is the English, not the Indians, who first suggest torture, not for delight's sake but "to bring him to a more ample confession of what he knew concerning his countrymen." Moreover, instead of "gratifying" this desire, Church "interceded and prevailed for his escaping torture." Nonetheless, the Nipmuck man was sentenced to die and the Mohegan who captured him "was allowed, as he desired to be, his executioner." If this scene followed Hubbard's direction, we would now expect Church to stand by and watch, but once again, Church's story takes a different turn. While the captured man is "brought before a great fire," Church, "taking no delight in the sport, framed an errand at some distance."[45] Church refused to form a part of the circle. He simply walked away. A year after this scene took place, after the fighting had ceased, Church was sent on a mission to "scour the woods of some of the lurking enemy." There he found an old Indian man who had fled from Swansea.

> The Captain asked his name, he replied, Conscience. Conscience, said the Captain, smiling, then the war is over; for that was what they were searching for.[46]

Forty years after King Philip's War had ended, when Benjamin Church recorded his tales, the stakes had changed. In 1716 Church portrayed himself as a man searching for Conscience, an independent moral agent, acting on the courage of his convictions, more moral than the Mohegans, but also more moral than the English. Benjamin Church had a different story to tell than William Hubbard. Because Church walked away, it is tempting to believe that the circle of spectatorship has been broken, that it no longer invites both eyewitnesses and readers to share in the complex pains and pleasures of cruelty. We are not Englishmen. We have not been influenced by reading "Spanish Cruelties." But still, in a sense, when we read Hubbard's account, we stand in that circle today. We can't help but be drawn into his narrative, but we can try to measure the genuineness of our compassion, the troubling fascination underlying our revulsion, and the curiosity behind our condemnation.[47]

PART ONE · *Language*

—*Signature of John Sassamon*

A.M. wrote Hist. of warr Indians. Sic P.M.
—*Increase Mather's diary,*
May 1, 1676

Chapter 1

BEWARE OF ANY LINGUIST

*I*n the late, chilly days of January 1675, John Sassamon set out for Plymouth. It was only a short journey from Namasket, the Christian Indian town where he served as minister, but for Sassamon, who carried urgent news, the road must have seemed almost unbearably long. Fifteen miles of lonely, snowy trails. At last, arriving in Plymouth, he sought an audience with none other than the colony's governor, Josiah Winslow. There, finally and feverishly, John Sassamon unburdened himself, whispering to Winslow that "Philip . . . was Indeavouring to engage all the Sachems round about in a warr." Perhaps the governor would offer a reward for such valuable information. Perhaps he would offer protection. Sassamon told Winslow he believed his life was in danger, that Philip would surely murder him if his betrayal was discovered. Winslow, alas, neither heeded Sassamon's warnings nor assuaged his fears. And he spoke of no reward. Instead, the governor dismissed Sassamon's information "because it had an Indian original, and one can hardly believe them [even] when they speak truth."[1] He sent the minister on his way.

If the road to Plymouth had seemed long, no doubt the road back to Namasket seemed longer still. Sassamon must have been startled by the noise of each cracking twig, each leaping deer. He had good reason to be afraid. Within a week of his meeting with Winslow, John Sassamon mysteriously disappeared. In February his bloated, bruised body was found under the ice at Assawompset Pond, not far from his home, and was buried without further delay. John Sassamon, it seemed, had been walking on thin ice.

All spring, as the ice thawed, rumors abounded. Many colonists and Indians alike suspected that Sassamon had been brutally murdered, as he himself had predicted. But by whom? Philip, of course, was the obvious suspect, but with Sassamon's death the Plymouth authorities were now more interested in determining whether he really was planning a war. At the end of February Philip voluntarily appeared before the Plymouth authorities to address Sassamon's allegations. "Upon a large debate" with Philip, the Plymouth Council concluded that there was "great reason to believe that the information against him might be in substance true," but they had no proof of his plans, and so, "hopeing that the descovery of it soe farr would cause him to desist they dismissed him frindly."[2] There remained the matter of Sassamon's murder, and on March 1, at its regular meeting, the Plymouth Court interrogated "many Indians" to no avail. Soon after the court adjourned, however, an eyewitness appeared who claimed to have seen three men kill Sassamon. At the next regular court session, on June 1, these three men, Mattashunannamo, Tobias, and Tobias's son Wampapaquan (three of Philip's chief counselors), were formally charged:

> being accused, that they did with joynt consent, upon the 29 of January . . . , att a place called Assowamsett Pond, wilfully and of sett purpose, and of mallice fore thought, and by force and armes, murder John Sassamon, an other Indian, by laying violent hands on him and striking him, or twisting his necke, untill hee was dead; and to hide and conceale this theire said murder, att the time and place aforesaid, did cast his dead body through a hole of the iyce into the said pond.[3]

An unusual jury of twelve Englishmen and six "of the most indifferentest, gravest, and sage Indians" was empaneled to consider the evidence. First, there was Patuckson, the eyewitness who, "unseen by those three that killed Sausaman, beheld all that they did to him, and spake of it, so that a Praying . . . Indian William Nahauton by name, heard of it, and he forthwith revealed what he knew to the English."[4] (Both Patuckson and Nahauton probably testified at the trial.) Second, there was the forensic evidence. Governor Winslow had ordered Sassamon's body dug from its grave and had commissioned "a Coroners Inquest, to make enquiry how he came by his death: And they found he had been murthered, for his neck was broken by twisting of his head round, which is the way the Indians some times use when they practice murther; also, his head was extreamly swollen, and his body wounded in several parts of it." Testimony may also have been offered that when the body "was first taken out of the pond, no water issued out of it, which argued that the Body was not drowned, but dead before it came into the water." Finally, there was the supernatural evidence: the court ordered Tobias to approach Sassamon's dead body and, as he did, Sassamon's body fell "a bleeding afresh, as if it had been newly slain." The experiment was repeated with the same result, supplying irrefutable testimony of the guilt of the accused.[5]

At the end of the trial, the jury, "both English and Indians . . . joyntly and with one consent" declared Tobias, Wampapaquan, and Mattashunannamo "guilty of the blood of John Sassamon" and pronounced the sentence of death.[6] The execution took place on June 8. "This so Exasperated King Philip," one colonist recalled, "that from that Day after, he studied to be Revenged on the English."[7] In just three days, on June 11, Wampanoags were reported arming outside Plymouth "in a posture of war," and by June 24 they had attacked Swansea, killing nine colonists.[8] Two days later, the earth's shadow eclipsed the moon. That night, English soldiers marching from Boston to Swansea made camp in the darkness on the banks of the Neponset River and waited for the eclipsed moonlight to creep out again. Staring at the brightening sky they saw a strange black spot, shaped like the scalp of an Indian, or maybe, some said, like an Indian bow. Both were terrible, terrifying omens, portending a deadly war.[9] It was three weeks since John Sassamon's body had spoken from beyond the grave. King Philip's War had begun.

I

WHO KILLED John Sassamon?

No doubt most colonists "believed that [Philip] was the Author of [the] murther" and the accused merely "the Actors," but John Easton, deputy governor of Rhode Island, had cause to wonder whether John Sassamon had really been murdered at all. "Sum English suposed him throne in," Easton acknowledged, but "sum indians that I judged intelegabell and impartiall in that Case did think he fell in and was so drouned."[10] Patuckson claimed to have seen Philip's men violently murder Sassamon and then conceal their crime by shoving the body through a hole in the ice, deliberately leaving Sassamon's hat and gun upon the surface, "so others might suppose him to have there drowned himself."[11] (It was also rumored that the murderers left "sum foulle" by Sassamon's body to suggest that he had accidentally drowned while hunting.) But the Wampanoags Easton spoke with found this story ridiculous. Although they admitted that "sumtimes na[ugh]ty indians wold kill others," they had never heard of an Indian who would "obscuer as if the dead indian was not murdered." Moreover, they suggested that William Nahauton had invented his testimony because he knew "it wold pleas the English so to think him a beter Christian."[12] (Nahauton, a minister at the praying town of Punkapoag, served the English as both soldier and spy during the war; the Massachusetts Council would later refer to him as one of "the cheef of our Indians."[13]) Easton's Wampanoag informants claimed that, far from having been strangled to death and then thrown into the water, John Sassamon had drowned and "the ies did hurt his throat" as he struggled to save himself.[14]

Murder? Suicide? Accidental drowning? Any reconsideration of this case would be compromised by the potential bias of nearly all the participants: Nahauton and Patuckson might have perjured themselves to gain the colonists' favor; the six Christian Indians on the jury probably had little choice but to concur with the twelve English jurors; the "intelegabell and impartiall" Wampanoags Easton interviewed might well have misled him about Sassamon's death to justify Philip's subsequent actions in attacking Swansea; and Easton, a Quaker, might have made up parts of his story to better condemn the Puritans' conduct.

Perhaps the most serious bias of all is the possibility that the Plymouth Court wrongly prosecuted Philip's men to send him a warning or even to deliberately provoke the war. But if so, why go to the trouble of framing three men for a murder that was really an accident or a suicide? If the English wanted to start a war, there were easier, faster, and less ambiguous ways to do it, means they had resorted to before and would again.[15] The Plymouth Court might have wanted to provoke Philip, and may even have supplied lying witnesses, but it seems unlikely (and all too unnecessary) that the murder itself was a fiction. The evidence that John Sassamon was indeed murdered is compelling. First, the absence of water in his lungs, if true, proves that Sassamon was dead before he entered the water. Second, both the coroner's inquest and Easton's Wampanoags agreed that Sassamon's throat was severely injured, but people who drown in frozen ponds are usually bruised or cut on the hands, arms, and chest from trying to hoist their upper bodies over the ice's sharp edge. The universally acknowledged injuries to Sassamon's neck and throat, in other words, strongly suggest foul play—namely, strangulation.[16]

To insist that there was a murder at the heart of this matter is not to deny a possible miscarriage of justice. John Sassamon seems to have been killed, but the evidence against Tobias, Wampapaquan, and Mattashunannamo is slim to vanishing. Patuckson and Nahauton appeared on the scene all too conveniently, and neither is an entirely credible witness. Even Wampapaquan's alleged eleventh-hour confession—just after the noose broke and temporarily interrupted his execution—must be discounted, since he was simply, and quite literally, trying to save his own neck.[17] Still, with no other evidence at hand, it is difficult to identify additional suspects. Perhaps the better strategy is to identify not the murderer but the motive.

Why was John Sassamon killed?

At first blush the answer seems obvious: dead men tell no tales. In other words, Philip had Sassamon killed (by Tobias, Wampapaquan, and Mattashunannamo, or by others) either as punishment for his treasonous betrayal or to prevent further leaks of information to the English. Boston merchant Nathaniel Saltonstall claimed that "King Philip suspecting he either would divulge or had already made known this Secret to the English, took Councel to kill this Sosoman." The Reverend Increase Mather said of Philip's men that "the main ground why they murthered him seems to be, because he discovered their subtle and malicious designs, which they were complotting against the English." In Rhode Island even John Easton conceded that "it was reported Sausimun before his death had informed of the indian plot, and that if the indians knew it thay wold kill him."[18]

This motive seems simple enough, and yet each of these three observers—Mather, Saltonstall, and Easton—suggested other, broader reasons behind the murder. First among these was Sassamon's religion: he was a Christian and a minister at the Indian "praying town" of Namasket, not far from Mount Hope, Philip's home. According to Mather, "no doubt but one reason why the Indians murthered John Sausaman, was out of hatred against him for his Religion." Saltonstall asserted that Wampapaquan, Tobias, and Mattashunannamo killed Sassamon because they were annoyed at his preaching: "Not liking his Discourse, [they] immediately Murthered him after a most Barbarous Manner."[19] Others claimed Philip had Sassamon killed because he himself was tired of Sassamon's proselytizing. And Sassamon's death was also attributed to his greed: he had served as a translator for Philip and had cheated him. The Wampanoags John Easton interviewed said Sassamon "was a bad man that king Philop got him to write his will and he made the writing for a gret part of the land to be his but read as if it had bine as Philop wold."[20]

Unfortunately, the surviving reports conflict so greatly that it is impossible to determine with any certainty the exact motive for Sassamon's murder. But the exact motive may not matter. Although the shape and size of the possible motives vary, they cast an identical shadow: behind each of them lies the specter of John Sassamon's position as a cultural mediator, as a man who was neither English nor Indian but who negotiated with both peoples.[21] And for Sassamon, the ability to hold this mediating position was predicated on his bilingualism and his literacy—his skill at speaking, reading, and writing English was intricately intertwined with his loyalty to the English, his conversion to Christianity, his betrayal of Philip, and even his ability to cheat Philip in the writing of his will. In a sense, literacy killed John Sassamon. And herein lies one of the fundamental paradoxes of the waging and writing of King Philip's War: the same cultural tensions that caused the war—Indians becoming Anglicized and the English becoming Indianized—meant that literate Indians like John Sassamon, those most likely to record their version of the events of the war, were among its earliest casualties.

II

IN THE EARLY seventeenth century Samuel Purchas declared that the "literall advantage" meant that literacy makes history possible: "By speech we utter our minds once, at the present, to the present, as present occasions move (and perhaps unadvisedly transport) us: but by writing Man seemes immortall." [22] Twenty-five years ago, social scientists resurrected Purchas's argument. Not only does the invention of writing mark the advent of history proper, they claimed, but the ability to write down and record events also creates a "historical sensibility," an awareness of the "pastness of the past." People who communicate orally can understand the past only in terms of their present-day face-to-face relationships; thus they create "myths" that emphasize continuity between past and present. Yet literate people, with their written records, cannot fail to notice the distinction between what was and what is. And since there are often inconsistencies between what was and what is, literate cultures invented history to document and interpret change over time. The concept of history, these scholars argued, was thus a direct consequence of literacy. [23]

In the years since this ambitious theory was proposed, anthropologists, historians, and other literacy scholars have unraveled its frayed edges so that today little of its fabric remains intact. While anthropologists have demonstrated that oral peoples quite self-consciously preserve history through oral tradition, historians have become increasingly aware that literate peoples (including historians themselves) are prone to myth-making. [24] Postmodernists are no longer confident in the ability to tell the difference between myth and history. And the "great divide" between orality and literacy, once clearly marked by the boundary between myth and history, has been challenged on other grounds as well. Scholars have insisted that literacy is not simply a technology we acquire but is also a value whose worth is culturally constructed; others suggest that we would do better to look at the "uses" of literacy than at its "consequences." [25]

Nonetheless, in the specific case of Native American history, some historians continue to argue, in essence, that while Europeans think in terms of history, Indians think in terms of myth. Unfortunately, this romanticized distinction between the "thoughtworlds" of contemporary white historians and historical Native Americans takes us back to the "great divide" theories all over again. As a result, many scholars continue to labor under the assumption that the acquisition of literacy inevitably leads to the recording of history or, if it doesn't, that this is the result of the persistent power of myth for non-Western peoples.[26] Clearly, this assumption is often correct, which partly explains its great staying power. Still, it occasionally obscures a much more complicated relationship between a people's literacy and their ability to pass down rich sources to eager historians—a relationship that is always mediated by culture, and by the conditions under which literacy is acquired and the uses to which it is put. In late-seventeenth-century New England a great number of Indians were literate—yet none of them wrote an account of King Philip's War, even though many English colonists thought fit to do so. Several of those literate Indians were ministers, like John Sassamon, and at least one, James Printer, worked as a printer for the press in Cambridge. And still none of them left a written, much less a printed, account.

Clearly, literacy is not an uncomplicated tool, like a pen or a printing press. Instead literacy is bound, as it was for New England's Indians, by the conditions under which it is acquired; in this case, at great cost. To become literate, seventeenth-century Indians had first to make a graduated succession of cultural concessions—adopting English ways and English dress, living in towns, learning to speak English, converting to Christianity. But these very concessions made them vulnerable. Neither English nor Indian, assimilated Indians were scorned by both groups and even were subject to attack. Because the acquisition of literacy, and especially English-language literacy, was one of the last steps on the road to assimilation, Indians who could read and write placed themselves in a particularly perilous, if at the same time a powerful, position, caught between two worlds but fully accepted by neither.

The predicament of literate Algonquians in seventeenth-century New England suggests that there may be a few more questions to be asked about the "consequences" and "uses" of literacy and its relationship to the recording of history. If literacy is employed as an agent of assimilation, can one of its uses be the devastation of a society's political autonomy and the loss of its native language and culture? Can literacy destroy? And, in the context of a broader cultural conflict, can one of the consequences of literacy be the death of those who acquire it? Can literacy kill? Perhaps most important, if literacy can be wielded as a weapon of conquest and can effectively compromise a native culture, what then of that culture's history and who is left to tell it? If the very people most likely to record their story, those who are so assimilated as to have become literate, are also the most vulnerable, does it then make sense to explain that culture's lack of written history by simply pointing to its attachment to mythical thinking?

To address these questions we must take a few more steps back and start at the very beginning of the story of John Sassamon's life. This will, unfortunately, prove a difficult task, since Sassamon, like the infamous Archduke Ferdinand, is best remembered for his death. Before that fateful day in the winter of 1675 when he sat uncomfortably in the governor's house and quietly whispered that "Philip was undoubtedly indeavouring to Raise new troubles," John Sassamon had entered the historical record only a handful of times—and most of these were brief appearances indeed.[27] Yet, however speculative, the story of Sassamon's life bears telling.

III

WHEN THE FIRST English settlers arrived in Massachusetts Bay in 1630, John Sassamon's parents might have welcomed the newcomers warmly. Among the few survivors of epidemics that plagued coastal Algonquians between 1616 and 1618, Sassamon's family perhaps looked to the English for protection against hostile inland neighbors.[28] Sassamon's parents saw fit, at any rate, to remain among the English in Dorchester and eventually to convert to Christianity, possibly during a devastating smallpox outbreak in 1633.[29] Interpreting the disease as supernatural evidence of the power of the Puritans' God, many Algonquians converted to Christianity on their deathbeds, leaving their orphaned children in the care of English families. "But now I must die," said one man, "yet my Child shall live with the English, and learne to know their God when I am dead." A Puritan promotional tract written in 1643 boasted that such children were "long since civilized, and in subjection to us," their civility and subjection measured by their literacy and their piety: many "can speak our language familiarly; divers of whom can read English, and begin to understand in their measure, the grounds of Christian Religion."[30]

As an orphaned Indian raised in an English home, John Sassamon would have learned to speak and even to read and write English at a relatively young age (he was probably in his early teens when his parents died). By 1637 Sassamon had evidently demonstrated his civility and subjection well enough to serve as an interpreter and to fight on the colonists' side during the war against the Pequot Indians.[31] "Sosomon, the Indian" served with Sergeant Richard Callicott of Dorchester and may have been the interpreter Captain John Underhill described in his account of the war. "We had an Indian with us that was an interpreter," Underhill wrote. One day, a group of Pequots noticed this man, who was "in English clothes, and a gun in his hand," and called out to him, "What are you, an Indian or an Englishman?" "Come hither," he shouted back, "and I will tell you." As soon as the curious Pequots came within range, the interpreter "pulls up his cock and let fly at one of them, and without question was the death of him."³² When confronted with a question about his identity, the young Sassamon, if indeed it was he, answered with startling violence.

At the end of the war, Sassamon and Callicott returned to Dorchester along with their own Indian captives: Sassamon brought a Pequot woman who may have later become his wife, while Callicott returned with a Montauk slave named Cockenoe, who was to become an interpreter for John Eliot, a minister in the adjacent town of Roxbury who had immigrated to Massachusetts in 1631.³³ Eliot had probably known Sassamon before the Pequot War, but by the time he began working with Callicott's slave in the early 1640s he had probably come to know Sassamon very well. For John Sassamon this would prove to be a fateful, even a fatal connection.

John Eliot was the first Englishman to make a serious effort at learning Massachusett, the Algonquian language spoken by eastern New England Indians in the seventeenth century (and now extinct). From the time of their arrival, English settlers were baffled by the native languages they heard spoken, but few bothered to learn them, relying instead on Indian interpreters such as the famous Squanto. In 1634 William Wood observed that "the language is hard to learn, few of the English being able to speak any of it, or capable of the right pronunciation, which is the chief grace of their tongue." Although Wood had noticed that the Indians "love any man that can utter his mind in their words," few colonists were willing to learn even the most basic Algonquian vocabulary.³⁴ Consistent with European attitudes about native cultures, most colonists considered the local languages barbaric, even satanic, and found in the Indians' lack of a writing system powerful evidence of the primitiveness of their culture. (Cotton Mather once wryly remarked that Indian words were so long he thought they must have been growing since the confusion at Babel.³⁵) Yet the colonists' disdain for native illiteracy and the supposed barbarity of native languages was not lost on their Algonquian neighbors, one of whom told a missionary it was no use for an Indian to pray "because Jesus Christ understood not what Indians speake in prayer," since He had "bin used to heare English man pray" and "was not acquainted with [the Indian language], but was a stranger to it."³⁶

In the early years, most communication between the two peoples was aided by gestures, native interpreters, and Indians' use of pidgin English. Matters had not improved much by 1643, when Roger Williams wrote his *Key to the Language of America*, a pragmatic phrasebook designed to aid travelers and settlers. (Williams had learned a good bit of the Narragansett language, a very close relative of Massachusett.) That distrust and misunderstanding characterized communication between the English and the natives can be seen in Williams' many translations for phrases such as "I cannot speake your language," "I lie not," and "Wee understand not each other."[37] But if Williams attempted to use his ill-fitting key to unlock the Indians' language, John Eliot hoped to swing the doors wide open.

Eliot, known to hagiographers as the "Aspostle to the Indians," is widely credited with translating and printing the entire Bible, as well as a host of primers, catechisms, and religious tracts, in the Massachusett language, a set of works collectively known as the "Indian Library."[38] In an effort to fulfill the colonists' original mission, as documented in the Massachusetts Bay Colony seal ("Come Over and Help Us"), Eliot labored for decades to convert Indians to Christianity, always stressing literacy as an absolutely necessary step toward conversion, since true (Protestant) Christians could only encounter God by reading the Scriptures. By translating the Bible and other devotional literature into Massachusett, Eliot hoped to bring the "heathen" Indians into the Christian fold.[39]

Yet Eliot did not act alone in his linguistic and missionary work; instead, he relied to a great extent on Indian translators, interpreters, and teachers.[40] Over the course of his lifetime John Sassamon would serve Eliot in each of these capacities; there is an almost uncanny parallel between the careers of the two men. Like Eliot, Sassamon was well known for both his linguistic and his missionary skills. He was typically described as "a very cunning and plausible Indian, well skilled in the English Language." Increase Mather wrote that "being of very excellent parts," Sassamon had "translated some part of the bible into the Indian language." This "Indian Schollar and Minister" might have worked with or known Eliot for forty years or more. Eliot himself noted Sassamon's death in his diary with sorrow, calling him "a man of eminent parts & wit."[41] John Sassamon seems to have spent some portion of his childhood or adolescence living in or near Dorchester, perhaps in the home of an English family (the Callicotts) and, as all evidence indicates, in close proximity to John Eliot in nearby Roxbury. When Eliot's interpreter Cockenoe returned to Long Island in the late 1640s, Sassamon must have proved a convenient replacement.[42]

Yet John Sassamon seems to have been always ambivalent about Puritan society, alternately embracing and rejecting it. The damning discipline of Puritanism was difficult enough for the colonists' children, and must have been more difficult still for young people raised in another culture. Nowhere is the agony of inadequacy that must have plagued Algonquians engaged in cultural and religious conversion better captured than in notes several wrote in the margins of their own Indian Bibles, perhaps none more poignant than the careful handwriting from a Bible owned by a Christian Indian on Martha's Vineyard: "I am forever a pitiful person in the world. I am not able clearly to read this, this book."[43]

John Sassamon's ambivalence registered itself in rebellion, probably from the start. He may even have been the Indian boy mentioned in an early Puritan tract "who for some misdemeanour that laid him open to publique punishment, ran away; and being gone, God so followed him, that of his owne accord he returned home, rendred himselfe to Justice, and was willing to submit himself, though he might have escaped."[44] If so, it may well have been Eliot who received the errant Christian back into the fold: William Hubbard claimed that Sassamon was subject to "the frequent Sollicitations of Mr. Eliot, that had known him from a Child, and instructed him in the Principles of our Religion, who was often laying before him the heinous Sin of his Apostacy."[45]

If Eliot had really "known him from a Child," Eliot himself probably taught Sassamon to read. It is also possible, of course, that Sassamon learned from a member of the English family with whom he lived or that he attended an Indian School in Dorchester.[46] In any case, Sassamon was very likely taught with methods similar to those Eliot would later describe: "When I taught our Indians first to lay out a word into syllables, and then according to the sound of every syllable to make it up with the right letters . . . They quickly apprehended and understood this Epitomie of the art of spelling, and could soon learn to read." While Sassamon learned to read and write English, Eliot himself was learning the Massachusett language. Eliot's description of his methods of learning the language are remarkably similar to those he used in teaching Indian students:

> Such as desire to learn this language, must be attentive to pronounce right, especially to produce that syllable that is first to be produced; then they must spell by art, and accustom their tongues to pronounce their syllables and words; then learn to read such books as are printed in their language. *Legendo, scribendo, Loquendo,* are the three means to learn a language.[47]

In effect, Eliot and Sassamon were engaged in similar projects. Syllable by syllable and word by word, both were mastering new languages, pulling letters apart and pushing them back together again, making familiar meaning out of unfamiliar sounds. Eliot taught Sassamon, but Sassamon also taught Eliot—their relationship would have been in some important ways a reciprocal one.[48] Once Eliot's linguistic apprenticeship ended, however, the power would have shifted dramatically in the Englishman's favor. Eliot's mission, after all, was to eradicate native cultural practices and replace them with English ones.

John Eliot had a scholar's interest in the study of linguistics, but his reigning passion was the conversion of the Indians to Christianity, and it was for this reason, and this reason above all, that he had painstakingly learned the Massachusett language. For the twin purposes of converting and Anglicizing Indians, Eliot established the first "praying town" in Natick in 1650, a place where Christian Indians, he hoped, could live and worship like Englishmen, free of the cultural influences of their non-Christian peers. (Before King Philip's War, Eliot would organize fourteen praying towns in Massachusetts Bay.)[49] Like Eliot, Sassamon was engaged in this project from the start: he literally helped build the town of Natick, and he soon become one of its schoolmasters. In his accounts for the year 1651 Eliot recorded distributing tools to several Indian and English assistants, including two axes to "John Sosoman." The same year Eliot gave thanks that "whereas I had thought that we must have an Englishman to be their School-Master, I now hope that the Lord will raise up some of themselves, and enable them unto that work, with my care to teach them well in the reason of the sounds of letters and spelling." Five years later Eliot recorded a payment of £30 to "Sosaman, Monequason, and Job," identified in his ledger as "three Indian Interpreters & Schoolmasters."[50] In describing the Indian schools at Natick during the time when Sassamon was either becoming a schoolteacher or already teaching, Eliot wrote, "we aspire to no higher learning yet, but to spell, read, and write."[51]

Evidently Sassamon was at this time one of Eliot's favorite and most talented students, because by 1653 Eliot had arranged for the Natick schoolmaster to attend Harvard College.[52] As Eliot had written in 1649, "there be sundry prompt, pregnant witted youths, not viciously inclined, but well disposed, which I desire may be wholly sequestred to learning and put to school for that purpose."[53] For at least one semester in 1653, John Sassamon was a classmate of the fortunate sons of Massachusetts Bay, among them Samuel Bradstreet; Thomas Shepard; Samuel Hooker; John Eliot's son, John, Jr.; and a very young Increase Mather.[54]

JOHN SASSAMON, JOHN ELIOT, AND THE PATH TO WAR

1631 Eliot immigrates to New England.
1637 Sassamon serves with the English forces in the Pequot War.
1646 Eliot begins preaching in the Massachusett language.
1647 Eliot begins publishing promotional tracts in England.

1650 Natick is settled.
1651 Sassamon becomes a schoolmaster at Natick.
1653 Sassamon attends Harvard College.
1654 Eliot publishes his first book in Massachusett.
1655 The Indian College is built at Harvard.
1658 Eliot imports press, fonts, and a pressman.
1659 James Printer begins an apprenticeship at the Cambridge Press.
1662 Massasoit dies; Alexander succeeds him.
      Sassamon begins working for Alexander.
      Alexander dies.
      Philip assumes the sachemship and Sassamon begins working for
        him.
1663 The first edition of the complete Massachusett Bible is printed at
      Cambridge.
1664 Eliot reports that Sassamon is teaching Philip to read.
      Sassamon continues to serve Philip as scribe and translator.
1671 Philip is reported arming for war but is subdued.
      Eliot orders Sassamon to attempt to convert Philip.
1673 Sassamon is deeded land in Namasket, where he becomes minister.
1675 Sassamon is killed; war breaks out.

Soon after John Sassamon left Cambridge, a special Indian College was opened at Harvard. Although a college specifically for Indians had been proposed as early as 1635, no concrete arrangements were made until 1651, when Harvard president Henry Dunster began soliciting funds for the Indian College to be built. It was finally erected in 1655. Yet, of the four other Indians who attended Harvard in the seventeenth century, all that we really know is that three fell victim to the fatal consequences of extended contact with the English: one died of consumption, one died of unknown causes, and one was killed by other Indians.[55] As Daniel Gookin, superintendent of the Indians in Massachusetts explained, many colonists attributed the deaths of "these Indian scholars" "to the great change upon their bodies, in respect of their diet, lodging, apparel, studies; so much different from what they were inured to among their own countrymen."[56] While Sassamon's academic career at Harvard remains a mystery, surely his survival alone must be counted a success.

Despite surviving Harvard, John Sassamon may have fallen from Eliot's favor in 1654. As part of his plan for Christian Indians' full participation in the Puritan religious community, Eliot had scheduled a day of examination for members of the Natick church. Unhappily for Eliot, about ten days before the examination, three Natick Indians became drunk and, to make matters worse, forced liquor on the young son of a more pious Natick resident. Eliot lost heart, "For one of the offendors (though least in the offence) was he that hath been my Interpreter, whom I have used in Translating a good part of the Holy Scriptures; and in that respect I saw much of Satans venome, and in God I saw displeasure."[57] If he committed these shameful sins and acts of apostasy, Sassamon would have sorely disappointed Eliot.[58]

Meanwhile, Eliot's missionary work continued. Beginning in 1647 he had been involved in the publication of a set of promotional pamphlets printed in London and designed to solicit funds for the propagation of the gospel in New England. Almost immediately he began funneling these funds into printing supplies. While the first books in the Indian Library had been printed on the colony's only press at Cambridge, the press was inadequate for the great works Eliot planned. In 1658 he arranged for the purchase of a new printing press and extra trays of fonts to refresh a supply of worn type (and possibly to accommodate the many *k*s, *m*s, and *w*s of the Massachusett language). He also sent for a typographer from England, Marmaduke Johnson, and in 1659 a former student of Eliot's joined the press as Johnson's apprentice.[59] (As Eliot wrote, "we have but one man, viz. the Indian Printer, that is able to compose the sheets, and correct the press with understanding." By virtue of his employment, this Indian apprentice soon became known as James Printer.[60]) By 1663 Eliot, having been aided by former schoolmasters Job Nesutan and John Sassamon as translators and by James Printer as typesetter, had produced two editions of an Indian primer, two books of psalms, and the entire Bible—the first Bible printed in North America. In coming years he would also translate works of devotion popular in England, including Baxter's *Call to the Unconverted* and Bayly's *Practice of Piety*. In 1669, in his *Indian Primer*, Eliot was able to recommend a sequential program of study:

> Wa-an-tam-we us-seonk ogke-
> tam-un-at. Cate-chi-sa-onk.
> Ne-gon-ne og-kee-tash Primer.
> Na-hoh-to-eu og-kee-tash
> Ai-us-koi-an-tam-oe weh-kom-a-onk
> Ne-it og-kee-tash Bible.[61]

> [Wise doing to read Catechism
> first, next read Primer. Next
> read Repentance Calling
> next read Bible.]

ELIOT'S "INDIAN LIBRARY," 1647–89		
Brief (English) Title	*Languages*	*Number Printed*
1654 A Primer or Catechism	Mass. only?	500 or 1,000
1655 Genesis	Mass. only?	
1655 gospel of Matthew	Mass. only?	
1658? A Few Psalms in Metre	Mass. only?	
1660? A Christian Covenanting Confession	Mass. & Eng.	
1661 The New Testament	Mass. only	1,500
1662 A Primer or Catechism (2nd ed.)	Mass. only?	1,500
1663 The Holy Bible	Mass. only	1,000 or 2,000
The Metrical Psalmes	Mass. only	
1664 Baxter's Call to the Unconverted	Mass. only	1,000
1665 Bayly's Practice of Piety	Mass. only	200
1666 The Indian Grammar Begun	Mass. & Eng.	500
1669 The Indian Primer	mostly Mass.	
1670 A Christian Covenanting Confession	Mass. & Eng.	
1671 The Indian Dialogues	English only	
1672 The Logick Primer	Mass. & Eng.	1,000
1680 The New Testament (2nd ed.)	Mass. only	2,500*
1685 The Holy Bible	Mass. only	2,000
Bayly's Practice of Piety (2nd ed.)	Mass. only	
Dying Speeches	English only	
1687? The Indian Primer (3rd ed.)	mostly Mass.	
1688 Baxter's Call (2nd ed.)	Mass. only	
1689 Shepard's Converts		

*Two thousand of these copies were reserved to be bound with the Old Testament, printed in 1685, joined with the 1680 copies of the New Testament, and issued as complete Bibles.

The labor behind the Indian Library was phenomenal, and the output of the Cambridge Press unparalleled. (The paper used to print two editions of the complete Bible was more than the total amount of paper used at the Cambridge Press since its beginning in 1639.) Each of the instructional and devotional books in the Indian Library was printed in huge print runs, resulting in more copies than, on the face of things, seems necessary: all told, one Bible was printed for every 2.5 Christian Indians.[62] Today, precious few copies of any of these works survive (and most of those that do can be traced to English, not Indian owners), a situation that has puzzled historians and bibliographers alike. The mystery of the surplus Indian Bibles is made all the more intriguing when it becomes clear that the vast majority of Christian Indians were likely not as literate as Eliot wanted his benefactors in England to believe.

MAMUSSE
WUNNEETUPANATAMWE
UP-BIBLUM GOD
NANEESWE
NUKKONE TESTAMENT,
KAH WONK
WUSKU TESTAMENT.

Ne quoſhkinnumuk naſhpe Wuttinneumoh *CHRIST*
noh aſoowesit

JOHN . ELIOT·

CAMBRIDGE·
Printeuoop naſhpe *Samuel Green* kah *Marmaduke Johnſon*.

I 6 6 3·

The Massachusett Bible printed in Cambridge in 1663. *Courtesy of the Houghton Library, Harvard University*

While Eliot boasted that "we have schools; many can read, some write, sundry able to exercise in publick," he may well have exaggerated.[63] A survey conducted in 1674 revealed rather low literacy rates for Indians living in praying towns in Plymouth Colony, where Richard Bourne served as missionary. Of 497 converted Indians, 142 (29%) could read the Massachusett language, 72 (14%) could write, and 9 (2%) could read English.[65] (These numbers are decidedly lower than literacy rates among New England's colonists: in 1660, about 60% of English men and 30% of English women in New England seem to have been literate.[66]) Unfortunately, no data exist for native literacy rates in Massachusetts Bay, where Eliot himself preached. Rates there must have been higher than in Plymouth, but probably not by much.

	Population	Number Who Can Read	Number Who Can Write	Number Who Can Read English
A CENSUS OF CHRISTIAN INDIAN TOWNS IN 1674[64]				
MASSACHUSETTS BAY COLONY				
Natick	145			
Punkapoag	60			
Hassanamesit	60			
Okommakamesit	50			
Wamesit	75			
Nashobah	50			
Magunkaquog	55			
Manchage	60	(n/a)		
Chabanakongkomun	45			
Maanexit	100			
Quantisset	100			
Wabquissit	150			
Pakachoog	100			
Waeuntug	50			
Total	1,100			
PLYMOUTH COLONY				
Meeshawn	72	25	16	0
Potanumaquut	44	7	2	0
Manamoyik Sawkattukett	71	20	15	1
Nobsquassit Matakees Weequakut Satuit	122	33	15	4
Pawpoesit Mashpee Wakoquet	95	24	10	2

	Population	Number Who Can Read	Number Who Can Write	Number Who Can Read English
Codtaninut				
Ashimuit	22	13	7	2
Weesquobs				
Pispogutt				
Wawayontat	36	20	7	0
Sokones				
Cotuhkikut				
Namasket	35			
Total	497	142	72	9
		29%	2%	14%

While these literacy rates only further complicate the question of why Eliot printed so many Indian Bibles (and why so few survive), they do clarify another matter: they suggest that John Sassamon, who could speak, read, and write both the Massachusett and the English language, was undoubtedly among the elite of Christian Indians, especially in the 1650s, twenty years before this survey was taken, when the number of literate Indians was smaller. Yet, just as Eliot ushered in his biggest success, the completion of the printing of the Indian Bible, John Sassamon left him. In 1662, a year that marked a dramatic turning point in Indian-colonial relations in southeastern New England, John Sassamon seems to have switched sides. That year the Wampanoag sachem Massasoit died and his eldest son, Alexander, succeeded him. While Massasoit's fidelity to the English had been reasonably well assured, the colonial authorities were unsure of the loyalty of Alexander, alias Wamsutta, and his younger brother Philip, alias Metacom. Now, during this critical transition in power, John Sassamon appeared on the scene. On a land deed between Alexander and the town of Providence from March 1662, John Sassamon signed as a witness. Since Alexander signed with a mark, Sassamon probably also served as Alexander's scribe and translator.[67] Soon after this land deal, Alexander died under suspicious circumstances (some Wampanoags believed the English had poisoned him), and Philip assumed the sachemship.[68] Later that same year Sassamon set his signature down as witness to Philip's oath of loyalty to the English.[69] Perhaps Sassamon had a falling out with Eliot. William Hubbard claimed that Sassamon had "upon some Misdemeanour fled from his Place [at Natick] to Philip, by whom he was entertained in the Room and Office of Secretary, and his Chief Councellor."[70]

Whether as scribe, interpreter, secretary, counselor, or some combination thereof, Sassamon assumed a role of considerable importance to Philip because in 1664, 1665, and 1666 Sassamon's name appeared again and again as witness in Philip's land transactions.[71] Cotton Mather would later report that Sassamon "apostatiz[ed] from the profession of Christianity, [and] lived like an heathen in the quality of a Secretary to King Philip; for he could write, though the King his master could not so much as read."[72]

In other words, the same skills that had made Sassamon valuable to Eliot now made him almost indispensable to Philip: the ability to speak, read, and write both English and Massachusett. But, while Sassamon used his literacy skills as a tool in acquiring status and prestige in the Indian community, it is difficult to know if Sassamon's work for Philip at this time represents a genuine change of heart or whether he was essentially acting as a spy for the English (attempting to evaluate Philip's loyalty) or as a missionary for Eliot (infiltrating Philip's counsel in order to convert him). That Eliot wanted passionately to convert Philip is clear. Most missionaries believed that "when a sachem or sagamore is converted to the faith, and yields himself up to embrace the gospel, it hath a great influence upon his subjects."[73] Philip, however, apparently had no desire to be converted. An anecdote recorded by Cotton Mather told of Philip taking a button off John Eliot's coat and declaring defiantly "that he cared for his gospel, just as much as he cared for that button."[74] Nonetheless, Eliot at one point rejoiced over an indication that Philip was finally succumbing. In 1664, at the very time when Sassamon was working closely with Philip as a scribe and witness to treaties, Eliot asked the commissioners of the United Colonies "to give incouragmt to John Sosaman, who teacheth Phillip and his men to read." Eliot claimed that Philip "did this winter past, upon solicitations and means used, send to me for books to learne to read, in order to praying unto God, which I did send unto him, and presents with all." Sassamon, Eliot believed, was "a means to put life into the work."[75]

Apparently neither Sassamon's work nor the books Eliot sent were successful in converting Philip, because seven years later Eliot made the same attempt all over again, sending even more Indian missionaries to visit Philip at a time when tensions between Philip and Plymouth were high and war was rumored. In March 1671, after Philip's men marched through Swansea displaying their weapons, Plymouth called Philip to court, where he admitted he was preparing for war. On April 10 at Taunton, Philip signed a treaty in which he agreed to turn his arms over to Plymouth. The crisis was not well resolved, however, and in the coming months Massachusetts authorities attempted to arbitrate. In September 1671 Philip, encouraged by John Eliot, traveled to Boston to solicit support in his conflict with Plymouth. Failing to find it (and instead finding himself facing the wrath of Massachusetts, Connecticut, and Plymouth), he opted instead to sign yet another treaty with Plymouth, agreeing to pay £100 in fines over three years.[76]

The events of 1671 were, in effect, a dress rehearsal for the events of 1675—except that in 1671 Philip backed down. John Sassamon played a critical role in both conflicts, serving as both messenger and missionary. At the height of the 1671 conflict, in August, the Natick church sent Anthony and William Nahauton to preach to the Wampanoags at Plymouth and requested "John Sausiman to join them."[77] (This, of course, was the same William Nahauton whose testimony would later become so pivotal at the trial of Sassamon's alleged murderers.) Philip was apparently not pleased to see Sassamon and had come to consider him untrustworthy. In September Massachusetts emissaries sent to Mount Hope found that Philip "exclaimed much against Sausiman" for giving him false information (about the whereabouts of several Narragansett sachems, who were, at this time, enemies of the Wampanoags).[78]

Perhaps enraged with Sassamon for his seeming duplicity in 1671, Philip may well have blamed Sassamon for his troubles with the English; meanwhile, since Philip was not converted, Eliot may have blamed Sassamon for this failure. Later in 1671 Eliot published a tract called *Indian Dialogues*, a set of conversion conversations he claimed were "partly historical, of some things that were done and said, and partly instructive, to show what might or should have been said, or that may be (by the Lord's assistance) hereafter done and said." In one lengthy, imaginary dialogue, two barely fictionalized Praying Indians, "Anthony" and "William Abahton," speak with "Philip Keitasscot," sachem of "Paganoehket." That Eliot left Sassamon out of his *Indian Dialogues* suggests either that Sassamon left the company of Anthony and William Nahauton and never made it to Plymouth to preach to Philip, or that Eliot considered Sassamon's contributions unworthy.

Indian Dialogues, however, remains interesting, if only for how much it reveals about Eliot's frantic desire to convert Philip. In one scene "Philip" expresses his "serious thoughts of accepting the offer, and turning to God, to become a praying Indian," but is concerned about whether his conversion would mean a diminishment of his authority as a sachem. The eloquent and persuasive Indian missionaries assuage his every fear and soon a very humbled "Philip" confesses, "I am drowned and overwhelmed with the weight of your reasonings." Much of the dialogue concerns the goodness of the Bible, to which "Philip" meekly and gratefully responds, "Your discourse doth breed in my heart an admiration at that excellent book." Again and again, "Philip's" objections to conversion are defeated by the wisdom of Anthony and William: "Who can oppose or gainsay the mountainous weight of these arguments?" a helpless "Philip" asks. Finally deferring to the missionaries' superior knowledge, he proclaims, "I am more than satisfied. I am ashamed of my ignorance, and I abhor myself that ever I doubted."[79]

Yet, in spite of the shipment of books, the visits by William and Anthony Nahauton, and Eliot's richly detailed fantasies, neither Sassamon nor Eliot nor any other missionary ever converted Philip to Christianity. But the missionary work continued. During the early 1670s Eliot continued to expand the Indian Library, while Sassamon apparently left Philip's employ to return to the Christian fold (or was told by Eliot to give up trying to convert Philip), and became minister in the praying town of Namasket. In 1673 he was given a tract of land to induce him to stay, and the same year he deeded this land to his daughter Betty and her husband, Felix.[80] Two years later Sassamon was either working for Philip or spying on him when he found out about Philip's plans to attack the English and nervously confided them to the governor of Plymouth. Just four years after Eliot published his fictional dialogues, Philip, instead of peaceably and humbly converting to Christianity, waged war against the English settlers.

IV

WE HAVE COME full circle and arrived once more at icy Assawompset Pond. Here we must ask yet again: Why was John Sassamon murdered? Was he killed simply because he betrayed Philip's plans to the English? Remember, Increase Mather was convinced that "No doubt but one reason why the Indians murthered John Sausaman, was out of hatred against him for his Religion, for he was Christianized, and baptiz'd, and was a Preacher amongst the Indians, being of very excellent parts, he translated some part of the bible into the Indian language, and was wont to curb those Indians that knew not God on the account of their debaucheryes." Daniel Gookin agreed, claiming that "this John Sasamand was the first Christian martyr of the Indians; for it is evident he suffered death upon the account of his Christian profession, and fidelity to the English." And Nathaniel Saltonstall argued that Philip's men killed Sassamon because they didn't wish to be converted. According to Saltonstall, Sassamon "was by the Authority of New-Plimouth sent to Preach . . . to King Philip, and his Indians: But King Philip (Heathen-like) instead of receiving the gospel, would immediately have killed this Sosomon, but by the Perswasion of some about him did not do it, but sent him by the Hands of three of his Men to Prison." On the way to "prison," Sassamon preached to his three captors, who, "not liking his Discourse, immediately Murthered him after a most Barbarous Manner" and returned to tell Philip of their deed.[81]

Clearly Philip was tired of listening to missionaries and angry that so many of his people had become Christians. When John Easton asked Philip and his counselors to list their grievances against the English, they responded "that thay had a great fear to have ani of ther indians should be Caled or forsed to be Christian indians. thay saied that such wer in everi thing more mischivous, only disemblers, and then the English made them not subject to ther kings, and by ther lying to rong their kings." Easton admitted, "we knew it to be true."[82] The Wampanoags Easton interviewed provided a good example of this kind of despised duplicity, claiming that instead of converting Philip, Sassamon was cheating him—"report was he was a bad man that king Philop got him to write his will and he made the writing for a gret part of the land to be his but read as if it had bine as Philop wold, but it Came to be knone and then he run away from him."[83]

This last explanation provides perhaps the most unequivocal instance of Sassamon's exploitation of his literacy. Pretending to write down what Philip dictated, Sassamon instead substituted his own words and then, when asked to read the document aloud, read as though he had written what Philip requested. No "will" of Philip's exists, but Sassamon did serve as scribe and witness for important land deeds in 1666 and 1668 in which Philip authorized certain lands to be sold. (Philip may have even drawn the map on the 1668 deed, in which he declared, "I Phillip ame willing to sell the Land within this draught," but it was probably Sassamon who "set downe all the principall names of the land wee are not willing should be sold," and he may not have followed Philip's orders.) This was the power that Sassamon wielded, "for he could write, though the King his master could not so much as read."[84] While it may or may not be true, this particular story about the writing of the will, told to Easton by a group of Wampanoag Indians, suggests that it had special significance for them. To the Wampanoags, at least, Sassamon's literacy was mysterious, potent, and dangerous. And it marked him as a man who could not be trusted.

But it wasn't just being literate that made Sassamon untrustworthy; it was how he got that way in the first place. Learning to read and write, and especially learning to read and write English, were among the very last steps on the path to cultural conversion. Steps taken earlier along this same path were considered not nearly as corrupting. Many New England Indians were bilingual; speaking English was useful for trading, among other things, and did not necessarily signify any particular loyalty to the English. Dressing as an Englishman and worshiping the Christian God were of course much less ambiguous; those practices clearly marked an Indian as having a compromised relationship with the English. Still, many Indians lived and attended church in praying towns simply because they needed the food and shelter, and then only temporarily, taking off English clothes as easily as they put them on. Literacy, however, was a special kind of marker, one that branded its possessor, perhaps most especially in his own eyes, as an Indian who had spent years and years with the English and whose very "Indianness" was thus called into question. After King Philip's War began, Indian interpreters like Sassamon became even less trustworthy, and colonists feared they would join the enemy at the first opportunity. In September 1675 John Allyn advised Fitz-John Winthrop, "beware of haveing any linguist in your company, least he so hide himselfe as that you leave him behind you!"[85]

In the end, although John Sassamon "was observed to conform more to the English Manners than any other Indian," the facts of his life are by no means clear on the question of whether his primary attachment was to one people or the other.[86] What is clear is that it was his linguistic skills, and especially his literacy, that made it possible for him to switch sides with such facility. But those same skills, and the untenable position they put him in, eventually led John Sassamon to his death, a death that signaled the failure of the English and native peoples to live together peaceably, the gradual loss of native political autonomy, and the eventual extinction of the Massachusett language. And, by the war's end, the Algonquian population in New England had been drastically and permanently reduced.

King Philip's War also marked the decline of English attempts to convert and educate the Indians; in some ways, Eliot's missionary program died with Sassamon.[87] The imprisonment of Christian Indians on Deer Island in Boston Harbor for the duration of the war spoiled not only their allegiance to the English but also their links to the Puritans' religion. As Eliot wrote in his diary, "When the Indians were hurried away to an iland at half an hours warning, pore soules in terror thei left theire goods, books, bibles, only some few caryed their bibles, the rest were spoyled & lost."[88] By the war's end, only a tiny number of copies of the much-celebrated Indian Bible survived. Dutch traders who ran into Eliot three years after the war asked him for a copy of the Indian Bible, but Eliot apologized that "in the late Indian War all the Bibles and Testaments were carried away and burned or destroyed, so that he had not been able to save any for himself; but a new edition was in press, which he hoped would be much better than the first one, though that was not to be despised."[89] The best explanation of the mystery of the disappearing Bibles is that, in their fury, Algonquians hostile to Christianity seized the books as a symbol of the pernicious influence of English culture and destroyed any they came upon.[90]

Although Eliot was able to secure the funds for a new printing of the Bible, the Society for the Propagation of the gospel became more and more reluctant to publish any more works in the Indian language, instead urging missionaries to simply teach the Indians English. While a handful of praying towns, including Natick, survived into the eighteenth century, they soon lost first their religious zeal, next their political autonomy, and finally their ability to preserve their native language. In 1698 the church membership at Natick had dropped to seven men and three women; by the 1720s the largely secular community was no longer self-governing. The Massachusett language also languished. In 1710 Cotton Mather would write,

> It is very sure the best thing we can do for our Indians is to Anglicize them in all agreeable instances; and in that of languages, as well as others. They can scarce retain their language, without a tincture of other savage inclinations, which do but ill suit, either with honor, or with the design of Christianity.[91]

By 1720 the paucity of books written in Massachusett made the preservation of the language increasingly difficult, even for literate Indians.[92] In 1745 one observer claimed that there were fewer than twenty families of Massachusett speakers, "and scarce any of these can read." Of the Indian Bible, he would ask, "*Cui bono?*"[93] And at Harvard, the building so hopefully erected as an Indian College in 1655 was soon put to other purposes. By 1677, two years after King Philip's War ended, the Indian College building's only use was to house the Cambridge Press. Originally imported by Eliot to print Indian Bibles and save Indian souls, the press at Cambridge was soon put to another, altogether different use: to print the colonists' war narratives, damning Indian devils.[94]

V

MURDER MAY HAVE silenced John Sassamon, but something else silenced John Eliot. In his diary at the end of 1675, Eliot looked back at the year's devastations, "the history whereof," he wrote helplessly, "I canot, I may not relate." Much later, after the war had ended, Eliot recalled, "I desisted fro[m] this work of recording p'ticular matters," partly because "I thought not my selfe so fitting." Moreover, "knowing that it was comited to othrs," Eliot explained, "I declined it."[95] Short of the printers and the licensers of the Cambridge Press, John Eliot was probably more familiar with the workings of the press than any other colonist in New England. And the man who supervised the printing of an entire Indian Library no doubt knew that any account he might write of the war would not be printable.

Eliot also knew that the task of recording the story had been committed to others, to men like William Hubbard and Increase Mather. Meanwhile, as

Daniel Gookin leafed through the pages and pages about King Philip's War written by people like Mather, Hubbard, and Saltonstall, he became increasingly frustrated. Gookin had noticed something disturbing:

> Forasmuch as sundry persons have taken pains to write and publish historical narratives of the war, between the English and Indians in New England, but very little hath been hitherto declared (that I have seen) concerning the Christian Indians, who, in reality, may be judged to have no small share in the effects and consequences of this war.

Boldly, Gookin decided to remedy the situation and to tackle the job himself, resolving "to give a particular and real account of this affair." It probably did not occur to Gookin that he might instead have encouraged one of the literate Indians he knew to write such an account; in fact, he did not so much notice the absence of accounts written *by* Indians as the lack of discussion, in English accounts, *about* Indians, and here he referred only to converted, Christian Indians. Still, Gookin's sympathy with the Indians may have been subversive enough—his "Historical Account of the Doings and Sufferings of the Christian Indians in New England," a manuscript presented to the Society for the Propagation of the Gospel in London in 1677 and presumably written for immediate publication, was put aside to gather the dust of more than a century. (Gookin had himself at one time been a licensor of the press in Cambridge, but during the war his standing in the colonial community diminished dramatically. In May 1676 he lost a reelection bid for the Court of Assistants.)[96] When John Eliot read Daniel Gookin's account of the war, his measured response hinted at resignation: "Here is enough to give wise men a taste of what hath passed. Leave the rest unto the day of judgment, when all the contrivances and actings of men shall be opened before the seeing eye of a glorious Judge."[97]

The accounts of King Philip's War that *were* printed, of course, were rarely to the credit of the Indians John Eliot had long labored to convert. Whether they wrote to justify the war or simply to document it, most colonists who described the war were likely to portray Indians, both Christian and non-Christian, in the worst possible light. Although earlier writing about the Indians had emphasized their potential for conversion, the King Philip's War narratives transformed New England's natives into irredeemable monsters. In his dedicatory poem to William Hubbard's *Narrative*, Benjamin Tompson suggested that the writings of men like Roger Williams and John Eliot had been rightly replaced by Hubbard's account of the Indians' barbarity:

Their grand Apostle [Eliot] writes of their Return [to grace];
[Roger] William's their Language; Hubbard how they burn,
Rob, Kill and Roast, Lead Captive, Slay, Blaspheme[.][98]

Tompson welcomed the replacement of Eliot's idealism with Hubbard's realism; Gookin mourned it. Yet, in noticing the war narratives' neglect of Indians (albeit only Christian Indians), Gookin was not only more perceptive than most of his contemporaries, he was also more perceptive than most of the historians who succeeded him, many of whom failed to consider even the possibility of an Indian perspective. This is an error very recent historians are not likely to make; instead, they usually cite the absence of Indian documents, acknowledge the inherent bias of the existing sources, and adopt one of three approaches to the colonists' accounts: read them with a "hermeneutics of suspicion" and accept or reject them according to whether or not they are corroborated by other evidence; claim that questions of truth and falsehood are irrelevant and that "verisimilitude" is a more appropriate indicator of a source's value; or piece together the sparse Indian sources to create a new, Indian-centered narrative.[99]

All of these strategies have their merits, just as all have limitations, but they all take the absence of Indian sources more or less for granted. They begin with the assumption that there are few or no such sources because historically people like seventeenth-century Algonquians have had no indigenous writing systems. In this they echo the observations of men like Cotton Mather, who was careful to note the natives' lack of letters or any written system of recording their past:

Reading and Writing is altogether unknown to them, tho there is a Rock or two in the Country that has unaccountable Characters engrav'd upon it.[100]

Yet, even in an age and in a place where such "unlettered" peoples were taught to read, historians have continued to assume that most were illiterate and hence unable to record the events of their lives. Rates of illiteracy prove this to be true enough. But behind this assumption lies the more troubling belief that these "inarticulate" peoples lacked not only the tools to communicate with us across the centuries but the sensibility as well, that people who lack the ability to read and write also lack historical awareness, the sense of existing on a time line. Yet, contrary to Samuel Purchas's seventeenth-century contention that writing makes man immortal, and contrary, too, to the theories proposed by anthropologists two decades ago that literacy makes history possible, the story of John Sassamon suggests that literacy might sometimes make history *im*possible, at least temporarily.

When John Sassamon learned to read and write he did not magically cross an invisible boundary between orality and literacy; he did not spontaneously abandon mythological concepts and begin to think historically. But with his acquisition of literacy came an extraordinarily complicated and tenuous cultural position as a mediator between two very different cultures. And Sassamon exploited this position in ways that had fatal consequences. The first casualty may have been the Pequot man whom an Indian interpreter, possibly Sassamon himself, shot dead in 1637, furious at being asked the question that haunted him: "What are you, an Indian or an Englishman?" The unanswerableness of this question would eventually kill Sassamon, too. His life, and his death, serve as a metaphor for tensions that would prove fatal to the thousands of literate and nonliterate Indians who died in King Philip's War. It was not until the Pequot William Apess in 1836 that a New England Indian writer would emerge to write the history of King Philip's War. If Sassamon had survived the consequences of literacy, he might have written such a history a century and a half earlier.

On the other hand, he might not have. Even though literate, John Sassamon might never have thought to write a history of his life, his people, or their calamitous war. Because little evidence survives to tell us how he thought, it remains a possibility that Sassamon did in fact lack the kind of "historical sensibility" anthropologists have commonly attributed to literate peoples. An early eighteenth-century missionary on Martha's Vineyard noted that most literate Indians read only at the "rate that poor Men among the English are wont to do."[101] Frustratingly, we will never know what kind of a writer John Sassamon might have been.[102] Certainly several New England Indians (including James Printer) *did* survive the consequences of literacy, but they can be no more faulted for their silence than Eliot himself: perhaps they, too, chose to "leave the rest unto the day of judgment."

War is a contest of words as much as it is a contest of wounds. This connection, between waging war and writing about it, was not lost on New England's colonists. For some, the war's injuries were signs from God, as legible as any scriptural text. "Why should we suppose that God is not offended with us," asked Increase Mather, "when his displeasure is written, in such visible and bloody Characters?"[103] God might write with an ink of blood, but so, too, did John Sassamon, when his decayed corpse fell "ableeding afresh," as Tobias approached it. And so, too, did Philip. One Englishman said that the war, through the wounds Indians inflicted on English bodies, was Philip's only chance to be "found in print," "drawing his own reportt in blud not Ink."[104] Maybe dead men do tell tales.

Chapter 2

THE STORY OF IT PRINTED

*I*ncrease Mather observed the John Sassamon murder trial with dismay. And, as the fighting began and began to worsen, he came to call it "the saddest time with New England that ever was known."[1] Although Mather had never intended to write a history of the war, he kept careful track of it. "I was not altogether negligent," he later confessed, "in Noting down such Occurrences, respecting the present War with the Heathen in New-England, as came to my knowledge." Still, he insisted, with strained humility, "what I did that way, was merely for my own private use." Never had he "the least thought of publishing" any of his observations of the bloody conflict. But coming across someone else's version of the story convinced him that publish he must. In early 1676 Mather read an early printed narrative of the war, "which it seems," he remarked gloomily, "met with an imprimatur at London in December last." The "abounding mistakes" in this account inspired Mather to pick up his pen to write "a true history of this affair." No sooner had the Boston minister filled his inkwell than he came upon "another Narrative of this war, written by a Quaker in Rhode Island, who pretends to know the truth of things." "But," Mather complained, "that narrative being fraught with worse things than mere mistakes, I was thereby quickened to expedite what I had in hand."[2]

The first account Mather came across was Boston merchant Nathaniel Saltonstall's *Present State of New-England with Respect to the Indian War,* printed in London in December 1675; the next, "written by a Quaker in Rhode

Island," was John Easton's "Relacion of the Indyan Warre," written in February 1676.[3] But the competitor Mather came to despise most was the Reverend William Hubbard, who, in addition to writing a narrative of the war, was chosen to deliver the colony's annual Election Day sermon on May 3, 1676—a sermon Mather had hoped to deliver.[4] Two days before Election Day, Mather began writing a history of the war: his May 1 diary entry reads simply: "A.M. wrote Hist of warr Indians. Sic. P.M." He wrote steadily through the summer, and on August 21 noted in his diary, "A.M. Finished History." Three days later Mather visited John Foster's Boston print shop, and within months his "true" story of King Philip's War, *A Brief History of the War with the Indians in New-England*, was printed in both Boston and London.[5]

Mather must have been elated: he had beaten Hubbard to the presses (Hubbard's *Narrative of the Troubles with the Indians in New-England* was not printed until the spring of 1677). All things considered, however, both ministers were latecomers, especially to the London publishing scene. Long before Mather completed his *Brief History*, several accounts of the war had already been published, some within weeks of the first attacks in June 1675. By the end of that year four printed reports were available to anxious readers in London, not only Saltonstall's *Present State* (which had so annoyed Mather) but also Edward Wharton's *New-England's Present Sufferings under Their Cruel Neighboring Indians*, the anonymous *A Brief and True Narration of the Late Wars Risen in New-England*, and Benjamin Batten's account in *The London Gazette*. At least three more accounts (by Wait Winthrop, Peter Folger, and John Easton) are said to have been printed that year, though no printed copy survives.[6] In the colonies, only one printed narrative appeared in 1675 (the Massachusetts Council's official broadside declaring the causes and progress of the war), but during the next year, when Mather published his *Brief History* as well as his sermon about the war, *An Earnest Exhortation to the Inhabitants of New-England*, Benjamin Tompson published an epic poem in both Old and New England, and Thomas Wheeler's sermon, *A Thankefull Remembrance of Gods Mercy*, was printed in Cambridge. Meanwhile, in London, readers relished two more installments of Saltsonstall's chronicle, as well as three more anonymous pamphlets. Between 1675 and 1676 several other colonists wrote accounts that were to remain unpublished: Josiah Winslow and Thomas Hinckley detailed the origins of the war; Daniel Gookin drafted his treatise on the sufferings of Christian Indians; Philip Walker composed a quirky, lyrical poem; William Harris sent an account to the British secretary of state; and a visiting English official, Edward Randolph, sent a report to the lords of the Privy Council.

Philip's death may have ended the war in August 1676 but it barely slowed the printing spree. In 1677 William Hubbard finally finished his *Narrative* (printed in London under the title *The Present State of New-England*), Richard Hutchinson joined the fray with *The Warr in New-England Visibly Ended*, and Increase Mather added two more tracts: *A Relation of the Troubles which Have Hapned in New-England* and *An Historical Discourse*. Then, in 1678, Samuel Nowell, official minister to the colonial army, published his sermon about the war, and finally, in 1682, probably at the urging of Reverend Mather, Mary Rowlandson made public her narrative of captivity among the Indians.[7]

NARRATIVES OF KING PHILIP'S WAR, 1675–82

Author	Brief Title	Where Printed
1675		
Anonymous	*A Brief and True Narration of the Late Wars*	London
Batten, Benjamin	(reported in *The London Gazette*)	London
Folger, Peter	*A Looking Glasse for the Times*	possibly published
Massachusetts Council	*To Our Brethren* (broadside)	Cambridge
Saltonstall, Nathaniel	*The Present State of New-England*	London
Wharton, Edward	*New-England's Present Sufferings*	London
Winslow, Josiah and Hinkley, Thomas	"Narrative shewing the manor of the beginning . . . Warr"	unpublished
Winthrop, Wait	*Some Meditations*	possibly published
1676		
Anonymous	*A Farther Brief and True Narration*	London
Anonymous	*News from New-England*	London
Anonymous	*A True Account*	London
Easton, John	*Relacion of the Indyan Warre*	possibly published
Harris, William	[untitled letter]	unpublished
Mather, Increase	*A Brief History of the War*	Boston and London
Mather, Increase	*An Earnest Exhortation*	Boston
Randolph, Edward	"Short Narrative of My Proceedings"	unpublished
Saltonstall, Nathaniel	*A Continuation of the State of New-England*	London
Saltonstall, Nathaniel	*A New and Further Narrative*	London
Tompson, Benjamin	*New England's Crisis*	Boston
Tompson, Benjamin	*New England's Tears*	London
Walker, Philip	"Captan Perse & his coragios Company"	unpublished

Wheeler, Thomas	*A Thankefull Remembrance of Gods Mercy*	Cambridge
1677		
Gookin, Daniel	"Historical Account of the Doings and Sufferings"	unpublished
Hubbard, William	*A Narrative of the Troubles with the Indians*	Boston and London
Hutchinson, Richard	*The Warr in New-England Visibly Ended*	London
Mather, Increase	*A Relation of the Troubles*	Boston
Mather, Increase	*An Historical Discourse*	Boston
1678		
Nowell, S.	*Abraham in Arms*	Boston
1682		
Rowlandson, Mary	*The Soveraignty & Goodness of God*	Cambridge, Boston, and London

Eight years after King Philip's War began, the printing presses finally stiffened to a weary halt. In those eight years, at least twenty-one different accounts had been printed, many in more than one edition, for a total of no fewer than thirty separate printings in London, Boston, and Cambridge. Fortunately, one very revealing letter provides an important clue about the number of copies printed and sold. In early 1677 Richard Chiswell, a London bookseller, wrote to alert the Reverend Mather that his *Brief History* was not selling well in Old England. Embarrassed, Chiswell admitted that "some people here made it too much their business to cry it downe, & sayd a better narrative was comeing, which did very much disappoint me, so that I never sold 5 hundred of them." By way of apology and "as a token of my thankfullness to you for your respects," Chiswell sent Mather two dozen copies of the unpopular book.[8] ("And good riddance to them," Chiswell may well have muttered under his breath.) Chiswell's letter suggests both that the original (and typical) press run was more than five hundred and that his inability to sell even that many copies of such a book was unusual. Indeed, as the printer explained, Mather's history failed only because of tough competition in the form of yet another account of the war—Hubbard's *Narrative*.

It is difficult to imagine the horror with which Mather greeted this news, but his disappointment is our gain, since Chiswell's letter suggests that despite the failure of the London edition of Mather's history, stories chronicling this cruel and bloody war were clearly popular, and at least moderate press runs must have been the rule. Even in an era profoundly less print-oriented than our own, several of the accounts, including Mary Rowlandson's dramatic captivity narrative, America's first "best-seller," probably sold in the thousands.[9] And even if the runs averaged only a moderate five hundred copies per printing, a minimum of fifteen thousand copies of printed accounts of King Philip's War would have descended on the very small Anglo-American book market between 1675 and 1682.[10] A literal advantage indeed.

Yet, despite thousands of books detailing the colonists' devastating losses at the hands of the cruelest of Indian enemies, Boston poet Benjamin Tompson found New Englanders strangely quiet, so quiet that he felt compelled to ask, "What means this silence of Harvardine quills / While Mars triumphant thunders on our hills?"[11] It is an unusual question, made all the more unusual because, to us, the more profound silence, of course, was not the colonists' but the Indians'. Nonetheless, we would do well to investigate why some colonists wrote so much while others wrote nothing at all.

I

IN HIS DIARY for the year 1675 Simon Bradstreet wrote about a shipboard accident, the trial of an Anabaptist, a nasty summer storm, and the untimely death of a former president of Harvard College. He barely mentioned "the Indian warre begun by Philip in Plymouth," noting only early on that so far "neer 200 English have been killed." Admittedly, Bradstreet was a laconic man. If more widely read, his pithy diary entries would humble wordy writers everywhere. Nonetheless, a flair for brevity cannot explain the Massachusetts colonist's failure to elaborate on the war. Nor can indifference. Simon Bradstreet was far from apathetic about the suffering and destruction around him; on the contrary, he was overwhelmed—too overwhelmed, in fact, to describe it. The war, he remarked grimly, "is a matter of [such] great Importe that I cannot here note it." In any event, he pointed out, "I suppose a Record of it will be publickly taken & the story of it Printed."[12] Why bother to write a personal account, Bradstreet asked himself, when a "public" record would soon appear?

Simon Bradstreet, deputy governor of Massachusetts, was well acquainted with the public record and with the machinations of men like Increase Mather. Even after beating Hubbard to the presses, Mather had remained obsessed with discrediting the Ipswich minister, especially after his jealousy was further fueled by Chiswell's letter. Mather had been a licensor of the press since 1674, and it was probably through this position that he obtained a copy of Hubbard's manuscript in early 1677. Disgusted, Mather passed the manuscript along to his brother-in-law, the Reverend John Cotton of Plymouth Colony, to solicit a critical reading from the Plymouth authorities. Cotton wrote back to Mather that Governor Winslow and others had given the manuscript a "cursory perusall" and "the mistakes are Judged to be many more than the truths in it." Cotton only wished that he had been able "to have kept your booke a few days longer, whereby it might have bin filled with marginal notes of Erratas." [13]

Hubbard, no fool, countered by courting an endorsement from the Massachusetts authorities, who, above Mather's protestations, stamped Hubbard's book with an official government imprimatur in March 1677:

> The worthy Author of this Narrative (of whose Fidelity we are well assured) by his great Pains and Industry, in collecting and compiling the several Occurrences of this *Indian Warre,* from the Relations of such as were present in the particular Actions, hath faithfully and truly performed the same, as far as best Information agreeing can be obtained, which is therefore judged meet for publick View. [14]

Simon Bradstreet was among the signers. In 1675, when Bradstreet wrote in his diary, "I suppose a Record of it will be publickly taken & the story of it Printed," he had not yet been called upon to endorse Hubbard's narrative, but surely he knew very well that some accounts of the war would be considered worthier, and more printable, than others.

Although Increase Mather's campaign to discredit Hubbard's account ultimately failed (and encouraged Bradstreet and the Massachusetts Council to add their imprimatur), it is nonetheless suggestive of the power wielded by the Puritan elite and offers a simple and important answer to Benjamin Tompson's question about the "silence of Harvardine quills": most colonists kept quiet out of deference to the official record. Merchant John Hull demurred on these grounds, too, omitting almost all mention of the war in his diary for 1675–76 and leaving instead only a cross-reference: "See the history of the war, printed 1676." In his own diary, John Eliot also had declined to write about the war, knowing that it was "comited to othrs." Like Simon Bradstreet, Eliot had special cause to be familiar with the workings of press censorship: a theological treatise he wrote in the 1650s had been banned and destroyed because of its potentially heretical content. [15] And, while prominent men like Bradstreet and Eliot declined to write at length, less powerful colonists were likely to apologize for writing as much as they did. In Providence, Mary Pray excused herself for writing about the war by claiming her grief had compelled her, and when the poor and elderly John Kingsley wrote to the Connecticut War Council begging for aid, he wondered whether he had a right to write at all. "It may be in som of your minds to say, why doe not the he[a]d men write, but onely this ould pore man," Kingsley apologized. "There is but too [2] that knowes of my writing, & the won descoriged me." [16] Even more than Bradstreet and Eliot, Kingsley and Pray knew that the war was not theirs to narrate.

It was, in fact, rather rare for people like Kingsley and Pray, who had directly experienced the worst of war, to write about it in any detail. Instead it was far likelier for wealthier people living farther away from the most awful scenes of war to write the lengthiest accounts. Surely this has something to do with the relative comfort and leisure of ministers like Increase Mather or Boston merchants like Nathaniel Saltonstall, but it also directs us to an even more obvious answer to Tompson's question: not all colonists could write about the war, even if they wanted to. As William Hubbard wryly noted, "All Soldiers are not like Caesar, able to describe with their Pens, what they have done with their swords." [17] Or, in this case, all soldiers or noncombatants, however Caesar-like, do not necessarily own pens or even possess the ability to write.

Literacy in early America took a particular, "traditional" form, characterized by its religious context, the scarcity of printed materials, and the habit of repetition. Colonists had contact with a limited number of books—most often Bibles, primers, and catechisms—which they were likely to read again and again, often to the point of committing them to memory. Because reading was taught before writing, many colonists, especially women, could do one but not the other, and as many as 40 percent of men and 70 percent of women could not even sign their own names. Seventeenth-century New England was, at the same time, a "world of wonders" in which belief in the occult coexisted with church theology and in which books were both especially valuable and especially magical: during King Philip's War one colonist sat in the town common reading the Bible in the midst of an Indian attack, believing he couldn't be killed that way (instead, he was the single casualty of the day). Not only the presses but other avenues of information were also controlled by the clerical elite and, even to a literate colonist, the idea of writing a personal account of an event of political import would have seemed radical indeed. [18]

These two explanations—low literacy rates and the elite monopoly of information—go a long way toward answering Benjamin Tompson's question, but not far enough. In particular, to explain some colonists' silence by focusing exclusively on the hierarchical nature of colonial society and the role of Massachusetts magistrates and ministers in the workings of the Cambridge and Boston presses would be to overlook the real diversity of contemporary accounts of King Philip's War. In large part this diversity was made possible by the option nonconforming colonists had of printing their accounts in London, although it had consequences for readers in the colonies as well. To answer Tompson's question we must look more closely at the printed narratives themselves.

The twenty-one separate accounts printed between 1675 and 1682 actually represent several different types of writing, aimed at different kinds of readers. The shorter tracts often take the form of letters written by New Englanders to solicitous friends in London. These were also the quickest off the presses; the earliest, *A Brief and True Narration of the Late Wars Risen in New-England*, was licensed for printing on November 16, 1675. Even before this account was printed, however, vague news of the war traveled throughout the colonies and across the Atlantic by word of mouth. "'Tis not to be doubted," began *A Brief and True Narration*, "but that Fame ere this hath sounded in your Ears that the Indians in New England, have, by a late Rupture disturbed the long and orderly Peace, that hath been enjoyed by us." [19] Unprinted, handcopied newsletters distributed in England also supplied news about the war, and on August 16 the first of two reports was printed in *The London Gazette*. [20] As Increase Mather would later write, "the report of poor New-England's Calamity, hath caused those that are in Lands afar off to be amazed and troubled." [21]

These epistolary accounts, clearly written for an inquisitive English audience, were always published in London, often aggressively advertised, and occasionally printed as supplements to *The London Gazette*. [22] Nathaniel Saltonstall's writings are typical of this genre. Appending a postscript to his first letter "to his Friend in London," Saltonstall explained:

> I have here enclosed you as large an Account as I can at Present of the State of this Wilderness, in Respect to the Heathens: I must confess, I was the willinger to take a little the more Pains in the collecting thereof, for the Sakes of those with you, who wish us well. Which if it may answer its intended End therein, the Labour in Writing will be well bestowed. [23]

Each of Saltonstall's narratives was announced in the *Term Catalogues*, the brochure of London booksellers. His books were cheap ("Price sticht," 6d or 8d) and, in a word, prurient. [24] They catered to a London reading public that delighted in tales of executions, cruel murders, and sensational crimes. [25] To that end, the title pages of Saltonstall's narratives, probably added by a cunning publisher, emphasized body count: they promised to relate "the true number of the Slain and Wounded," or "a Catalogue of the Losses in the

News of the war as reported in *The London Gazette*, August 1675. *Courtesy of the Houghton Library, Harvard University*

whole, sustained on either side since the said War began."[26] In this regard they borrowed from the tradition of the lists of the dead that had been printed in London during the great plague of 1664 and 1665. As Benjamin Tompson wrote,

> When London's fatal bills were blown abroad
> And few but specters travelled on the road,
> Not towns but men in the black bill enrolled
> Were in gazettes by typographers sold:
> But our gazettes without erratas must
> Report the plague of towns reduced to dust.[27]

Nathaniel Saltonstall's accounts were also published in a large format, the same size as *The London Gazette:* they looked like news reports. The contents of Saltonstall's accounts dwelled on brutal acts of torture and the magnitude of casualties. (It was Saltonstall's entirely secular perspective that so enraged Mather.) In addition, whether at the urging of the printer or by his own accord, Saltonstall's letters included definitions of Indian words ("*Wigwams* are Indian Huts or Houses," "A *Sachem* is a King, Prince, or Chief"), providing further evidence that he wrote for an English audience, since colonists would have been quite familiar with such terms.[28]

Many of these published letters were apocalyptic. "This may inform thee," a nervous Edward Wharton announced to his London correspondent, "that a most bitter Spirit is entred the English, and Indians; in which they greatly endeavour the utter destruction one of another."[29] Others, after pages detailing horrifying battles and terrifying losses, made sure to end on an optimistic note. The printer of *News from New-England* felt compelled to tack on a final paragraph of late-breaking news before letting a single book out of his shop. The bottom of the last page boldly, if prematurely, reassured readers:

We have Received very late news that the Christians in New England have had very great Victory over the Infidel Natives.
FINIS.[30]

Of the remaining published accounts, several are sermons, one is an epic poem, one a captivity narrative, and only Mather's and Hubbard's are what we would recognize as actual "histories" of the war. Significantly, all of these were first published in Boston or Cambridge, although several were soon after reprinted in London. New Englanders, who acquired their books by borrowing from friends, neighbors, or relatives, or by buying them from itinerant booksellers or at one of the nine bookshops in Boston, evidently had different literary tastes than their English cousins.[31] While the letters to London are clearly news reports, many of them critical of the Puritan oligarchy, the remaining narratives are more self-consciously literary, historical, and religious in nature. The Boston and Cambridge publications, endorsed by the Massachusetts government, emphasized the devastation and violence of the war, but always with a simple and much-stated purpose: moral instruction. Thus Thomas Wheeler included a preface addressed to "The Christian Reader" in his sermon *A Thankefull Remembrance of Gods Mercy,* in which he explained his reasons for writing: "Wherein the Providences of God towards us in his wayes about us were so Remarkable, in our sore Exercises, and gracious Deliverances that they ought never to be forgotten by us, but kept in Remembrance all our dayes."[32]

The difference between accounts printed in Boston and Cambridge and those printed in London is not as dramatic as it might seem. We need not take high-minded intentions like Wheeler's as chief indicators of the accounts' appeal; the London reprintings of Boston and Cambridge narratives suggest that even sober Puritan sermons might have satisfied readers interested in gore for gore's sake. Several of these narratives were also advertised in the *Term Catalogues* as well as in *The London Gazette.*[33] Moreover, accounts printed only in New England did not always remain there. The colonial authorities sent important narratives of the war to King Charles, and more than a few colonists shipped books to friends and family across the Atlantic.[34] John Hull of Marblehead wrote to an English cousin, "I have sent you three Bookes of the History of our War; one for Mr. Sam Burfoot, one for your self, & Cousin Dan Quinscy, and one for Cousin Buckam."[35] Similarly, Samuel Sewall sent copies of Mary Rowlandson's captivity narrative to his English uncles.[36] Nor did printed materials only travel eastward. In August 1675 Joseph Eliot wrote to a fellow Connecticut colonist to see if he could borrow some of his English "gazets": "My intreaty therefore is unto your self, that you would do me the favor to lend me such as are gainable there, and I shal carefully return them: it is one addition to the advantage of reading them, that in this our calamtou[s] times we can the better sympathize with the European stories of the sad effects of these warrs."[37]

The sending of so many books across the Atlantic confirms the view, widely held by historians of the book, that seventeenth-century New Englanders lived in a world of print continuous with that of Europe.[38] Perhaps the best evidence about the transportation of books, both within and outside the colonies, comes from Increase Mather, who was meticulous about recording how he distributed copies of his own accounts of King Philip's War. When

Richard Chiswell returned two dozen unsold copies of the London edition of *A Brief History* to Mather, the Boston minister asked his brother-in-law John Cotton to help sell them in Plymouth and Connecticut.[39] Meanwhile, Mather shipped more than a few copies right back across the Atlantic, to friends in England, along with copies of his *Relation* and other works.[40] By all indications, Mather's friends and colleagues eagerly awaited his books. John Bishop wrote to Mather in July 1676, complaining anxiously, "we knew nor heard of any thing Printed, til of late Mr Alden told me there was, & wondred that we had it not."[41] William Goffe begged Mather for a copy of his *Brief History*: "I was tould that beside your Exhortation, you have also taken the pains to write a History of the War, which is also printed. But I have not had the happynesse as yet, to see it; and know not when I shall, tho: I much desire it." Goffe had even had difficulty keeping his copy of Mather's *Exhortation,* which, he said, was "was taken from me before I could read it a second time."[42] In Dublin, Ireland, Mather's brother Nathaniel made a similar complaint, acknowledging that he had received "3 of your historyes of the late war with the Indians, for which I heartily thank you & wish I had had more of them . . . they were so acceptable that save that I kept one of them, to read it over a few hours, I have not yet been able to keep any of them in my hands."[43]

The popularity and distribution of the war narratives must have varied greatly, of course, as did their content. Yet, whether printed in Boston, London, or Cambridge, in octavo or quarto, in two editions or four, on cheap paper or fine, one element is common to all of the published accounts of King Philip's War: all exhibit a pressing if not a frantic concern about truthfulness. This concern is reflected in the titles of some: *A True Account, A Brief and True Narration, A Farther Brief and True Narration;* and in the subtitles of others: "Being a True and Perfect Account," "being a True and last Account," "The most Exact Account yet Printed," "an Account of the true Reason thereof, (as far as can be judged by Men)," or a narrative that has been "Faithfully Composed."[44] Such titles can be partly explained by convention; news and historical accounts published in England commonly asserted their truthfulness on their title pages. Yet, like Mather's assertion that his was the "*true* history of this affair," many chroniclers of King Philip's War also provided lengthy prefatory statements establishing their narratives' authenticity. Saltonstall's first letter began by noting, "There being many and various Reports concerning the Causes of the present War amongst us, it may not be amiss in the First Place, to give you a true Account of the Reasons thereof."[45] Another account offered a "true Narrative of those Indians Stirs." And William Hubbard's preface contained an extended discussion of the sources for his history, all of whom were "Persons worthy of Credit."[46]

Like Mather, who was disgusted by the "abounding mistakes" in Saltonstall's *Present State* and, he believed, the equally uncreditable account of John
Easton, several writers established their own legitimacy by casting aspersions
on other reports. "What hath been made Publick from the beginning hath not
been represented so exactly as it might have been," complained the author of
A True Account. "I shall therefore upon a review of some Papers lying by me
Collect and Communicate a few lines so much of that Affair . . . [that] may
be depended upon as true, without partiality to either side." [47] Correcting the
errors of other authors was often cited as a principal reason for writing in the
first place. And when colonists like Thomas Wheeler explained that they
wrote not only "for the help of our memories" but also for "the preventing of
mistakes in Reports," they had cause to be concerned. [48] No matter how much
the colonists wrote and wondered about their war, the truth always seemed
elusive.

II

LONG BEFORE Wheeler's *Remembrance,* before Hubbard's *Narrative,*
before even the earliest accounts in *The London Gazette,* news of the war had
spread quickly throughout the colonies. Most people got their news face to
face, from friends, neighbors, or relations. Seventeenth-century New England
was, after all, primarily an oral culture. To William Harris it seemed that
"Mesengers like Jobes came soone one after another," all telling "of burneing
houses, takeing cattell, killing men & women & Children: & carrying others
captive." Or, as Noah Newman lamented, colonists "dayly herd of houses
Burned & People ded & killed at severall Places." Much news also came by
letter. Benjamin Tompson put a common sentiment into verse when he complained, "Posts daily on the Pegasean steeds / Bring sad reports of worse than
Nero's deeds." [49]

If little of the news was good, even less was reliable. "Reports are so many
& various that one knowes not what to believe," wrote one confused colonist.
Or, as another complained, "Wee have many Lame reports & blinde relations
of such things & without Cleerer grounde know not well how to direct prayers
or prayses." As a result of all the confusion, some news was conveyed in qualified terms: "We have newes that Plimouth Deauxborough, and Bridgwater
are great part destroyed and that Capt. Bradford and his Son both are Slayne,"
wrote a beleaguered Bostonian. Yet, he added with failing optimism, "all
Communication by land betweene this and that land obstructed; Soe that
there is roome for hope that matters are not soe bad as reported but hitherto
they have comonly prooved worse." [50]

In their attempts to keep up with false reports, many colonists engaged in fact-checking correspondences. In July 1675 John Winthrop, Jr., wrote to his brother to warn him that "that which hath beene reported, as you mention that Quabage was burnt, is utterly falce." And, Winthrop continued, as to the news that some of Philip's men had fled to another sachem, "being only a report, I can write nothing positively." In a reply to a letter from Winthrop, William Leete informed him, "As to those misreports about Indians westward stirring, &c., I understand you have already bin better informed & so I need say nothing."[51] Not all colonists, of course, were so careful about verifying the reports they sent and received. "People are apt in these dayes to give credit to every flying and false report," Samuel Gorton complained, "and not only so, but they will report it againe, as it is said of old, report and we will report; and by that meanes they become deceivers and tormenters one of another, by feares and jealousies." John Pynchon, too, noted the proliferation of false reports. To Winthrop he wrote, "Yours was the first and all the intelligence I have had except flying reports."[52]

That information was sent did not necessarily mean it would arrive, since roads were often impassable. "The way of Sending is Soe enterupted by the war," complained William Harris, "that ther is noe safe Sending nor pasing to & fro (without danger of life)." After John Pynchon sent a post to Brookfield, he later found out that "they were obstructed by 15 or 16 Indians . . . who endeavored to get the way of our messengers." Daniel Witherell intercepted and opened a letter that was intended for John Winthrop, Jr., and later apologized to Winthrop: "This morneing I Recaved the Narrative of the Bloody Designs of the Indians Which was Directed to your Honour; and Conceiving it might give uss herer fuller Information than wee had formerly Receved[, we] presumed to open [it] hopeing wee shall obtayne your honours pardon therein." An old man, deserted and alone, John Kingsley added a postscript to a letter to the Connecticut War Council, begging that a message be sent to his son in Massachusetts: "If aney know or here that Enoes Kingsley be alive, at Northamton, let know that I his father am a live tho no shelter for my gray head."[53]

Of all the unreliable news of the war, most colonists considered news conveyed by Indians to be the most dubious. Samuel Hooker cautiously passed on "the last report which cometh to mee (which is Indian newes) but said to be true" and Roger Williams warned that "all the fine words from the Indian Sachims to us were but words of policie, falshood & Treacherye."[54] Communication between the two sides was usually assigned to literate Christian Indians temporarily released from Deer Island, but they commonly met with little success. When the Massachusetts Council sent a Christian Indian to

Wachusett to negotiate the release of Mary Rowlandson, they sent him with "paper pen and Incke" and carrying a white flag. That the Council saw fit to explain that such a flag "is used by civil nations in tyme of warre when any messengers are sent in a way of treaty" suggests the difficulties and dangers inherent in such exchanges.[55] Meanwhile, Algonquians who did not wish to be found often successfully thwarted Christian Indians, as when Sam Namphow, carrying a message for the sachem Wannalancet, was sent on a wild goose chase. "We cam to pamakook," Namphow reported, and "there we soe sum of the pumakook indians and asked them w[h]ere wamsait was they sait he was a[t] pomachowasick we went to wanneposokick . . . w[h]ere they sat he was but when we cam to wunnippasakick there we saw sum more indians we asked them were is the sachem they sait he went away three weeks agone from pomaschowasick."[56]

Algonquians who fought against the colonists had their own lines of communication: news reports, whispered rumors, prophecies, diplomatic envoys, stories told in wampum beads. Unfortunately, colonists took little note of how their enemies communicated news of the war—Nathaniel Saltonstall warned that "these Heathenish Stories are consonant to their Barbarous Crueltie, and ought to be valued accordingly"—except to observe, as they often did, that "the Indians have their scouts out."[57] Instead, colonists were more likely to express amazement at how well Algonquians *hid* information. Colonial soldiers could never be certain how many of the enemy had been killed, since the Indians almost always "adventured back and took their dead Men away with them."[58] But, while hiding the extent of their own losses, Algonquians celebrated English losses by making marks on trees and shouting or "co-hooping" to count the enemy dead—messages designed to be seen and heard by Indians and colonists alike. As John Russell wrote, "when [the Indians] heard of the Massacre at Quaboag, they made in the Fort eleven Acclamations of joy, according to the number of our men that were slain."[59] Writing about the attack on Marlboro, Richard Jacob described how a group of Indians, "as theire accustomed maner is after a fight, began to signifie to us how many were slaine. They Cohoop'd seventy-four times, which we hoped was only to affright us seing we have had no intelegence of any such thing, yet we have Reason to feare the worst Considering Theire Numbers."[60]

For most of the war, colonists everywhere had reason, like Jacob, "to feare the worst": most news was bad news. Yet, however bad the news was likely to be, people were desperate to hear it. "We long to here some good tidings from Boston," Mary Pray wrote from Providence, since "we have But littel here But such news as Increaseth our sorrowes."[61] Similarly, Thomas Whalley told John Cotton, "We dayly long to heare from our army," and later begged him, "What

[news] you have i pray you send me." With the enemy "round about us," colonists in isolated towns felt particularly cut off from the flow of important information: "We are a distressed people. We hear nothing since from the army." In August 1675 the Connecticut Council wrote to John Pynchon, employing a poignant image in its request for news: "*We stand a tiptoe for intelligence.*"[62]

Colonists begged one another for news time and again, and especially for lengthy reports. "The Last heavy newes of the Indyan Warr hath put mee upon a bold request," Nathaniel Brewster wrote in July 1675, "to beseech yor honor for a few Lines, as an abstract, of the true state and progress of this sad Commotion." After receiving a letter from John Cotton, Noah Newman obliged a similar request. "As to your desir of the Hystory of [the] medfield tragedy," Newman replied, "I shall give you the best account I can."[63] Colonists sent lengthy letters not only to one another but also to friends and relatives in England, who often copied and distributed them. Writing from England, Jane Hook reminded Increase Mather, "we are much inquiring after the afares of our brethren in N:E:"; and toward the end of the war, Christopher Whichcot rejoiced at once hearing "some incouraging news by the last ships that come from new England."[64] Sketchy news of the war often left friends and relations in England anxious for fuller details. Stephen Dummor, distressed by a letter he received from his cousin Samuel Sewall detailing "the Barbarous and cruell proceedings of the Heathons," criticized another New England correspondent for his failure to supply eagerly awaited news: "In your Letter you have not sent me a word of the sad tydings that are fallen out amongst you." For John Hall, who worried from England about his mother in Massachusetts, no news was worse than bad news: "I have Lively Ideas in my minde of the fright and distractions that those salvages put you too."[65] No news was worse than bad news, but often enough, no news was all most colonists could give.

III

MUCH AS they yearned for news, much as friends, neighbors, and relatives begged them for it, many colonists, like Simon Bradstreet and John Eliot, found it difficult to write about the war at all. After witnessing the burning of the town of Springfield, John Pynchon felt utterly debilitated, admitting, "I know not how to write."[66] And often, even writers who supplied lengthy and vivid accounts apologized for the ineptness of their descriptions. "It is not my tongue, or pen can express the sorrows of my heart, and bitterness of my spirit," Mary Rowlandson wrote.[67] In his moving letter to the Connecticut War Council begging for help, John Kingsley confessed, "I am not able to beare the sad stories of our woeful day." As "the 1 man & onely left" in a town that he had seen destroyed and then abandoned, Kingsley was starving and near death. "I can say truely," he moaned, with weariness weighing down every word, "that since our wares begun my flesh is so gon with feare, care & grife & now this sicknes, my skin is redey to cleave to my bones." Moreover, he continued, "to tel you what wee have & how wee are like to sufer my hart wil not hould to write & sheetes would [not] contayne." [68]

Kingsley's dilemma is paradoxical. The magnitude of his suffering required him to write, but it also made writing impossible; however much he needed help, he could not bear the sad stories he must tell to get it. *To tell you what we have and how we are likely to suffer my heart will not hold to write and sheets would not contain.* It is, in fact, the uncontainability of Kingsley's pain that distressed him most, and it is here that his choice of imagery is most telling: his suffering, Kingsley suggested, is best measured by the paper needed to describe it. And no amount of paper is enough. Images like this, in which paper and books and pens and ink act as measurements of pain and evil, are peppered throughout the wartime writings. In a letter about the "trechoury" of the Narragansett Indians, for instance, Mary Pray claimed that "a vollum might be writ of their vilany." And Philip Walker employed the same metaphor when describing Indian attacks:

> The Impious actts off thes Infernal bests
> actted abroad & in ther helish nests
> would swell a volum to a magnitud.

Another common metaphor suggested that some horrors could never be described by the written word, and could only be measured by the physical evidence produced by the body. Thus Benjamin Tompson wrote,

> Not ink, but blood and tears now serve the turn
> To draw the figure of New England's urn.

Similarly, John Hall wrote to his mother in Ipswich, "though tears of water yea of blood if wee were able are not enough to bewaile the desolations that fire; blood, rapine, and cruelty hath made in N.E." [69]

The devastation of the war was, to many colonists, "hardly imaginable." [70] Indeed, the troubling result of all of the "flying reports" and miserable news was that colonists hardly knew what to believe unless they had seen it themselves or, better yet, had touched or felt it, since appearances, too, were sometimes uncreditable. Literary scholar Elaine Scarry has called this concern with communication during war "verbal unanchoredness" and argues that it is an inevitable result of the traumas of warfare. "Within the war itself," Scarry argues, "the indisputably physical reality of the mounting wounds has as its verbal counterpart the mounting unreality of language." That is, as the physical devastation becomes real, the language describing it becomes unreal. Lies, falsifications, misrepresentations, fictions, and misinformation are all typical of the spoken and written language of war, according to Scarry, and all combine to produce a suspended reality, a verbally "unanchored" world.[71]

In the fictive world of an unimaginable war, "eye or ear Witnesses" assumed new importance.[72] As Benjamin Tompson wrote, "the natives' treachery felt too fierce / For any but eyewitness to rehearse." And when James Oliver described an attack on an Indian settlement (in which he participated), he said his letter was "as nearly as I can a true relation" but felt compelled to add that he had "read the narrative to my officers in my tent, who all assent to the truth of it."[73] Words alone, whether written or spoken, could no longer qualify as evidence—only the physical damage itself, the burned houses, the maimed bodies, the brittle pools of blood, could be believed. In a physical reality of such traumatic intensity, in a world where wounds, fire, and famine spread as fast as lies, rumors, and fictions, language itself had become inadequate.

For John Kingsley it was paper that seemed inadequate; what his heart held, sheets would not contain. In Kingsley's and others' writings, such "volume" and "blood, ink, and tears" metaphors suggest that pain endured and pain inflicted could only barely be contained by language, if at all. Certainly these pains could not be adequately expressed in a single letter or piece of poetry; ink, paper, and even books were all inadequate containers. Some of this imagery is no doubt formulaic, especially when used in verse, as in Benjamin Tompson's couplet, "all the cruelties the foes devise / Might fill a volume," or in Wait Still Winthrop's stanza: "And now my frind, here I will End, no more here shall I write, Or lest I shall some Tears let fall, and spoil my Writing quite."[74] Yet when employed by writers like Kingsley and Pray, blood and ink metaphors take on a genuineness that suggests that even when these metaphors were used formulaically they expressed a widely and deeply felt sentiment about the inadequacy of language.

Other writers employed different strategies for "containing" the war's pain in prose. Some simply put a premature end to their descriptions lest the letters they were writing burst from the pressure of the pain they contained. Saltonstall, for instance, abruptly ended one of his missives by concluding that "to reckon up all their Cruelties, would be no lesse burthensome to compassionate Christians Ears, than too tedious for a Letter, which is already swelled too big." Still others wrote as a release, so their own selves would not burst from pain's pressure. "I canot forbear to writ I am so ful of grife for our frinds and conterymen," was the apology with which Mary Pray began a letter to a friend in Boston. William Leete, too, complained that he had "enough of other reall & sad storyes to exercise our thoughts & hearts."[75]

Some writers sought to contain the suffering of the war by organizing it. "Their outrages are so many and different," wrote the author of *News from New-England*, that "they will not be brought into a fluent Narration." Nonetheless, he urged the reader "to accept them plainly and dyurnuily according to the time, place, and manner as they were committed, which is the only way to avoid omissions, and consequently to Satisfie the inquisitive, who I suppose would willingly hear of all the extremities have happened to the suffering Christians in this New England War." In a like vein, Saltonstall recalled that when he first wrote about the war he was almost incapacitated by the pain of describing it: "My Hand Trembled, and my Heart almost fainted, when my Mind reflected on our present Miseries, and revolved for the Future what might be the Issue of that Deluge of Calamity which threatened us." The next time, however, he approached the endeavor more rationally, relying on the comforting structure of chronology to calm him: "But that I may set down Things in some Method, I shall reassume the Narritive of our Troubles, where I left off in my last Letter, and relate the most considerable Actions from that Time, in the same Order as they happened."[76]

Each of these three strategies—containing, censuring, and organizing the stories of the war—is consistent with Scarry's theory about what pain does to language. "One of two things is true of pain," according to Scarry. "Either it remains inarticulate or else the moment it first becomes articulate it silences all else."[77] A colonist faced with the trauma and suffering of King Philip's War could remain silent, like Simon Bradstreet, or could articulate his pain, like John Kingsley, and risk becoming overwhelmed by it. This all-or-none theory of pain's relationship to language helps explain the incongruency between how much some colonists wrote about King Philip's War and how little others wrote.

Colonists who kept quiet about King Philip's War had good reasons. Many were illiterate, or at least not quite literate enough to narrate their own experiences. Most deferred to the official record. And some were silenced by their own suffering. In a sense, these three different reasons are unified and embodied in the metaphors employed by Kingsley and Pray. Their metaphors—of paper, books, ink, volumes—testify not only to a relationship to pain and its uncontainability but also to a relationship to the authority of the written and especially the printed word in colonial New England.

IV

AT THE END of his almanac for 1676, Boston printer John Foster included several events of the war in his "Chronology of some memorable Occurrences hapning in New-England," but added that

> To particularize the memorable Transactions of this year would be sufficient to fill a Volume: It would therefore be in vain to . . . enumerate the horrid Massacres, Murthers, Savage Crueltyes, cowardize, ungrateful and perfidious dealings of Bloud-thirsty Barbarians.[78]

Here, Foster's use of a volume metaphor to describe the war's cruelties and explain his failure to write a more complete account of the war takes on a different cast than it had for John Kingsley. Kingsley was overwhelmed by the suffering he had endured and terrified at the idea of putting it into writing, but John Foster censored himself because he had other books in his shop to sell, among them Benjamin Tompson's *New England's Crisis* and Increase Mather's *Brief History* (and soon he would be peddling Hubbard's *Narrative*, too). As a printer, John Foster knew what it meant to "fill a Volume," and he knew to leave it to someone else, just as Simon Bradstreet knew well that a record of the war would be "publickly taken & the story of it Printed."

Blood as ink. Volumes of villainy. Pain that sheets cannot contain. The cruelty of King Philip's War invited these metaphors, this language of suffering and of the authority of the written, and especially the printed, word. By making the world unreal, a place where rumors abound and "mesengers like Jobes came soone one after another: [telling] of burneing houses, takeing cattell, killing men & women & Children: & carrying others captive," the war created a world full of distortions, fictions, and confusion.[79] For the colonists, that confusion created a war of words. But, whether illiterate or literate, New England's Indians had little chance to win this kind of war, or even to wage it, since literacy itself, and the cultural compromises it entailed, was potentially dangerous. Seventeenth-century New England was a world in which books were scarce, but the ability and the authority to write them were even harder to acquire. And harder still, of course, for those whose first language was not English, and for those, like John Sassamon, to whom literacy might prove fatal. In the end, of course, the crucial rivalry was not between the competing interpretations of Massachusetts ministers such as Hubbard and Mather, or between accounts printed in London or Cambridge or Boston, but between the differing views of the war held by English colonists and Indians. The real silence was not that of "Harvardine quills" but of Algonquian pens. And, in that regard, the writing about the war was as critical as the waging of it. In place of native accounts of the war, some English colonists offered their versions of what the Indians might have had to say (a technique John Eliot had employed when he wrote "Philip's" conversion narrative in the *Indian Dialogues*). Participating in a tradition that would last well into the nineteenth century, Benjamin Tompson imagined the speech Philip might have delivered to his warriors on the eve of the war:

> My friends, our fathers were not half so wise
> As we ourselves who see with younger eyes.
> They sell our land to Englishmen who teach
> Our nation all so fast to pray and preach:
> Of all our country they enjoy the best,
> And quickly they intend to have the rest.[80]

Whether these words in any way represent Algonquian motives in the war, they were, to the colonists, ultimately meaningless. As the colonists saw it, violence itself was the Indians' only vocabulary. When English soldiers fired on Indians and Indians fired back, the colonists said they were "answering our Men in the same Language." [81] And even while the English lamented their helplessness against Indian attacks, they took comfort in the knowledge that they controlled the pens and printing presses. When William Hubbard briefly digressed from the war's action in his *Narrative,* he quickly returned to the subject to "pursue the Rebellious Indians, and keep Pace with them in our History, though our Forces as yet could never overtake them in the Woods." [82] If war is a contest of both injuries and interpretation, the English made sure that they won the latter, even when the former was not yet assured.

PART TWO · *War*

Thou English man hath provoked us to anger & wrath & we care not though we have war with you this 21 years for there are many of us 300 of which hath fought with you at this town[.] we hauve nothing but our lives to loose but thou hast many fair houses cattell & much good things.

—*Anonymous note tacked to a tree,*
February 1676

Why should we suppose that God is not offended with us when his displeasure is written in such visible and bloody characters?

—INCREASE MATHER,
May 1676

Chapter 3

HABITATIONS OF CRUELTY

A True but Brief Account of our Losses sustained since this Cruel and Mischievous War began, take as follows:

In Narraganset not one House left standing.
At Warwick, but one.
At Providence, not above three.
At Potuxit, none left.
Very few at Seaconicke.
At Swansey, two, at most.
Marlborough, wholy laid in Ashes, except two or three Houses.
Grantham and Nashaway, all ruined but one House or two.
Many Houses burnt at Springfield, Scituate, Lancaster, Brookefield and Northampton.
The greatest Part of Rehoboth and Taunton destroyed.
Great Spoil made at Hadley, Hatfield, and Chelmsford.
Deerfield wholly, and Westfield much ruined.
At Sudbury, many Houses burnt, and some at Hingham, Weymouth, and Braintree.
Besides particular Farms and Plantations, a great Number not to be reckoned up, wholly laid waste, or much damnified.
And, as to Persons, it is generally thought, that of the English there hath been lost, in all, Men Women and Children, above Eight Hundred, since the War began: Of whom many have been destroyed with exquisite Torments, and most inhumane Barbarities; the Heathen rarely giving Quarter to those that they take, but if they were Women, they first forced them to satisfie their filthy Lusts and then

murdered them; either cutting off the Head, ripping open the Belly, or skulping the Head of Skin and Hair, and hanging them up as Trophies; wearing Men's Fingers as Bracelets about their Necks, and Stripes of their Skins which they dresse for Belts. . . . Nor have our Cattle escaped the Cruelty of these worse than Brute and Savage Beasts: For what Cattle they took they seldom killed outright: or if they did, would eat but little of the Flesh, but rather cut their Bellies, and letting them go several Days, trailing their Guts after them, putting out their Eyes, or cutting off one Leg, etc.

—NATHANIEL SALTONSTALL,
July 22, 1676

Nathaniel Saltonstall's "True but Brief Account of our Losses" is a standard portrait of New England during King Philip's War, a landscape of ashes, of farms laid waste, of corpses without heads.[1] A place where three-legged cattle wander aimlessly, dragging their guts after them, and Indians strut through the woods wearing belts of human skin and necklaces of rotting fingers. It is difficult to imagine a scene that could do more to assault English notions of order.[2] Towns have been razed and blood spills everywhere. Nearly all that was English has been destroyed—English houses, English farms, English crops, English livestock, English bodies. The tamed wilderness has become wild once again. English husbandry and agriculture have been ruined, leaving only scars on a landscape they once marked with fences and barns and fields of hay. Thousands of colonists have suffered; hundreds have died. As one frantic colonist reported, "Many of our miserable inhabitants lye naked, wallowing in their blood, and crying, and whilst the Barbarous enraged Natives, from one part of the Country, to another are on Fire, flaming forth their fury, Spoiling Cattle and Corn and burning Houses, and torturing Men, Women, and Children; and burning them alive." "I am greatly afflicted," Thomas Whalley lamented, "to see the danger we are in and the Confusion and sad disorder that we are fallen in." And, as Saltonstall wrote, "Nothing could be expected but an utter Desolation."[3]

Many colonists, sheltering themselves in garrisoned houses, could do little but watch as their towns were destroyed. While the people of Rehoboth looked on in horror, the Indians "fell presently to fyring of empty houses & burnt about 35 houses that had familyes belonging to them besides four other vacant houses that had no inhabitants & Barnes." "Thay burnt our milles, brake the stones, ye, our grinding stones," John Kingsley reported, "& what was hid in the erth they found, corne & fowles, kild catel & tooke the hind quarters & left the rest, yea, all that day . . . they burnt cartes wheeles, drive away our catel, shipe, horses." "In a word," Kingsley summarized, "had not the Lord restrayned [them] thay had not left won to have tould of our woful day." Having pitched camp at the edge of town, the Indians "rose up at day light the next morning," walked over to Providence, "& theire did likewise." "The buryall of the slaine," the town minister wrote, "tooke us 3 days."[4]

Such terrifying ravages strained even the most eloquent colonists' powers of description. Philip Walker called the war a "dredffull bludy shouer," and Edward Wharton said the Indians had made of the English settlements "a burdensome and menstruous cloth" that, having fouled, they might now cast out of the land.[5] Benjamin Tompson believed depicting this cruelest of wars required more than bloody metaphors, more, even, than the formidable skills of a poet. Since words alone could not suffice, Tompson wished a painter might "overtrack" his "pen." Of the Indians, Tompson urged, "Limn them besmeared with Christian blood & oiled / With fat out of white human bodies boiled. / Draw them with clubs like mauls & full of stains, / Like Vulcans anvilling New England's brains." Of the damage, "Paint here the house & there the barn on fire, / With holocausts ascending in a spire." Of loss, "Draw there the pastor for his bible crying, / The soldier for his sword, the glutton frying." And of torment, "Let here the mother seem a statue turned / At the sad object of her bowels burned."[6] Tompson, with the help of his "painter," presented a strikingly gruesome panorama, but Mary Rowlandson, unaided, provided perhaps the most arresting image of all. "Thus were we butchered by those merciless heathen, standing amazed, with the blood running down to our heels."[7]

Not only the colonists but their land, too, was bleeding, as Edward Wharton put it, like "a burdensome and menstruous cloth." What happened to English people, in the colonists' eyes, happened equally to English property, and the separation of the one from the other was counted among the greatest devastations of the war. Draw confusion everywhere, Benjamin Tompson instructed his artist, and paint the goddess of disorder ruling over all New England.

> Let Ataxy be mounted on a throne
> Imposing her commands on everyone . . .
> One she bids flee, another stay, a third
> She bids betake him to his rusty sword,
> This to his treasure, th'other to his knees,
> Some counsels she to fry and some to freeze,
> These to the garrison, those to the road,
> Some to run empty, some to take their load:
> Thus while confusion most men's hearts divide
> Fire doth their small exchequer soon decide.[8]

If, as Elaine Scarry has argued, there are three arenas of damage in war—bodies, possessions, and political identities—then New England's colonists conflated the three time and again.[9] Colonial writers understood the destruction of houses as a blow not only to their property but also to the very Englishness of the landscape. Meanwhile, nearly any attack could be understood metaphorically as an assault on the human body. "The body is a model which can stand for any bounded system," the anthropologist Mary Douglas has written. "Its boundaries can represent any boundaries which are threatened or precarious."[10] And the cultural proclivity to exploit the body as a symbolic system reaches its fullest expression during times of war when, by definition, boundaries are being breached. In the seventeenth-century world, war itself was even understood, by some, as "chirgury" undertaken on the body politic to heal a "wound," or breach of the body's boundary of skin. But surgery, like war, was itself invasive. "Warre is alwayes a Physick too strong," Anthony Ashcam wrote in 1648, "which entring the body with a force greater then the infirmity, must needs increase the distemper, and like thunder purging the bad qualities, corrupt the good."[11]

Nearly all of the damage to the English during King Philip's War—the burning of houses, the spilling of blood, the English becoming Indianized—was understood as attacks on bounded systems. While disorder threatened to rule New England, military strategists sought means to draw a line to keep Indians—and chaos—out. In Massachusetts, alarmed colonists even debated building an eight-foot-high wall of stone or wood all the way from the Charles River to the bay, "by which meanes that whole tract will [be] environed, for the security & safty (under God) of the people, their houses, goods & cattel; from the rage & fury of the enimy."[12] But the concern with barriers was not limited to physical, geographical boundaries. It extended also to violations of English bodies, and, perhaps most terrifyingly of all, to Algonquian encroachments on English culture. Everywhere, there were barbarians at the gate.

I

ON SEPTEMBER 9, 1675, George Ingersol heard three guns go off in the distance, and noticed "great smoke up in the River above Mr. Mackworth's." He sounded an alarm but could not assemble enough men to investigate safely. The next day, with reinforcements, Ingersol followed the smoke to what had been Thomas Wakely's home. "When I came to the place, i found an house burnt downe, and six persons killed, and three of the same family could not be found. An old Man and Woman were halfe in, and halfe out of the house neer halfe burnt. Their owne Son was shot through the body, and also his head dashed in pieces. This young mans Wife was dead, her head skined." The young woman, Ingersol reported, "was bigg with Child," and two of her children, "haveing their heads dashed in pieces," were found "laid by one another with their bellys to the ground, and an Oake planke laid upon their backs." The three missing family members, Ingersol later discovered, had been taken captive.[13]

Here is a family murdered: a pregnant woman scalped, her children mauled, their grandparents burned alive. Everyone died badly. Only the young man was shot, but even his corpse is in disarray, "his head dashed in pieces." All of the bodies have been mutilated, their physical integrity spoiled by the seepage of blood and brains. A tableau worthy of Benjamin Tompson's painting. Here, too, is a house destroyed, its beams and floorboards charred and crumbling. The house, built to shelter this family, has become, in a sense, its coffin. The two small children have been pressed underneath "an Oake planke laid upon their backs" while their grandparents are "halfe in, and halfe out of the house," their bodies "neer halfe burnt."

This house, whose ashes cover the old couple and whose torn planks entomb the children, is a crucial element in George Ingersol's account. More than the state of the corpses, the house, in a sense, explains the scene. Ingersol would have been confused to come upon these six bodies in the middle of the woods, but the house supplies the context for him to understand that this is an English family, killed by marauding Indians while seeking protection within their house. Ingersol is careful to note which bodies are inside the house and which are outside, since these details help him reconstruct the events that took place there. One imagines, for instance, that when the Indians first arrived the young man stepped outside to fend them off, only to be shot dead. Next, the Indians set the house on fire, forcing the pregnant woman and her children to run out to escape the smoke and flames. There they were quickly killed or taken captive. Meanwhile, the old man and his wife stayed inside almost until the very end, when finally, burning, they crawled halfway through the doorway and died.

If the house explains this scene, it also gives it its particular pathos—its utter failure to protect the family. Thomas Wakely, the old man, might have saved himself and his family if he had been willing to leave his house much earlier. He had been criticized for settling too far from his neighbors, too far away to get their help, and, when the war began, they must have urged him to seek protection in a nearby garrison. Surely Wakely himself must have considered leaving in early September when Thomas Purchase's house was plundered just a few miles away. But Wakely refused to abandon his homestead, perhaps thinking he and his son could defend it. He may have clung to this belief even as the Indians approached, when it was already too late for escape. Even at the very end, Wakely was too attached to his property to abandon it.[14] Still, this kind of attachment was not at all uncommon.

Thomas Wakely's "neer halfe burnt" corpse and his "burnt downe" house have a complicated relationship. The notion of property, of things that could be owned, was central to seventeenth-century Anglo-American culture. Property was, in a sense, foundational to culture, since English political economy rested on the private ownership of land, and the political economy, in turn, largely structured social relations. With the development of capitalist markets in the sixteenth and seventeenth centuries, private property had become increasingly important, and revolts against this change, like the Digger protests of the 1640s and 1650s, were met with violent censure. Gradually property became the defining character of social relations, the defining character, even, of an individual's identity.[15] By 1689 John Locke would be able to elaborate a theory of government based on the idea that "every man has a property in his own person."[16] If, at the level of political theory, identity would soon be defined as ownership of one's self, property had already become identity at the level of popular belief—what one owned defined who one was. As England moved away from a feudal land system and kinship-based social relations, this idea provided the basis of class relations in the emerging capitalist economy. In New England it would eventually play the same role, but in the decades of settlement leading up to King Philip's War, the idea of property as identity had much more to do with distinguishing an Indian from an Englishman than a merchant from a servant.

When the English first arrived in New England, they found the land to be "spacious and void," a place where the Indians "do but run over the grass, as do also the foxes and wild beasts" and the colonists had not "any houses or much less towns to repair to." "The country is yet raw," Robert Cushman wrote in 1621, "the land untilled; the cities not builded; the cattle not settled." Francis Higginson argued that "The Indians are not able to make use of the one fourth part of the land; neither have they any settled places, as towns, to dwell in; nor any ground as they challenge for their own possession, but change their habitation from place to place." Or, as John Josselyn observed, "Towns they have none, being always removing from one place to another for conveniency of food." The Algonquians' perceived nomadism, and their failure to "improve" the land, formed the basis for English land claims. New England, John Winthrop argued, was a *vacuum domicilum*, since only land that is fenced in, tilled, and built upon can be owned. Indians could not own the land, "for they inclose no ground, neither have they cattell to maintayne it, but remove their dwellings as they have occasion." [17] The English, then, could claim the land simply by improving it. (The concept of improvement even makes an appearance in Thomas More's sixteenth-century Utopia: "They consider it a most just cause for war when a people which does not use its soil but keeps it idle and waste nevertheless forbids the use and possession of it to others who by the rule of nature ought to be maintained by it." [18])

Establishing "plantations" in New England, colonists chopped down trees, built houses, erected fences, and planted crops. When they first settled, English colonists built hurriedly, and usually lived in sparsely furnished wattle-and-daub huts, so similar to the woven-mat buildings Algonquians constructed that they were called "English wigwams." By the middle of the seventeenth century the colonists rejoiced that such temporary—and to them inferior—dwellings had been largely replaced with more permanent, and more thoroughly English, architecture: "The Lord hath been pleased to turn all the wigwams, huts, and hovels the English dwelt in at their first coming into orderly, fair, and well-built houses, well furnished many of them." [19] By the 1670s, at the start of King Philip's War, the English could boast that "by their great industry," they had "of a howling Wilderness improved those Lands into Cornfields, Orchards, enclosed Pastures, and Towns inhabited." [20]

But during the war it seemed to many colonists that all that had made them English and all that had made the land their own—their clothes, houses, barns, churches, cattle, and crops—were being threatened. For most colonists, the loss of habitations became the central crisis of the war. Horrified by the devastation around him, Increase Mather asked himself, "How are we spoiled?" and could only answer, "We are greatly confounded because our dwelling places have cast us out." "Certainly," Nathaniel Saltonstall insisted, "it cannot but deserve both Wonder and Commiseration, that these Parts which were not many Moneths since hardly to be Parrallel'd for Plenty and Security, are now almost destroyed and laid Waste by the savage Cruelties of a Bloody (and sometimes Despicable) Enemy." Saltonstall no doubt believed that the best way to convey the extent of the devastation of the war, given such astounding losses, was with numbers, and he was not the only colonist to take this approach. "We Judg according to our best Computation," Samuel Symonds reported to the king's secretary in April 1676, "that Since the beginning of this Warre there hath been Slaine of his Majesties Subjects above five hundred," although "the houses burnt [are] not easy to be Numbered." [21] Whenever they could, English accountings of the war's casualties, like Saltonstall's "True but Brief Account of our Losses," tallied houses first, then people. (By contrast, Saltonstall's reckoning of Indian losses tallied people first—six thousand killed, enslaved, or subdued—and only briefly mentioned the loss of "vast Quantities of their Corn, Houses, ammunition, and other Necessaries.") And so the colonists recorded, for instance, that "at New Dartmouth . . . they burnt all their houses but one, viz. 29, and slew several persons. In Middlebrough the Indians burnt 21 houses. In Taunton they burnt ten houses and killed ten persons." Or, "the Indians burnt 17 houses & killed one man at Deerfield." Or again, "they Burnt near thirty Houses in Dartmouth . . . killing many People after a most Barbarous manner." Some reckonings also included cattle and crops: "They Burnt Twenty three Houses at Swansey, and killed many people there, and took much Cattle, as also Burnt the hay and Corn in great Quantities." Some figured in whether the Indians had "pulled down Fences."[22]

And not just towns but families, too, counted people, possessions, and property when measuring their losses. A grieving William Harris reported, "I have lost a deer son, a dillegent engenious Just man temperate in all things, whome the Indians lay in waite for by the way & kild him, and A negro man." (It is difficult to know if Harris counted his African slave as a person or a possession.) Not only that, Harris continued, but they "burnt our houses, & drove away aboute fifty head of Cowkind Cattell, and fourscore horse kinde of ours, & carryed away some goods, & burnt more than fifty loade of hay."[23] Seeing a town and its houses destroyed was extraordinarily painful. On finding Springfield burned, John Pynchon wrote to John Russell, "We came to a lamentable and woeful sight. The town in flames, not a house nor barn standing, except old Goodman Branch's, till we came to my house and then Mr. Glover's, John Hitchcock's, and Goodman Stewart's burnt, some with barns, corn, and all they had. . . . They tell me 32 houses and the barns belonging to them are burnt, and all the livelihood of the owners, and what more may meet with the same stroke the Lord only knows." The next day Russell reported to the Massachusetts Council that Springfield's "habitations are now become an heape."[24]

Colonists who were spared this fate gave abundant thanks. "Wee are yet in our habitations thro' Gods marsi," John Sharpe wrote to Thomas Meekins in April 1676, "but we are in expectation of the enimi everi day if God be not the more marsiful unto us."[25] Meanwhile, soldiers could be punished for abandoning the protection of houses too soon, and many colonists believed that it is not "for the safe gard of a people to forsake their places, but rather to keepe their stations, and listen to Gods calling of them forth to stand together as one man."[26] When families fled from their homes, whole towns were likely to be destroyed. In Springfield, "the Indians being too numerous," the town's inhabitants "were forced to Leave their houses & goods to the enemy (or rather) the rage & cruelties of the enemie: soo that towne is almost wholly lost."[27]

There were plenty of good reasons for the English to count their cattle, crops, and houses among their losses. Without these, they could not survive, especially during the harsh New England winters. Dismay at losing one's home is certainly a genuine expression of a very real, very devastating, and very practical loss. But there was more to the colonists' concern than simple practicality: English possessions were, in a sense, what was at stake in the war, for these—the clothes they wore, the houses they lived in, and the things they owned—were a good part of what differentiated the English from the Indians. These were not simply material differences, they were cultural, for every English frock coat was stitched with threads of civility, each thatched roof rested on a foundation of property rights, and every cupboard housed a universe of ideas.

II

WHEN JOHN PYNCHON returned to Springfield to find the town nearly burned to the ground, his property stripped of its buildings, he felt that he had himself been stripped naked: "Oh, that I may sensibly say with holy Job: naked came I and naked shall I return and blessed be the name of the Lord."[28] The connection between English property and English identity was so strong that many colonists employed a common metaphor for the loss of both, the metaphor of nakedness. All over New England, English bodies were said to have been left to "lye naked, wallowing in their blood," and English land, too, was left "naked," stripped of its buildings (as when, for instance, the Connecticut Court ordered towns to build garrison houses to cover "the nakedness of each and every place").[29] In images like Nathaniel Saltonstall's "True but Brief Account of our Losses," wartime New England had been stripped of its churches, houses, fences, and barns, while its people had been stripped of their clothes, their skin, even their heads and fingers (these were now "worn" by Indians).[30] As the colonists perceived it, their world had been made bare. Left naked, English bodies and English land were no longer recognizable—naked men, after all, were barbarians, and naked land a wilderness. It was, in fact, the "nakedness" of America and of its native peoples—signaling the land's vacancy and the Indians' savagery—that had made English colonization possible in the first place.[31] To the English who settled there, America had been naked land and, their descendants feared in 1675, it would soon be naked again. In establishing plantations in the wilderness, the English settlers had sought to mark the land as their own, to clothe the ground as they clothed their bodies, but King Philip's War undid their work, denuding both the landscape and its colonists.

Before the war, "naked Englishman" would have been almost oxymoronic. While the colonists clothed themselves in skirts, bodices, doublets, cloaks, breeches, caps, and boots, they perceived Indians as "wholly naked."[32] This distinction caused Roger Williams to wonder

> what should bee the reason of this mighty difference of One mans children that all the Sonnes of men on this side the way (in Europe, Asia and Africa) should have such plenteous clothing for Body, for Soule! and the rest of Adams sonnes and Daughters on the other side, or America . . . should neither have nor desire clothing for their naked soules, or Bodies.

Like Williams, English colonists perceived bodily nakedness as signaling both cultural and spiritual depravity, marking the Indians as doubly lacking. Thus the move "from Barbarism to Civilitie" could only be accomplished by the Indians' "forsaking their filthy nakedness."[33]

Algonquians, for their part, were keenly aware that the English dressed differently: the Narragansett word for European (English, Dutch, French, or Scotch) is "*Wautaconâug*," or, literally, "Coatmen," deriving from "*Waûtacome*," meaning "one that weares clothes."[34] The distinction seems to have had a metaphoric appeal for both cultures, even if it was not true that Indians were "wholly naked." Before Europeans arrived, Algonquians in New England commonly wore breechcloths and, especially in winter, leggings and cloaks of skins and furs. By the time of King Philip's War many had begun to wrap themselves in dyed wool blankets and other European fabrics and even to wear English clothes. Christian Indians, especially, commonly forsook their "nakedness," replacing traditional apparel with English dress.[35] And during the war, Algonquians stripped dead colonists of their clothes to wear them themselves, or to trade them for food and weapons.[36] (When Mary Rowlandson was a captive, Philip himself asked her to make a shirt and cap for his son, and before the war, Philip visited Boston wearing a coat, buckskins, beads, and a belt.[37])

In other words, the meaning of nakedness as a marker distinguishing civilized men from barbarians or Englishmen from Indians was not entirely stable. Nonetheless, as John Sassamon's story demonstrates, both peoples considered fully clothed Indians confusing and dangerous. Mary Rowlandson reeled with horror after she mistook a group of clothed Indians for Englishmen:

> My heart skipped within me, thinking they had been English men at the first sight of them, for they were dressed in English apparel, with hats, white neckcloths, and sashes about their waists, and ribbons upon their shoulders.: but when they came near, there was a vast difference between the lovely faces of Christians, and the foul looks of these heathens.[38]

Meanwhile, the idea of a naked Englishman, even one who was only spiritually naked, was always extremely disturbing. As Roger Williams wrote, "the best clad English-man, Not cloth'd with Christ, more naked is: Then naked Indian."[39]

In the years before King Philip's War began, the illusion that these meanings were stable had become increasingly important. (In the sixteenth century, the English in Ireland had been so plagued by this anxiety that they passed a law designed to draw a sartorial line between the civilized English and the savage Irish, decreeing that "every Irishman shall be forbidden to wear English apparel . . . upon pain of death."[40]) If the principal cultural anxiety behind King Philip's War was confusion of identity (would Englishmen degenerate into Indians?), then the colonists must have taken heart that one thing, at least, seemed more clear than others. One boundary, at least, was rarely broached: even if some Indians sometimes wore clothes, Englishmen and -women were never publicly naked. But during the war, of course, all that changed. While still alive, an English colonist attacked or captured by Indians was very likely to be "stript by them of all but his Skin." If tortured, he or she might not even be left with that, since a common torment involved the slow tearing off of skin and flesh. Many colonists died while Algonquians were "skinning them all over aliv, some only their Heads, cutting off their Hands and Feet." And if live Englishmen were likely to be stripped, skinned, or scalped, dead Englishmen fared no better. "Many of the English, when the Natives have killed them, they strip them naked, and leave their bodies to rot upon the ground." After burning Middleborough and Dartmouth, the Indians "barbarously murdered both men and women in those places, stripping the slain, whether Men or Women, and leaving them in the open Field, as naked as in the day wherein they were born." Naked and damaged bodies were often left to rot in highly visible places. After being slain by Indians attacking Groton, one Englishman was "strip'd naked, his Body mangled, and dragged into the High-way, and laid on his Back in a most shameful Manner." A dead man might even be stripped of his burial cloth. After destroying Groton, the Indians returned later to finish their business. "They strip'd the Body of him whom they had slain in the first Onset, and then cutting off his Head, fixed it upon a Pole looking towards his own Land. The Corpse of the Man slain the Week before, they dug up out of his Grave, they cut off his Head and one Leg, and set them upon Poles, and strip'd off his Winding-sheet." Stripping dead Englishmen was so common that Algonquians used English clothing as symbols of their victories. After killing several Englishmen near Deerfield, Indians retreated to the other side of the river, where they displayed "the Garments of the English in Sight of the Soldiers."[41]

Naked English bodies had been stripped of the clothes of civility, stripped, sometimes, of their English skin, just as the land had been stripped of its "improvements." The affinity between English land and English bodies was long-standing. When William Wood surveyed New England in 1634 he claimed that "that part of the country wherein most of the English have their habitations . . . is for certain the best ground and sweetest climate . . . , agreeing well with the temper of our English bodies."[42] The colonists' sense of the predestination of their settling in New England, their natural affinity with the land, and their cultural proclivity to conflate property with identity, all combined to produce this oneness of bodies and land. And this, in turn, became a vehicle that allowed them to express their concerns with both cultural and territorial boundaries between English and Indians. In the context of King Philip's War, concerns about the boundaries of the body became overlaid onto concerns not only about the boundaries of English property but also about the cultural boundaries separating English from Indian. Bodies were defined in relationship to houses, but houses, too, were metaphorical bodies. The physical integrity of houses could be compromised just as the physical integrity of bodies could. In English anatomical thought, skin, "an unseamed Garment covering the whole Body," was likened not only to clothing but also to buildings: "The Skin it self is the Wall of the Castle."[43] Open doors, then, could be like wounds on the body, the people spilling out like blood.

"These are perillous times which we now live in," Increase Mather preached during the war, "when men . . . can scarce look out of doors, but they are in danger of being seized upon by ravening Wolves, who lye in wait to shed blood, when men go not forth into the field, not walk by the way side, but the Sword of the Enemy, and fear is on every side."[44] The war, it seemed, redefined the physical landscape. No longer did fences mark the boundaries of safety, no longer town limits, but the walls of houses and the skin of bodies. Doors, then, became especially dangerous, deeply symbolic places separating safety from peril, life from death, order from chaos. Employing a common metaphor, the Connecticut Council warned, "an high handed enemie is at our doore." Or, as those in Massachusetts maintained, God had been provoked "to stir up many adversaries against us, not only abroad, but also at our own doors (causing the heathen in this Wilderness to be as thorns in our sides, who have formerly been, & might still be a wall unto us therein)." Even Benjamin Tompson made use of the evocative power of doorways, pitying the "Poor people spying an unwonted light," who "Leap to the door to fly, but all in vain, / They are surrounded with a pagan train."[45]

To emphasize the symbolic significance of doors and walls in the writing about the war is not to dismiss the very real protection that houses, especially those that were garrisoned, afforded during Indian attacks. When Brookfield was besieged and some eighty townspeople fortified themselves in a single garrison house, only those who "occasionally stept out" lost their lives. Thomas Wilson was shot when he went to get water, and Sargent Prichards' son had his head chopped off while running to fetch goods from his father's house. Henry Young never actually left the garrison but merely took a peek "out at a garret window"; for his curiosity, he was shot and mortally wounded. And when Providence was attacked, "all that were in Forts, Men, Women and Children, were Saved," but two colonists died that day nonetheless: Elizabeth Sucklin, who "was preparing to goe from Her own Hous to A Fort, but delaying they Killed Her," and Goodman Wright, who "could not be perswaded to come into any garrison" but remained in his own, unfortified home. (As Roger Williams remarked, "H. Wright would trust God in his own Hous. There they Killed Him with his own hammer.")[46] Indeed, it was because of these very real hazards that leaving the protection of a house or a garrison, walking out the door, or even sticking a head out a window took on new meaning during the war—it was the most dangerous thing a body could do.[47] Thomas Wakely's attachment to his property was, in fact, not unusual, and meeting death on the doorstep, as he did, was not an uncommon fate.

If building a house on a piece of land makes that land your own, and if the land you own defines who you are, then losing that house becomes a very troubling prospect indeed. With this in mind, Thomas Wakely's willingness to die with his house becomes easier to understand. Separated from his property, Thomas Wakely would no longer be Thomas Wakely, farmer, no longer Thomas Wakely, Englishman.[48] "Many people in these partes are like soules distracted, running hither and thither for shelter," Samuel Gorton observed with dismay, "whole families together not leaving there houses only, but goods and livelyhood also." By becoming as nomadic as Indians, they had lost not only their property but their identity as well, "blown / From place to place without an home to own."[49]

III

WHEN JOHN FOSTER engraved a map of New England to accompany William Hubbard's *Narrative*, he marked English territory with tiny houses and church steeples, and Indian territory with trees.[50] And when Benjamin Tompson recruited the assistance of a painter to help him portray New England's devastation, he instructed him to paint the Indians green:

> If painter overtrack my pen let him
> An olive color mix, these elves to trim;

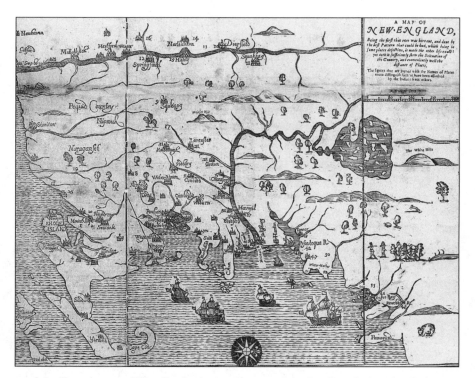

John Foster's map of New England, 1677. *Courtesy of the American Antiquarian Society*

> Of such an hue let many thousand thieves
> Be drawn like scarecrows clad with oaken leaves,
> Exhausted of their verdant life and blown
> From place to place without an home to own.

When Tompson turned his attention to the backdrop of his portrait of New England's Indians, he instructed the painter:

> Let round be gloomy forests with cragged rocks
> Where like to castles they may hide their flocks . . .

Far, far away from the homes and barns and fences and churches of colonial towns, Tompson's Indians are both naked and homeless. They are clad only "with oaken leaves," a symbol of their organic connection to the woods in which they live. In part, Tompson was speaking literally; Algonquians commonly camouflaged themselves with ferns, leaves, and branches.[51] (Mary Pray feared that summer, "when the leaves are green," was the Indians' best time for fighting.⁵²) But Tompson was also speaking metaphorically when he, like many colonists, portrayed the Indians as if they had no clothes and no homes and suggested, even, that the Indians had no bodies—they blended so well with the woods as to be almost invisible there, indistinguishable from the wilderness around them, more like plants than people or, if animate, more like animals.⁵³ In the first decades of settlement, the Indians' supposed oneness with the woods (and their corresponding lack of ownership of the land) had served the colonists well in claiming New England as a *vacuum domicilum*— during King Philip's War it made those same Indians frightful enemies. "Clad with oaken leaves," Indians could easily ambush English settlers or hide from English soldiers. As Tompson versified it, "The trees stood sentinels and bullets flew / From every bush (a shelter for their crew)." Or, again, "every stump shot like a musketeer, / And bows with arrows every tree did bear."⁵⁴

Swamps made the best cover of all. To the colonists' eyes, Indians were entirely invisible in swamps, disembodied, indistinguishable from the vegetation around them. Swamps were "so full of Bushes and Trees, that a Parcel of Indians may be within the Length of a Pike of a Man, and he cannot discover them."⁵⁵ "How many Indians we killed we cannot tell," wrote one Englishman, "for so thick were the bushes, that hardly one was to be seen."⁵⁶ In the chaos of swamps, the English might even mistakenly shoot one another: "Our Men when in that hideous place if they did but see a Bush stir would fire presantly, whereby 'tis verily feared they did sometimes unhappily shoot English Men instead of Indians."⁵⁷ As a result, English soldiers were quite appropriately terrified of swamps. Daniel Henchman and his forces

> were not willing to run into the Mire and Dirt after them in a dark Swamp, being taught by late Experience how dangerous it is to fight in such dismal Woods, when their Eyes were muffled with the Leaves, and their Arms pinioned with the thick Boughs of the Trees, as their Feet were continually shackled with the Roots spreading every Way in those boggy Woods. It is ill fighting with a wild Beast in his own Den.⁵⁸

To the colonists, swamps were hideous and dangerous places, the most foreign and un-English land in all the New World. The word itself, "swamp," only entered the English language with the first reports from North America in 1624.⁵⁹ And each time the colonists wrote about swamps they saw the need to offer a definition. "A *Swamp*," Nathaniel Saltonstall informed his English readers, "signifies a Moorish Place, overgrown with Woods and bushes, but soft like a Quagmire or Irish Bogg, over which Horse cannot at all, nor English Foot (without great Difficulty) passe." Or, as William Harris put it, a swamp is "a sorte of watery ground by brookes: or rivers: or pond sydes: very wooddy, & not pasable for horses, & very troublesome for men to pas." Usually swamps were defined as watery or waterlogged (as we think of them today), but the colonists occasionally used the term to describe simply a "thick wood" or a "Grove of trees and underwoods."[60] (So often did Indians hide themselves in swamps that the English came to use the word as a verb, as in the description they "in swamped them selves in a great Spruse swamp," or in the order "Apprehend them before they swamp themselves."[61])

Just as the fate of English bodies and English houses was inextricably linked, so Indians were fated to live or die in swamps. And if houses explain scenes of English devastation, swamps explain Indian scenes. The English called swamps the dens of wild beasts, "habitations of cruelty," and "habitations of darkness," but they were also, clearly—and especially in wartime—habitations of Indians.[62] Algonquians had long used swamps as "Refuges for Women and children in Warre" and as warehouses for corn and other foods to be consumed during winter months; and, from the earliest months of King Philip's War, they also used swamps as hideouts, since the English were particularly inept at navigating through them.[63] As Increase Mather declared, "every Swamp is a Castle to them."[64]

Much as men like John Josselyn had insisted, "Towns they have none," Algonquians were not nomads. They lived for most of the year in regular, settled communities, one in summer, one in winter. In summer, families gathered to live in villages near fertile agricultural lands; in winter, they moved closer to hunting grounds, returning to the same place for as many years as the lands could sustain them. Algonquian settlements were generally small, and consisted of a group of wigwams, sturdy buildings constructed of woven mats that could be easily disassembled and transported (and quite similar to the "English wigwams" the colonists had lived in when they first arrived). By the middle of the seventeenth century some wigwam construction included English hardware for doorframes and windows. In general, Algonquian wigwams were much more sparsely furnished than English houses, though many did contain items of English furniture: a chair, bed, table, or chest. What goods Indians owned, European or otherwise, needed to be portable, while the English cherished permanent property most of all. Colonists and Indians alike viewed this, and the temporary nature of wigwam construction, as a fundamental cultural difference. (Moreover, most Algonquians proved unwilling to adopt English ways. In Natick, John Eliot had made it a priority that Christian Indians cease to "live shifting up and downe to other Wigwams," but even when he provided supplies and house lots, Natick Indians rarely built English-style houses for themselves, preferring to live in more traditional homes.)[65]

During a bad year, native communities might move more often, and during war, they might move a good deal. Refuges in swamps lessened the strains of war, allowing women, children, and old men to stay put in safe havens. Yet, whatever their similarities to or differences from English homes, colonists refused to consider Indian settlements in swamps real "towns," or their wigwams true "houses."[66] Entering Pocasset Swamp, James Cudworth wrote, "the place we found was a hideous dismal swamp; the house or shelter they had to lodge in, contained, in space, the quantity of four acres of ground, standing thick together," but his labeling of a wigwam a "house" was extremely unusual.[67] More typical was Benjamin Tompson's scorn:

> Their myrmidons enclosed with clefts of trees
> Are busy like the ants or nimble bees:
> And first they limber poles fix in the ground,
> In figure of the heavens convex: all round
> They draw their arras-mats and skins of beasts
> And under these the elves to make their nests.
> Rome took more time to grow than twice six hours,
> But half that time will serve for Indian bowers.[68]

Here, Indian homes are animal "nests" or, at best, temporary "bowers." Mary Rowlandson came perhaps closer than any other chronicler of the war to considering Indian settlements in swamps analogous to English towns, but she, too, resisted the idea:

> When I came to the brow of the hill, that looked towards the swamp, I thought we had come to a great Indian town (though there were none but our own company). The Indians were as thick as the trees: it seemed as if there had been a thousand hatchets going at once: if one looked before one, there was nothing but Indians, and behind one, nothing but Indians, and so on either hand.[69]

Rowlandson at first thought she had come to a "great Indian town" but quickly corrected herself—this scene, too, was one of wild disorder, with Indians not living in settled communities but lurking "as thick as the trees."

Swamps, where "the Indians were as thick as the trees," were also the places where the English inflicted the most damage and practiced the greatest cruelties. Yet, in refusing to consider Algonquian settlements in swamps homes, the colonists absolved themselves of any possible violation of the laws of war in destroying them. English notions of just conduct dictated that soldiers were not to "plunder and burne houses, drive away the inhabitants, breake open the doores, and commit such like outrages," and it was just these violations that most alarmed colonists whose towns were thus destroyed.[70] But in swamps, English soldiers again and again mimicked Indian "outrages."[71] When the English managed to find a hidden, "enswamped" Algonquian camp, they usually burned the Indians' wigwams, just as the Indians burned English houses. Samuel Moseley reported in August 1675, "we did find A parsell of wigwoms beond the Swaimp about 20 which we burnt &c."[72] Often enough, the chief difference between English and Indian "cruelties" was simply the words they used to describe them: since Indian homes were "wigwams," not "houses," their settlements "camps," not "towns," fights in swamps were "courageous battles," not "massacres."

This particular manifestation of the moral vocabulary of warfare is best seen in the English attack on the Narragansetts' Great Swamp on December 19, 1675. On that day, a coalition of English soldiers from each of the United Colonies, aided by an Indian guide, entered the Great Swamp (near present-day South Kingstown, Rhode Island), where they found a palisaded fort sheltering hundreds of wigwams and, by some estimates, as many as three thousand or four thousand Narragansetts. Most were women and children hidden in the swamp for protection during the war, along with storehouses of winter supplies. English soldiers first set fire to the wigwams and then waited as the Narragansetts began fleeing over the palisade and through its doors and windows. Then the soldiers "ran on the very musles of thyr guns, up to the Indeans port holes: & fyred in at them, & leped over thyr brest workes, & run into theyr forte, & beat them out: & slew many of them." The fury of the English was so great that, rather than preserve the wigwams for their own shelter, or save the food, they burned everything and were forced to march back out of the swamp all through the night and the next several days, in driving snow, during which many English soldiers froze to death.[73]

The English attack on the Great Swamp has all the elements of an Indian assault on an English town, or upon a house like Thomas Wakely's: setting fire to buildings to drive the people out; then, as they fled the smoke and flames, killing them on their doorsteps, or "port holes"; and finally, destroying all who had remained inside. Surely this fight violated several English codes of just conduct during warfare, not least among them the rule that "To cut off a few nocent, wee are not to cut off multitudes of Innocents, such as are Weomen and Children (as in sieges, and other depopulations) of whom the one is to be spared for sex, the other for want of age."[74] Still, no English account of the "Great Swamp Fight" noted this inconsistency. Instead, most English accounts emphasized the justness of the attack and celebrated it as one of the few "fair" contests of the war: "The English Souldiers played the men wonderfully; the Indians also fought stoutly, but were at last beaten out of their Fort." Upon entering the fort, "It did greatly rejoice our Men to see their Enemies, who had formerly sculked behind Shrubs and Trees, now to be engaged in a Fair Field." Joseph Dudley noted the "great courage" of the English soldiers who "valiantly scaled the fort." And Benjamin Tompson wrote:

> Here English valor most illustrious shone,
> Finding their numbers ten times ten to one.
> A shower of leaden hail our captains feel
> Which made the bravest blades among us reel.
>
> Sundry the flames arrest and some the blade
> By bullets heaps on heaps of Indians laid.
> The flames like lightning in their narrow streets
> Dart in the face of everyone it meets.
> Here might be heard an hideous Indian cry,
> Of wounded ones who in the wigwams fry.

Bravery and valor thus overwhelmed the "hideous Indian cry," but even Tompson paused to recognize the extent of the slaughter: "Had we been cannibals here might we feast."[75]

IV

WHAT THE Reverend Noah Newman would have thought of the Great Swamp fight remains a mystery, but what he saw and heard in the town of Medfield horrified him. "The sight of this poore people was very astonishing," Newman recalled, and "the cry of terrifyed persons, very dreadfull." More dreadful still were the yells of the enemy, "shouting so as the earth seemed to tremble." Newman probably shivered to remember that day, when more than three hundred Indians attacked the town, but since his friend John Cotton had asked him for "the Hystory of the medfield tragedy," Newman was determined to give "the best account I can." Still, Newman could not recall the day without pain. "Oh what an Indian calamity was this," he said with a bitter sigh.[76]

A party of Nipmucks had infiltrated Medfield during the night of February 20, hiding in trees and barns, with the intention, Noah Newman surmised, "to take persons at their first Looking out at their doors in the morning." "Which," Newman admitted tersely, "accordingly they did." Thomas Wight's son, apparently an early riser, was "one of the first that was killed in that manner." Then the Indians threw pellets at Timothy Dwight's house "to provoke him to Looke out & when he did Looke out shot him through the shoulder." Soon Joshua Fisher's grandson, "going out at the door was shot att, the bullet passing through some flesh about his chollar bone." And when Henry Adams "stept but over the threshold," he "was shot through the windpipe & fell downe dead." So it continued throughout the morning. In listing the casualties, Newman soon dispensed with his description of the wounds and wrote, simply, "Goodman Bowers & his son was killed. Thomas Mason & his son kild."[77] All those who looked out, or, worse still, stepped out, were bound to be met with a volley of bullets and arrows. All of these, like Thomas Wakely, died in their doorways. The boundaries separating English from Indian had been breached.

The people of Medfield did not expect this tragedy. As Reverend Newman remarked, "few when they lay downe" the night before had "thought of such a dolefull morning." The town, after all, was occupied by more than a hundred colony soldiers and as many local militiamen. The nearby town of Lancaster (where Mary Rowlandson lived) had been destroyed a week before Medfield was attacked, and John Wilson, fearful of his town's meeting a similar fate, had written to the Massachusetts Council begging for help. "Now the rode from Nipmuck is fair for these caniballs, be pleased for God's sake to remember us, and let some considerable sufficient force be sent to us for our speedy releife, before it be to late, by the soonest, by the soonest that possibly can be, lest Medfield be turned into ashes and the smoke of it amaze such that shall behold it."[78] These, as it turned out, had been prophetic words. Although the council quickly sent in two companies, twenty horsemen and eighty foot, to add to Medfield's militia, the troops were scattered about town on the night of February 20. When morning came "they could not get together into a body to repel the enemy" (John Wilson estimated there were as many as a thousand), who showered arrows "into the bosome of the Town."[79]

Medfield had been particularly vulnerable to Indian attack because it was a frontier town, close to Indian "wilderness" and not yet fully "improved." As William Hubbard would later write, "Most of those inland Plantations being over run with young Wood (the Inhabitants being every where apt to engross more Land into their Hands than they were able to subdue) as if they were seated amidst of a Heap of Bushes."[80] John Foster's map suggests the extreme vulnerability of such frontier settlements. (Each number on the map corresponds to the site of an Indian attack.) On Foster's map, Medfield stands perilously close to ominous-looking trees. Other frontier towns also suffered for their woodiness. At Scarborough, Major Philips was trapped in his house because "the bushes being thick within shott of his house could not at ffirst See an Indian." "Our woods," Edmund Browne wrote from Sudbury, "are pestered with Indians." In Rehoboth, the townspeople were similarly trapped: "Wee are shut up in our garisones," John Kingsley reported, "& dare not goe abroad far to our outlandes." "They are like wild Deare in the Wilderness," John Hull complained, who "will Never stand to maintaine any fight but come upon some of our out plantations & burne some of the remote houses & kill one or two & take there scalps & get away that our souldiers can rarely find any of them."[81]

In Medfield, the fighting probably lasted most of the morning, as more and more Nipmucks jumped out from their overnight hiding places. After the initial shooting, the townspeople tried to hide in their houses, but soon their "dreadful hour" came, as it had come for the Narragansetts at the Great Swamp in December, and for Mary Rowlandson in Lancaster just days before. In Lancaster, Rowlandson and her family had endured two hours of shooting before considering leaving the protection of their house. Finally the Nipmucks succeeded in setting the house on fire. "Now," wrote Rowlandson, "is the dreadful hour come. . . . Some in our house were fighting for their lives, others wallowing in their blood, the house on fire over our heads, and the bloody heathen ready to knock us on the head, if we stirred out. Now might we hear mothers and children crying out for themselves, and one another, Lord, What shall we do?" "But," she resolved, "out we must go, the fire increasing, and coming along behind us, roaring, and the Indians gaping before us with their guns, spears and hatchets to devour us." (On the first night of her captivity, Mary Rowlandson's captors camped near a deserted English house. "I asked them whither I might not lodge in the house that night," Rowlandson recalled. But the Indians replied, mocking her, "What, will you love English men still?" Rising the next morning, Rowlandson recognized her fate: "I must turn my back upon the town, and travel with them into the vast and desolate wilderness, I knew not whither.")[82]

Similarly, in Medfield, while some Nipmucks had been shooting down people in their doorways, others had been busy setting fire to the houses and barns they had so recently hidden behind. Driven out by smoke and flames, still more townspeople were killed. In all, some fifty houses were destroyed and thirty inhabitants killed or taken captive. As William Hubbard wrote, "some were killed as they attempted to fly to their Neighbours for Shelter: some were only wounded, and some taken alive and carried Captive; in some Houses the Husband running away with one Child, the Wife with another."[83] If doors marked liminal spaces between inside and outside, order and chaos, and houses represented the English body, those same houses also represented the English family—a house destroyed was a family destroyed. To leave the house was to risk tearing the family apart, a husband running in one direction, his wife in another. And a family torn asunder was yet another sign of chaos. As Increase Mather asked rhetorically, "Is it nothing that Widdows and Fatherless have been multiplyed among us? that in a small Plantation we have heard of eight widows, and six and twenty fatherless children in one day? And in another of the Villages of our Judah, of seven Widows an about thirty fatherless children, all at once?" But to stay in a house was to risk being destroyed along with it and learning the gruesome lesson that the family that stays together is slain together. When Indians attacked William Clark's house in Plymouth, "the Indians destroyed them all, root and branche, the Father, and Mother, and all the Children. So that eleven persons were murdered that day, under one roof."[84]

In Medfield, Thomas Thurston's wife had been lodging at Seth Smith's house when the Nipmucks began their attack. She must have left the house early on, for soon she was "stricken dead to the enemys apprehension," upon which "they stript her & tooke of[f] her head cloths." Goodwife Thurston, alas, had not quite expired. On the contrary, she soon "came to her selfe, went into the house got a blanket & run to Mr. Wilson." But, as John Wilson later told a friend, this bloody and nearly naked woman was "a frightfull spectacle." When she arrived at Wilson's doorstep, even her closest neighbors failed to recognize her, "they not knowing who she was her hair hanging downe & her face covred with blood."[85] As she stirred to consciousness, Goody Thurston may have come "to her selfe," but her "selfe," it seems, was no longer obvious. Stripped, bloodied, and disheveled, she had lost her identity. No doubt she looked like the people Mary Rowlandson encountered on the streets of Lancaster, "Christians lying in their blood, some here, and some there, like a company of sheep torn by wolves. All of them stripped naked by a company of hell-hounds, roaring, singing, ranging and insulting, as if they would have torn our very hearts out." One of her neighbors, who had been "chopped into the head with a hatchet, and stripped naked," was still alive, and Rowlandson watched him "crawling up and down" in front of her.[86] No longer Englishmen and -women, the townspeople of Lancaster had become deranged sheep.

On that day in Medfield, Goodwife Thurston was unrecognizable partly because her face was covered with blood and her hair was "hanging down." Probably her attackers had begun to scalp her but had been unexpectedly interrupted. Stripping the skin off the head, or scalping, was a common practice among New England Indians: "When ever they wound, and their arrow sticks in the body of their enemie, they . . . follow their arrow, and falling upon the person wounded, and tearing his head a little aside by his Locke, they in the twinckling of an eye fetch off his head though but with a sorry knife." [87] Having stripped Goodwife Thurston and taken off her bonnet, or "head cloths," her attackers may have been pulling at her hair and cutting away at her forehead when they were unexpectedly attacked or otherwise interrupted in their work. Still, even an unfinished cut to the head would have bloodied Goodwife Thurston's face considerably. In their haste, or perhaps deliberately, they may have stripped the skin off part of her face; scalping often involved this type of "skinning." "Such also is their Inhumanity," Increase Mather commented, "as that they flay off the skin from their Faces and Heads of those they get into their hands." [88]

Either way, Goody Thurston's face was covered with blood and hair. To her neighbors, she was "a frightfull spectacle," mostly, no doubt, because of her own panicked aspect and her terrible injuries, but partly also because she had been shorn of all emblems of piety, civility, and Englishness. English faces were especially endowed as markers of English national superiority: as Edward Chamberlayne had written in 1671, "The complexion of the inhabitants . . . excells all other nations." [89] The idea that English bodies were physically distinct, and somehow purer than other peoples' bodies, gained considerable favor in the seventeenth century. In the shape of their noses, the fineness of their hair, the suppleness of their skin, Englishmen and -women were encouraged to think of themselves as closer to God's image, unaltered versions of the model of humankind, while foreign peoples, with their tanned skin, strange body piercings, tattoos, and mutilations, had distorted, artificially altered bodies. [90] The face, the English believed, "is a special glass wherein the glory and Image of God doth shine forth and appear," and to obscure it in any way was an offense against God. Long hair in men, or wayward hair in women, was considered excessive, "when it is so long, that it covers the eyes, the checks, the countenance, &c God hath ordeined those parts to be visible." Long hair was considered "a badge of cruelty and effeminacy" and was even vaguely associated with cannibalism. [91] Long or loose hair also, of course, distinguished Indians in New England from their English neighbors, making it possible, for instance, for short hair to be used as a disguise, as when, late in the war, "Phillip had cutt off his haire to disguise himself." [92]

Not only was Goodwife Thurston's face covered with blood and hair, but also her body was naked but for a blanket. Still, Goody Thurston's neighbors, however confused, must have very quickly realized she was an Englishwoman in great need, even if they didn't know exactly who she was. Two Thurston children died that day, and at least one was taken captive, but their mother is not listed among the casualties. When she arrived at John Wilson's doorstep, having just recovered consciousness after suffering a brutal attack, Goodwife Thurston probably did not speak clearly. She may have shrieked, or spoken in gibberish, or she may have been unable to speak at all. But, after a moment, she may have begun to speak clearly, and then her neighbors would have recognized that she was speaking English. (She told her neighbors that "all her afflictions was swallowd up in the loss of her poore child gone into Captivity."[93]) Speech was somewhat more reliable than appearance, as it could pierce through any darkness or disguise.[94] During another skirmish, "at the very instant" that an English soldier was about to start shooting at three Indians, "a child with them in the habit of an Indian papoos" cried out that "he was an English boy" and the soldier held his fire. Immediately, "the child ran to the English and escaped." On another occasion, fellow Englishmen "were ready to have shot at" Wheeler and his men, "till we discerning they were English by the Majors speaking."[95]

Language, in this story, may have been the final marker of Englishness. Like so many chroniclers of the war, Goodwife Thurston may have told her tale both as a way of making sense of her experience and as a way of reclaiming her identity. If the colonists' Englishness had been compromised before the war by becoming more Indian in their ways, it was further compromised during the war by the loss of their homes and clothes and, most of all, by their killing mercilessly and abandoning the codes of "civil nations." By telling about the war, and most especially by writing about it, the colonists could reclaim civility, could clothe their naked war with words. The writing itself would "dress" the English back up; it would undo the damage of the war by making clear once again who was English and who Indian, and what made a massacre and what a victory. All of this depended, however, on denying the possibility that the Indians might themselves "dress" the war with their own words. But that, alas, was a mistaken assumption.

V

WHILE THE TOWN of Medfield burned and Goodwife Thurston calmed down enough to speak English clearly and tell her neighbors who she was, a retreating Nipmuck, very possibly James Printer, hastily wrote a note and tacked it to a tree probably just a stone's throw from John Wilson's house:

> Thou English man hath provoked us to anger & wrath & we care not though we have war with you this 21 years for there are many of us 300 of which hath fought with you at this town[.] we hauve nothing but our lives to loose but thou hast many fair houses cattell & much good things.[96]

At the war's end, William Hubbard would scoff at the threat, remarking only that the Indians "fell short of their Expectation by ninteen [years]," but at the time the people of Medfield must have been terribly shaken by it. In just two short sentences the note offered an analysis that the colonists had failed to consider in any of the hundreds of letters and dozens of accounts they themselves had written about the war: that Indians attacked English towns for reasons other than the pure pleasures of wanton cruelty.

What the Medfield note suggests is that the Algonquians knowingly directed their attacks against the English acquisition of land and the introduction of livestock (their "fair houses cattell & much good things"), developments that dramatically undermined traditional Algonquian subsistence practices. English livestock strayed onto Indian land, ate Indian crops, dug up Indian clam beds, and always compelled colonists to take more and more Indian land for pasturage.[97] As a Narragansett man had explained to Roger Williams: "You have driven us out of our own Countrie and then pursued us to our Great Miserie, and Your own, and we are Forced to live upon you."[98] (While some Algonquians, including Philip himself, took to keeping livestock themselves, they kept only hogs, the wildest of all English domesticated animals, and retained their animosity toward other kinds of English livestock, especially cattle.[99]) As Philip and his counselors complained to John Easton, they had "thoft when the English boft land of them that thay wold have kept ther Catell upone ther owne land," but even if they moved thirty miles from English settlements, "thay Could not kepe ther coren from being spoyled" and "the English Catell and horses still incresed."[100]

Most importantly, the Medfield note called attention to the Nipmucks' vehement rejection of the English conflation of property and identity: "We hauve nothing but our lives to loose but thou hast many fair houses cattell & much good things." If this, as Noah Newman feared after reading the note, "is the summe they warr from," it was not an unwarranted calculus. It was, after all, this "computation" that the English themselves relied on in tallying up the damage of the war, counting burned houses, killed cattle, and toppled fences.[101] The precious few notes and letters written by warring Indians prove that the connection between English property and English lives was not lost on their enemies. "You know, and we know," one Indian wrote in a letter negotiating the release of captives, "you have great sorrowful with crying; for you lost many, many hundred men, and all your house, all your land, and woman, child, and cattle, and all your things that you have lost."[102] Not only notes but also rites of cruelty and the verbal taunts that often accompanied them attacked the English attachment to land. While burying several English captives alive, a group of Algonquians mocked English agriculture (and curiously echoed Samuel Gorton's fear that the Indians were trying to "root out the English"): "You English since you came into this Countrey have grown exceedingly above the Ground, let us now see how you will grow when Planted into the Ground."[103] (Meanwhile, Algonquians had always celebrated their detachment from goods and property. The Narragansetts traditionally engaged in a ritual in which participants offered "almost all the riches they have to their gods, as kettles, skins, hatchets, beads, knives, etc." and threw them "into a great fire."[104])

Almost without exception, the English interpreted Algonquian assaults, and the taunts that accompanied them, as expressions of mindless savagery or as divine retribution rather than as calculated assaults on the English way of life. Indian attacks on English livestock, for instance, appalled the colonists, who frequently reported finding the enemy driving away or "killing off Cattle."[105] (Edward Randolph later reported that the English had lost "eight thousand head of Cattle" during the war.[106]) On occasion Algonquians might even "torture" English livestock: "They took a Cow, knocked off one of her horns, cut out her tongue, and so left the poor creature in great misery. They put an horse, ox &c. into an hovil, and then set it on fire only to shew how they are delighted in excercising cruelty." As the English perceived it, the Indians did so only to "to shew what barbarous creatures they are."[107] But clearly, attacks on English livestock were attacks on the English practice of keeping livestock, animals who often ruined Indian crops and took over Indian hunting grounds.[108] When Joshua Tift was taken captive and brought to the Great Swamp, the Narragansetts who captured him brought along "5 of his Cattell and killd them before his face." Tift was "forc't to be Silent," but he nonetheless "praid the Sachim to Spare the rest," to which the sachem answered, "What will Cattell now doe you good?" The next day, the Narragansetts sent for the rest of Tift's cattle and killed them all before his eyes, symbolically suggesting that Tift, as a captive, must now turn his back on English ways and accept Indian ones.[109] Interpreted in this light, the reasons for killing Tift's cattle are clear enough, but not, it seems, clear enough for the colonists. As their voluminous writing about the war demonstrates, most colonists were either unwilling or unable to place Indian "cruelties" within the broader context of Algonquian culture, instead labeling them "barbarous" violations of English ideas of just conduct in war, or understanding them only, and somewhat ironically, as messages from a brutal and furious God.

Chapter 4

Where is Your O God?

*I*n late April 1676, a party of Nipmucks near Mount Wachusett prepared for battle. Forming a circle, they gathered around two figures: a powwaw, or shaman, who knelt on a deerskin, and a standing man who held a gun. Those in the circle fell to their knees, beat on the ground with sticks, and made a noise that sounded to Mary Rowlandson, who witnessed the scene, like "muttering or humming." The powwaw spoke, and all assented to what he said. A tightly orchestrated series of actions followed: The standing man who held the gun was made to leave the circle and then asked to return. He was given a second gun, and asked to leave once more.

> Then they called him in again, but he made a stand; so they called him with greater earnestness; but he stood reeling and wavering as if he knew not whither he should stand or fall, or which way to go. Then they called him with exceeding great vehemency, all of them, one and another: after a little while he turned in, staggering as he went, with his arms stretched out, in either hand a gun.

Those in the circle rejoiced, again the powwaw spoke, all assented, and "so they ended their business, and forthwith went to Sudbury-fight."[1]

To Rowlandson, the ritual of the circle seemed satanic. "When they went, they acted as if the devil had told them that they should gain the victory," and when they returned, the powwaw looked "as black as the devil."[2] But to the

Nipmucks, the circle was sacred. In listening to the powwaw and in at first rejecting but ultimately arming and rousing the standing man, they expressed
their resolve to fight, called upon the power of animal and other spirits, or
manitou, to aid them in battle, and sought, from the powwaw, prophecy of
victory.[3]

Meanwhile, in Boston, a day of humiliation was declared. At the old
Meeting House, three ministers dressed in black stood on a raised platform,
reading from a large printed book and preaching to hundreds of men and
women assembled before them in long rows of wooden benches. They knelt
in humility before God; they stood and sang His praise. Increase Mather
preached that day, no doubt reflecting on the causes and course of the war and
praying for God's help. Preparing for an earlier day of humiliation, Mather
had prayed to God "That Hee would sanctify these awfull Judgments on the
Countrey. And Reverse them in due Time." After the April 20 day of humiliation, Mather wrote in his diary, as he did on many days, that he had been
"graciously assisted in [the] Lords worke." Perhaps he expected that the day
of humiliation would turn the tide in the war and bring the colonists greater
victories. Surely it would bring the people of Boston closer to God. But as
Mather later wrote in his history, "The next day sad tidings came to us."[4] A
party of Nipmucks had destroyed Sudbury.

Despite the powwaw's prophecy, the assault on Sudbury was a mixed success. On April 21 five hundred Nipmucks attacked the town (less than twenty
miles west of Boston), killing more than thirty of the enemy but losing a half
dozen of their own men.[5] In a letter later printed in London, one death was
described in detail:

> an elderly English man endeavouring an Escape from the Indians by run-
> ning into a Swamp, was overtaken by an Indian, and being Destitute of
> Weapons to Defend himself or Offend him, the Indian insulted over him
> with that Blasphemous Expression (Come Lord Jesus, save this poor Eng-
> lishman if thou canst, whom I am now about to Kill).

The Nipmuck's taunt "was heard by another Englishman, who was Hid in a
Bush close by" and who watched "that Bloody Wretch . . . Knock [the elderly
man] down and leave him Dead." The shocked chronicler of this scene concluded weakly, "We hope the Lord is Arisen to Avenge those blasphemies."[6]

At Sudbury, a Nipmuck warrior who, the day before, had called upon his
own manitou to fight with him in battle, now mocked the colonists' god. And
an elderly Englishman who had likely once prayed to his Savior for strength
in adversity (and whose Boston neighbors had spent the previous day humil-

iating themselves before God) found himself dying at the hands of a man he considered a heathen uttering words he considered blasphemous: *Come Lord Jesus, save this poor Englishman if thou canst.*

Taunts, prayers, prophecies. All raise an intriguing question: Was King Philip's War a holy war? And if so, whose?

I

APPALLED BY their astounding losses during the war, many colonists in New England believed that God was punishing them for their sins, not least among them their failure to convert the Indians to Christianity. "Betwixt God & us," John Eliot confided to the governor, "I think that our sins have ripened us for so seveare a scourge as the warre hath, & is likely to prove." War, Increase Mather maintained, is "the greatest of all outward Judgements"; or, as John Kingsley put it, "general sin cales useley for generall plague; which is now."[7] After describing an Indian attack, Philip Walker wondered "what god in such a scrug Intends":

> in this owr great Advercitee
> let us Consider what may bee
> the Ca[u]se owr glorious angry god
> so hevi on us Lays his rod
> shure wee ow Arant have forgott
> that makes us ffeele the hethens shot.[8]

The English had always looked for supernatural messages in the natural world—in the skies, in "monstrous" births, in diseases, in bad crops.[9] During the war they strained their eyes to see messages within the devastation around them. As Mary Pray wrote, "we . . . know not what to do; but our eyes are upward."[10] Everywhere the English found God writing his judgment onto New England's landscape or onto English bodies. He had made New England into "a looking glasse" whose ravages reflected the colonists' own spiritual corruption. He had filled the colonists' "cup of sorrow," He had made his hand "heavie upon the land." He had taken away the churches of those who were unfaithful, the houses of those who were greedy, the clothes of those who were proud, and the lives of those who sinned.

In the colonists' eyes, all of the devastation around them, the destruction of their world, carried with it a message from God, often through the world of the occult. Houses burning, dead bodies piling up, and blood spilling everywhere: images like these pervaded the colonists' descriptions of the war, and each had a special significance. Blood that flowed uncontrollably, for instance, signaled filth and chaos. Blood, the colonists believed, ought to be contained within the body, where it regulated all the vital forces. Blood might be "let" to cure "plethora," but carefully, and, one hoped, by someone who could stop it. Within Galenic physiology, the prevailing physiology of the day, all bodily fluids were thought to be reducible to blood. Three of the bodily "humors"—phlegm, choler, and melancholy—were simply imperfect forms of the fourth and perfect humor, blood. To upset the balance of these humors, and especially to lose too much blood, would not only put one's life in danger but would also fundamentally alter one's disposition, since humoral balance dictated temperament. Indians, after all, were considered "prone to injurious violence and slaughter, by reason of their bloud dryed up." [11] Uncontrollable bleeding was also akin to menstruation, and, as such, was cause for shame.[12] While expelling menstrual blood was thought to purify women, the blood itself was considered an excrement.[13] With such a great loss of blood, then, the colonists themselves might become as "dryed up" and vicious as the Indians or, at the very least, as filthy as menstruous women.

Spilled blood, however, also signaled God's judgment. Most colonists would have agreed with the English anatomist who wrote that the body was the very "*Book of God.*"[14] Or, as 1 Corinthians 6:19 decreed, "your body is a temple of the Holy Spirit." Among the many symbolic functions of the body was its role as God's writing tablet, on which He might write with "bloody characters." And, in seventeenth-century medical parlance, wounds were themselves called "lips."[15] Spilled blood, then, told not only of slaughter but also of judgment. "Why should we suppose that God is not offended with us," Increase Mather had asked, "when his displeasure is written, in such visible and bloody Characters?"[16]

God's bloody writing may have been in full view, but to many His penmanship was terrible. Reading what God had written, or hearing what He had to say, required both vigilance and diligence. "Ah, the burden that I beare night & day," Kingsley moaned, "to see the blessed & loving God thus angrey, & wee have not a Profet to tel how longe, & to say this or these are New Englandes sinn." "The Busines of the Day in N.E.," Roger Williams commanded, "is not only to keepe our selves & ours from murthering[,] our Howses Barnes & from firinge, to destroy & cut off the Barbarians or subdue & reduce them, but our main & Principall Opus Diei is to listen to what the Eternal speaketh." The Lord, Williams insisted, "will speake peace to his people," and, as David had pledged, "I will listen to what Jehovah speaketh." And there was to be no talking back to Jehovah. "Oh that we may be silent before him," John Pynchon prayed, "and not open our mouths, but lie at his foot."[17]

Just as Puritan ministers interpreted signs from God, so Algonquian powwaws looked for messages from the spirit world. Wampanoags attacking Bridgewater saw a spirit "in the Shape of a Bear walking on his 2 hind feet" and the powwaw Tispaquin ordered a withdrawal. If the omen had taken the form of a deer, "they would have destroyed the whole Town & all the English." And when a violent seaside storm blew down English houses in August 1675, Nathaniel Saltonstall wrote that "The Indians afterwards reported that they had caused it by their *Pawwaw*. They farther say, that as many Englishmen shall die, as the Trees have by this wind been blown down in the Woods."[18]

Algonquian powwaws, like Puritan ministers, also played an important role in determining whether a war ought to be waged at all. In 1660 the Pawtucket powwaw Passaconaway had warned his people not to fight the colonists:

I was as much an Enemy to the English at their first coming into these Parts, as any one whatsoever, and did try all Ways and Means possible to have destroyed them, at least to have prevented them sitting down here, but I could in no way effect it; . . . therefore I advise you never to contend with the English, nor make War with them.[19]

In the 1670s, powwaws among the Narragansetts, Nipmucks, Pocumtucks, and Wampanoags apparently contradicted Passaconaway's earlier warning, now commanding that war was the only means available to preserve their way of life.

Predictably, the colonists thought powwaws received their orders straight from Satan. (Indeed, Eliot and other missionaries had long railed against powwaws, believing that all "serve the Devill."[20]) Philip Walker believed that Indians adored and served the Devil, who

by ther powas . . . prescribes t[o them] his Law will & plesur declaring to them he [is] The princ of darknes . . . he perswads them darknes is Light & [evil] is good.[21]

Looking back at the war, Cotton Mather considered it inevitable because

these parts were then covered with nations of barbarous indians and infidels, in whom the prince of power of the air did work as a spirit; nor could it be expected that the nations of wretches, whose whole religion was the most explicit sort of devil-worship, should not be acted by the devil to engage in some early and bloody action, for the extinction of a plantation so contrary to his interests, as that of New England was.[22]

Yet, if the English believed that powwaws served the devil, they found it no contradiction to believe that the Indians were also the instruments of God. By far the most humbling of all the messages of the war was that God did not speak to His chosen people directly. Instead, He used Indians, in a sense, as His translators: He made the Indians a "rod" with which to chastise the colonists for their failure to convert their heathen neighbors. As the Massachusetts government declared,

> The Righteous God hath heightned our Calamity and given Commission to the Barbarous Heathen to rise up against us, and to become a smart Rod, and severe Scourge to us, in Burning and Depopulating several hopeful Plantations, Murdering many of our People of all sorts, and seeming as it were to cast us off . . . hereby speaking aloud to us to search and try our wayes and turn again unto the Lord our God from whom we have departed with a great Backsliding.[23]

Eager to encourage wayward colonists to reform their ways, Puritan clergy, especially, interpreted God's messages as suggestions that He was not on the colonists' side in the war. Increase Mather told the story of one soldier who, hearing his fellow soldiers use "many profane oaths," and considering the bad weather and the recent losses against the enemy, took these as signs "that God was against the English; whereupon he immediately ran distracted, and so was returned home a lamentable Spectacle." And when another soldier accidentally shot and killed an Englishwoman, it was taken as "a sign God is angry, when he turns our Weapons against our selves." As Mather declared, "the Lord himself seemeth to be against us, to cast us off, and to put us to shame, and goeth not forth with our Armies."[24]

Puritan divines were not without their critics. The Quaker Edward Wharton had abundant criticism for the prophecies and preachings of Massachusetts magistrates and ministers:

> Our Rulers, Officers, and Councellors are like as men in a maze, not knowing what to do: but the Priests spur them on, telling them the Indians are ordained for destruction; bidding them go forth to Warr, and they will Fast and Pray at home in the mean time: yet their General, with some other Officers, complain and say, with tears, They see not God go along with them.[25]

(Intriguingly, Wharton's criticism here sounds very much like the Puritans' indictment of the pernicious influence of powwaws on the natives.) Yet Wharton, too, saw the war as a message from God. Like many other religious nonconformists, including Peter Folger and Samuel Groome, he understood the war as punishment for the Puritans' persecution of dissenters. The irony was not lost on Richard Hutchinson, who observed that, however "various are Men's Thoughts why God hath suffered [the war], all acknowledge it was for Sin."[26]

To atone for the sins that had brought them such misery, conforming colonists observed days of fasting, prayer, and humiliation throughout the war. Plymouth declared the war's first fast on the very day the fighting began, June 24, 1675, and Massachusetts Colony followed suit four days later, printing and posting a broadside to announce it. In Connecticut, every Wednesday from September 1675 to July 1676 was a day of fasting. Puritan churches in Boston, Plymouth, and other towns marked their own days of religious observation, while colony governments declared dozens more, especially when things were going badly. In December all of the United Colonies observed a general day of fasting and humiliation, in preparation for the attack on the Narragansetts' Great Swamp. In 1675 Connecticut canceled its annual autumn thanksgiving and in Massachusetts Bay no days of thanksgiving were declared until June 29, 1676 (exactly a year after that colony's first wartime day of humiliation), when the tide had finally turned in the colonists' favor.[27]

DAYS OF FASTING, HUMILIATION, AND THANKSGIVING

1675

June 24	Plymouth Colony observes a fast day.
June 29	Massachusetts Bay Colony observes a day of humiliation.
July 8	Massachusetts Bay Colony observes a day of humiliation.
July 21	Plymouth Church observes a day of humiliation.
September 1	Beginning on this date, counties in Connecticut begin holding weekly fasts.
September 17	Boston observes a day of humiliation.
October 7	Massachusetts Bay Colony observes a day of humiliation.
October 14	Plymouth Colony observes a fast day.
December 2	All of the United Colonies observe a day of fasting and general humiliation, in preparation for the campaign against the Narragansetts.

1676

January 5	Plymouth Church observes a day of humiliation.
February 2	Plymouth Church observes a day of humiliation.
February 5	Boston observes a day of humiliation.
February 23	Boston observes a day of humiliation.
	Connecticut Colony, departing from its weekly fasts, observes a day of thanksgiving, postponed from the fall.

1676

April 20	Boston observes a day of humiliation.
June 29	Massachusetts Bay Colony observes a day of solemn thanksgiving (the first colonywide thanksgiving there since the war began).
July 21	Connecticut Colony shifts from weekly fasts to weekly days of thanksgiving.
August 17	Plymouth observes a day of thanksgiving.
August 30	Connecticut Colony observes a special day of thanksgiving.
November 1	Connecticut Colony observes a special day of thanksgiving.
November 9	Massachusetts Bay Colony observes a day of thanksgiving.

Meanwhile, even as English colonists gathered to damn the Algonquians' religion and to beg God to go to battle with them, the Indians answered them in kind. After decades of learning about the colonists' religion—visiting their churches, holding their Bibles, meeting their ministers—Algonquians in New England were well prepared to attack the colonists' spiritual Achilles' heel: their fear that their God had forsaken them. And attack it they did. As Wharton reported, "The Indians, I hear, insult very much, and tell the English Warriors that God is against them, and for the Indians; and that the English shall (for their Unrighteousness) fall into their hands." Wharton, as a Quaker, had an ulterior motive in making this point, but we need not take his word for it. Algonquian attacks on Christianity, and especially blasphemies like the one reported at Sudbury ("Come Lord Jesus, save this poor Englishman if thou canst") were not at all uncommon. When the Nipmucks returned from a fight they typically celebrated by mocking their victims, scoffing that "They had done them a good turn to send them to heaven so soon." In Groton, Indians destroyed the church and then asked the minister, "What will you do for a house to pray in now we have burnt your Meeting-house?" While under siege in Brookfield, an English captain tried to encourage his soldiers by declaring, "God is with us, and fights for us, and will deliver us out of the hands of these Heathen," to which the Nipmucks, who had heard this rallying cry, responded by "sending in many shots" and shouting, "now see how your God delivers you." To provoke the English into leaving their garrisoned house, a group of Nipmucks went into the church next door and "in Contempt made an hideous noise somewhat resembling singing." Laughing at the Puritans' solemn practices of piety, the Nipmucks called out to the besieged colonists, "Come and pray, & sing Psalmes." But the people of Brookfield restrained themselves, "the Lord giving us Courage to resist them." To the colonists' great horror,

Indians were also especially likely to attack people on the Sabbath, or on a declared day of religious observation, even as colonists were on their way to church: "At Springfield . . . these devillish Enemies of Religion seeing a man, woman, and their Children, going but towards a meeting house, Slew them (as they said) because they thought they Intended to go thither."[28]

Algonquian attacks on Christianity could be symbolic as well as verbal. When Goodman Wright "had a strange Confidence, or rather Conceit, that whilst he held his Bible in his Hand, he looked upon himself as secure from all kinde of Violence," the Indians who killed him "deriding his groundless Apprehension, or Folly therein, rippe[d] him open and put his Bible in his Belly."[29] Retreating Indians might also leave particular objects behind, objects that could be made to operate as powerful symbols: books, goats, hoes, cows, clogs, aprons, church bells. When used by Indians to leave a trail of signs, even these everyday objects, like a "Hat shot through" found in the road, could become terrifying.[30] In June 1675, for example, English soldiers were tracking the enemy in Rhode Island when, "after they had marched about a Mile and Half, they passed by some Houses newly burned: not far off one of them they found a Bible newly torn, and the Leaves scattered about by the Enemy in Hatred of our Religion." But this was just the beginning. "Two or three Miles further they came up with some Heads, Scalps, and Hands cut off from the Bodies of some of the English, and stuck upon Poles near the Highway, in that barbarous and inhuman Manner bidding us Defiance."[31] First the houses, then the pages of the Bible, and then the body parts themselves. Scenes like this seemed to carry the Indians' message within them: We will first take away your shelter, then your beliefs, and only then will we take your lives, leaving you, not as men, but as bare, butchered flesh. As one colonist aptly put it, "Our Enemies proudly exault over us and Blaspheme the name of our Blessed God; Saying, Where is your O God?"[32]

II

JUST AS Increase Mather claimed he never had "the least thought" of publishing his account of King Philip's War, he also maintained that he never had any intention of writing about "the Grounds of this Warr, and the justness of it on our part," since such a discussion would make his *Brief History* "too voluminous." In the end, of course, Mather found the space to "adde a few words" on the subject.[33] According to his version of events, the English had worked for peace even after the first Wampanoag attacks on Swansea. On June 25, 1675, a delegation of colonial diplomats traveling to Mount Hope to negotiate with Philip was stopped in its tracks by the bodies of "divers Englishmen on the ground, weltering in their own blood, having been newly murdered by the Indians." Appalled by the sight, "they could not proceed farther" and decided that "a Peace now could not honourably be concluded after such barbarous Outrages." The next day, the earth's shadow eclipsed the moon and English soldiers marching to Swansea feared the worst. "Since the Enemy did shed the blood of some of ours who never did them . . . the least wrong," Mather concluded, "no man can doubt the justness of our cause."[34]

Yet doubt it they did. "It is never safe to take a Dog by the ears," William Hubbard warned. In other words, avoid war at all costs. During his Election Day sermon in May 1676, Hubbard preached that Christians everywhere should beware of waging "an unnecessary war" because while war is on both sides a judgment, it is always on one side "an hainous evil or murder."[35] Hubbard disagreed with a purely providential interpretation of the war (epitomized by Mather's preaching), and, to a certain extent, condemned the war on practical and even ethical grounds. He was not alone. Perhaps with a resolve weakened by listening to Indian taunts, many colonists in New England were plagued with doubts about the justness of their war, especially early on. "Uncomfortable & dishonorable reports" had made it "very difficult dissatisfying, & uncomfortable to conscientious parents and other Relations, to send out their children, & other dear relations unto the war, where many of them were slain, & all in danger of their lives." Even more importantly, perhaps, was the worry that "the dishonor would redound to the Name of God, if N.E. should goe to war in a bad cause, or not every way justifiable in the sight of God & all the world." To some colonists, one sign from God was more distressing than all the others: they worried that "our bad Success: did exspres: our bad cause: & unJust war."[36]

Criticism of the war seemed to come from all quarters, both divine and human. As Josiah Winslow complained, not only Indians but also many English colonists were "pleased to sensure us highly as if wee had ungroundedly enterprized this warr."[37] And Edward Randolph, an agent for the Crown, reported that Massachusetts magistrates had provoked the war by repeatedly calling Philip to court on contrived charges.[38] Such criticism caused the colonial authorities to justify their actions at great length, offering confused and even contradictory accounts of the origins and progress of the war.

From the very start of the war, both sides insisted that their cause was just. As Roger Williams had observed, "all men of Conscience or Prudence, ply to Windward & wisely labour to mainteine their Wars to be defensive." The Wampanoags claimed "thay had dun no rong, the English ronged them," while the English just as vehemently insisted that the Indians' "unmanly barbarous practices" came from "no provocation nor unfairness in the least from us."[39] Since many colonists continued to doubt "whether our English were wholy inocent on that account, viz. our freinds of Plimouth parts," Governor Winslow found it necessary to insist that, "as respecting the enemy . . . wee stand as innocent as it is possible for any person or people to be towards theire neighbour." Nonetheless, in July 1675 John Eliot was still waiting for a satisfactory explanation from the Plymouth authorities. "What the causes of the warre were," he grumbled, "I suppose Plimoth will declare." Three months into the war, Winslow was sufficiently agitated to write a "Narrative shewing the manor of the begining of the present Warr with the Indians," in which he attempted to demonstrate how "slow were wee and unwilling to engage ourselves and Naighbours in a warr," but that, provoked by Indians "of whose hands wee had deserved better," war had become unavoidable. Soon those with doubts began to resign themselves. Although in August he was still "of a differing mind from our friends," John Pynchon considered his objections no longer worth mentioning since "it is now too late, a war being already begun."[40]

By fall, even those New Englanders who had initially criticized the war had been drawn into its action. After reading Winslow's "Narrative," the commissioners of the United Colonies issued a declaration that "the said warr doth appeer to be both Just and Nessesarie; in its first Rise a defensive warr; and therefore wee doe agree and conclude that it ought now to be Joyntly prosecuted by all the united Collonies."[41] In December the Massachusetts Council wrote its own account of the origins of the war and distributed it in broadside form to be posted on trees, courthouses, and meetinghouse doors all over the colony, no doubt in response to lingering criticism. (They also sent the broadside to officials in England and New York.)[42] Nonetheless, for some colonists, war of any kind was to be greatly regretted. Even if Plymouth had acted lawfully, Roger Williams confessed, "I fear the Event of the justest War."[43]

The colonists' ideas about what made a war just derived, in part, from a philosophical tradition most fully articulated by a Dutch jurist and theologian named Hugo Grotius. (Increase Mather considered Grotius "one of the Learnedest men that this age has produced," and other sources suggest that Grotius, if not necessarily widely read, was deeply influential on New Englanders' political ideas.)[44] In his *De Jure Belli Et Pacis*, first printed in 1625, Grotius had established the fundamental tenets of what would come to be called international law. Relying on ancient authorities as well as departing from them—and, most especially, rejecting the concept of holy war—Grotius had set out to prove that war is not without law but is in fact in accordance with both the "law of nature" (a set of principles known to all humans who possess reason) and the "law of nations" (a set of legal and moral principles guiding the conduct of sovereign nations).[45]

In the tradition elaborated by Grotius, the evaluation of whether a war is just or unjust is based on two criteria: just cause (*jus ad bello*) and just conduct (*jus in bellum*). The first is concerned with why war is waged, the second with how. In the words of the political scientist Michael Walzer, "War is always judged twice, first with reference to the reasons states have for fighting, secondly with reference to the means they adopt. The first kind of judgment is adjectival in character: we say that a particular war is just or unjust. The second is adverbial: we say that the war is being fought justly or unjustly."[46] Belonging, as it did, to their European intellectual heritage, seventeenth-century English colonists commonly made this distinction when they wrote about war. Thus John Leverett, governor of Massachusetts, said that the Indian enemy violated the standards of both *jus ad bello* and *jus in bellum*. According to Leverett, Philip, "with others his wicked complices and abettors," began the war "without any just cause, or provocation given them," and then proceeded to fight unfairly, perpetrating "many notorious barbarous and execrable murthers, villanies and outrages."[47]

Following the tradition of just war doctrine, New England's colonists believed that "war, in some cases is lawful and at sometimes necessary," but "a woe to him that is the unjust cause of them."[48] Colonial writers justifying King Philip's War always insisted that it was a strictly defensive war, begun only after the Wampanoags attacked Swansea.[49] Thus, Thomas Wheeler wrote, "Philip the Sachem of the Wampanogs, lying about Mount-hope, having done some Acts of Hostility against Plimouth Colony by murdering men, burning Houses and killing Cattel: the said Colony was necessitated to warr with him in their own defence."[50] Massachusetts and Connecticut had joined the fight only to aid Plymouth and, when the Narragansetts and Nipmucks allied with Philip, they, too, were fought on defensive grounds.

Yet, while Wheeler and others explained that the English had fought a just war with a secular cause, many New Englanders also understood fighting Indians in religious terms, worrying, for instance, about whose side God was fighting on. Like their English counterparts, American Puritans also employed warfare as a metaphor when writing about religious conflicts, urging all men to become "spiritual soldiers."[51] New Englander John Richardson preached that war "is an ordinance appoynted by God for subduing and destroying the Churches Enemies here upon Earth," and in killing Indians Puritan colonists claimed to be acting as God's instruments, ridding the land of "the perfect children of the Devil."[52] To some New Englanders, King Philip's War was thus a holy war—that is, a war fought for the goals of the

Church and subject to few limits of conduct (since the Indians were infidels, "blud ffor blud shal bee ther portion Just").[53]

As defined by St. Augustine in the fifth century, a holy war "sanctioned by God" was intended to enforce discipline in the Christian world.[54] And, as Pope Innocent IV had pronounced in the thirteenth century, Christians could wage wars against infidels solely on the basis of their nonbelief in God.[55] Commanded by God, soldiers fighting in a holy war were required to be personally godly (the Massachusetts Court passed "Lawes and Ordinances of warr" outlining punishments for soldiers who blasphemed or skipped church[56]) but must also be prepared to abandon all moral restraints in the execution of war. A just war was expected to be fair, legal, and limited; a holy war, divinely ordained and unrestrained.

By the time Hugo Grotius began writing his *De Jure Belli Et Pacis* in 1623, the idea of holy war had become moribund in the Protestant world. Alberico Gentili had declared in the 1590s that "There is no religion so wicked as to order an attack upon men of a different belief."[57] Still, although most Europeans, including the vast majority of Englishmen and -women, had come to find the idea of holy war increasingly anachronistic, reports of the death of holy war were greatly exaggerated for, during Grotius' own lifetime, some late-sixteenth- and early-seventeenth-century English writers resurrected the idea of a holy war to justify the Puritan revolution.[58] For these English Puritans, even offensive wars were just if waged for religion. (Among the writers who endorsed this view was William Ames, an English Puritan minister whose writings exerted a tremendous influence on New England Puritans.[59])

Swayed by the competing traditions of just and holy war, New England's colonists often seemed at odds with one another when they wrote about war. In part, this confusion, or rather coexistence, of traditions was possible because of Hugo Grotius' failure to answer a critical question: What happens when a Christian nation wars against a non-Christian nation?[60]

In the sixteenth century this question had been elaborately addressed by Francisco Vitoria, a friar and political theorist whose most notable writings defended the Spanish conquest. Disagreeing with Pope Innocent IV, Vitoria insisted that difference of religion cannot be a just cause of war. For proof, he argued that infidels have the natural right to defend themselves against Christians who wage war against them to convert them, in which case, if it is just for Christians to wage such a war, then it would be just on both sides, a most confusing and quite impossible circumstance.[61] Vitoria argued that Indians could not be dispossessed of their property simply because they did not know Christ. Indians, he claimed, had "dominion," which could not be alienated by virtue of their unbelief, any more than it would be lawful to take away the possessions of Jews or Saracens. Dominion, as Vitoria defined it, was predicated on whether a people "were true masters of their private chattels and possessions, and whether there existed among them any men who were true princes and masters of the others." To Vitoria's thinking, the Indians satisfied both these conditions. They were "true masters," Vitoria argued, because Thomas Aquinas had proven that "all forms of dominion derive from natural or human law; therefore they cannot be annulled by lack of faith." Only madmen were not true masters, but Indians, since they had organized societies and a form of religion, were clearly not mad. "If they seem to us insensate and slow-witted," Vitoria wrote, "I put it down mainly to their evil and barbarous education. Even amongst ourselves we see many peasants (*rustici*) who are little different from brute animals." And the Indians also had "true princes," he concluded, because their social order was observed to be similar to the hierarchical, monarchical systems of Europe. Finally, Vitoria argued that Indians could not be forced to become Christians. "Even if the barbarians refuse to receive Christ as their lord," he declared, "they cannot for that reason be attacked or harmed in any way" because Christ and Christianity "are things for which they cannot be furnished with evident proof by natural reasonings." And war, he scoffed, "is no argument for the truth of the Christian faith."[62]

Although Vitoria believed that converting the Indians was an unjust cause for war, he found that the Spanish conquest of Mexico was just on other grounds. He agreed with Aquinas that knowledge of God is not necessary for knowledge of natural law (since natural law can be known through the use of human reason). Therefore, inhabitants of America, who had never heard of Christ, could still know the natural law.[63] For Vitoria, the pope had no particular mediating role in relations between nations because he "is not the civil or temporal master of the whole world." Instead, a universally applicable system of social rights and duties, deducible from natural law, pertained to all peoples. And if the Indians failed to act in accord with the law of nature and with the law of nations, they could be forced to comply. Now, instead of waging war against non-Christians to convert them to Christianity, Christians might wage war to make non-Christians conform to the dictates of natural and international law.[64] Unlike Christianity, the law of nations could be demonstrated by reasoning and even if the Indians had not intuited it themselves, once taught by the Spanish, they were obliged to abide by it.[65] To wage war lawfully, then, the Spanish had only to demonstrate that the Indians violated natural law by practicing such barbarous outrages as idolatry and cannibalism or that they had violated international law by failing to follow its dictates.[66]

Nearly two centuries after the Spanish conquest, Hugo Grotius dismissed Vitoria and writers like him with disdain. "Most of them have done their work without system," Grotius complained, "and in such a way as to intermingle and utterly confuse what belongs to the law of nature, to divine law, to the law of nations, to civil law, and to the body of law which is found in the canons."[67] Instead of providing a straightforward answer to the question "What happens when Christians wage war against non-Christians?" Grotius instead established two different sets of rules of war, one for Christians and one for non-Christians. Both Christians and non-Christians, Grotius argued, are answerable to the law of nature in the waging of war. Since they do not know God, natural law is all that non-Christians can be expected to know, and in waging war against one another they rely on that law exclusively. Christians, however, must also follow the dictates of Scripture, which impose additional moral constraints. When Christian nations fight one another, Grotius claimed, they supplement natural law with Christian morality.[68] Nowhere, however, did Grotius directly address the question of which set of laws prevails when a Christian nation wages war against a non-Christian nation.

To argue that warring non-Christians rely exclusively on natural law for guidance, Grotius had to assume that non-Christians, who know neither Scripture nor the law of nations, lack any kind of religious and secular mores that might impose additional restraints on war. In making this assumption, Grotius may well have been influenced by his interest in the New World; in 1642 he even published a short tract called *On the Origin of the Native Races of America* (in which he confidently concluded that America's indigenous inhabitants were primarily descended from Germans and Chinese).[69] Like many political theorists of his time, Grotius was fascinated by the peoples of the New World who, in the eyes of theoretically minded Europeans, lived in a world free from the conventions of civilized society, and as such provided partial inspiration not only for just war doctrine but also for social contract theory.[70] Whether they saw Native Americans as living in a state of nature or a state of war, seventeenth-century political theorists, most famously John Locke and Thomas Hobbes, were quick to exploit the example provided by the peoples of the New World, at least as a rhetorical device. "In the beginning," according to Locke, "all the world was America."[71] And Hobbes, who argued that the state of nature is a state of war "of every man, against every man," pointed to the New World as proof, "for the savage people in many places of America . . . have no government at all; and live at this day in that brutish manner."[72]

Europeans who had had more contact with Native Americans than Grotius, Locke, and Hobbes were likely to see things differently, but many made similar assumptions, especially English colonists in New England. Thomas Morton, for instance, wrote in 1637 that "these people are *sine fide, since lege, & since rege.*[73] And Roger Williams said the Indians, "having lost the true and living God their maker, have created out of the nothing of their owne inventions many false and fained Gods and Creators."[74] Meanwhile, even though some early visitors to New England argued that Indians recognized the law of nations,[75] and some colonists attempted to "teach" Indians certain codes of conduct (as when the Massachusetts Council explained how a white flag is "used by civil nations in tyme of war"[76]), most were pessimistic about introducing the Indians to the laws of war, "they being a people not so acquainted with such waies, nor the usages of civill nations."[77]

Most colonists in New England were unable to believe that Algonquians were truly like themselves—humans, possessed of both reason and the knowledge of God, and members of sovereign nations that abided by universally binding rules. While the colonists cannot be said to have taken a consistent or consensual position in defending their war, they did manage, in a rather paranoid fashion, to defend themselves on nearly every possible grounds: not only were the Indians infidels, they were also devils and barbarians who lacked both reason and dominion and who perpetrated atrocities violating both the law of nations and the law of nature. As the colonists insisted, Indians had few if any codes of conduct, engaging in "savage" wars with wanton motives.[78] On a practical level, this meant that the colonists themselves were freed to abandon the laws of war. As historian Barbara Donagan has argued of seventeenth-century England, "Against a Christian foreign enemy, the laws of war, posited on hostilities between sovereign states, were straightforwardly applicable. In a colonial war, especially one with strong racist, religious, and retributive elements, many argued that the laws of war were abrogated, since barbarian or heretic 'others' or outsiders did not merit the protections due to the civilized and Christian."[79]

The historian who pores over the records of King Philip's War will search in vain for a coherent political ideology or a single legal, moral, or religious justification of the war. Living in a world in which the laws of nature and of nations were, in effect, being invented, and in which the idea of holy war lingered even as a secular conception gradually replaced it, colonial writers participated in these debates more than they followed preexisting notions. And always, they covered their bases. In condemning Indian cruelties, New England's colonists often lumped violations of the laws of nations and of the laws of nature together, as when Roger Williams said that the Indians "*had Forgot they were Mankind,* and ran about the Countrie like Wolves tearing and Devouring the Innocent, and peaceable."[80] Predictably, supposed Indian violations of the laws of war produced some of the colonists' most vitriolic prose. In the colonists' words, enemy Algonquians fought like beasts, marauders, and fiends, or even like women, not truly fighting but "skulking": "creeping: & cruching: behinde any bush, tree, rock, or hill, Sometimes one alone: two or three to gether, & then (as they See need) start up & run away (Soe fast) among the Shrubs & rocks: that noe horse (as the place & man may be) can catch them." [81] John Freeman reported to Governor Winslow in July 1675, "We see their design is not to face the army; but to keep a flying army about the woods, to fall on us and our army, as they have advantage." [82] Or as Philip Walker put it, "Thes murthres Rooges like wild Arabians thay / Lurk heare & there of every thing make p[rey]." [83]

Perhaps more definitively than any other Algonquian practice, skulking violated every English code of conduct. To the English it implied cowardice and deceit and, as Josiah Winslow maintained, "unmanliness." [84] Similarly, Samuel Gorton believed "the manner of their warre appears to be such that a rascall like boy may take his opertunitie to be the fall of the most hardy and puisassant souldier." [85] Roger Williams wrote that "all their War is Commootin they have Commootind our Howses, our Cattell, our Heads &c & that not by their Artillerie but our Weapons: that yet they are so cowardly, that they have not taken one poore Fort from us in all the Countrey, not won (no scarce fought) one battell since the beginning." [86] After the war, Urian Oakes would recall fighting against "a despised & despicable Enemy, that is not acquainted with books of military Discipline, that observe no regular Order, that understand not the Souldier's Postures, and Motions, and Firings, and Forms of Battel, that fight in a base, cowardly, contemptible way." [87] The Massachusetts Council declared in August 1675 that "it is the manner of the Heathen that are now in Hostility with us, contrary to the practice of the Civil Nations, to execute their bloody Insolencies by stealth and sculking in small parties, declining all open decission of their controversie, either by Treaty or by the Sword." [88]

To some, the Algonquians' multiple violations of the laws of civil nations and even of the laws of nature meant that their fighting ought not to be dignified by being classed with European conflicts. After all, William Hubbard refused to call the conflict of 1675 and 1676 a war because, "being rather Massacres, barbarous inhumane Outrages, than Acts of Hostility or valiant Atchievements," it didn't "deserve the Name of a War." [89] But did Algonquians have their own laws of war? [90]

III

NEARLY ALL human cultures that practice war follow rules of their own prescription. When cultures with different rules go to war they may well borrow from each other's traditions, but perhaps more important, their fundamental differences are brought into sharp relief. Warring societies may even exaggerate their differences to make the killing easier; the more foreign the enemy, the better.[91] And war sometimes causes people to call into question their own basic assumptions about the world—ideas, for instance, about what it is to be human, or what God's role is in human affairs. Although we are less likely to find sources discussing how Algonquians felt about these matters, it is clear that King Philip's War precipitated just such a moral and epistemological crisis for New England's colonists. Nowhere is this crisis more visible than in the colonists' justifications for the war itself and for their conduct within it. King Philip's War was not an easy war for the English settlers to justify, but the language they employed to that end pulled the peoples of seventeenth-century New England farther and farther apart. Meanwhile, Algonquians communicated their ideas about war in ways that the colonists largely ignored or deliberately silenced.

Benjamin Tompson declared that "Indian spirits need / No grounds but lust to make a Christian bleed" and most English colonists insisted, with John Leverett, that the Indians began the war "without any just cause, or provocation given them."[92] Thomas Wheeler prayed "The Lord avenge the Blood that hath been shed by these Heathen *who hate us without a Cause.*"[93] And, much as the English justified their own conduct at great length, embracing and accommodating a wide diversity of opinions and philosophies, what possible cause might have driven their Indian neighbors to war, the colonists professed not to know. Hearing that Philip had taken up arms, Samuel Gorton confessed himself mystified. "On what hinge the ocation thereof turned," he admitted, "I know not."[94] Josiah Winslow insisted, "Wee have not soe much as heard of any thing that hee alleageth as ground of his discontent and taking arms against us." And Benjamin Batten wrote in a letter published in *The London Gazette,* "the reason of this taking of Armes Wee knowe not."[95]

But Winslow and Batten knew very well what initially propelled Philip to war. Batten supposed that the execution of Sassamon's alleged murderers, "thay being [Philip's] Cheife men," may have "Inraidged him."[96] And Winslow said he knew nothing about Philip's justification, "save only hee sayth *wee* had began a war" by "the execution of three Indians for a murther." (Such a claim was absurd, Winslow implied, because the Sassamon trial was fair and legal, "the three Indians after sentenced to day acknowledging the justice of the Courte and giveing us thanks for our fayer tryall of them, and the last of them that was executed, at execution confest the fact; so that hee had no ground of complaint of injury to him or his, in that or any other respect [that we know of].")[97] Just weeks after the execution, a group of Narragansetts asked Roger Williams "why Plymmouth pursued Phillip." At first

Williams offered a brisk, formal reply: "He broke all Laws and was in Armes of Rebellion against that Colony." Then, with more candor, Williams added, "it is believed that [Philip] was the Authour of murthering John Sossiman for revealing his plots to the Govr of Plymmouth." Williams failed to mention how the Narragansetts responded to this explanation, but two days later he noted that many in Rhode Island "wish that Plymouth had left the Indians alone [or] at least not put to death the 3 Indians upon one Indians Testimony a thing which Philip fears."[98] As John Easton reported, Philip had listed among his grievances against the English that "if 20 of there [h]onest indians testefied that an Englishman had dun them rong, it was as nothing, and if but one of ther worst indians testefied against ani indian or ther king when it plesed the English that was sufitiant."[99]

When pressed, then, most colonists admitted that the execution of Sassamon's alleged murderers seemed to have been the immediate cause for war, the "irruption of this flame," but few were willing to look beyond that, at broader economic, cultural, or religious tensions. Even Easton was ultimately uninterested in the Wampanoags' grievances. "We knew what ther Cumplaints wold be," Easton recalled, and so tried to put the Wampanoags off, saying "it was not Convenient for us now to Consider of," since they had more urgent business to attend to. But Philip would not be silenced. He "Charged it to be disonesty in us to put of the hering of the complaints," and eventually Easton's delegation "Consented to here them." The Wampanoags then proceeded to offer a long list of grievances, including the colonists' taking Indian lands, interfering with Indian agriculture, and attempting to convert Indians to Christianity.[100]

If nearly all of the colonists' explanations for the war boiled down to John Sassamon's death and the execution of his alleged murderers—the same immediate cause Wampanoags and Narragansetts cited—why then did the English continue to profess their ignorance of Indian motives, denying even the possibility that such motives might exist? One answer, of course, is that the colonists rarely put the question to Indians themselves. And when, on occasion, colonial authorities did interrogate Indians about their reasons for fighting, full and candid answers were hardly forthcoming: captured or surrendering Indian men and women were not likely to court execution by speaking defiantly. When Peter Awashonks presented himself to the Plymouth Council to make peace with the English in June 1676, he was quick to declare that "The English never did us any hurt or wronge to this day." "If they had," he assured his examiners, "we would speak of it." Although his questioners urged him to "Speake freely, without fear," it seems unlikely that Peter would have wanted to do so, despite his and their assurances to the contrary.[101]

Yet, even if the surviving sources tell us little, or little that is credible, about Indian justifications for the war, that doesn't mean that Algonquians had nothing to say on the subject. Most, no doubt, had strong opinions about why they were fighting. And certainly they had rules of war and codes of conduct, however unfamiliar these may have been to their English neighbors.[102] It is, in fact, that very unfamiliarity that should interest us most. Unfortunately, historians, like the colonists themselves, have rarely been interested in exploring this unfamiliar territory. As one scholar has recently pointed out, historical scholarship has largely ignored "the possibility that the non-state societies of aboriginal North America may have waged war for different—but no less rational and no more savage—purposes than did the nation-states of Europe."[103]

Algonquians in New England had well-developed ideas about war. That their standards were at variance with those held by the English is illustrated by the colonists' condemnation of certain Algonquian practices, including the torture of captives. Yet the two cultures undoubtedly shared some common assumptions about war. There is considerable evidence that Algonquian standards included a distinction between concepts roughly equivalent to *jus ad bello* and *jus in bellum*. Narragansetts who fought with the English in the Pequot War, for instance, agreed with the waging of the war in the first place, but then refused to participate in acts they found unacceptable to their notions of just conduct. When the English burned hundreds of women and children trapped in a compound, the Narragansetts backed off, crying, "*Mach it, mach it;* that is, It is naught, it is naught, because it is too furious, and slays too many men."[104]

Many Algonquians also either shared or quickly learned and borrowed from English codes of conduct, using them to protect themselves in combat or to defend their own actions before the colonial authorities. On one occasion, during the early years of settlement, Plymouth authorities went to arrest a sachem they thought to be hidden in a house occupied by a group of Indians. On arriving, the colonists announced that they "would not at all hurt their women or children," and then began firing. Hearing the shots, several Indian boys in the house cried out, "*Neen squaes!* that is to say, I am a woman."[105] Another example, from King Philip's War, reveals a curious irony. Accused of the murder of a colonist and his family, William and Joseph Wannuckkow and John Appamatogoon were quick to excuse their involvement by making reference to an English war doctrine. Although they admitted to having been present at the attack, the three Indians claimed that they "neither killd nor Burnt not tooke away any thing there, But were Instrumental to save Goodman Eames and his children alive." "Besides," they continued, they ought to be immune from prosecution since "It was a time of ware when this Mischiefe was done; and though It was our unhappy Portion be with the Enimies, yet we conceive that depredations and Slaughters in warre are not Chargable upon Particular persons."[106] In jail for crimes committed during wartime, William and Joseph Wannuckkow and John Appamatogoon excused their actions by claiming the special exemptions due to soldiers during wartime.[107]

One common purpose for Algonquian war was to gain captives to increase a diminished population, a practice anthropologists call "mourning-war."[108] Often such wars were initially waged in response to the deaths of valued members of a tribe; in the case of King Philip's War, the three Wampanoags executed for the murder of John Sassamon. Among the nearby Iroquois, "warfare was a specific response to the death of specific individuals at specific times, a sporadic affair characterized by seizing from traditional enemies a few captives who would replace the dead, literally or symbolically, and ease the pain of those who mourned."[109] Traditional warfare among Algonguians in New England may have sometimes met similar needs, where wars of retaliation ended as soon as retribution had been inflicted and "native hostilities generally aimed at symbolic ascendancy, a status conveyed by small payments of tribute to the victors, rather than the dominion normally associated with European-style conflicts."[110] Yet, although retaliation was one of many possible motives, attributing such wars to simple revenge is unfair, according to one historian, since they can be better understood as "justified reprisals." Or, in short, just wars.[111] One seventeenth-century Lenape Indian in Pennsylvania, for example, propounded a just war protocol whose complexity might have won even Hugo Grotius' admiration. "We are minded to live at peace," the Lenape man declared.

> If we intend at any time to make War upon you, we will let you know of it, and the Reasons why we make War with you; and if you make us satisfaction for the Injury done us, for which the War is intended, then we will not make War on you. And if you intend at any time to make War on us, we would have you let us know of it, and the Reasons for which you make War on us, and then if we do not make satisfaction for the Injury done unto you, then you may make War on us, otherwise you ought not to do it.[112]

Anthropologists used to say that there are two kinds of warfare, "primitive" and "civilized." Today the terms have changed—"nonstate" is usually used instead of "primitive," and "state" for "civilized"—but, in large part, the categories themselves have remained intact.[113] Primitive or nonstate warfare has been understood to be limited, not especially lethal, and usually immediately motivated by prestige, revenge, or sport, but ultimately driven by resource scarcity or the need to regulate the population; civilized or state warfare, by contrast, has been understood to last longer, to be both better organized and more fatal, and usually to be motivated by economic, territorial, or political concerns.[114] This view has its origins in Europeans' earliest New World encounters and was commonly expressed in early-seventeenth-century New England in the decades before King Philip's War. During the Pequot War in 1637, Captain John Mason said the Pequots' "feeble Manner . . . did hardly deserve the name of fighting" and in 1643 Roger Williams observed that Indian conflicts were "farre less bloudy and devouring than the cruell Warres of Europe."[115]

This view, however, has recently been questioned. In arguing that Indian assaults, far from being too "feeble" to deserve the name of fighting, were too *brutal* to deserve the name of war, William Hubbard anticipated an important late twentieth-century anthropological revision. With the critical work of anthropologist Lawrence Keeley, the notion that war in nonstate societies is less frequent and less deadly than war in state societies has come under focused attack. As Keeley argues, nonstate warfare is actually both more frequent and more fatal than state warfare.[116] While King Philip's War can be understood as a war between a nonstate society and an encroaching state, war was a serious and deadly matter in both cultures. Those Narragansetts, Nipmucks, Pocumtucks, and Wampanoags who chose to fight against the English and their Mohegan, Pequot, and Christian Indian allies had complicated reasons, reasons that extended beyond mourning or retributive war. They were fighting to protect their territory and to preserve their way of life.

If the English had examined Algonquian actions not as signs from God but as signs from Indians, they might have seen a great deal about Algonquian motives. Still, some few recognized that such acts of "cruelty" were also a form of communication, not from God, but from the Indians themselves. Philip Walker, after all, complained of Philip "drawing his own reportt in blud not Ink."[117] Much as most colonists denied it, Algonquian attacks and Algonquian tortures were not random or arbitrary. On the contrary, they were deliberate and deeply symbolic.[118] This is not surprising, since ritual behavior increases in times of uncertainty. And ritual, as the anthropologist Mary Douglas reminds us, "is pre-eminently a form of communication."[119]

Ritual cruelty is a symbolic language that can be "read" and then "translated" into spoken or written language. Algonquians in New England often provided this translation themselves, leaving notes explaining their actions, or sending letters, or, most often, mocking and taunting the English verbally while they assaulted them. And as the acts themselves make clear, New

England's Algonquians were attempting, in small, physical dramas, to turn the English world inside out and upside down. (Remember the Indians burying English captives alive and taunting them, "You English since you came into this Countrey have grown exceedingly above the Ground, let us now see how you will grow when Planted into the Ground."[120]) That fighting Algonquians sought to cultivate chaos is demonstrated again and again in the piquancy of their ridiculing of English values. "Ritual," according to Douglas, "recognises the potency of disorder," and in these ritualistic acts of cruelty, the Indians disordered English society.[121] Or, taken another way, Algonquians sought to restore their world to a balance, to recover it from the chaos into which it had been falling ever since the English first arrived.

Nevertheless, English colonists were either unwilling or unable to place such practices within the broader context of Algonquian culture and to read them as partial explanations for what had provoked the Indians to wage war (English incursions on Indian land, English attempts at converting the Indians to Christianity). Since "there can be no War just on both sides," it was critical that the English deny the possibility that the Indians might have had grounds to wage war against the settlers—and that the colonists elaborate on the justness of their own cause in the war.[122] The language of "provocation" and "cause" was applied not to the Indians but to God.[123] If the English had sinned, they had "rebelled greatly rebelled" against the Lord, not against their Algonquian neighbors.[124] Those who considered the Indians God's messengers knew that the Bible commanded God's people to "mind what the Messengers of God speak in his name" (Amos 3:7).[125] But, busily interpreting Indian actions as messages from God, New England's colonists utterly failed to see Indian actions as messages from *Indians,* or even simply to pay attention to Indian explanations for the war.[126]

Ultimately, of course, all Indian explanations for or interpretations of the war were dismissed—*"these Heathenish Stories are consonant to their Barbarous Crueltie, and ought to be valued accordingly"*—because they compromised the justness of the colonists' own cause.[127] Meanwhile, the English labeled all Indian assaults "barbarous" violations of English ideas of just conduct in war, thereby masking their own violations. Quaker John Easton believed that "new England prists . . . ar so blinded by the spiret of persecution" that they failed to see that they themselves had violated "the law of nations and the law of arems."[128] In looking at Indian actions, English colonists most often "read" and "translated" Indian cruelties either as random acts of savagery or as messages from God. What they utterly failed to consider was that the war might not only be an obscure message from a distant but reproachful God but also a loud shout from extremely disgruntled but very nearby neighbors, communicating a complex set of ideas about why they were waging war.

IV

ON MARCH 29, 1676, a party of Narragansetts attacked Providence, destroying the town. To Roger Williams, who considered himself a friend of the Narragansetts (and who had hoped that, as a result, Rhode Island would be spared in the war), the attack was a profound betrayal. With a rage fueled by distress, Williams walked to the outskirts of town to meet with the Narragansetts and force them to answer for their perfidy. Pointing to his own house, which, he said, "hath Lodged kindly Some Thousands of You these Ten years," but which was then burning to ashes behind him, Williams asked "Why they assaulted us With burning and Killing who ever were kind Neighbours to them." In a heated discussion, the Narragansetts offered three answers:

> [firstly] they Confessed they were in A Strang Way.
> 2ly we had forced them to it.
> 3ly that God was [with] them and Had forsaken us for they had so prospered
> in Killing and Burning us far beyond What we did against them.

Enraged by this reply, Williams let his fury fly, insisting that, far from taking the Indians' side in the war, God favored the English. "God had prospered *us* so that wee had driven the Wampanoogs with Phillip out of his Countrie and the Nahigonsiks out of their Countre, and had destroyed Multitudes of them in Fighting and Flying, In Hungr and Cold etc.: and that God would help us to Consume them." [129]

This is indeed a startling encounter. Its attempt at dialogue is, to say the least, unusual. And, as a record of Indian motives in the war, it is, sadly, unparalleled. Compare, now, this list to another. In a sermon delivered before the Artillery Election Company on June 3, 1678, Samuel Nowell, who had served to minister to the colonial army during King Philip's War, attempted to explain the colonists' reasons for waging war. "There are commonly reckoned three causes of War," he declared:

> 1. For defence of ourselves.
> 2. To recover what hath been taken away.
> 3. To punish for injuries done. [130]

While the Narragansetts' list combined secular reasons ("we had forced them to it") with religious ones ("God was [with] them and Had forsaken us"),

Nowell's list of the possible causes of war is entirely secular. (Although Nowell made no explicit reference to it, his list was derived from Grotius' own list of the three causes of just war—"defence, recovery of property, and punishment"—a list that Nowell, a half-century later, would reproduce exactly.) Yet, preaching before the Artillery Election Company four years earlier, Joshua Moodey had exhorted New Englanders to "take, kill, burn, sink, destroy all sin and Corruption, &C which are professed enemies to Christ Jesus, and not to pity or spare any of them."[131] Samuel Nowell may have believed he had fought a just war, fair, legal, and limited, but Joshua Moodey was ready for holy war, divinely ordained and unrestrained.

The Narragansetts' explanation for why they burned Providence provided Roger Williams with precious little comfort as he watched his house become a heap of ashes. But their words, like those of Nowell and Moody, suggest that both sides in King Philip's War believed they were fighting to save their lives—and their religions. And perhaps both peoples knew that, in the chaos and excess of a cruel war, they were "in A Strang Way," disoriented by loss, fear, and gods who had forsaken them.

PART THREE · *Bondage*

And I only am escaped to tell the news.
—Job 1:15, *as quoted by*
Mary Rowlandson, *1682*

Philips boy goes now to be sold.
—John Cotton,
March 9, 1677

Chapter 5

COME GO ALONG WITH US

O n February 10, 1676, Nipmuck Indians attacked the town of Lancaster, Massachusetts, and took several colonists captive, among them Mary Rowlandson. For the next three months, Rowlandson, the wife of a prominent Puritan minister, lived among the Indians; she ate Indian food, slept in Indian wigwams, learned Indian ways. And always, she prayed. In long treks through the bitter winter, on foot and on horseback, across rivers and through swamps, she accompanied a group of Nipmucks and their captives as they traveled westward and then, in early spring, turned eastward again. Finally, on May 2, Mary Rowlandson was "redeemed" when a twenty-pound ransom was paid for her release. The following day she arrived in Boston, where she remained until April 1677, when she and her husband, Joseph, resettled in Wethersfield, Connecticut.¹ Sometime during the year and a half between her move to Wethersfield and her husband's death in November 1678, Mary Rowlandson wrote an account of her captivity among the Indians.² In March 1682 that account, piously titled *The Soveraignty* [sic] *and Goodness of God,* was printed in Boston. Within months, second and third editions were printed in Cambridge, and by November 1682 the first London edition of Rowlandson's narrative was advertised in a catalog of English booksellers. It would become America's first best-seller. Today, *The Soveraignty and Goodness of God* is considered a foundational work in American literature; it is better remembered than any other account of King Philip's War and is more widely read than any other Indian captivity narrative.³

Yet within Mary Rowlandson's captivating tale—quite literally in the very ink on its pages—lies another story: the story of James Printer. Printer, himself a Nipmuck Indian, was converted to Christianity by John Eliot and, in the years before King Philip's War, he worked with Eliot at the Cambridge Press, translating manuscripts and setting type (hence, James *Printer*). At the start of the war, Printer was living in the "praying town" of Hassanemesit (present-day Grafton, Massachusetts). In early November 1675 Nipmucks allied with Philip came to Hassanemesit and carried away its townspeople. For the next several months, Printer, the brother of a prominent Indian minister, trekked through the woods of New England with the enemy Nipmucks. When Rowlandson was taken captive by the same group little more than three months later, Printer realized that his future lay with her (and hers with him). In the coming weeks Printer served as scribe during negotiations for Mary Rowlandson's redemption. Then, when amnesty was offered to Christian Indians who had joined the enemy, Printer turned himself in to colonial authorities, bringing with him, as required by special instruction, the heads of two enemy Indians—testaments to his fidelity. Eventually Printer returned to his work at the press in Cambridge and, in 1682, in one of the most sublime ironies of King Philip's War, James Printer set the type for *The Soveraignty and Goodness of God*.[4]

Mary Rowlandson and James Printer are indeed a curious pair. Their intricately linked stories are at once uncannily similar and crucially divergent. Before the war, Mary's husband, Joseph Rowlandson, was the minister of her town, while James' brother, Joseph Tukapewillin, was the minister of his. Both Rowlandson and Printer spent the winter of 1675–76 with enemy Nipmucks. Both returned to Boston months later to live, again, among the English. But while Rowlandson came to terms with her time among enemy Indians by writing a book, Printer supplied body parts. In the end, the divergences tell us more than the similarities, and together they suggest that the most important legacy of Mary Rowlandson's narrative is not its coherent statement of Puritan typology, its poignant psychological portrait of terror, or even its paradoxically defiant yet submissive female voice. The lasting legacy of Mary Rowlandson's dramatic, eloquent, and fantastically popular narrative of captivity and redemption is the nearly complete veil it has unwittingly placed over the experiences of bondage endured by Algonquian Indians during King Philip's War.

I

"ON THE TENTH of February 1675, came the Indians with great numbers upon Lancaster." So begins Mary Rowlandson's narrative, and so began her captivity, on what she called "the dolefullest day that ever mine eyes saw."

Reckoning the losses, Rowlandson invited her readers to imagine witnessing the scene in Lancaster that day:

> *Come, behold the works of the Lord, what desolations he has made in the earth.* Of thirty seven persons who were in this one house, none escaped either present death, or a bitter captivity, save only one, who might say as he, Job 1:15, *And I only am escaped to tell the news.* There were twelve killed, some shot, some stabbed with their spears, some knocked down with their hatchets. . . . There was one who was chopped into the head with a hatchet, and stript naked, and yet was crawling up and down. It is a solemn sight to see so many Christians lying in their blood, some here, and some there, like a company of sheep torn by wolves. All of them stripped naked by a company of hell-hounds, roaring, singing, ranting, and insulting, as if they would have torn our very hearts out.[5]

Rowlandson wrote about her captivity to reflect on "the Sovereignty & Goodness of God, Together With the Faithfulness of His Promises"; her narrative was devotional. As a Calvinist, she believed affliction of any kind was cause for spiritual reflection; before the war, she had even prayed that her devotion might be tested by such trials. And, beginning on February 10, her prayers were answered in abundance. "Before I knew what affliction meant, I was ready sometimes to wish for it. . . . Affliction I wanted, and affliction I had, full measure (I thought) pressed down and running over."[6] Captivity was a special brand of affliction, uniquely suited to increasing piety, as suggested in a tract published in London in 1675 that promised to help captives everywhere make their captivity "instrumental towards the attainment of an eternal weight of glory."[7] Despite their sufferings or, indeed, because of them, captives were blessed with abundant time for spiritual reflection. It was in this spirit that Rowlandson wrote about her experience:

> *It is good for me that I have been afflicted.* . . . It was but the other day that if I had had the world, I would have given it for my freedom, or to have been a servant to a Christian. I have learned to look beyond present and smaller troubles, and to be quieted under them, as Moses said, Exodus 14. 13. *Stand still and see the salvation of the Lord.*[8]

Yet, within this Calvinist framework, Mary Rowlandson was not only redeemed from captivity, captivity also redeemed her. "Redemption" had, and has, several shades of meaning. In one sense (emancipation through payment), the ransom redeemed Rowlandson from physical bondage; in another sense (delivery through spiritual salvation), her bondage itself redeemed her from sin by teaching her to stand still and accept God's will. Twenty pounds bought her freedom; captivity saved her soul.[9]

But there is yet another sense of redemption (expiation of guilt) that played a role in Rowlandson's release. In writing her narrative, Mary Rowlandson was attempting, at least in part, to "redeem" herself from both the horrors—and the complicity—of captivity. Perhaps she believed that, if only she could describe it fully, the "dolefull sight" that had "so daunted" her spirit would free her from the nightmares that continued to haunt her.[10] ("I can remember the time, when I used to sleep quietly without workings in my thoughts, whole nights together, but now it is other wayes with me."[11]) Having been "in the midst of those roaring lions, and salvage bears, that feared neither God, nor man, nor the devil," Mary Rowlandson had journeyed, she believed, into the belly of the beast. Writing an account of that journey was part of her escape. Clearly she wrote, most of all, to testify to God's wonderful providences, but Mary Rowlandson also wrote to redeem herself, to deliver herself from the demons of memory and to reconcile herself with her first, fateful choice: choosing captivity over death.

Before the war, Mary Rowlandson had pledged to accept death before captivity: "I had often before this said, that if the Indians should come, I should choose rather to be killed by them than be taken alive."[12] And her sister had done just that: "Seeing those woeful sights, the infidels haling mothers one way, and children another, and some wallowing in their blood . . . she said, And Lord, let me die with them; which was no sooner said, but she was struck with a bullet, and fell down dead over the threshold."[13] "Those woeful sights" made Mary's sister wish for death, but they made Mary cling to life. Indeed, the sight of such horrors led her to abandon her pledge: "When it came to the trial my mind changed; their glittering weapons so daunted my spirit, that I chose rather to go along with those (as I may say) ravenous beasts, than that moment to end my days."[14]

Here, in recounting the defining moment of her captivity, Mary Rowlandson's phrases swell with ambiguity. As she described it, she had been "captivated," overwhelmed not by charm, as we would take the word to mean today, but by force, as seventeenth-century usage implied. "The Indians laid hold of us, pulling me one way, and the Children another, and said, Come go along with us; I told them they would kill me: they answered, If I were willing to go along with them, they would not hurt me." To be taken captive is to be taken by force, against one's will, but Rowlandson, curiously, admitted she was "willing to go along with them." True, she was wounded and terrified, and had clearly been threatened; still, captives were not supposed to be "willing." Like Mary's sister, not a few colonists, after all, had allowed themselves be killed rather than be taken captive. They did so, no doubt, out of fear about what lay ahead—the deprivations and difficulties of captivity—but also out of a fear that they might never return. The Indians' main purpose of taking captives was to adopt new members into their communities; many captives, especially children, became thoroughly Indianized, living out their lives with their new Algonquian families and losing even the ability to speak English. Some later resisted rescue and refused to return to live with their English families.[15] While prominent captives, like Rowlandson, might be traded for ransom money or swapped in an exchange of prisoners, most who survived the initial hardships were expected to abandon English ways and to become, eventually, wholly Indian.[16] The choice between death and captivity must have felt to some colonists like a choice between salvation and damnation. That Rowlandson described this experience with phrases that swell with ambiguity should not surprise us.

No doubt the vividness of Rowlandson's prose helped convince readers that, in her position, they could have done no better than to act as she had. Rowlandson employed all the strategies of description available to contemporary chroniclers of the war—numbers, stark images, and biblical references. And she invoked all the most powerful signs of chaos—spilled blood, diabolical Indians, naked Englishmen. Her words must have had a powerful effect on those who read them. And yet Rowlandson still feared that her readers, in the comfort of their orderly, peaceful homes, could never fully understand what it felt like to stand outside that burning house in Lancaster. "When we are in prosperity, oh the little that we think of such dreadfull sights, and to see our dear friends and relations lie bleeding out their heart-blood upon the ground."[17]

Like Rowlandson, many colonists had probably pledged to die rather than be taken captive by Indians, but, if tested, few would have been able to keep such a pledge, awestruck, as she was, by "their glittering weapons" and by the prospect of a violent death. Still, adult, able-bodied, and especially male colonists who offered little resistance to capture may have been judged harshly (and at least one was executed), their easy capitulation seen as a sign not only of weakness but also, possibly, of a willingness to embrace the Indian way of life or, at the very least, of a willingness to abandon English ways. Returning captives were no doubt welcomed back into English society, but some were also probably feared and, to a certain extent, mistrusted. A few colonists may have even believed that having lived among the Indians left a former captive contaminated by the influences of Indian society and Indian culture. The colonists' greatest cultural anxiety, after all, was the fear that they were becoming Indianized. "How many that although they are Christians in name,"

Increase Mather asked, "are no better then Heathens in heart?"[18] Being taken from one's home was terrifying enough, but being taken to live among the Indians was just the kind of blurring of boundaries that colonists feared most.

In describing her captivity, Mary Rowlandson made clear that even while she lived among the Indians she had always remained, at heart, thoroughly English. Even as she embraced the indignities she suffered and reveled in her humility before God (she cited Psalms 38:5–6: "My wounds stink and are corrupt, I am bowed down greatly"[19]), she recoiled from her heathen surroundings, stressing her revulsion at nearly all things Indian—Indian food ("filthy trash"), Indian houses, Indian dances—at the same time as she proclaimed her fondness (and her homesickness) for all things English. When she came upon signs of English habitation, for instance, Rowlandson was powerfully moved: "As we went along, I saw a place where English cattle had been: that was comfort to me, such as it was: quickly after that we came to an English path, which so took with me, that I thought I could have freely lain down and died."[20] This feeling was so strong that at times during her captivity Rowlandson almost forgot where she was:

> I cannot but remember how many times sitting in their wigwams, and musing on things past, I should suddenly leap up and run out, as if I had been at home, forgetting where I was, and what my condition was: but when I was without, and saw nothing but wilderness, and woods, and a company of barbarous heathens, my mind quickly returned to me.[21]

And Rowlandson made sure to tell her readers that she had been spared the kind of heathen contamination they would have feared most: "Not one of them ever offered me the least abuse or unchastity to me, in word or action." (There is very little evidence that Algonquians ever sexually abused their captives.)[22]

For being spared rape, and for all other blessings, Mary Rowlandson gave abundant thanks to God: "O the wonderful power of God that I have seen, and the experience that I have had!"[23] She expressed her gratitude both in writing her narrative and in allowing it to be printed. According to the published narrative's preface (presumed to have been written by Increase Mather), Rowlandson initially resisted publication, but her reticence was soon overcome.[24]

> Some friends having obtained a sight of [the manuscript], could not but be so much affected with the many passages of working providence discovered therein, as to judge it worthy of publick view, and altogether unmeet that

such works of God should be hid from present and future generations: and therefore though this gentlewomans modesty would not thrust it into the press, yet her gratitude unto God made her not hardly persuadable to let it pass, that God might have his due glory, and others benefit by it as well as herself. I hope by this time none will cast any reflection upon this gentlewoman, on the score of this publication of her affliction and deliverance.[25]

In a transaction that mimicked the scene at Lancaster on February 10, Rowlandson was again forced through a doorway, out into public view. Not her body this time, but her manuscript, was "captivated," and put into God's service.[26] In both cases Rowlandson was "persuadable" only because she sought to follow God's will. In exonerating Mary Rowlandson for allowing her manuscript to be published, the writer of the preface similarly exonerated her for allowing herself to be captured by Indians. He wrote,

> I may say, that as none knows what it is to fight and pursue such an enemy as this, but they that have fought and pursued them: so none can imagine what it is to be captivated, and enslaved to such atheisticall proud, wild, cruel, barbarous, bruitish (in one word) diabolical creatures as these, the worst of the heathen; nor what difficulties, hardships, hazards, sorrows, anxieties and perplexities do unavoidably wait upon such a condition, but those that have tried it.[27]

If "none can imagine what it is to be captivated . . . but those that have tried it," Rowlandson could not be judged for her actions. Nor could her testimony be ignored, or she be condemned for offering it. Far from thinking ill of Rowlandson, either for her involvement with the Indians or for her immodesty in writing about it, readers were encouraged to consider her a "worthy and precious Gentlewoman" deserving of "both commendation and imitation." "No serious spirit then (especially knowing any thing of this Gentlewomans piety) can imagine but that the vows of God are upon her. Excuse her then if she come thus into publick, to pay those vows."[28]

II

JOSHUA TIFT CAME into public, too, though not to pay the vows of God. And, far from being excused, he was executed—hanged and quartered—for treason. Under interrogation, Tift, a farmer, claimed to have been taken captive by Narragansetts. Questioned by Roger Williams on January 14, 1676, Tift testified that his captivity had begun soon after he hired an Indian man to keep his cattle while he traveled to Rhode Island. On the day he was to depart, in mid-December 1675, a party of Narragansetts came to Tift's house and "told him he must die." Unlike Rowlandson, Tift made no pretense of having once preferred death to captivity; instead, he admitted that he had simply "begd for his Life and promised he would be servant to the Sachim while he lived. He Saith the Sachim then Caried him along with him having given him his Life as his Slave." Tift was then taken to the Great Swamp, along with five of his cattle, who were then killed before his eyes.[29]

If all that Joshua Tift had done was to choose captivity over death, and to serve an Indian sachem to spare his own life, he was guilty of no more than Mary Rowlandson.[30] Indeed, many of two captives' experiences were similar. The killing of Tift's cattle, and especially the mocking that answered his pleas to spare them ("what will Cattell now doe you good"?), mimicked the taunting Rowlandson was subjected to when she asked if she could sleep in a deserted English house on the first night of her captivity ("What will you love English men still?"). Both captives were forced to leave English ways behind, especially things such as cows and houses, potent symbols of English agriculture and notions of property ownership, things that would do them little good during their new life among the Indians. (Since one purpose of taking captives was to eventually adopt them into the tribe, captives were typically subjected to rituals of initiation during which they were encouraged to abandon their native culture.) But while Rowlandson was eventually redeemed from captivity and welcomed back warmly into English society, Tift was interrogated and executed. How did they come to such different ends?

Some differences are obvious and critical. Mary Rowlandson told her story to give thanks to God and to spiritually and psychologically redeem herself. Tift told his story to save his neck. And Tift's admission that, at the fateful moment, he "begd for his Life," contrasts markedly with Rowlandson's emphasis on how her resolve was broken by the persuasive power of "their glittering weapons." Tift's credibility was always in doubt, compromised partly by the conditions under which he told his story, partly by his much more ambiguous involvement with the Indians he claimed had captured him, and partly by his sex. Tift was never released from captivity as Rowlandson was, by ransom money or by an exchange of prisoners, nor did he escape; instead, English soldiers found him living among the Narragansetts on January 14, 1676, and they had reason to believe that Tift had actually fought on the side of the Narragansetts during the Great Swamp fight a month earlier. Finally, Tift, as an able-bodied man, had little excuse for not violently resisting capture, while Rowlandson, an injured woman carrying an injured infant, had abundant reason to submit.

The first crack in Tift's story was its noticeable absence of any mention of torture: he did not report being beaten or injured during an attack or having been tied up or staked down once captured; the worst he endured was seeing his cows killed. The complete absence of any reference to torture (either endured or witnessed) is, in fact, a rather unusual characteristic of Tift's account, distinguishing it from other male captives' reports. Thomas Warner, for instance, told of how his captors "kill'd one of the Prisoners presently after they had taken him, cutting a Hole below his Breast out of which they pull'd his Gutts, and then cutt off his Head," upon which they threatened Warner with the same fate. Warner himself was not entirely spared, for soon the Indians "burnt his Nayles, and put his Feet to scald them against the Fire, and drove a Stake through one of his Feet to pin him to the Ground."[31] Another freed captive, a fourteen-year-old English boy, said he was bound to a tree "two Nights and two Days" and threatened with torture before he managed to escape.[32] (As a woman, and especially as the wife of a well-known and powerful Puritan minister, Rowlandson was likely to have been spared torture or the threat of it.)[33]

Yet, while Tift's failure to mention torture made his story unusual, it did not necessarily make it unbelievable. It was only when he told what happened next that Tift lost any credibility he might have established in telling earlier parts of his story. Tift claimed that after being captivated he had been taken to the Narragansett fort and, when the English attacked on December 19, 1675, he had had no choice but to remain among the Indians. When his English interrogators accused Tift of fighting on the side of the Narragansetts, Tift insisted he had not even had a gun: "Being askt whether he was in the Fort in the fight, he Saith yes and waited on his master the Sachim there untill he was wounded . . . but he saith Himselfe had no Arms at all."[34] Nathaniel Saltonstall reported that Tift had "pretended that he was taken Prisoner by the Indians, and by them compelled to bear Arms in their Service," but that this was "proved to be false." The evidence for such a conclusion, however, is limited. Like most events of the war, several accounts of the story of Joshua Tift contradict one another. Captain James Oliver suggested that Tift had lived with the Indians for years and had "married an Indian woman, a Wampanoag." Tift, Oliver said, was "a sad wretch" who "never heard a sermon but once these 14 years" and whose father, on going to rescue Tift, had been killed by Indians.[35] Meanwhile, Increase Mather claimed Tift had "apostatized to the Heathen"; Saltonstall said Tift was an English soldier who had recently deserted the colonial army because of a disagreement with his commanding officer; and an Englishwoman who had been captive among the Narragansetts was said to have claimed that Tift was "their encourager and conductor."[36] And, while Tift was "said to wound Capt. Sealy" in the fight, and Oliver claimed Tift had "shot 20 times at us in the swamp," Saltonstall maintained that Tift never had the chance to get off a shot but that when he was captured by the English his musket was "found deep charged, and laden with Slugs."[37]

Frustratingly, it is impossible to determine with any certainty which of these claims is true. Yet, whether he had deserted the army, apostatized from Christianity, or married a Wampanoag woman, all versions of the story, except Tift's own, suggest that he joined the Narragansetts willingly. Perhaps there was good reason to disbelieve Tift's story—maybe he never was "captivated"; maybe he had fought against the English. On the other hand, Tift may have been telling the truth, at least in part. If Tift were really holding a loaded gun when he was captured, for instance, it seems unlikely that he would have later testified that he "had no Arms at all." He might, of course, have been lying wildly during his interrogation, with no regard for the inconsistencies in his story, and certainly, if he had willingly fought alongside the Narragansetts during the Great Swamp fight, he had every reason to lie about it. But if Tift was telling the truth, and he actually was an unarmed captive, then he was simply, and fatefully, in the wrong place at the wrong time. And yet, even if Tift told the truth, he was still guilty, in a sense, for failing to fight *against* the Narragansetts when the English attacked. Tift may not have had a gun, but his "master," after all, was shooting at English soldiers, and apparently Tift did nothing to stop him.

Mary Rowlandson was "willing to go along with them," but even if his version of the story were true, Joshua Tift had done more than that: he had been willing to stand aside and watch as his captors shot at English soldiers. Tift's relinquishment of his liberty was far more complete than Rowlandson's. And since Tift was a man and Rowlandson a woman, Tift's submission, his surrendering of his will, his willingness to go along with the Indians, were all the more culpable. As an English woman, Mary Rowlandson was not supposed to have very much will of her own to give away; submission was her gender's mandate.[38] And submission was also the posture required of her as a Christian. "In my travels," Rowlandson recalled, "an Indian came to me and told me, if I were willing, he and his squaw would run away, and go home along with me: I told him No: I was not willing to run away, but desired to wait God's time, that I might go home quietly, and without fear."[39] If Mary Rowlandson's captivity was willful, it followed God's will, not her own. Mary Rowlandson's piety, and her femininity, meant that the "vows of God" were upon her and that her will was not her own. For Puritans in New England, captivity among the Indians was easily put to spiritual ends, but it is no coincidence that the first and most popular captivity narrative was written by a woman. The tension between resistance and surrender was best managed by gendered explanations. Mary Rowlandson had already surrendered her will to her husband, and to God, and to surrender to Indians in God's name was consistent with what her culture expected of her, or at least more consistent for her than such behavior was for a man. Even as a captive, Joshua Tift was still expected to possess a will of his own.[40]

Joshua Tift did not call himself a captive; he called himself a "servant" or a "slave" to the sachem who captured him. This was not unusual. In the early months of captivity, before being formally adopted, captives often underwent a difficult period of initiation, somewhat akin to enslavement. Mary Rowlandson, for instance, belonged to an Indian couple (a Narragansett leader named Quinnapin and a "squaw sachem," Weetamoo, from Pocasset), whom she called her "master" and "mistress," terms a servant would have used. Indian captives would have been better able to predict what fate awaited them, but Europeans had little idea of what to expect, or what their true status was in this new community, and came to understand it in whatever terms seemed appropriate to them.[41] The people who suffered forms of bondage during King Philip's War were called by many names: captives, servants, slaves. Even today these terms can be confusing, but to us, some fundamental differences dictate their usage. A captive is someone who has been kidnapped and held by force, usually temporarily. A servant is someone required (often by force) to work for another in exchange for housing, food, and occasionally wages. A slave is a permanent, unpaid servant, whose children inherit that status.

During King Philip's War these three terms were sometimes used interchangeably. Increase Mather wrote that on June 7, 1676, the English "came upon a party of Indians not far from lancaster, and killed seven of them, and took nine and twenty of them Captive: some of which not long since had English Captives under them. Thus did they that had led into Captivity, go into captivity."[42] The twenty-nine Indian "captives" taken that day (some of them Rowlandson's own former captors) were almost surely sold into foreign slavery or, if children, placed into service with an English family. The "captivity" they would have experienced differed dramatically from the "captivity" Mary Rowlandson experienced. Yet, if they didn't always maintain distinctions between their terms, the English in New England maintained distinctions in their minds. English people owned themselves; Indians did not. Ultimately, Indians could be enslaved, while English people could not. But this racialized distinction had a gendered dimension as well. In its most common usage, captivity meant being held against one's will and kept in confinement, usually temporarily; but a captive, especially a male captive, still possessed a will. Slavery, on the other hand, meant becoming the property of another human being, completely divested of freedom and personal rights. Even if Joshua Tift told the truth, he failed to exonerate himself because he was, in effect, unredeemable. For standing by idly while his "master" shot at English soldiers, Joshua Tift was either a traitor or a slave; either way, he was no Englishman.

III

JAMES PRINTER WAS no Englishman either, but he, too, might have claimed to have been taken "captive" (and not been believed). In early November 1675 three hundred Nipmuck Indians arrived in Printer's town of Hassanemesit—not with the violence with which they would later assault Lancaster, but with much the same intention: acquiring captives. Like Mary Rowlandson and Joshua Tift, James Printer was given a choice. If the people of Hassanemesit would "go with them quietly," the Nipmucks "would spare their lives; otherwise they would take away all their corn, and then they would be famished." While Rowlandson chose captivity and Tift begged for his life, Printer had the option, it seemed, of refusing to go along with the Nipmucks, and simply fleeing to the English when provisions ran out in Hassanemesit. But this, alas, was a false choice. By the time the Nipmucks arrived in Hassanemesit, the Massachusetts authorities had already removed hundreds of Christian Indians to islands in Boston Harbor and shipped hundreds more Christian and enemy Indians out of the colonies to be sold as slaves in the West Indies and other places within English dominion. "If we do not kill you," the Nipmucks rightly argued, and "you go to the English again, they will either force you all to some Island as the Natick Indians are, where you will be in danger to be starved with cold and hunger, and most probably in the end be all sent out of the country for slaves." Printer and his townspeople had a choice, then, between captivity among the Indians and confinement on a barren island in Boston Harbor (which might in turn lead to perpetual slavery in a far more remote land). As Daniel Gookin later reported, "many of them at last were inclined, in this strait, of two evils to choose the least, as it to them appeared, and to accompany the enemy to their quarters." In defense of the Hassanemesits, Gookin pointed out that "perhaps if Englishmen, and good Christians too, had been in their case and under like temptations, possibly they might have done as they did." [43] Mary Rowlandson could not have said it better.

Within days of the Nipmucks' confrontation with Printer and his townspeople, Captain Daniel Henchman reported finding Hassanemesit a hauntingly empty town.[44] He was not convinced, however, that the Christian Indians had been "captivated" and claimed there were "no signs of an enimy that had been there; but a flight of Indians, i fear, real or feined, by apples, corn, nuts and other things lying up and down."[45] On the other hand, authorities in Boston seem to have become gradually convinced that the Christian Indians had in fact been taken captive. In a letter written November 6, the Massachusetts Council reported that the Hassanemesit Indians had been taken by the Nipmucks—"whether with their consent or without their consent we are not certayne"—but on November 16 the Council seemed less ambiguous, informing Captain Appleton that "a considerable party of [Nipmucks] have appeared (within this 14 dayes) in the Nipmoke country, and have *surprised and carried away* or slayne about 180 men women & children of the praying indians that lived at & were confyned unto a place called Hassanemesit." And, in a letter written a week later, Boston authorities used even more forceful terms, reporting that the Hassanemesit Indians had been "*seased & carred away.*"[46]

Whether the Christian Indians of Hassanemesit were truly "captivated" or whether they joined the Nipmucks willingly is certainly subject to debate, but before attempting any conclusion we would do well to first consider the options they were faced with. If James Printer had refused to go with the Nipmucks and instead fled to the English for protection, he might well have been shot during his travels eastward. In August 1675 Captain Samuel Moseley, widely known as the cruelest captain in the colonial army (he had once ordered an Algonquian woman to be "torn to peeces by Doggs"), had accused Printer and fourteen other Christian Indians of the murder of seven colonists at Lancaster on August 22. Moseley's evidence was entirely circumstantial, and a single confession had been elicited from one of the group only after he had been tortured and threatened with death, but public sentiment against Christian Indians was so strong that Moseley was able to bring the case to trial. On August 30 Moseley brought James Printer and fourteen other Christian Indians into Boston, "pinioned and fastened with lines from neck to neck."[47] In September Printer lingered in a Boston prison until he and his companions were brought to trial, at which point all but two of the accused were declared innocent. Even then,

> Some men were so violent that they would have had these Indians put to death by martial law, and not tried by a jury, though they were subjects under the English protection, and not in hostility with us; others had received such impressions in their minds, that they could hardly extend charity to the jurors and magistrates that acquitted them.[48]

A lynching was narrowly averted, and for coming to the defense of the accused, Daniel Gookin and John Eliot were themselves threatened.[49]

James Printer, in other words, was well acquainted with the colonists' vigilante justice. And on August 30, the very day that Printer and the other accused Hassanemesit Indians were marched to Boston, tied neck to neck, the Massachusetts Council issued an order declaring that all Christian Indians be forthwith confined to their towns, "for security of the English & Indians in amity with us"—and, surely, to prevent exactly the kind of depredations of which the Hassanemesits stood accused. If a wayward Indian happened to be shot, "the Council do hereby declare that they shall account themselves wholly innocent, & their blood, or other damage by them sustained will be upon their own heads."[50] If Printer had chosen to flee from the Nipmucks when they arrived in Hassanemesit in November, he could have been killed in the woods and no one would have had to answer for his death.

On the other hand, Printer might have made it safely to an English town, in which case he would have been taken away and confined to Deer Island in Boston Harbor within days of his arrival. On October 13 the Massachusetts authorities had ordered that all Indians from the praying town of Natick be removed to Deer Island, and the evacuation of other praying towns soon followed.[51] (Plans to confine Christian Indians had been considered almost as soon as the war began; in September the minister of nearby Mendon proposed that the Hassanemesit Indians be ordered to built a fort in Mendon and to move there with their families as soon as their corn crop was harvested, though the plan was never executed.)[52] Most Christian Indians in the newer, more western praying towns ("being but raw and lately initiated into the Christian profession") had already joined the enemy; now, those who had remained loyal to the English, residents of the fourteen "old" praying towns, were to be indefinitely confined.[53] Fear of the misery of Deer Island inspired Christian Indians in Wamesit to leave the colony entirely and to "go towards the French." In a letter explaining their decision to abandon their town, the Wamesits wrote, "As for the Island, we say there is no safety for us, because many English be not good, and may be they come to us and kill us. . . . We are not sorry for what we leave behind, but we are sorry for the English have driven us from our praying to god and from our teacher."[54]

When the Nipmucks came to his town in November 1675, James Printer could not have known exactly what fate would have awaited him on Deer Island, but he had his own recent experience of English confinement to call to mind, and he had probably heard rumors about the condition of the Indians on the island, and, then too, it would have taken little imagination to conclude that things would only worsen over the winter. Printer would have been right in expecting the worst.

Those Indians who tried to escape from Deer Island could be killed, while others were illegally taken from the island and sold as slaves. When John Eliot met with a group of Natick Indians on the shores of the Charles River just before they were to depart, he "comforted and encouraged and instructed and prayed with them, and for them," but many were afraid that "they should never return to their habitations, but be transported out of the country."[55] On November 3 the General Court, referring to "sundry Indians (that have subjected to our government)" who had been placed "upon some islands for their and our security," proclaimed "that none of the sayd indians shall presume to goe off the sayd islands voluntarily, uponn payne of death" and "that if any person or persons shall presume to take, steale, or carry away either man, woeman, or child of the said Indians, off from any the said islands where they are placed, without order from the Generall Court or council, he or they shall be accounted breakers of the capitall law printed & published against man stealing." The Court's orders, however, often proved ineffectual. Even though the Court had stipulated that provisions be "sent downe to Deare Island, so as to prevent their perishing by any extremity that they may be put unto for want of absolute necessaries," the hundreds of Indians on the small island had few resources with which to feed and shelter themselves for the winter, and the provisions they received were inadequate.[56] By the end of November the Deer Island Indians' condition was so bad that the Massachusetts Council grudgingly appointed two colonists to "take care that none of the Said Indians do desert the Island nor are injured by any persons Indians or English nor that they suffer for want of necessarys."[57] In December, when Gookin and Eliot traveled to the island "to visit and comfort the poor Christian Indians," they found about five hundred starving men, women, and children; "the Island was bleak and cold, their wigwams poor and mean, their clothes few and thin."[58]

Outside of Gookin and Eliot, however, there was little sympathy for the plight of the Indians confined to Deer Island. Not a few colonists believed confinement was too good a treatment for Indians, Christian or not. Even Christian Indians who served the English as soldiers were believed by many to be disloyal. Mary Pray, for instance, complained that "those Indians that are caled praying Indians never shut at the other Indians, but up into the tops of the trees or into the ground; and when they make shew of going first into the swamp they comonly give the Indians noatis how to escape the English."[59] This suspicion had been vindicated by Tift himself, who informed his interrogators that "if the Monhiggins and Pequts had bene true [to the English] they might have destroyed most of the Nahiggonsiks, but, the Nahigonsiks parlied with them in the beginning of the [Great Swamp] Fight so that they promised to shoote high which they did and kild not one Nahigonsik man except against their Wills."[60] If Christian and allied Indians fighting alongside

English soldiers were disloyal, Christian Indians living with enemy Indians were thought to be far worse. To punning Puritans, praying Indians had now become "preying Indians."[61]

In February, after the attacks on Medfield and Lancaster (where Mary Rowlandson was "captivated" by Indians believed to include the former Christian Indians of Hassanemesit), several colonists contemplated taking revenge against the Christian Indians on Deer Island. As Daniel Gookin reported, "This intelligence of burning Medfield coming to the General Court, and so soon after the burning of Lancaster, occasioned many thoughts of hearty and hurrying motions, and gave opportunity to the vulgar to cry out, 'Oh, come, let us go down to Deer Island, and kill all the praying Indians.' "[62] At about the same time, in mid-February, there was a rumor that the Indians themselves were planning an escape off the island, after which they were expected to return to Boston and "make Boston especially the magistrates pay deare for sundry hours they have been kept there."[63] On February 22 a group of nervous Bostonians petitioned the Council urging stronger measures against all Indians, enemy or not, and that the Christian Indians be removed to "some place farther more from us."[64]

Responding to rumors of possible assaults and escape attempts, the General Court convened a debate on the fate of the Indians on Deer Island on February 23. As Gookin reported, "Some would have them all destroyed; others, sent out of the country; but some there were of more moderation, alleging that those Indians and their ancestors had a covenant with the English about thirty years since, wherein mutual protection and subjection was agreed." The records indeed revealed such an agreement, made in 1644, which the Court decided to abide by.[65] (Meanwhile, for his advocacy of the Indians on Deer Island, Gookin was threatened with death. On February 28 three Englishwomen heard Richard Scott call Gookin "an Irish Dog, that was not faithfull to his country, the Sonne of a whoare, a Bitch, a Rogue, God confound him & God rott his Soul, saying if I could roast him alive, I would."[66] Soon afterward, a note signed by "the Society A.B.C.D." and probably authored by Scott was posted in Boston calling Gookin a traitor and warning him "to prepare for deathe."[67]) Finally, on February 29, 1676, the Massachusetts Council, "having seriously considered the state of the Indians now Confyned to deare Island," issued a four-part order. This stipulated, first, that "a guard of six or eight English men" be posted to ensure that no Indians escaped the island; second, that these guards put all the Indians to work, "some to spining, others to breaking up land to plant on, others to gett fish & clams"; third, that the colonists who owned Deer Island and other islands used to confine the Indians (these included Long Island, Potuck Island, and the Brewster

Islands) be compensated for the use of their land; and fourth, that Captain Daniel Henchman, the officer in charge of the island, ensure that the Indians "live soberly & religiously." [68]

The condition of the Indians living on the islands, however, continued to deteriorate. In March Henchman reported to the Council that "the said Indians are in great distress for want of food for themselves [and their] wives & children." [69] By early May the Massachusetts Council, "considering the present distressed condition of the Indians at the island, they being ready to perish for want of bread, & incapacitated to make provission for the future, doe order, that there be a man with a boate provided, who, with some of the Indians, shallbe imployed in catching of fish for theire supply." [70] Several weeks later, those Indians on the island who had survived the winter were finally released. Daniel Gookin reported that "God was pleased to mollify the hearts and minds of men towards them, little and little; partly by the true reports brought to the General Court, of their distressed estate, and the great unlikelihood they were to plant or reap any corn at the Islands . . . and the General Court then sitting passed an order, giving liberty to remove them from the Islands." Their "deliverance" may have been, as Gookin claimed, "a jubilee to those poor creatures," but more than half of the Christian Indians confined to Deer Island had died during the winter, and many no doubt were too sick to enjoy their liberty for long. [71]

IV

WITH THE FATE that might have awaited him at Deer Island in mind, then, James Printer did not flee to the English when the Nipmucks came to Hassanemesit in November 1675, only to be released weak and starving the following May. But his brother, Joseph Tukapewillin, eventually did. [72] Tukapewillin, the minister of Hassanemesit, at first went along with the Nipmucks when they came to the town that fall, but after several months of captivity, he planned his escape. In February 1676 Tukapewillin met with a Christian Indian named Job Kattenanit, a preacher from Magunkog, who had been employed by the English to serve as a spy among the Nipmucks. With several other Indians, Kattenanit had been temporarily released from confinement on Deer Island to undertake an especially dangerous mission. [73] (Among the information Kattenanit supplied to the English was a warning of the February 10 attack on Lancaster, though it came too late to save Mary Rowlandson and her family.) [74] While Kattenanit was in Nipmuck territory, he spoke to Joseph Tukapewillin, and the two men arranged to meet in a designated woods later in March, when Tukapewillin would escape with his wife and children, bringing with him Kattenanit's own children, who, according to Kattenanit, were also being held captive among enemy Indians. Returning to Boston, Kattenanit petitioned the Massachusetts Council for permission to rescue his family from captivity, declaring,

> in my jorny I found my 3 children with the enimy together with some of my friends; that continue their fidelity to God & to the English & do greatly mourn for their condition & longe desire to returne to the English.[75]

Unfortunately for the aptly named Job, however, Captain Samuel Moseley found out about his plan and successfully subverted it. Instead of meeting Kattenanit, Tukapewillin and his companions were captured by Captain Benjamin Gibbs and his soldiers, who, Gookin claimed, took all of Tukapewillin's goods, including "a pewter cup, that the minister had saved, which he was wont to use at the administration of the sacrament of the Lord's Supper, being given him by Mr. Elliot for their use." On being brought to Marlborough, the captured Indians were harassed and abused by the English, so much so that Tukapewillin's wife and eldest son and another woman and her daughter ran off and "escaped away into the woods," probably regretting ever having left the Nipmucks. (Tukapewillin's wife even left a nursing child behind with the English.) Soon afterward, Tukapewillin and his remaining companions were sent to endure yet another form of captivity on Deer Island. (On his own return, Job Kattenanit was shipped back to Deer Island.)[76]

During a brief release from the island, Tukapewillin was brought to John Eliot's house. Questioned by Eliot and others, Tukapewillin mourned the absence of his wife and son but insistently declared his loyalty to the English: "I nevere did join with them against the English. Indeed they often solicited me, but I utterly denied & refused it. I thought within myself it is better to die than to fight the church of Christ." Tukapewillin's statement to Eliot is the most eloquent surviving description of the extreme vulnerability of Christian Indians during the war, a vulnerability that had taken more lives than just John Sassamon's. Tukapewillin pleaded,

> Oh Sir I am greatly distressed this day on every side, the English have taken away some of my estate, my corn . . . my plough, cart, chaine, & other goods. The enemy Indians have also taken a part of what I had, & the richest Indians mock & scoff at me, saying now what has become of your praying to God. The English also censure me, & say I am a hypocrite. In this distress, I have no where to look, but up to God in Heaven to help me.[77]

From Tukapewillin's statement, it appears that non-Christian Algonquians hated the "preying Indians" as much as the English did. Tukapewillin reported that Philip had even given his men orders to make sure to bring the most notable Christian Indians to him alive, "that he might put them to some tormenting and cruel death."[78]

Because Joseph Tukapewillin was captured by English soldiers while running away from enemy Indians and because Eliot advocated his cause, Tukapewillin was spared from fates worse than confinement on Deer Island: execution and foreign slavery. Other Hassanemesit Indians were not as fortunate. A Christian Indian named Captain Tom, who, along with Printer and Tukapewillin, had been compelled to go with the Nipmucks when they came to Hassanemesit in November 1675, was captured by the English in June 1676 and tried for treason. While Captain Tom claimed to have been captivated by the Nipmucks, his story, like Joshua Tift's, was not believed. On June 12 Captain Tom was brought to Boston and, as John Eliot reported in his diary, "a great rage was against him." On June 14 Captain James Cowell and other English soldiers "testified thei saw him at Sudbury fight," but Captain Tom denied this charge, claiming that he had been sick during the attack on Sudbury and had "never ingaged against the English." He had only joined the Nipmucks, he claimed, because "a devil put it into his head to be willing to goe with them [and] knowing the rage of the English."[79] On June 19 the Massachusetts Council issued a warrant for several witnesses to appear to testify regarding Captain Tom's loyalty.[80] A Christian Indian named James Quanapaug, who had served with Job Kattenanit as a spy for the English, testified that when he was among the Nipmucks he had seen Captain Tom and "heard him say that he was caried away from Hassanmiku by the enimy though he was also afraid to goe to deere island." Furthermore, Quanapaug had

> heard som of the enimy mock Tom & som heard of the indians carried captive that they cryed when they were caried away, more like squas than men. Capt. Tom also told me that hee was wearing of living among those wicked indians, & greatly desired to bee among the praying indians & englisshe againe . . . [he] told me that hee never had or would fight against the english.

(Job Kattenanit was also available to corroborate Quanapaug's story.)[81]

Although Quanapaug's testimony provided compelling evidence that Captain Tom had in fact been a captive among the enemy Indians, several Englishmen contradicted this account. Edmond Rice, who had served under

Captain Wadsworth, testified that he "well knew Capt Tom Indian . . . that lived withe the Indians" and that he had seen Captain Tom at the fight at Sudbury, "walking with a long staffe Grinning as he went."[82] Even more damning was the testimony of John Partridge of Medfield, who declared that "When the Indians came to our towne of Medfield, and were partly about my house in the fyring of it & . . . I did heare the very reall voice of Captaine Tom." Partridge recognized the voice, he claimed, because he had heard it before the war, when Captain Tom, as a leader in the praying town of Natick, had come "with his natick Souldiers to medfeild & comanded them."[83]

If Quanapaug's version of the story was true, Captain Tom, like Joshua Tift, was judged harshly for choosing captivity over death. Neither Tom nor Tift was able to redeem himself by telling his story or, in Tom's case, by having his story corroborated by Indians loyal to the English. Daniel Gookin claimed Captain Tom was "a pious man" who was simply "tempted beyond his strength; for, had he done as he ought, he should rather have suffered death, than have gone among the wicked enemies of the people of God," but that, instead, he had "yielded to the enemies' arguments, and by his example drew most of the rest."[84] When that "dreadful hour" had come and enemy Indians said, "Come go along with us," Captain Tom and Joshua Tift were expected to give their lives rather than be taken captive and so, in a sense, were Mary Rowlandson and Joseph Tukapewillin, but only two were able to exonerate themselves.

The unredeemability of Captain Tom and Joshua Tift rested, in part, on their sex—it was more difficult for men to explain why they had chosen captivity over death than it was for women. Quanapaug's testimony in this regard is particularly revealing. He said that he had heard that Tom and other captives "cryed when they were carried away, more like squas than men." Intimately familiar with English gender conventions, Quanapaug perhaps realized that Tom's only hope of redemption lay in making him seem as weak as a woman. In a similar fashion, William Nahauton, another Indian intimately familiar with English ways (he had testified against Sassamon's murderers), played to English ideas about gender when petitioning for the release of a female relative being held prisoner in Boston. "Although she did belong to phillip his Company," Nahauton wrote, "shee being a woman whatever her mind hath been it is very probable she hath not dun much mischefe."[85] Nahauton's strategy, seeking exoneration for his kinswoman on the basis of her sex, was successful; she was ordered released.[86] But Quanapaug's suggestion that Captain Tom was as weak as a woman could not save him.

On June 20 John Eliot visited Captain Tom in prison. That same day the Massachusetts Council declared the war's first day of thanksgiving (to be held on the twenty-ninth) to give thanks for their signal victories over the enemy. On June 21 Eliot went to the governor "& intreated that Capt Tom might have liberty to prove that he was sick at the time when the fight was at Sudbury & that he was not here." The governor spoke of "how bad a man Tom was," and Eliot, with unusual rage, told the governor that "at the great day he should find that christ was of anothr mind." The next day, as Eliot walked to attend a sermon in Boston, a marshal handed him a sheet of paper announcing the upcoming thanksgiving. After the sermon was over, the same marshal ushered Captain Tom to the gallows. In his diary, Eliot reported that Tom addressed the crowd and said: "I did never lift up hand against the English, nor was I at sudbury, *only I was willing to goe away with the enemise that surprized us.*" [87] In his own diary, Bostonian Samuel Sewall reported more blandly, "Two Indians, Capt. Tom and another, executed after Lecture." [88]

V

IN NOVEMBER 1675, when James Printer was faced with choosing among captivity among the Nipmucks, confinement to Deer Island, execution, or foreign slavery, he chose captivity. If calling what he endured "captivity" seems somehow inaccurate, that is partly the legacy of Mary Rowlandson, whose narrative established the defining elements of what would prove to be a sturdy genre, the American story of captivity in the wilderness. And yet Printer's captivity made Rowlandson's redemption possible. Increase Mather said the return of English captives was the result of prayer. "For some, prayer hath been more abundantly poured forth; so for Mr. Rowlandson his wife and two children, and we have seen the Lord returning them all again." [89] But in reality, Mary Rowlandson's redemption depended not only on the assistance of Englishmen such as Mather (who intervened on her behalf before the Massachusetts authorities) but also on the negotiations of Indians who had either been temporarily released from Deer Island or had been taken captive by enemy Indians. In a sense, Rowlandson's release from captivity was predicated on those same Indians' own bondage.

On March 31, 1676, the Massachusetts Council released a Christian Indian named Tom Dublett (also known as Nepanet) from Deer Island and instructed him to travel to the central part of the colony to deliver a letter to Mary Rowlandson's captors. "Inteligence is Come to us," the Council wrote, "that you have some English (especially weomen and children) in Captivity among you. Wee have therefore sent this messenger offering to redeeme them either for payment in goods or wampum, or by exchange of prisoners." The Council asked that the sachems respond by letter ("if you have any among you that can write your Answer to this our messenger, wee desire it in writting, and to that end have sent paper pen and Incke") or send a messenger ("provided he Come unarmed and Carry a white flagg upon a staffe vissible to be seene, which wee call a flagg of truce; and is used by civil nations in tyme of warre").[90]

On April 12 Tom Dublett dutifully returned to Boston carrying a letter signed by the Nipmuck sachems Sam and Kutquen Quanohit and transcribed by Peter Jethro, a Christian Indian who had been taken captive by the Nipmucks at Hassanemesit. Although the sachems made assurances regarding the safety of the captives and followed the Council's instructions in the manner of their reply, its contents were disappointing. As one Englishman remarked, theirs was "a very insolent Letter, that as yet they had no need to accept of Ransom for our Captives."[91] Clearly the sachems were aware of the strength of their negotiating position, and the damage the war had done to the English:

> You know, and we know, you have great sorroful with crying; for you lost many, many hundred men, and all your house, all your land, and woman, child, and cattle, and all your things that you have lost.[92]

Apparently the Nipmuck sachems (or Jethro himself) were not especially pleased with Tom Dublett. "We now give answer by this one man; but if you like my answer, send one more man besides this Tom, and send with all true heart, and with all your mind, by two men."[93] Accordingly, when Dublett was sent back for further negotiations, he was accompanied by another Christian Indian named Peter Conway. When Dublett and Conway arrived, Mary Rowlandson spied them and learned their task. "Though they were Indians, I got them by the hand, and burst out into tears; my heart was so full that I could not speak to them."[94] On April 27 Dublett and Conway returned to Boston with another letter, this written by James Printer and not signed by the sachems:

> I am sorrow that I have don much wrong to you and yet I say the falte is lay upon you, for when we began quarel at first with Plimouth men I did not think that you should have so much truble as now is: therefore I am willing to hear your desire about the Captives. Therefore we desire you to sent Mr Rolanson and goodman Kettel: (for their wives) and these Indians Tom and Peter to redeem their wives, they shall come and goe very safely: Whereupon we ask Mrs Rolanson, how much your husband willing to give for you she gave an answer 20 pounds in goodes.[95]

The Council, however, was disappointed with Printer's reply. On April 28 the Council sent the sachems another letter, this time asking for "a plaine & direct answer to our Last Letter." "Wee received your Letter by Tom & Peter, which doth not answer ours to you, neither is subscribed by the sachims nor hath it any date, which wee know your scribe james Printer doth well understand should be." Dublett and Conway, along with an Englishman named John Hoar, returned to Nipmuck country to deliver this message.[96]

When the Council delegation arrived, Mary Rowlandson asked to see John Hoar: "I begged them to let me see the English man, but they would not." During a break in negotiations, however, she was finally allowed to meet with him, and learned of the possibility of her imminent release. Afterward she addressed her captors eagerly: "I now asked them, whether I should go home with Mr. Hoar? They answered No." At the end of another day of negotiations, James Printer visited Rowlandson and Hoar to inform them of the likelihood of Rowlandson's release. The next morning, according to Rowlandson, the Indians "called their General Court (as they call it) to consult and determine, whether I should go home or no: and they all as one man did seemingly consent to it, that I should go home; except Philip, who would not come among them."[97] Mary Rowlandson was released on May 2 and returned to Boston on May 3.

Within two months of Mary Rowlandson's reunion with her husband in Boston, James Printer, responding to an offer of amnesty, returned to Boston as well.[98] On July 8, 1676, as Increase Mather reported,

> Amongst others, James an Indian, who could not only reade, and write, but had learned the Art of Printing, notwithstanding his Apostasie, did venture himself upon the mercy and truth of the English Declaration which he had seen and read, promising for the future to venture his life against the common Enemy.[99]

Like all returning Indians, Printer was required to demonstrate his loyalty to the English. Some submitting Indians began by "crying out against King Philip, and other ill Counsellors, as the Causes of their Misfortunes," and Printer himself had lain the foundation for a possible reconciliation with the English when he wrote in April, "I am sorrow that I have don much wrong to you."[100] It was deeds and not words, however, that the English required. As Thomas Whalley reported, "those that come in are conquered and help to conquer others." Most often, surrendering Indians were required to join the English army in capturing and killing enemy Indians "that Soe lately wear theyre friends" (with the result that "the Indeans are a great teror one to the other & afrayde of the sighte of each other").[101] Thus on July 3 the Massachusetts Council had instructed Daniel Gookin to order Printer, who had likely expressed an interest in securing amnesty for himself, to demonstrate his fidelity "by bringing som of the enemies heads."[102] (Here, "heads" may mean "scalps.")[103] Apparently Printer succeeded in securing the necessary badges of fidelity and returned to English society; he soon returned to his work at the Cambridge Press.

Mary Rowlandson reconciled herself to her captivity by writing about it; James Printer reconciled himself with the English by bringing in the scalps or heads of enemy Indians. Words and wounds are not equivalent, but they are sometimes analogous. James Printer picked up a hatchet and killed Indians, Mary Rowlandson picked up a pen and wrote about them. Both responses helped these former captives redeem themselves and return to English society. Others, such as Joshua Tift and Captain Tom, were not so successful. Of course, Rowlandson's welcome was never truly in doubt; a pious pastor's wife, she was never in danger of being executed on her return. Unlike Joshua Tift, Mary Rowlandson had nothing to answer for—except, perhaps, the memories and the guilt that haunted her. James Printer and Captain Tom, meanwhile, had every reason to worry, despite their former close relations with the English. In the end, what was at stake for Mary Rowlandson and James Printer could not have been more different. Printer killed to save his life; Rowlandson wrote to save her soul.

Mary Rowlandson wrote her way out of captivity and back into the Christian, English fold, freeing herself from memories of life among savages. James Printer could never fully belong to English society (and we might wonder whether would he have wanted to), but he did resume his former place as a printer at the Cambridge Press. And herein lies the greatest irony in the two captives' tales. The abundance of phonetic misspellings in the Cambridge edition of Rowlandson's narrative ("Second Addition," for instance, instead of "Second Edition") has led several scholars to conclude that the type was set by the only worker at the press who was not a native English-speaker: James Printer.[104] Printer, then, not only wrote the letter negotiating Rowlandson's redemption by ransom, he also set the type documenting her redemption by prose.

"Come and hear what she hath to say," the preface to Rowlandson's narrative urged.

> Read therefore, peruse, ponder, and from hence lay by something from the experience of another against thine own turn comes, that so thou also through patience and consolation of the scripture mayest have hope.

Title page of the "Second Addition" of Rowlandson's
narrative. *Courtesy of The Trustees of Boston Public Library*

James Printer placed these inky letters side by side on the type tray: *lay by
something from the experience of another against thine own turn.* It is impossible
not to wonder what he thought. Did he measure Rowlandson's sufferings
against his own? The author of the preface boasted that "no Friend of divine
Providence will ever repent his time and pains, spent in reading over these
sheets, but will judge them worth perusing again and again."[105] Whether
Printer found inspiration or desperation in reading Rowlandson's narrative
will remain a mystery, but the truth of the preface's prediction about the book's
popularity cannot be denied. *The Soveraignty and Goodness of God,* the last and
most enduring of the King Philip's War narratives, was printed four times in
1682. It proved so popular that it was literally read to pieces; of the first edition, only four tattered leaves survive.[106]

Chapter 6

A DANGEROUS MERCHANDISE

O n August 2, 1676, a party of English and Indian soldiers led by Captain Benjamin Church captured Philip's wife, Wootonekanuske, and his nine-year-old son (whose name has not survived).[1] That day, Philip himself escaped, but as even the viciously unsympathetic Increase Mather observed, "It must needs be bitter as death to him, to loose his Wife and only Son (for the Indians are marvellous fond and affectionate towards their Children)."[2] Ten days later, Church's forces caught up with Philip at Mount Hope and executed him on the spot. Meanwhile, Wootonekanuske and her son were sent to a prison in Plymouth, where they lingered for weeks that stretched into months. In small, dark cells, despised by their jailers, they must have suffered an especially horrible captivity.

What eventually befell Wootonekanuske was never recorded, but the fate of Philip's son was greatly debated. The young boy (sadly for him) posed a theological conundrum. On the one hand, vengeful colonists were eager to see him executed. On the other hand, the most obviously relevant scriptural passage, Deuteronomy 24:16, specifically argued against such a punishment: "The fathers shall not be put to death for the children, neither shall the children be put to death for the fathers: every man shall be put to death for his own sin."

While the Puritan clergy debated over whether to abide by Deuteronomy, Captain Thomas Smith's sturdy ship, the *Seaflower*, sailed from Boston Harbor. In the cramped cargo hold, at least 180 "heathen Malefactors men, women, and Children"—and probably more—groaned under the weight of their own misery. Seventy had been sold into slavery by the authority of Massachusetts Bay; 110 came from Plymouth. In the captain's cabin, documents ensuring the legality of the venture were safely stowed away: two certificates bearing official colony seals, one from John Leverett, governor of Massachusetts Bay, and one from Josiah Winslow, governor of Plymouth. Leverett's letter was addressed "To all people," Winslow's "To all Christian People"; Leverett called Philip "an heathen Sachem," Winslow called him "an heathen Prince."[3] But with these and other minor exceptions, the two certificates were nearly identical. Both promised prospective buyers that "by due & Legal procedure the said heathen Mallifactors . . . have beene sentenced & cndemned to Perpetuall Servitude & slavery."[4] With these words the fates of 180 Algonquian men, women, and children were sealed.

Philip's son did not sail on the *Seaflower*. Instead, New England's leading theologians continued agonizing over what to do with him. Samuel Arnold and John Cotton were called on to reflect upon the matter, and on September 7 they issued an opinion that seemed, at first, cut and dry:

> The question being propounded to us by our honored rulers, whether Philip's son bee a child of death! our Answer hereunto is: That we do acknowledge that Rule, Deut. 24.16 to be Morall and therefore perpetually binding, viz. that in a particular act of wickedness, though capital, the crime of the parent doth not render his child a subject of punishment by the civil magistrates.

Clearly not satisfied with this scriptural precedent, Arnold and Cotton had apparently pored over their Bibles for an answer more to their liking. "Yet, upon serious consideration," they continued (adding, and then crossing out, the phrase "& mature deliberation"),

> we humbly conceive, that the children of notorious traitors, rebels and murtherers, especially of such as have been principall leaders and actors in such horrid villanies, (and that against a whole country, yea the whole people of God,) may bee involved in the guilt of their parents, and may, salva republica, be adjudged to death, as to us seems evident, by the Scripture instances of Saul, Achan, Haman, the Children of whom were cut off by the sword of justice for the transgressions of their Parents, although concerning some of those Children it be manifest that they were not capable of being co-actors therein.[5]

Even a young boy like Philip's son, then, could have been "involved" in his father's perfidious treason and hence subject to execution.

Philip's son, however, was not then executed. Perhaps the prospect of hanging a nine-year-old child was simply too grisly, even for those intent on his death. Instead, he remained in prison while the debate continued. On October 20 Increase Mather wrote to John Cotton, offering his own opinion about what should be done with the boy:

> It is necessary that some effectual course be taken with him. This makes me think of hadad, who was a little child when his Father, Chief Sachem of the edomites, was killed by Joab, & had not others fled away with him, I am apt to think that David would have taken a Course that Hadad should never have proved a scourge to the next Generation.[6]

(Mather was here referring to 1 Kings 11:17: "That Hadad fled, he and certain Edomites of his father's servants with him, to go into Egypt; Hadad being yet a little child.") Countering the leniency dictated by Deuteronomy, Mather cited a scriptural passage that could be loosely interpreted as an argument for exile and possibly execution: if hanging was too brutal, perhaps it would yet be moral to sell Philip's son into foreign slavery. But still the boy and his mother lingered in prison. On October 30 James Keith wrote to Cotton, "I long to hear what becomes of Philips' wife & his son." Hoping that New England would continue to be "the habitation of justice and the mountain of holiness," Keith added two more conflicting scriptural references to the debate: Psalms 137:8–9 ("O daughter of Babylon, who art to be destroyed; happy shall he be, that rewardeth thee as thou hast served us. Happy shall he be, that taketh and dasheth thy little ones against the stones"), and 2 Chronicles 25:4 ("But he slew not their children, but did as it is written in the law in the book of Moses, where the Lord commanded, saying, The fathers shall not die for the children, neither shall the children die for the fathers, but every man shall die for his own sin"). Keith wrote,

> I know there is some difficulty in that Psalm 137.8.9 though I think it may be considered whether there be not some specialty and somewhat extraordinary in it, that law Deut. 24.16 compared with the commended example of Amasias 2 Chron.25.4 doth sway much with me in the case under consideration. I hope God will direct those whom it doth concern to a good issue.

When the Reverend Cotton received Keith's letter he succinctly summarized the debate in its margin. On the one hand, "Evil doers shall be cut off," but on the other, "The Children shall not be put to death for the Fathers."[7]

How and when the colonial authorities came to a final decision about what to do with Philip's son remains a mystery, as does the fate of Wootonekanuske. And, were it not for a seven-word postscript John Cotton appended to a letter to Increase Mather in March 1677, we would have no clues at all. All we do know is that Cotton remarked, rather casually, "Philips boy goes now to be sold."[8] Still, these seven words tell us a great deal. Fully eight months after he and his mother were first imprisoned, Philip's son was finally released from prison, only to be sold into slavery and shipped, most likely, to the West Indies. (Wootonekanuske probably met the same end, or else died in prison.)

By the time Philip's son was sold, hundreds of other captured Algonquians, like those who boarded the *Seaflower*, had already been sent out of the colonies as slaves. The Puritan clergy may have decided that Philip's son could neither be killed nor spared, and settled on selling him into slavery as a middle course and, as they believed, a merciful one. Slavery was considered to be just this kind of a compassionate compromise: notorious Indians, like Philip himself, were executed; harmless enemies, mainly women and young children, were forced into servitude for a period of years; and those who were neither notorious enough to be hanged nor harmless enough to remain in New England were routinely sold into foreign slavery.[9]

But deciding to sell Philip's son as a slave was probably not as simple as choosing a middle course between death and service. The surviving correspondence suggests that the decision rested on the nature of Philip's evil-doing. Deuteronomy 24:16, which dictated leniency, applied only to cases of capital crimes. It was, in this sense, inadequate, since the colonists considered Philip to be more than a murderer, to be, instead, a traitor, a treasonous rebel, who had revolted against "a whole country, yea the whole people of God." For that reason his son must be punished so as not to become "a scourge to the next Generation." In other words, it was Philip's political position, his sachemship (a position the colonists always misunderstood), that meant that his son must suffer for the deeds of the father, since only by wielding authority as a leader of his people could Philip commit the kind of crimes of state that would doom his son. (Mather had made this point by calling Hadad's father "Chief Sachem of the edomites.")

And so Philip's boy went to be sold. And so, too, did hundreds of other Algonquian men, women, and children. Yet the sad tale of the nameless boy is unlike that of all the others: his fate sparked a debate; theirs did not. With the important exception of an impassioned plea by John Eliot, the mass enslavement of Algonquian Indians proceeded without any delays of conscience. Instead, a precarious legal apparatus was hastily erected by which their bondage could be justified. Certificates legalizing their enslavement were stowed on board the ships that took them across the ocean. But, paradoxically, the slave certificates' legal justification rested on denying Philip's political authority—the very authority that, in another context, condemned his son to slavery.

Surely it should come as no surprise that the colonists' legal and theological rhetoric was riddled with contradiction, nor that the idea of chattel slavery found easy acceptance in colonies whose population included slaves of another sort: Africans. Still, the story of how English colonists came to sell hundreds of Algonquians into perpetual servitude bears telling, if only because, like the kinds of bondage endured by men like James Printer, it is a story that has been largely overshadowed by Mary Rowlandson's captivity. And, more than any other story of King Philip's War, it suggests just how furiously the colonists had come to despise a people they had once hoped to convert.

I

THE SALE OF Indians into foreign slavery began early in the war, in the summer of 1675, although widespread, systematic enslavement came only a year later, when large numbers of Indians surrendered or were captured. No doubt the colonial authorities hoped the labor provided by Indian servants retained within New England would aid struggling colonists in rebuilding their ravaged towns, while the sale of Indians into foreign slavery would help fill the coffers emptied by wartime expenses.[10] In effect, captured Algonquians were the rewards of war, to be punished to the public's satisfaction or distributed in the same manner as relief funds. The Connecticut Council, for instance, stipulated "that the divission of persons be made proportionably to every County, the quallity of persons allso to be considered, to be as equall as may be, and then to be divided by the committee men to the severall townes in like proportion."[11]

Trading in Indians was lucrative. Between June 25 and September 25, 1676 alone the Massachusetts Bay Colony received £397.13 for 188 "prisoners of war sold."[12] (The going rate for Indian prisoners was about three pounds a head, a rate consistent with Samuel Sewall's observation, made on July 1, 1676, that "9 Indians sold for 30£," but somewhat more than James Oliver received when he sold "47 Indians, young and old, for 80£ in money."[13]) Given the potential for profit, colonial governments jealously competed over who owned which captured Indians.[14] Eager to join this profitable endeavor, independent merchants and privateers also became involved in the trade. In July 1676 Samuel Shrimpton proudly reported to his wife, "I doe verryly thinke that the warr with the Indians draws nigh an End. Wee have lately killed abundance of them & taken as many Captives. I bought 9 the other day to send to Jamaica but thinke to keep 3 of them." [15] (Christian Indian soldiers also profited from Indians they sold into slavery.) [16]

Much of the trade was conducted illegally, and even Indians who worked as servants in English households were vulnerable to being stolen and sold as slaves. In October 1675 John Paine, who lived on Prudence Island in Narragansett Bay, wrote to the commissioners of the United Colonies pleading for the release of several Narragansett men who worked and lived with him but who had been taken away under cover of night. [17] Since the colonial governments had money at stake in remaining in charge of the sale of Indians, those who sold Indians illegally might be prosecuted. William Waldron was jailed in August 1676 for "Conveighing away a Sagamore Indian and other Indians to the Eastward to fyall [Fayal] or to the lands beyond Sea." [18]

The prosecution of such abuses, however, must have been rare, especially since the sale of Indians was, from the start, a confused and at times arbitrary process. Chief among the confusions was the colonists' uncertainty—and even unconcern—about which Indians should be sold and which spared. In principle, those who were not too dangerous were to remain in New England as servants for a ten-year term or, if children, until age twenty-four or twenty-five; more villainous Indians were either to be tried and executed or shipped out of the colonies as slaves. Meanwhile, the most notorious Indians were likely to be executed at the time and at the site of their capture. And so in August 1676 Benjamin Church and his soldiers captured an Indian named Sam Barrow and "told him that because of his inhuman murders and barbarities, the Court had allowed him no quarter, but was to be forthwith put to death." [19] Some well-known Indians, however, did make it to trial in Plymouth, Boston, Hartford, or Newport. [20] Records of such trials are most abundant in Rhode Island, where captured Algonquians were prosecuted as subjects who "trayterously, rebelliously, royetously, and routously arm, weapon, and array themselves with Swords, Guns and Staves, &c., and have killed and bloodely murthered many of his said Majestys good Subjects." Thus Quinnapin, the Narragansett sachem who had "owned" Mary Rowlandson, was there tried and found guilty and summarily executed (Weetamoo, herself a sachem as well as Rowlandson's former "mistress" and Wootonekanuske's sister, drowned in a river while attempting to escape the English and later had her head cut off and placed on a pole). [21]

The vast majority of Algonquians, of course, were not so well known to colonial authorities as Quinnapin or Weetamoo. Most were, to the colonists' eyes, anonymous. And, with masses of surrendering and captured Indians crowding New England capital towns in the summer of 1676, colonial authorities were eager to disperse them as quickly as possible, even if they had little idea about which Indians had surrendered with a promise of amnesty (the offer James Printer responded to) and which had been captured while fighting against the English. Added to this mix were Christian Indians recently released from the islands in the harbor, some of whom had the misfortune to be found among their non-Christian peers.

Efforts to separate these three groups appear to have been largely unsuccessful. In August 1676 the Massachusetts Council admitted that "the Indians lately come in, & have submitted themselves to the mercy of this Government, are scattered up & downe to the great dissatisfaction of many English." The Council ordered an English captain to "take the number of the said Indians & call them all together into one place, & see that they be not permitted to scatter up & downe," but clearly he met with little success.[22] A month later, the Council appointed a special committee to decide how "to dispose of such Indians as are peaceable amongst us, and also of such as are come in upon former proclamations or articles, or may come in upon future proclamation, and submitt to mercy." The committee, in turn, decided that it might be better to kill the worst of the enemy Indians instead of selling them: "Such of them as shall appear to have imbrued their hands in English blood should suffer death here, and not be transported into forreigne parts."[23] Similarly, the Connecticut Council, faced with the same dilemma, set up regulations "respecting the Indians which have or shall before january next surrender themselves to mercy of this Government": all those who "cannot be proved murtherers shall have theire lives and shall not be sould out of the Country for slaves," while the rest would be put into service among the English.[24] But whether anyone in the colonies had the ability to make these determinations remains questionable. Meanwhile, the swift and dubious trials of captured Algonquians had an unintended consequence: discouraging surrender. After an Indian named Wotuchpo (possibly an escapee from Deer Island) was hastily tried and executed for the murder of an Englishwoman named Sarah Clarke, the Plymouth authorities nervously announced that this punishment was an exception, and would not be meted out "against such as killed his enimie in the feild in a souldier like way."[25]

Confusing Christian, surrendering, and captured Indians probably only became more common as the war progressed and the need to quickly dispose of Indians in English territory became more pressing. Predictably, the best-documented cases of mistaken identity, miscarried justice, and revoked promises are those involving Christian Indians, men and women who recorded their own harrowing tales.[26] That such cases were commonplace is evidenced in the many petitions for the release of relatives made by Indians to whom the colonists owed favors. In July 1676 the ever-supplicating William Nahauton petitioned for the release of a five-year-old Indian girl, "kindred to my wife," asking that "shee not bee sold away out of the contry."[27] And Anthony and James, Natick Indians who had attempted to convert Philip to Christianity before the war, also petitioned on behalf of imprisoned friends.[28] Such records further suggest that even Indians who had served the English in a variety of ways—as missionaries, spies, or soldiers—were not necessarily rewarded with their liberty. In August 1676 Daniel Gookin was ordered to send out two Indian spies "to procure all the English captives they can find among them & to bring them away with them" and that if they returned with English captives, the spies "shal have their lives given them & freed from foreign slavery."[29] On their return, however, these Indian spies may have met with considerable difficulty. Peter Jethro, a Christian Indian from Hassanemesit who, with James Printer, had been imprisoned in Boston by Moseley in September 1675, joined the Nipmucks in November 1675, and served as a scribe during negotiations for Mary Rowlandson's release, apparently believed he, like Printer, had been promised his freedom in exchange for bringing in enemy Indians. Major Richard Waldron, however, denied having made such a pledge. "I Promised neither Peter Jethro nor any other of that company life or liberty it not being in my Power to doe it," Waldron wrote in November 1676. "All that I promised was to Peter Jethro vizt that . . . I would acquaint the Governor with what service he had done & Improse my Interest in his behalfe."[30] Similarly, in November 1676, Gookin had to intervene to ensure that Mary Nemasit, the wife of an Indian who had served with the English in the war, might be bought out of slavery. Waldron, who had been unable to protect Peter Jethro, had also mistakenly placed Nemasit with a group of enemy Indians to be sold. "How she came among that company I know not," Waldron wrote to Gookin, professing ignorance of the arrangement by which she was promised liberty and adding, "twas her own fault in not Acquainting mee with it." (Waldron, however, agreed to pay back the men who had bought Nemasit and she was eventually released.)[31]

The colonists' inability to tell the difference between "good" and "bad" Indians led the Massachusetts Council to award a brass medal to some Christian Indians who had served the English. On one side of the medal was engraved an Indian woman, much like the Indian on the Massachusetts colony seal; and on the other, the words, "At A COUNCIL, Held at Charlestown, June the 20th, 1676, In the present Warr with the Heathen Natives of this Land, they giving us peace and mercy at there hands. Edward Rawson." A hole in the top of the medal suggests that the Algonquian who owned it wore it on a string around the neck, probably for years.

A brass medal given to Christian Indians as a reward for service. *Courtesy of the National Museum of the American Indian, Smithsonian Institution, New York*

If the idea that "there's no such thing as a good Indian" has a history, surely this chapter in the story of King Philip's War plays a part in it. For the colonists there seemed to have been literally no way to know which Indian was a friend and which a foe, except by the mark of the medal. (Nathaniel Saltonstall lamented that the English "cannot know a Heathen [Indian] from a Christian [Indian] by his Visage, nor Apparel.")[32] More than the terrified petitions and harrowing tales, the Christian Indian medal suggests the colonists' difficulty in discriminating between Indian allies and enemies, a discrimination that must have seemed irrelevant to colonists who believed that all Indians had become *preying* Indians.

II

IN AUGUST 1675 John Eliot sent a letter to the governor and Council of Massachusetts, voicing his strident opposition to the sale of Indians into foreign slavery. One of his objections was practical. He argued

> That the terror of selling away such Indians, unto the Ilands for perpetual slaves, who shall yeild up themselves to your mercy, is like to be an effectual

prolongation of the warre & such an exasperation of them, as may produce, we know not what evil consequences, upon all the land.

In making this argument, Eliot was joined by the only other colonist to protest Algonquian enslavement.[33] In September 1675 William Leete, deputy governor of Connecticut, wrote to the colony's governor, John Winthrop, Jr., and warned that the harshness of the punishment combined with its indiscriminate application was likely to exacerbate the war. Indians working for the English, Leete reported, rightly

> plead . . . some difference betwixt such [enemy Indians] as are taken by them, & those that so have surrendered themselves to mercy, especially sundry of them being of their blood relations & affinity, whome to surrender for slaughter or forraigne captivity, doth run hard against the graine of nature.

As Leete argued, "in so difficult a time, actuall murderers excepted," it was better to determine "some expedient of a placide composition for those captives, then by an over vigorous & hasty attempt to inforce their delivery of them in hostile wise, least the cuntry should be more enflamed."[34] Leete's and Eliot's prediction that enslaving Indians would exacerbate the war was borne out: fear of foreign slavery compelled Christian Indians like those at Hassanemesit to consider joining the enemy, and the knowledge that surrender could well lead to perpetual servitude led enemy Indians to fight longer than they might have otherwise.[35]

But the bulk of John Eliot's argument was essentially a moral protest and, in that regard, entirely singular. First, he declared that "this usage of them is worse than death," and that death was the proper (and more merciful) punishment for the most dangerous Indians: "To put to death men that have deserved to dy, is an ordinance of God, & a blessing is promised to it." Next, Eliot reminded the Massachusetts authorities that the colony's charter required "the indeavour of the Indians conversion, not theire exstirpation."[36] (Here he echoed Roger Williams' 1654 warning that the fate of New England lay between two extremes: on the one hand, "the Glorious Conversion" of the Indians, and on the other, "the Unnecessary Warrs & cruell Destructions" of them.)[37] Eliot asserted that his own attempts at converting the Indians had been effective and suggested that "To send them away from the light of the gospel, which Christ hath graciously given them, unto a place, a state, a way of perpetual darknesse, to the eternal ruine of theire soules, is (as I apprehend) to act contrary to the mind of Christ." Having been charged by God and by the king of England with the care of the Indians' souls, the colonists would fail their mission miserably if they were to sell those same Indians into foreign slavery:

> Gods command is, that we should inlarge the kingdom of Jesus Christ, Esay 54.2. enlarge the place of thy tent. it seemeth to me, that to sell them away for slaves, is to hinder the inlargment of his kingdom. how can a Christian soule yeild to act, in casting away theire soules, for when, christ hath, with an eminent hand provided an offer of the gospel?

Nor should the colonists consider profiting from such trade, for, as Eliot warned, "to sell soules for mony seemeth to me a dangerous merchandize."[38]

On the whole, Eliot cared not so much for the lives or liberty of captured Indians but for the salvation of their souls, a salvation that could only be achieved if the Indians remained, dead or alive, among the Puritans in New England:

> If thei deserve to dy, it is far better to be put to death, under godly governors, who will take religious care, that meanes may be used, that thei may dy penitently. to sell them away from all meanes of grace, when Christ hath provided meanes of grace for them, is the way for us to be active in the destroying their soules, when we are highly obliged to seeke theire conversion, & salvation, & have opportunity in our hands so to doe.

Finally, citing the bad example of the Spaniards "in destroying men & depopulating the land," Eliot maintained that "the Country is large enough, here is land enough for them & us too. p. 14.26. in the multitude of people is the kings honor."[39]

In making this argument, Eliot followed closely the writings of Bartolomé de Las Casas, the Spanish Dominican friar who had written a defense of the Indians conquered in Mexico that was later published in England as "Spanish Cruelties." In 1550 Las Casas, along with other scholars, theologians, and jurists, was summoned by Charles V to Valladolid, Spain, to debate the legitimacy of waging war against and, in particular, enslaving the native peoples of the Americas.[40] At Valladolid a great debate emerged between Las Casas and the royal historian Juan Ginés de Sepúlveda, a debate that, at heart, centered around the issue of whether it was lawful to wage war against the Indians before converting them to Christianity so that, once subjected to Spanish rule, their conversion could be more easily accomplished.

Sepúlveda declared Spain's war against the Indians both lawful and necessary and, among his reasons, asserted that the rudeness of the Indians' natures obliged them to serve the more refined Spaniards. In making this point, Sepúlveda relied on Aristotle's theory of "natural slavery," by which people of barbarous customs are considered slaves by nature.[41] Referring, largely, to the Aztecs (whom he had never seen), Sepúlveda cited the Indians' cannibalism, idolatry, and savagery as evidence of their barbarous nature. "How can we doubt that these people, so uncivilized, so barbaric, so contaminated with so many sins and obscenities . . . have been justly conquered by such an excellent, pious, and most just king as was Ferdinand the Catholic and as is now Emperor Charles, and by such a humane nation which is excellent in every kind of virtue?" The Aztecs were to the Spanish, Sepúlveda declared, "as children are to adults, as women are to men. Indians are as different from Spaniards as cruel people are from mild people." Among the badges of civilization that the Indians lacked, Sepúlveda offered a list that would come to characterize New Englanders' perceptions of the deficiencies of Algonquian culture. The Aztecs, Sepúlveda argued,

> lack letters and preserve no monument of their history except certain vague and obscure reminiscences of some things in certain paintings. Neither do they have written laws, but barbaric institutions and customs. They do not even have private property.[42]

Rebutting Sepúlveda, Las Casas argued that missionaries must be the vanguard of colonization and that it was unlawful to wage war before attempting to convert the Indians. Aristotle's theory of natural slavery, according to Las Casas, did not apply to the Indians in America, since they were not barbaric in the sense Aristotle required.[43] Moreover, Las Casas rejected Aristotle, "who was ignorant of Christian truth and love," because his theory of natural slavery seemed to imply that God had intended half of humanity to be enslaved to the other. "He who wants a large part of mankind to be such that, following Aristotle's teachings, he may act like a ferocious executioner toward them, press them into slavery, and through them grow rich, is a despotic master, not a Christian." Or, as Las Casas put it succinctly, "Good-bye, Aristotle!" As a missionary Las Casas most especially mourned the loss of potential converts that accompanied the enslavement of the Indians: "The results of such a war are very surely the loss of the souls of that people who perish without knowing God and without the support of the sacraments, and, for the survivors, hatred and loathing of the Christian religion."[44] More than a century later John Eliot would rephrase this argument, modifying it only slightly by adding a Protestant twist: "To send them away fro the light of the gospel, which Christ hath graciously given them, unto a place, a state, a way of perpetual darknesse, to the eternal ruine of theire soules, is (as I apprehend) to act contrary to the mind of Christ."[45]

No verdict was offered by the judges assembled to evaluate the arguments of Sepúlveda and Las Casas in 1550, but the debate itself, and especially the writings of Las Casas, however papist, exerted a tremendous influence over John Eliot, who, like Las Casas, opposed slavery because it led to the destruction of the Indians' souls. In 1550, while the debate at Valladolid raged, Charles V suspended all expeditions to the New World, but in New England in 1675, no such interruption of King Philip's War or of the sale of Indian slaves accompanied Eliot's petition to the Massachusetts governor and Council. There is no evidence to suggest that Eliot's petition even sparked a debate among the Council members.[46] Of all the contestations for meaning and morality in the war, the question of slavery would seem most likely to cultivate debate, yet Eliot's letter stands alone in its declaration of moral outrage.[47]

For Las Casas and for Eliot, the question of Europeans' right to enslave Indians hinged on their potential for conversion, the redeemability of their souls. For Sepúlveda, it was a matter of the barbarousness of their customs, including their lack of letters. But for New England's civil magistrates, their right to enslave enemy Algonquians turned on the justness of the war itself. In New England, legal precedent for the enslavement of Indians had been established in 1641, in a document known as the "Body of Liberties." There, colonists celebrating their own freedom had declared that "there shall never be any Bond-slavery, Villenage or Captivity amongst us, unless it be lawful Captives taken in just Wars."[48] In decreeing that "lawful Captives taken in just Wars" could be legally sold into slavery, the Massachusetts authorities obligated themselves to demonstrate the justness of any war whose captives they wished to enslave. (Thus, in 1645, when it seemed as if a war with the Narragansetts was imminent, Emmanuel Downing wrote to John Winthrop, "If *upon a Just warre* the Lord should deliver them into our hands, wee might easily have men and woemen and children enough to exchange for Moores." Downing relished the possibility, adding, "I suppose you know verie well how wee shall maynteyne 20 Moores cheaper than one Englishe servant.")[49]

While the colonists justified their war in many ways, the particular justification upon which enslavement rested was most fully expressed in the certificates Governors Leverett and Winslow sent on board Thomas Smith's *Seaflower*.

> *Boston in the Mattachusetts Colony of New-England*
>
> *To all People unto whome these prsente may come, John Leverett Esq. Governor: greeting &r: Bee it known, and manifest that whereas Philip an heathen*

Sachem inhabiting this Continent of New-England, with others his wicked complices and abettors have treacherously and perfidiously rebelled against and revolted from theire obedience unto the Government our Sovereign Lord his Majesty of England Scotland ffrance and Ireland, here Established in and other of our confederate Colonies, unto which they had willingly Subjected themselves & have been protected by and enjoyed this priviledge of the English Laws, having entred into a solemn League and Covenant with the Authority of the sd Respective Colonies, and have without any just cause, or provocation given them, broken their League and Covenant, which they had often renewed, and contrary thereunto have taken up arms, used many acts of hostility, and have perpetrated many notorious barbarous and execrable murthers, villanies and outrages both upon the persons and Estates of many of his sd Maties Subjects in all the sd Colonies; without giving any account of their controversys and refusing (according to the manner of civill nations) an open decision of the same by Treaty or the Sword: and Whereas many of the sd Heathen have of late been captivated by the Arms of his sd Maties Subjects, and been duly convicted of being actors and Abettors of sd Philip with sd inhumane and barbarous crueltys murder, outrages and vilainies. Wherefore by due and legall procedure the sd heathen Malefactors men, women, and Children have been Sentenced & condemned to perpetuall Servitude and by speciall Li-cense Seventy of the sd Malefactors are transported in ths Ship—Sea-fflower-Thomas Smith Comander to be made Sale of in any of his sd Majesties Dominions or the Dominions of any other Christian Prince. In Testimony whereof I the sd Govr have Signed this prsent with my hand and caused them to be Sealed with the publique Seal of the aboue written Colony this twelfth day of Septembr . . . Annos Dm. 1676.

—JOHN LEVERETT,
September 12, 1676

Leverett's and Winslow's slave certificates were intended to guarantee the legality of the means by which the Indians had been enslaved, and that guarantee, in turn, rested on establishing the justness of the war itself. To that end the two governors made three important points:

1. Philip and his allies had once "willingly Subjected themselves" to the king of England, "having entred into a solemn League and Covenant" with his colonies in New England.

2. They had since "treacherously and perfidiously rebelled against and revolted from theire obedience" to the king by taking up arms and attacking his subjects.

3. They had resisted all efforts at negotiation, diplomacy, and treaty, having failed to give "any account of their controversys and refusing (according to the manner of civill nations) an open decision of the same."[50]

To demonstrate the Wampanoags' subjection to the king of England, Leverett referred to the leagues of covenant that Philip and, before him, Massasoit had signed. In the most recent of these covenants, signed in 1671, Philip and his people had "formally submitted ourselves and our People unto the Kings Majesty of England, and to the Colony of New Plimouth."[51] (Leverett simply cited these covenants, but several printed accounts of the war reproduced them in full.) In betraying this covenant, Leverett argued, Philip and his "wicked complices" had "rebelled" against a government to which they had previously pledged their "subjection," and now practiced "many notorious barbarous and execrable murthers, villanies and outrages."[52] Implicitly, Leverett also denied the possibility of native sovereignty in his choice of words, since only subjects "rebel" while true nations wage war.[53]

Yet in this very argument there lies a critical contradiction. On the one hand, Philip and his allies were said to be sovereign peoples, competent, though unwilling, to engage in negotiation and diplomacy with other nations. On the other hand, Philip and his allies were declared subjects of the king of England, with all the rights and responsibilities such subjection affords. (This ambiguity, over whether Indian peoples are sovereign or subjected, would lie at the heart of Indian-white relations in the colonies and later the union, until the U.S. Supreme Court ruling in *Cherokee Nation* v. *Georgia* in 1831, in which John Marshall would assign Indians the unique status of "domestic, dependent nations.")[54] Moreover, it is unclear whether either of these statuses legally justified the Indians' enslavement by the standards of the day. If Philip and his allies were truly treasonous subjects of the king of England, execution, not enslavement, was their proper punishment. And if sovereign, surely they could not be consigned with such equanimity to the ultimate unsovereignty of chattel slavery.

The two conditions of sovereignty, by European standards, were authority and possession. As the sixteenth-century Spanish friar Francisco Vitoria had articulated it, the question of whether Indians had sovereignty or "dominion" rested on whether they "were true masters of their private chattels and possessions, and whether there existed among them any men who were true princes and masters of the others."[55] (Vitoria died in 1546, or else he, too, would surely have been invited to the debate at Valladolid in 1550.) While Vitoria determined that the Indians of New Spain satisfied both of these conditions, English colonists in New England were, at first, far more ambivalent about Indian sovereignty and, later, certain that it was an impossibility. Regarding possession, the English typically considered Indians to be homeless nomads who could not own land since they did not "improve" it, while at the same time believing those same Indians could legally sell their land to eager

English purchasers.[56] Meanwhile, some early English observers recognized Indian "authority" in the form of an established, hierarchical government (Vitoria's "true princes"), and were quick to identify sachems as monarchs: "For their governors they have kings, which they call saggamores, some greater and some lesser, according to the number of their subjects."[57] Others, however, disagreed, arguing that "their sagamores are no kings, as I verily believe, for I can see no government or law amongst them but club law; and they call all masters of ships sagamores, or any other man that they see have a command of men."[58] In the end, the colonists' evaluation of Indian sovereignty was merely an extension of their thinking about Indian possession: Indians were only sovereign enough to give their sovereignty away.

Yet, in spite of the colonists' insistence that leaders like Philip had the authority to submit "their people" to the king of England, this was most likely a misperception, and, as such, part of a broader misunderstanding of native political culture. Nowhere is this misunderstanding better illustrated than in the colonists' fears of an Indian conspiracy. New England colonists feared, above all else, that Philip headed a "generall (if not universall)" plot whose full extent was ultimately unknowable—"how far his tribes may spread is with the Lord our God to order."[59] Most colonists claimed to have "Great Reason to beleeve that there is an universall Combination of the indians," even if evidence of a conspiracy was lacking, and nearly all were convinced that "the confederacy of the indians is larger than yet we see."[60] Samuel Gorton, who concluded that such fears were unfounded, was, as usual, of a different mind than his fellow colonists. "There is a rumour as though all the Indians were in combination and confederacie to exterpate and root out the English," Gorton observed. "For my own part," he boasted, "I fear no such thing."[61]

Gorton was almost certainly right, but it is easy enough to see why the English were prone to suspect such a conspiracy. They believed, after all, that the Indians would behave as they themselves had and ally with their "countrymen." Meanwhile, most Indians expected the English to behave as they themselves did, loyal largely to a single tribe, and failed to understand why the colonists were obligated to what must have seemed to them a distant and weak authority. When a group of Narragansett Indians asked Roger Williams "why the Massachusets and Rode Island rose, and joynd with Plymmouth against Phillip and left not Phillip and Plymmouth to fight it out," Williams found it necessary to give them a lesson in English political culture. "All the Colonies were Subject to one King Charls," Williams explained, "and it was his pleasure and our Dutie and Engagement for one English man to stand to the death by Each other in all parts of the world."[62] A few weeks earlier John Easton had considered it necessary to issue a similar warning to the Wampanoags.

If "blud was spilt" in a war against the English, Easton cautioned, "that in-gadged all Englishmen for we wear to be all under one king."[63]

When both the Narragansetts and Wampanoags fought against English colonists, the colonists assumed that the two tribes (and possibly others, some as far away as Maryland and Virginia) had formed a powerful alliance, but when colonists from both Plymouth and Massachusetts allied, the Indians assumed that each colony must have a separate grievance.[64] These twin reactions—the colonists' fear of a widespread Indian conspiracy, and the Indians' perplexity at the ties that bound all colonists to a distant monarch—suggest just how poorly the two peoples understood each other's political cultures and systems of government. For the Indians, the colonists' (perhaps willful) mis-understanding of the nature of Indian political authority had far-reaching consequences, the most important of which was the denial of Indian sover-eignty, a perception that formed the underpinnings of the legality of their enslavement.

Exactly because the enslavement of Indians gave few New England colonists pause, it must be considered as a critical step in the evolution toward an increasingly racialized ideology of the differences between Europeans and Indians. Unlike the sixteenth-century Spanish, seventeenth-century English colonists in New England failed to articulate an elaborate or cohesive philos-ophy of racial difference. Yet a growing perception of difference, however poorly stated or unelaborated, had begun to pervade the colonists' thinking. Much as New England's colonists might seem to borrow bits and pieces of moral or political philosophy articulated during the debate about the Spanish conquest (Leverett drawing, implicitly, from Vitoria, or Eliot explicitly citing Las Casas), most of these borrowings were uncredited. Even as the specter of "Spanish Cruelties" haunted Englishmen and -women in New England, its moral underpinnings had become largely incorporated into their own world-view. There was no need for the Massachusetts Council to debate the legality and morality of enslaving captured Indians; the 1641 Body of Liberties an-swered any legal arguments, and the sneaking though widespread suspicion that Indians were in fact less than human (and thus satisfied Aristotle's con-ditions for what constituted natural slaves) answered any moral complaints. Most important, a public response to Eliot's petition was unnecessary, at least in part, because that question had already been settled, in a sense, in Val-ladolid more than a century earlier.

In every measurable way King Philip's War was a harsher conflict than any Indian-English conflict that preceded it. It took place on a grander scale; it lasted longer; the methods both sides employed were more severe; and the language the English adopted to justify and document it was more dismissive of Indian culture—Indian religious beliefs; Indian warfare; Indians' use of the land; and, ultimately, Indian sovereignty—than it had ever been before. In some important ways King Philip's War was a defining moment, when any lingering, though slight, possibility for Algonquian political and cultural autonomy was lost and when the English moved one giant step closer to the worldview that would create, a century and a half later, the Indian removal policy adopted by Andrew Jackson.

What the colonists moved toward (but never fully embraced) in their writing about King Philip's War was the idea that Indians were not, in fact, truly human, or else were humans of such a vastly different race as to be considered essentially, and biologically, inferior to Europeans. Europeans had contemplated this possibility from their first encounters with America, but, as many historians have pointed out, a rigid system of racial classification would be centuries in development. Although the excessive concern about Indian and English identities and the reinforcement of boundaries between the two peoples are arguably the most salient features of King Philip's War, colonists rarely expressed this concern in explicitly racial terms. For the most part this concern can be better understood as part of a set of anxieties about cultural or even ethnic identities and, for the English to a limited extent, about an emerging sense of national identity (as English men and women, not as Americans). Nevertheless, signposts pointing toward racial taxonomies can be spotted at occasional moments of intense cultural conflict. A sense of racial identity emerges by the English, for instance, when the colonists persistently make ideological, if not necessarily always linguistic, distinctions between "slaves" and "captives"; only because Indians are somehow less than human can they be fully enslaved in a way Europeans never could.

III

WHEN NATHANIEL SALTONSTALL'S *Continuation of the State of New-England* was printed in early 1676, it appeared, as advertised on the title page, *Together with an Account of the Intended Rebellion of the Negroes in the Barbadoes.* To readers in London, King Philip's War and the Barbadian rebellion must have seemed bound together even more tightly than the stitching in the book's binding. In the summer of 1675, while King Philip's War raged in New England, hundreds of African slaves in Barbados had allegedly contrived a massive rebellion that, had it not been discovered, might have forced the English colonists to flee the island. Terrified English colonists in Barbados believed that the Africans had "intended to Murther all the White People there," just as panicked English colonists in New England feared that the

Indians had "risen almost round the countrey."[65] The parallels between the two uprisings were uncanny and profoundly disquieting. Barbados and New England, Saltonstall suggested, had *tasted of the same Cup.*"[66]

Meanwhile, in Virginia, still more terror loomed. In the winter of 1676, bands of Indians began attacking outlying English settlements, and William Berkeley, the colony's governor, was not inclined to see this series of events as mere coincidence, either. If Barbados and New England tasted of the same cup, so did Virginia. "The infection of the Indianes in New-England," Berkeley maintained, "has dilated it selfe to the Merilanders and the Northern parts of Virginia."[67] Jonathan Atkins, governor of Barbados, agreed. In November 1675 Atkins warned London officials that "the ships from New England still bring advice of burning, killing, and destroying daily done by the Indians, and the infection extends as far as Maryland and Virginia."[68] Fearful of a similar "infection," Atkins must have resolved that ships from New England might bring bad news to Barbados, but they would not be allowed to bring bad Indians. In June 1676 the Barbadian legislature passed an act "to prevent the bringing of Indian slaves, and as well to send away and transport those already brought to this island from New England and adjacent colonies, being thought a people of too subtle, bloody and dangerous inclination to be and remain here."[69] Now, New Englanders' vicious words of war, calling Indians "subtle, bloody and dangerous," came back to haunt them, making one of their most valuable wartime commodities, Indian slaves, almost entirely unmarketable.

Jonathan Atkins and the Barbadian legislature no doubt learned of the abominableness of New England's Indians through letters or informal reports or by reading any one of the printed pamphlets, gazettes, or books about the war brought by ship to ports throughout the English-speaking world. Yet they need not have looked so far. When New England authorities shipped captured Indians to the nether parts of the English empire to be sold as slaves, they literally advertised the odiousness of their cargo. As Leverett and Winslow's slave certificates declared, these were "heathen Malefactors" capable of "notorious barbarous and execrable murthers, villanies and outrages."

No one knows what happened to most of the men, women, and children sold out of New England as slaves. Captain Thomas Smith's *Seaflower* arrived in Jamaica in early November 1676, but whether he was able to unload his cargo there is unclear. The ship itself was seized by the French at Jamaica in 1690, and Smith seems to have died in Boston in 1688. We do know a bit more about Smith himself, however. Thomas Smith was more than a mariner; he was also a painter. His remarkable self-portrait (perhaps the earliest self-portrait in the English colonies) tells us a good deal about the man. He painted himself with a seascape in the window to mark his seafaring and with his right hand resting on a skull, a paperweight holding down a page on which is written Smith's versified philosophy of life and death, and of the "wiles" of war:

> Why why should I the world be minding
> therein a World of Evils Finding
>> Then Farwell World: Farwell thy Jarres
>> thy Joies thy Toies thy wiles thy Warrs
> Truth Sounds Retreat: I am not sorye.
>> The Eternall Drawes to him my heart
>> By Faith (which can thy Force Subvert)
> To Crowne me (after Grace) with Glory.[70]

Thomas Smith's self-portrait, Boston, 1670–91. *Courtesy of the Worcester Art Museum, Worcester, Massachusetts. Museum purchase*

Of Smith's cargo, and the hundreds of other Algonquians shipped out of the colonies, including Philip's son, we know precious little. By the time Philip's son left the colonies, Barbados and Jamaica had both passed legislation preventing the importation of Indians from New England, "being thought a people of too subtle, bloody and dangerous inclination."[71] Turned away at port after port, it is possible that slave ships from New England simply dumped their now valueless cargo somewhere in the Caribbean Sea, or abandoned groups of New England Indians on uninhabited islands. Perhaps some number of them were illegally smuggled into English colonies in the West Indies. Yet one small piece of evidence, a letter from John Eliot to Robert Boyle written in 1683, suggests that at least some New England Indians, after being bounced from port to port, were shipped all the way to Africa. Greatly distressed, Eliot reported that

> A vessel carried away a great number of our surprised Indians, in the times of our wars, to sell them for slaves, but the nations, whither she went, would not buy them. Finally, she left them at Tangier; there they be, so many as live, or are born there. An Englishman, a mason, came thence to Boston, he told me they desired I would use some means for their return home. I know not what to do in it; but now it is in my heart to move your honour, so to mediate, that they may have leave to get home, either from thence hither, or from thence to England, and so to get home.[72]

It is unlikely that Eliot received any assistance from Boyle, or that any Algonquians still alive in Tangier or elsewhere ever made it to England, much less to New England. Twenty years later Cotton Mather found their destination scripturally appropriate:

> 'tis a Prophesy in Deut. 28, 68. The Lord shall bring thee into Egypt again with ships, by the way whereof I spake unto thee. Thou shalt see it no more again; and there shall we be sold unto your Enemies, and no Man shall buy you. This did our Eliot imagine accomplished, when the Captives taken by us in our late Wars upon them, were sent to be sold, in the Coasts lying not very remote from Egypt on the Mediterranean Sea, and scarce any Chapmen would offer to take them off.[73]

Now the New England clergy who had decided to sell Philip's son into slavery might well cite Jeremiah 22:12: "But he shall die in the place whither they have led him captive, and shall see this land no more."[74]

PART FOUR · *Memory*

Our Indian wars are not over yet.
—COTTON MATHER, *1692*

Every white that knows their own history, knows there was not
a whit difference between them and the Indians of their days.
—WILLIAM APESS, *1836*

Chapter 7

THAT BLASPHEMOUS LEVIATHAN

O
n a sultry day in August 1676, in a swamp near Mount Hope neck, Captain Benjamin Church triumphantly announced to his soldiers that Philip had been shot dead, "upon which the whole army gave three loud huzzas." Church then ordered that the slain sachem "be pulled out of the mire to the upland." Some Indian soldiers taking "hold of him by his stockings, and some by his small breeches (being otherwise naked)," Philip's body was dragged along a narrow path, out of the muddy swamp, "and a doleful, great, naked, dirty beast he looked like." Standing over the corpse, Church announced that since Philip "had caused many an Englishman's body to be unburied, and to rot above ground, not one of his bones should be buried." This, however, was not the last indignity the dead man would suffer. Soon Church called an "old Indian executioner," who briefly eulogized over Philip, saying that "he had been a very great man, and had made many a man afraid of him, but so big as he was, he would now chop his arse for him."[1]

Next the executioner beheaded and quartered the body. (In Boston, Increase Mather would later relish the image of Philip being "hewed in pieces before the Lord.")[2] That done, Church had Philip's four quarters hung from four trees, but he gave one bit of butchered flesh, Philip's hand, to Alderman, the Indian who had shot him, "to show to such gentlemen as would bestow gratuities upon him." Alderman earned "many a penny" by this employment (as tradition has it, he preserved the hand in a bucket of rum).[3] Other soldiers may have taken other trophies; in the nineteenth century, dozens of objects said to have once belonged to Philip would turn up in New England museum collections—Philip's belt, his bow, his bowl, and, most famously, his war club.[4] In late August 1676, when Church captured one of Philip's chief advisers, Annawon, he was given "Philip's royalties," which, appropriately enough, may have ended up in Windsor Castle. In the spring of 1677 Josiah Winslow sent "the best of the ornaments and treasure of sachem Phillip the grande Rebell" (his "Crowne, his gorge, and two belts") to the king of England.[5] But the biggest prize of all was Philip's bloody, decapitated head.

Philip was killed on August 12. On August 17 Plymouth Colony celebrated a day of thanksgiving. Such days of prayerful gratitude, like days of fasting and humiliation, had been observed in the colonies for years. Philip's father, Massasoit, is best remembered today for having attended the Pilgrims' "first thanksgiving," in 1621. That thanksgiving, however, was only an autumn harvest festival, not a declared religious holiday.[6] But in 1676, Massasoit's son Philip—or, rather, his son's *head*—made an appearance at a true thanksgiving. On August 17, soon after the Reverend John Cotton finished his thanksgiving day sermon, Captain Benjamin Church and his soldiers arrived in Plymouth, carrying Philip's head. (Church received thirty shillings for it, which he considered to be "scanty reward, and poor encouragement.")[7] Philip's head was then staked on a tall pole for public viewing. It must have been the centerpiece of the celebration. To Increase Mather, the timing seemed providential: God had given Philip's head "to be meat to the people inhabiting the wilderness . . . the very day of their solemn Festival."[8] Even after the feasting of thanksgiving had come to an end, Philip's head remained at its post. For decades. In 1718, when Benjamin Church fell off his horse, died, and was buried, Philip's decaying, desiccated skull may still have cast a shadow over the town of Plymouth.

One fine day, years after Philip's death, Increase Mather's son Cotton made a pilgrimage to Plymouth to visit the head. There, with an outstretched arm, he reached up and "took off the Jaw from the Blasphemous exposed Skull of that Leviathan." Wasn't this a bit much? Philip had already been shot, quartered, and decapitated. Why steal his jaw? Revenge, perhaps. Although Cotton Mather was only twelve at the time of the fighting, he still remembered how "this bloody and crafty wretch" had taught other Indians to "*Philippize* in barbarous murders." (More prolific even than his father, the younger Mather also studied the war and later wrote about it in his *Magnalia Christi Americana*, published in 1702.)[9] But if he was motivated only by vengeance, however belated, why not simply spit at the skull, or smash it to dust? Perhaps Cotton had a more metaphorical motive: to shut Philip up. By stealing Philip's jawbone, his *mouth*, he put an end to Philip's blasphemy (literally, his evil utterances). Perhaps Cotton Mather grabbed the blasphemous bone for the same reason that his father had picked up his pen to write his *Brief History*—to symbolically silence other versions of the story of King Philip's War. Just as Increase had tucked his bulky manuscript under one arm and raced down the streets of Boston to John Foster's printing shop, so Cotton rode out to Plymouth and yanked the decrepit jawbone loose from its skull.

For Cotton Mather, as for his father, King Philip's War was a holy war, a war against barbarism, and a war that never really ended. Some of the tensions that had brought colonists and Indians to war in 1675 were no more resolved when Increase wrote his *Brief History* than when Cotton wrote his *Magnalia Christi Americana*. Questions about the sovereignty of Indian peoples and the legitimacy of English land claims had been more avoided than answered, and, most distressingly, the colonists' fears about "degenerating" into Indians had only been exacerbated by their own "savage" conduct in the war. The incompleteness of the colonists' victory meant that preserving the memory of the war, and preserving a particular kind of memory, one that depicted Philip as a barbarous villain, became as desperately critical to the colonists' sense of themselves as waging the war had been in the first place. Waging the war, writing about it, and remembering it were all part of the attempt to win it, but none of these efforts ever fully succeeded. No matter how much the colonists wrote about the war, no matter how much or how eloquently they justified their cause and conduct or vilified Philip, New England's colonists could never succeed at reconstructing themselves as "true Englishmen." The danger of degenerating into Indians continued to haunt them.

Philip was more than dead, but his war still raged.

I

IN HIS DIARY for the year 1676, Samuel Sewall neatly wrote, "*Philippus exit.*" across from that fateful day, August 12.[10] Sewall hoped, with Increase Mather, that the war would "dye with Philip."[11] (Richard Hutchinson had even optimistically titled his printed account of Philip's death *The Warr in New-England Visibly Ended*.) And, indeed, hostilities did end in southeastern New England—at least temporarily. But the colonists' victory over the Wampanoags, Narrangansetts, and Nipmucks was far from an unambiguous military success. Although colonial forces and their Indian allies had killed or captured thousands of enemy Algonquians, especially in the six months before Philip's death, in the end, the greatest killers of Indians had been disease and starvation, not English soldiers.[12] And the colonists' strongest ally was no ally at all; one reason why many Algonquians had submitted to the English in the summer of 1676 was that they had been driven from their western retreats by Mohawks. (Philip may have made a failed effort to form an alliance with the powerful Mohawks, the eastern arm of the Iroquois League and the Algonquians' traditional enemies.)[13] If Philip's forces had been better supplied and had not had to fight three wars at once—one with the English, one with their Pequot, Mohegan, and Christian Indian allies, and one with the Mohawks—the colonists might well have lost everything. And they knew it. At the end of the war, William Harris claimed that had "the Indeans not bin devided, they might have forced us to Som Islands: & there to have planted a litle Corne, & fished for our liveings."[14] And Increase Mather declared, "as to Victoryes obtained, we have no cause to glory in any thing that we have done, but rather to be ashamed and confounded for our own wayes."[15]

A page from Samuel Sewall's 1676 almanac, noting Philip's death. *Courtesy of the Watkinson Library, Trinity College, Hartford, Connecticut*

King Philip's War did not end with King Philip's death. No peace treaty was signed after August 12, and in many ways the fighting simply became less intense, less organized, and, from the perspective of colonists living in more populated seaboard towns, more distant. In October even Samuel Sewall admitted that while "most Ring leaders" were dead ("having themselves had blood to drink"), "Yet there is some trouble and bloodshed still in the more remote Eastern parts."[16] Related fighting went on for months, especially in Maine, where Abenakis (later also known as Penobscots) systematically attacked English settlements well into 1677. Meanwhile other groups, both Iroquois and Algonquian, would continue to assault frontier towns throughout New England until at least the French and Indian War some seventy years later. In 1704, towns in the Connecticut River Valley that had been partially rebuilt after 1676 were again destroyed in Indian fighting. As a result, historians today are unable to agree on when King Philip's War actually ended. Some consider Philip's death merely a convenient marking point whose military significance was wishfully exaggerated by the colonists themselves and has been similarly exaggerated ever since.[17] Meanwhile, other scholars have argued that King Philip's War never ended because, in a figurative sense, it was the archetype of all Indian wars to follow.[18]

To English families living in southeastern New England, however, Philip's death made a difference. It marked an end to the destruction even if, in some places, it turned out to be only a temporary respite. But when displaced colonists returned to their ravaged homes, reminders of the war were everywhere: in still-abandoned neighboring towns, on gravestones, at battle sites, in the wounds on people's bodies.[19] The war proved impossible to forget; it would take the colonists more than three decades to rebuild what had been destroyed.[20] Writing in 1677, Increase Mather recalled, "we cannot but remember, how near this Tree was to cutting down a year or two agoe."[21] In the years to come, captives taken during the war continued to return from captivity, adding fresh stories to those already being told around firesides all over New England. War mementos—bullets, arrowheads, hatchets, and even body parts—were probably widely collected and passed around at family and community gatherings. Meanwhile, church sermons no doubt dwelled on the lessons of the war, especially on important anniversaries. And accounts of the war would continue to be published in 1677, 1678, and 1682, and to be read and circulated long afterward. Many printed chronicles made their intention clear: "This shall be written for the Generation to come," read the title page of Mather's *Historical Discourse,* quoting from Psalms 102:18. Several also quoted from Exodus 17:14: "And the Lord said unto Moses, Write this for a memorial in a book, and rehearse it in the ears of Joshua."

All over New England, colonists commemorated the end of the war even as they relived its brutalities. When Samuel Sewall wrote the words "*Philippus exit.*" in his almanac, it must have calmed him to contemplate this momentous event in somber Latin syllables (a far cry from the more emotional responses of Church's soldiers, who gave "three loud huzzas"; of Church himself, who damned Philip "to rot above the ground"; and especially of the Indian executioner who told Philip "he would now chop his arse for him"). Yet Sewall soon found quiet, cerebral celebration inadequate to the powerful feelings the end of the war had provoked in him. Seeking a more emotionally cathartic celebration, Sewall probably attended one or more of the public executions of captured Indians that took place in Boston in August and September 1676—he noted several of them in his diary (including that of Captain Tom). And after one of those executions Sewall, along with his friend the poet and physician Benjamin Tompson and five other doctors, conducted an anatomical dissection of "the middlemost of the Indian executed the day before." Standing above the split corpse, one of the men reached into the abdomen and, "taking the heart in his hand, affirmed it to be the stomack."[22] Sewall might have laughed at the wittiness of the remark. The joke, purposefully mistaking an Indian's heart for his stomach, mocked Indians' supposed heartlessness (who have only guts), and, knowingly or not, echoed Benjamin Tompson's own couplet ("Indians spirits need / No grounds but lust to make a Christian bleed"). Marking Philip's death in his calendar in Latin might have satisfied Sewall's intellectual need to document the end of the war, but in dissecting the corpse of an executed Indian, Sewall staged for himself a physical encounter with the "remains" of the war and a vivid verification of the colonists' victory. He, too, needed to soak his hands in blood.

Much of war's immediate commemoration, like Sewall's dissection, was bloody. Not only Philip's head but also other, perhaps less gruesome memorabilia were displayed and distributed throughout the colonies. Josiah Winslow's affection for what he called "Indian rareties" was neither unique nor novel. From the earliest months of the war, mementos of the enemy, mainly body parts but also bits of clothing, had been cherished by Indians and colonists alike, a practice anthropologists call a "war trophy complex."[23] English colonists paid bounties for Indian scalps, collected body parts as pledges of fidelity, and were willing to travel considerable distances to visit the shrines of English victories. In the days and weeks following Philip's death, colonists from all over New England journeyed to Plymouth to gaze at Philip's newly decapitated head, perhaps meeting Alderman on the road for a look at Philip's shriveling, scarred hand (or, as Edward Rawson called it, his "paw").[24] The head must have had a reassuring effect on colonists who needed ocular proof that the war had really, finally, come to an end.

Many English soldiers, like their Indian allies and enemies, also relished witnessing the deaths of their enemies. When the Narragansett sachem Canochet was captured he was not immediately put to death but was instead sent to Stonington, Connecticut, where he was treated by Indians in much the same way Church's company had treated Philip:

> that all might share in the Glory of destroying so great a Prince, . . . the Pequods shot him, the Mohegans cut off his Head and quartered his Body, and Ninnicrofts Men made the Fire and burned his Quarters, and as a Token of their Love and Fidelity to the english, presented his Head to the Council at Hartford.[25]

Like the English, Algonquians often dismembered English bodies during the war, carrying away body parts as prizes or erecting them as monuments. In July 1675 the Connecticut Council complained that Wampanoags who had killed dozens of Plymouth colonists "still are carrying thier heads about the countrey as trophies of their good succer in their cruell designes against the English."[26] On another occasion, Hezekiah Willet was slain "a little more than Gun-shot off from his house, his head taken off, body stript," and though the Narragansetts carried the head away with them, they left "the Trunk of his Body behind, as a sad Monument of their inhumane Cruelty." (Willet's head was afterward recovered.)[27] Similarly, during the siege of Brookfield, a colonist named Prichard ventured out of the garrison but "was Caught by those Cruel Enemies," who then "cut off his head, kicking it about like a Football, and then putting it upon a Pole . . . before the door of his Fathers house."[28] Decapitation was the most common form of dismembering, but chopping off hands and fingers was also typical, and, if Nathaniel Saltonstall can be believed, enemy Indians might wear necklaces of human fingers around their necks.[29]

During the war, the Indians' purposeful display of body parts was clearly intended to frighten the English, and in this effort it met with indubitable success. When Captain Beers' company was ambushed, "the barbarous Villains showed their insolent Rage and Cruelty, more than ever before, cutting off the Heads of some of the Slain, and fixing them upon Poles near the Highway . . . by which Means they thought to daunt and discourage any that might come to their Relief, and also to terrifie those that should be Spectators with the Beholding so sad an Object."[30] When Major Treat's forces came upon this scene, the Indians' intended end was achieved: "His men were much daunted to see the heads of Captain Beers's Souldiers upon Poles by the way side."[31]

Much as the English expressed their horror at the barbarity of these practices, they engaged in many of them themselves. When English soldiers came upon English heads on poles, they often simply took them down and put Indian heads in their place.[32] Nonetheless, there are critical differences between the Algonquian and English "war trophy complexes." While Algonquians beheaded almost any enemy, English soldiers were inclined to reserve this punishment for prominent leaders (in England, beheading was a punishment reserved for the nobility).[33] And while the English displayed body parts in the commons of colonial towns, where they encouraged the public celebration and commemoration of English victories, Indians placed their displays where English soldiers were likely to find them. Algonquians hoped to terrorize their enemies; the English hoped to cheer themselves.[34]

Unlike its English counterpart, the Algonquian practice of decapitation had religious significance. Narragansetts believed that the soul (*Cowwewonck*) resided in the brain. After death, the *Cowwewonck* traveled to Cautantowwit's house, a land of perpetual prosperity—good weather, good harvests, good death. To separate a head from its body was to deny the soul entrance to Cautantowwit's house, to deny it a blissful afterlife. In this sense, beheading enemies was a way of winning the war forever, of beating the English for eternity, especially in cases where Indians dug up English corpses specifically to decapitate them.[35] While this meaning was probably lost on the English, it must have had a powerful effect on those Algonquians who saw the heads of their enemies (and later in the war, of their leaders) erected on poles, doomed to restless wandering.

Meanwhile, English colonists who made the pilgrimage to view Philip's decaying skull or who butchered the corpses of dead Indians or fingered the beads of a belt once worn by a great sachem, wanted not only to celebrate the end of the war but also to remember it, to keep the memory of the war fresh in their minds. Samuel Sewall in particular wanted no one to forget. Late in 1676 Sewall, who was by then running the Cambridge Press, printed an almanac for 1677, on the final page of which he issued a boldface warning to his readers: "New-England Remember,—Forget not thy last yeares Miseries, Mortalities, Mercyes."[36]

Possibly responding to Sewall's "New-England Remember" command, the Boston printer John Foster went one step farther in encouraging colonists to remember the war: he included the anniversaries of important events of the war on the pages of his almanacs. In Foster's almanacs there was no need to write in *"Philippus exit."* by hand; the printer had done it already. On the page for August in his almanac for 1679, Foster set type to read: "August 12. 1676. Philip Sachem of Mount-Hope, who first began the War with the English, was slain by Capt. Church of Plymouth." The pages of Foster's almanacs were nearly filled with anniversary notices.[37] The March page, for instance, listed the following reminders: "March 13, 1676. Groton surprised by the Indians,

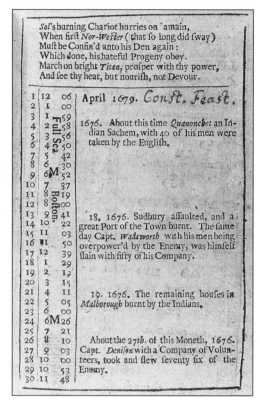

Sol's burning Chariot hurries on amain,
When firſt *Nor-Weſter* (that ſo long did ſway)
Muſt be Confin'd unto his Den again :
Which done, his hateful Progeny obey.
March on bright *Titan*, proſper with thy power,
And ſee thy heat, but nouriſh, not Devour.

April 1679. *Conſt. Feaſt.*

1676. About this time *Quanoncbet* an Indian Sachem, with 40 of his men were taken by the Engliſh.

18. 1676. Sudbury aſſaulted, and a great Port of the Town burnt. The ſame day Capt. *Wadsworth* with his men being overpower'd by the Enemy, was himſelf ſlain with fifty of his Company.

19. 1676. The remaining houſes in *Malborough* burnt by the Indians.

About the 27*th*. of this Moneth, 1676. Capt. *Deniſon* with a Company of Volunteers, took and ſlew ſeventy ſix of the Enemy.

A page from John Foster, *An Almanack . . . 1679* (Boston, 1679). *Courtesy of the Watkinson Library, Trinity College, Hartford, Connecticut*

and the greatest part of it burnt"; "March 14. 76 Northampton assaulted by the Indians, several houses burnt and some persons slain"; "March 17 1676. Warwick assaulted and burnt by the Indians"; "March 26. 1676. Marlborough assaulted and a great part of it burnt. The same day an hot conflict between the Indians and English on Seaconk-plain"; "28. 1676. Rehoboth assaulted."[38]

Foster's anniversary notations shaped New Englanders' memories of the war, both by defining which events were important to commemorate and by setting the tone for the way in which they ought to be commemorated. At the anniversary of the Great Swamp fight, Foster offered a glib couplet: "'Tis fear'd a thousand Natives young and old, / Went to a place in their opinion cold." Foster had no sympathy for the Narragansetts who died that day, and he expected his readers to feel the same. For January 20, the day Joshua Tift was executed, Foster wrote simply, "O Wretched *Tift!*"[39]

But as the years passed, Foster's reminders became less detailed and less frequent. What had been in the 1679 almanac "September 1. 1676. the Indians assaulted Deerfield, and laid waste the greatest part of that hopeful plantation" became in the 1681 version simply "Deerfield laid waste." Now the events of March were lumped together: "In this moneth Groton, Northhampton warwick, Marlborough and Rehoboth assaulted by the Indians."⁴⁰ With time, the war inevitably receded in importance in the colonists' popular culture.⁴¹

Elaine Scarry has argued that the lingering evidence of a war's destruction documents and reinforces its ending: "The very endurance of the record partly explains why the outcome is abided by." Without visible signs of the war's devastation, "etched into their bodies and their material culture," warring peoples can simply continue to fight from one generation to the next. Visible reminders of war mark its end, Scarry argues, and discourage people from resuming it.⁴² Yet there is something deeply ambiguous in the early commemorations of King Philip's War, the etching of it onto bodies and land. Displaying Philip's skull seems to have kept the war alive as much as it put it to rest. The desperation with which the war's artifacts were preserved, its memories cherished, seems, if anything, to testify to the fragility of the colonists' victory.

As early as July 1676 Increase Mather was already warning his congregation against complacency: "Why then should carnal security grow upon us? When some said unto the holy Prophet, Watchman, what of the night? Watchman what of the night? He replyed, The morning cometh and also night."⁴³ In 1677 Urian Oakes cautioned his parishioners against being lulled into a false sense of peace: "These are not Times wherein the Nations beat their Swords into plough-shares, and their Spears into Pruning-hooks."⁴⁴ And then, in 1679, Increase Mather again despaired: *People are ready to run wild into the woods again and to be as Heathenish as ever.*⁴⁵ After fourteen months of bloodshed, followed by three years of intermittent fighting, the colonists were right back where they started, as "Heathenish," as Indian, as ever. Philip's death was only a hollow victory. Depravity still soiled New England. In 1681 an Englishman named Thomas Saddeler fornicated with a mare "in a certaine obscure and woodey place, on Mount Hope," Philip's former home. Tempted by the devil, corrupted by the Indian wilderness, Englishmen were still degenerating into beasts. (Saddeler was branded on the forehead with a "P," not for Philip, but for pollution.)⁴⁶ In 1692 Cotton Mather would echo his father: "We have [become] shamefully Indianized in all those abominable things," he warned. "Our Indian wars are not over yet."⁴⁷

II

IN 1681, five years after King Philip's War had ended, two men met in the woods outside Providence. One was English, the other Indian. Both carried guns. When the Englishman, Benjamin Henden, saw the Indian (whose name was never mentioned), he ordered him to halt, but the Indian "would not obey his word, and stand at his Comand." Furious, Henden raised his gun and fired, "with an Intent to have killed him." Luckily for the Indian, Henden was a lousy shot and missed his target entirely. And luckily for Henden, the Indian was not a vengeful man. "Notwithstanding the said violence to him ofered did not seek to revenge himselfe by the like return; although he alsoe had a gunn and might have shott at Henden againe if he had been minded soe to have done." Instead of shooting Henden, the Indian man "went peaceably away," stopping only long enough to use "some words by way of Reproof; unto the said Hernden blaming him for that his Violence and Cruelty, and wondering that English men should offer soe to shoot at him and such as he was without cause."[48]

Had these same two men met in the same woods five or six years earlier, when King Philip's War was still raging, it is unlikely that both would have survived the encounter unharmed. Henden, if he had traveled at all in Massachusetts, was probably familiar with the law passed in that colony in 1675 dictating that "it shall be lawful for any person, whether English or Indian, that shall finde any Indian travelling or skulking in any of our Towns or Woods . . . to command them under their Guard and Examination, or to kill and destroy them as they best may or can."[49] But that law was, of course, no longer in effect (and never was in Rhode Island), and for his anachronistic and misplaced aggression, Henden landed himself in court, condemned for his "late rash turbulent and violent behavior." The case even led the Rhode Island General Assembly to pass "an act to prevent outrages against the Indians, precipitated by a rhode islander shooting an indian in the woods." In the first place, as the Assembly declared, agreeing with Henden's intended victim, Henden had "noe Authority nor just cause" to command the Indian to halt. "Noe person," the Assembly proclaimed, "shall presume to doe any such unlawfull acts of violence against the Indians upon their perrills." And more importantly, Henden and others like him must learn to "behave themselves peaceably towards the Indians, in like maner as before the warr."[50]

That the Rhode Island General Assembly saw fit to pass a law "to prevent outrages against the Indians" implies that Benjamin Henden was not alone in failing to adjust to peacetime. Random, unprovoked attacks on Indians were probably not uncommon in the years immediately after the war. In July 1677, when two captured Indians were brought to Marblehead Harbor, a group of Englishwomen beat them to death, leaving their bodies "with their heads off and gone, and their flesh in a manner pulled from their bones."[51] As a result, those Narragansett, Wampanoag, and Nipmuck Indians who survived the war, fearing persecution, enslavement, or execution, were likely to go underground, hiding out with other tribes, or to leave New England entirely "to

quitt their old and seeke new habitations farr remote in the wildernesse."[52] Yet
the commonly held assumption that southern New England's Indians "vanished" in the wake of King Philip's War is woefully mistaken, an unfortunate
product of nineteenth-century romanticism.

After the war, significant numbers of Indians lived among the English,
while others lived in small native enclaves. Pequots and Mohegans, who had
been allied to the English, remained on their lands in Connecticut (though
those lands gradually dwindled). A small Narragansett community continued
in Rhode Island. In Massachusetts some Christian Indians resettled primarily in two remaining Christian Indian towns, Natick and Punkapoag, while
Wampanoags on Martha's Vineyard and Nantucket, who had been largely in-
sulated from the war, remained on those islands.[53] (Some number of Indians
also stayed on land near Assawompset Pond, where John Sassamon died, on a
piece of property still known as Betty's Neck, named after Sassamon's daughter.)[54] Perhaps most importantly, a community of Wampanoags living in the
Mashpee area of Cape Cod became a refuge for considerable numbers of
Indians from all over New England.[55]

How those Algonquians who survived King Philip's War commemorated
and remembered the war is, sadly, mere speculation. Like their colonial counterparts, surely they told stories, visited sacred sites, and cherished mementos.
In 1761 Ezra Stiles (a future president of Yale College) visited a Rhode Island
settlement of about 350 Narragansetts, where he met "the oldest Indian alive,
and who remembers K. Philip's War and the Swamp Fight, A.D. 1675."[56] Even
after the last participants died, however, stories of the war were handed down
from one generation to the next and survive today in rich oral traditions.

Algonquians who remained in southern New England after King Philip's
War found themselves in a different world. Many lived as slaves or servants.
Some lived in hiding. But other than on Cape Cod and the islands, few lived
outside English supervision. Nonetheless, as historians Daniel Mandell and
Jean O'Brien have demonstrated, those Indians who remained in eastern
Massachusetts reorganized themselves and even formed a "new Indian identity, based, in part, on their relationship to the land itself."[57] Organized into
churches headed, in many instances, by native preachers, and into towns led
by sachems, Indians in Massachusetts managed to preserve much of their traditional culture, continuing, for instance, to rely on clan boundaries as the primary form of social organization. While they adopted many English ways,
including concepts of land ownership, they often retained native practices. In
late seventeenth-century Natick, where the majority of Indians who survived
confinement on Deer Island had eventually resettled, Indians attended services at an English meetinghouse and organized their town into English-style

house lots, but they lived, by and large, in traditional Algonquian homes, rather than in English clapboard houses.[58] Their culture was neither English nor Algonquian, but a combination of the two.

In the eighteenth century, the external pressures of trespass, poaching, and fraudulent land sales, combined with the internal pressures of alcoholism within native communities, meant that many Indians in Massachusetts came to live more and more like their English neighbors. More spoke only English. By the middle of the century, native languages had more or less died out in New England (though they survived a bit longer in more remote areas, such as Martha's Vineyard and Nantucket).[59] Probate inventories and other eighteenth-century evidence suggest that native communities in New England also increasingly adopted English agricultural and subsistence practices and English furnishings and house styles.[60] This change is well expressed in a petition written in 1726 by Samuel Abraham, a Christian Indian living in Natick:

> whereas I have a great desire to live more like my Christian English neighbors, than I have hitherto been able to do; being weary of living in a wigwam . . . which I hope I should be able to do with more comfort and satisfaction, if by any means I could be able to build such a house, as the English live in.[61]

Elements of native culture survived, however, especially in crafts and trades.[62] And Wampanoags in Mashpee practiced communal land ownership until well into the nineteenth century.[63]

In the century following King Philip's War, New England's Indians did not simply vanish. Instead they became increasingly integrated into the wider colonial community. When Ezra Stiles visited Hassanemesit in 1760 he wrote in his diary, "At Grafton, als. Hassimanisco, I saw the Burying place & Graves of 60 or more Indians. Now not a Male Ind. in the Town, & perh. 5 Squaws who marry Negroes."[64] Stiles did not find the "Indians" he was looking for at Hassanemesit, but he simply may not have recognized them. Because there was considerable intermarriage between Indians and free blacks, some Algonquians passed as white and some were considered black. Stiles would not have counted these people as "Indian," even if they themselves did. In the nineteenth century, census-takers often recorded people of Indian descent as "people of color," "black," "negro," or "mulatto," and thus continued to underestimate the continued Algonquian presence in New England.[65] Algonquians in southeastern New England did not vanish, but at least to whites, they did become invisible.[66]

III

ON DECEMBER 31, 1775, the Reverend Nathan Fiske delivered a hair-raising sermon. The American Revolution had begun just months before, and in Brookfield, Massachusetts, just a day's ride from Lexington and Concord, concerned townspeople sat in rows of pews as Fiske began his sermon. At first he preached not about Tories and patriots but about Wampanoags and Narragansetts. Delivering a commemorative sermon, Fiske marked the centennial anniversary of King Philip's War. To start, he quoted from Deuteronomy: "Remember the days of old." Full of fervor, Fiske asked his listeners to give thanks that through God's mercy New England was no longer in a state of unimproved chaos:

> Instead of a desolate uncultivated wilderness—instead of mountains and plains covered with thick untraversed woods—and swamps hideous and impassable, the face of the earth is trimmed, and adorned with a beautiful variety of fields, meadows, orchards and pastures. . . . Instead of the smoaky huts and wigwams of naked, swarthy barbarians, we now behold thick settlements of a civilized people, and convenient and elegant buildings.

Fiske recalled the brutalities of 1675 and gave thanks that in 1775,

> We are not anxious lest the frightful Savage should spring from his thicket with his murderous tomahawk, or drive the leaden death through our bodies before we are aware; nor lest, when we return home, we should find our dwellings in ashes, our little ones dashed against the stones and our wives carried captive through a perilous, dreadful wilderness, by those whose tender mercies are cruelty.

And yet, Fiske added ruefully, all is not well:

> . . . is there not something that imbitters the relish and lessens the value of these possessions and enjoyments? are not the dangers and distresses, the cruelties and sufferings which our forefathers underwent, renewed in part in our day and practised upon some of their posterity? But what do I say? Are the deceased tribes of Indians risen out of their graves with their hatchet, and bows . . . ? Or has any other nation of a fierce countenance, a hard language, and harder hearts, invaded our territories?

Of this new enemy, Fiske concluded, "When [our forefathers] purchased lands of the natives, they thought them their own: and when they cultivated them for their children whom they hoped to leave free and happy, they little thought their posterity would be disturbed in their possessions by *Britons,* more than themselves were by savage Indians." [67]

Philip had been dead for a century, but now the story of his war was put to a new end. With an uncanny sense of political expediency, Fiske and others of his revolutionary generation resurrected the story of King Philip's War to employ it as a propaganda tool against the British. In depicting the British as more savage enemies than the Indians of King Philip's War, Fiske had hit on a powerful source of revolutionary rhetoric. He was not alone.[68] King Philip's War had become suddenly popular. All over New England, centennial addresses and sermons were delivered, and beginning in 1770, many of the original narratives of the war were reprinted. Benjamin Church's narrative had been out of print since 1716, but, along with several seventeenth-century accounts of the war, it gained a new readership in the 1770s when, with added prefaces and illustrations, the original chronicles were updated for the revolutionary generation. In an illustration from a 1770 edition of Mary Rowlandson's captivity narrative, Rowlandson is refashioned as an American daughter of liberty (in a widely used woodcut), and the title page of a 1773 edition shows Rowlandson under attack from men who look more like redcoats than Indians.[69]

Frontispiece of *A Narrative of the Captivity, Sufferings, and Removes of Mrs. Mary Rowlandson* (Boston: Z. Fowle, 1770). *Courtesy of the American Antiquarian Society*

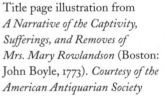

Title page illustration from
*A Narrative of the Captivity,
Sufferings, and Removes of
Mrs. Mary Rowlandson* (Boston:
John Boyle, 1773). *Courtesy of the
American Antiquarian Society*

John Boyle, the Boston printer who published the 1773 edition of Rowlandson's narrative, was an ardent patriot, and in 1775, at the start of the Revolutionary War, he also resurrected and reprinted William Hubbard's history
of King Philip's War, which had lain dormant since its last printing in 1677.[70]
Tellingly, the preface to Boyle's 1775 edition of Hubbard, like Fiske's sermon,
drew an analogy between New England's old Indian enemies and its new
British adversaries: "We of this province, with inconsiderable intermissions,
from that early period, at unknown expense and loss, have been called to defend our lives and properties against the incursions of more distant savages."[71]
In the 1770s, due to the efforts of printers like Boyle, colonists looking for inspiration with which to fight their own war could read William Hubbard,
Benjamin Church, and Mary Rowlandson. Clothed in revolutionary rhetoric,
the memory of King Philip's War was invoked to urge the colonists to free
themselves from the "captivity" they now suffered under British tyranny.[72]
Colonists commemorated King Philip's War during the American Revolution
because of the centennial, and also because the war had a particular resonance
as a metaphor.

Meanwhile, even as seventeenth-century Indians were being used as a
metaphor for the redcoats, seen as simply "more distant savages," many of
their descendants were quite nearby, fighting alongside the patriots. Mashpees

from Cape Cod, Penobscots and Passamaquoddies from lower Maine, and Pequots and Mohegans from Connecticut all fought on the colonists' side in the War for Independence. (All also suffered severe losses, casualties that led, in turn, to more racial intermarriage, as Indian war widows married men from other communities.) But since large numbers of native peoples in the colonies, including most Iroquois, fought on the side of the British, New England's Indians failed to benefit from their service. As historian Colin Calloway has argued, "the fiction that *all* Indians had fought for the British in the Revolution justified massive dispossession of Native Americans in the early republic, whatever their role in the war."

For Indians in New England, the American Revolution signaled not a gain but a loss of liberty. In 1788 Massachusetts repealed a 1763 ruling by which Mashpee had been incorporated as a separate, self-governing district, appointing, instead, a board of white overseers. Pequot and Mohegan soldiers who fought in the Revolution returned to Connecticut only to find whites encroaching on their lands. And the state of Maine gradually claimed most of the Penobscots' and Passamaquoddies' lands in the years after the war. Each of these groups petitioned their state governments for redress. Each failed. The Passamaquoddies even argued their case before Congress, employing the rhetoric of revolution and asking "that we may Enjoy our Privileges which we have been fighting for as other Americans."[73] But none of these groups succeeded in winning their cases.

Perhaps more distressing, American popular culture denied these peoples' very existence. In 1782, when J. Hector St. John Crèvecoeur asked his famous question "What then is the American, this new man?" his answer did not include Indians. While Crèvecoeur acknowledged that Wampanoags still lived in Mashpee and on the islands, his general conclusion was that New England's natives had disappeared:

> They are gone, and every memorial of them is lost; no vestiges whatever are left of those swarms which once inhabited this country . . . : not one of the descendants of Massasoit, father of Mètacomèt (*Philip*), and Wamsutta (*Alexander*). . . . They have all disappeared either in the wars which the Europeans waged against them, or else they have mouldered away, gathered in some of their ancient towns, in contempt and oblivion: nothing remains of them all, but one extraordinary monument, and even this they owe to the industry and religious zeal of the Europeans, I mean the Bible translated into the Nattick tongue.[74]

For Crèvecoeur, Eliot's Indian Bible was the only "monument," the only surviving evidence that there were ever Indians in New England. Just how wide the chasm was between white perceptions of vanished Indians and the lived experience of real Indians had become is suggested in an encounter that took place just thirteen years before Crèvecoeur wrote. In 1769 the missionary Joseph Fish found that Narragansetts in Rhode Island were uninterested in learning to read the Bible; they countered Fish's argument that Christians needed Scripture to know God by claiming they knew the spirits directly.[75] Even as whites came to identify Eliot's Indian Bible as the only surviving monument of Indians in New England (as, in effect, their only "voice" from the past), real Algonquian men and women continued to speak for themselves and even to resist the very culture on which Eliot's Bible rested: the culture of Protestantism, the culture of literacy.

IV

THE COLONISTS' public and private commemorations of King Philip's War in the early years—the almanacs, the skulls on poles, the books, the stories told out loud, the bullet holes shown to children—were intended to keep the story of King Philip's War alive for the edification of generations to come, but most public commemorations were also intended to keep a particular version of the story alive, a version that excluded alternate interpretations.[76] They succeeded. Because few Indians in early New England learned to read and write after Eliot's missionary efforts failed, it remains difficult today for historians to discover those alternate interpretations. But some evidence nonetheless survives of the rich traditions of storytelling by which Algonquians in eighteenth- and nineteenth-century New England preserved memories of the war, perhaps none more tantalizing than a Narragansett tradition recorded in the 1930s. According to this Narragansett story,

> when Philip was killed his faithful warriors, not being able to steal the whole body, for fear of detection, stole the head of their chief and hid it . . . until they could safely bury it, with all the sacred rituals due the mighty chief, who [died] for home and people.

Though "the great sachem's head is buried between Taunton and Mt. Hope, . . . no one knows its resting place." Perhaps attempting to find his way to Cautantowwit's house, Philip's ghost "walks abroad" every three generations and reveals the true site of his head's final resting place to a medicine man.[77] Forget Benjamin Church, forget Alderman, forget the Plymouth day of thanksgiving. This account fully contradicts every contemporary description of Philip's execution. It lends to Philip's grisly death an air of quiet dignity, even as it leaves him wandering, restlessly, forever. Philip is long dead, but his war still rages. But is the skull missing its jaw?

Chapter 8

The Curse of Metamora

O n the evening of December 15, 1829, on the stage of the Park Theater in New York City, "Philip" died again. But this time, Philip
(here also known as "Metamora") did not die silently. This time, at
least, Philip had the last word. When Benjamin Church and his soldiers fired,
Metamora fell, but cried,

> My curses on you, white men! May the Great Spirit curse you when he
> speaks in his war voice from the clouds! Murderers! The last of the
> Wampanoags' curse be on you! May your graves and the graves of your chil-
> dren be in the path the red man shall trace! And may the wolf and panther
> howl o'er your fleshless bones, fit banquet for the destroyers! Spirits of the
> grave, I come! But the curse of Metamora stays with the white man!

On hearing Metamora's final speech, the audience at the Park Theater rose in
wild and reportedly "rapturous" applause.[1]

Beginning with this, its opening night, *Metamora; or, the Last of the
Wampanoags* resurrected the story of King Philip's War for generations of
Americans; it was performed until at least 1887 and was one of the most widely
produced plays in the history of nineteenth-century theater. *Metamora* rein-
terpreted not only Philip's death scene but also many of the main events of the
war. It told of "Sassamond"'s betrayal of Philip and of his subsequent murder
("So should the treacherous man fall, by the keen knife in the darkness"); of

the colonists' suspicion of conspiracy ("Philip, 'tis thought you . . . plot with the Narragansetts, and contrive fatal disorder to our colony"); of Philip's struggles with the colonists over land ("No! White man, no! Never will Metamora . . . let the plough of the strangers disturb the bones of his kindred"); and of the capture of his wife, "Nahmeokee," and their son (after which Metamora warns the English, "If one drop fall from Nahmeokee's eye, one hair from her head, the axe shall hew your quivering limbs asunder").[2]

At its peak, in the 1830s and 1840s, *Metamora* held enormous popular appeal. Lines from the play became household words, "as familiar upon the public's tongue as the name of Washington." Across America "boys of ten years old could be seen and heard almost anywhere taking the position of Metamora . . . and exclaiming: 'Metamora cannot lie!' Older persons would frequently quote: 'The good man's heart should be a stranger to fear and his tongue ever ready to speak the words of truth.'"[3] Many Americans, no doubt, also committed to memory Metamora's devastating, dying curse.

Meanwhile, just a week before that late-fall day in 1829 when *Metamora* debuted in New York, a very different scene was taking place in the nation's capital. There, on December 8, 1829, the newly elected president, Andrew Jackson, delivered his first annual address, an address with fateful consequences for American Indians. Even as stagehands at the Park Theater prepared the sets for *Metamora's* opening, Jackson declared his intention to implement a policy that had come to be called "Indian removal." Jackson proposed to relocate large numbers of southeastern Indians—Cherokees, Choctaws, Chickasaws, Creeks, and Seminoles—to lands west of the Mississippi, by force if necessary. Such a move would at once clear eastern tribal lands for white settlers and rid southern states—Georgia, Alabama, Louisiana, Mississippi, Florida, and Jackson's home state, Tennessee—of their pernicious "Indian problems": illicit trading, violent skirmishes, and fraudulent land sales. In the 1830s Jackson's Indian removal policy would divide the nation, its Congress, and its highest court. It would also bring untold misery to thousands of native peoples. Most infamously, the Trail of Tears would claim the lives of one of every four Cherokees marching from Georgia to Oklahoma in 1838. Disease, malnutrition, and exposure would cut the population of other tribes in half. When the furious dust settled, those "removed" Indians who survived to cross the Mississippi were left in a strange land with few resources.[4]

Presidents before Jackson had advocated Indian removal, just as plays about Indians had been performed before *Metamora*. But *Metamora's* debut and Jackson's address, separated by seven short days in December 1829, intensified and accelerated two developments: the popularity of Indian plays and the pursuit of Indian removal.[5] Two developments? Or were they one? Did the same forces that brought thousands of Americans to see *Metamora* also lead them to support sending thousands of Cherokees to Oklahoma? And if so, why a play about Philip alias Metacom alias Metamora, "last of the Wampanoags"? A century and a half after Philip's death, why did Americans crane their necks in crowded theaters everywhere to see him die yet again—this time defiantly—even as Cherokees fell by the roadside, collapsing with exhaustion?

Metamora, the play, is a tragedy. Metamora, the Indian removal–era phenomenon, is a many-layered mystery. Old cruelties, new cruelties. Old curses, new curses. Peel back all the layers—the play's origins, its actors, its audiences, its critics—and what remains is a struggle for American and Indian identity. Through plays like *Metamora,* white Americans came to define themselves in relation to an imagined Indian past. That definition, however, required that there be no Indians in the present, or at least not anywhere nearby. While *Metamora* played across the country and Americans everywhere read Cooper's *Leatherstocking Tales* by the fireside, the federal government sought support for removing eastern Indians west of the Mississippi partly by invoking images like those popularized in Indian plays and Indian fiction. At the same time, Indians in New England (and possibly elsewhere) turned such images to their own advantage, negotiating the tangled logic of the noble savage and the rhetoric of Indian removal to hold on to their tribal lands and even build momentum for a movement to found a new kind of Indian identity. In the nineteenth century, Philip would come to be the central figure in the story of the war that bears his name, and that story would prove to be even more malleable than it had been during the American Revolution. Those who told it put the story of King Philip's War to many, and often contradictory, uses.

No story about King Philip's War was more popular than *Metamora,* and no act of historical ventriloquism is more intriguing than Metamora's dying curse.[6] When Philip was shot on August 12, 1676, Benjamin Church had damned him: "Forasmuch as he had caused many an Englishman's body to be unburied, and to rot above ground . . . not one of his bones should be buried." After Philip had been drawn and quartered, Increase Mather had prayed, "So let all thine Enemies perish, O Lord!" Even the Indian who hacked up the corpse had made a "small speech" to Philip, saying "he would now chop his arse for him."[7] But Philip himself said nothing (or, if he did, no one recorded it). A century and a half later, when *Metamora* debuted in New York in 1829, Philip finally spoke up. As Metamora fell, dying, he cried, "My curses on you, white men!" . . . and white audiences applauded, rapturously.

I

THE MAN who delivered Metamora's curse was the incredible Edwin Forrest. Far and away the most celebrated American actor of the nineteenth-century stage, Forrest was a burly, broad, and muscular man, much mocked for his unusually large calves (a favorite subject of cartoon caricatures). In later life he would become embittered by a very public and very scandalous divorce, but in the 1820s the young Forrest was just emerging as America's dramatic darling, a theatrical star large enough to rival the fame of more established European actors.[8] In 1828, in the spirit of cultivating "native" American literature dealing with distinctly American themes (and acquiring a play whose title role would be designed to exploit his unique acting talents), Forrest offered five hundred dollars for "the best tragedy, in five acts, of which the hero, or principal character, shall be an aboriginal of this country."[9] The Committee of Award, headed by William Cullen Bryant, selected a script written by John Augustus Stone, a playwright and actor originally from Concord, Massachusetts.[10] Metamora; or, the Last of the Wampanoags quickly became, and remained, Forrest's most successful moneymaker. When he held a lengthy engagement in Mobile, Alabama, in 1844, for instance, his theater receipts for Metamora were far greater than for any other performance—twice the receipts for Macbeth and King Lear in an age when Shakespeare typically thrilled the theatergoing public. In twenty-five years Philadelphia had only two seasons without Metamora.[11]

Metamora made Forrest so much money that the play inspired dozens of imitations and, later, parodies. Fueled by Metamora's success, serious and silly "Indian plays" came to dominate American big-city theaters and small-town playhouses, much to the dismay of many highbrow critics, who found the melodramatic Metamora and its imitators irretrievably schmaltzy.[12] By 1846 James Rees could complain that Indian dramas "had become a perfect nuisance."[13] But Metamora remained one of the most popular of them all. In the frontier states of Indiana, Ohio, Illinois, and Michigan, towns (and probably streets, too) were named after the play's Indian hero.[14] King Philip fever ran high. Antiquarians collected and displayed newly "discovered" relics from the war—King Philip's bowl, King Philip's war club, King Philip's pipe and belt—while a Metamora-inspired Philip became the subject of everything from dime novels to nursery rhymes.[15] Such excesses prompted one observer to complain in 1838 that the "bloody Indian" was now "glorified in Congress; canonized by philanthropists; autobiographed, and lithographed, and biographed, by authors, artists, and periodicals."[16]

Dime novel about King Philip, alias Metamora, c. 1870. *Courtesy of the John Carter Library, Brown University*

Poster for *Metamora*, 1854. *Courtesy of the Crawford Theatre Collection, Yale University*

Although Edwin Forrest prepared for the role of Metamora well before the proliferation of Philip paraphernalia, he was not wholly without source material. The most promising clues about what those sources might have been come from an inventory of Forrest's library taken in 1863 (the year he had many of his books and personal effects cataloged and sold, including his Metamora wardrobe).[17] Forrest owned more than a few books about King Philip's War. The bulk of these were published before 1829, and it seems likely that Forrest purchased them while studying for *Metamora*. Among these works, for instance, was James Fenimore Cooper's 1827 novel about King Philip's War, *The Wept of Wish-ton-Wish* (which failed as a novel but became a successful play and even a ballet).[18] More significantly, Forrest owned an essay by Washington Irving called "Philip of Pokanoket," first published in 1814 and widely reprinted in Irving's popular *Sketchbook* collection.[19] Irving's

King Philip was a warrior bold,
Whose deeds are writ in records old;
He through New England's woods did roam,
And sorrow brought to many a home.

King Philip nursery rhyme, 1853. *Courtesy of the American Antiquarian Society*

portrait of Philip would come to be closely associated with *Metamora*—some newspapers went so far as to reprint "Philip of Pokanoket" alongside reviews of the play, while the Princess Theatre included a lengthy excerpt from the essay on its advertising poster for *Metamora*—and it requires careful consideration.[20]

Washington Irving decided to write about Philip after consulting several early histories of King Philip's War and finding himself disgusted with the colonists' accounts, especially Increase Mather's *Brief History,* in which, he claimed, Mather

> dwells with horror and indignation on every hostile act of the Indians, however justifiable, whilst he mentions with applause the most sanguinary atrocities of the whites. Philip is reviled as a murderer and a traitor without considering that he was a true born prince, gallantly fighting at the head of his subjects to avenge the wrongs of his family; to retrieve the tottering power of his line; and to deliver his native land from the oppression of usurping strangers.

Offering a corrective to Mather's history, Irving urged his readers to see beyond the prejudices of the early historians of the war that they might better appreciate Philip's virtue and mourn that he had died "like a lonely bark foundering amid darkness and tempest—without a pitying eye to weep his fall, or a friendly hand to record his struggle."[21]

While the Mathers had considered Philip a devilish, barbarous villain and even, in Cotton's words, a "blasphemous leviathan," Washington Irving recast the Wampanoag leader as an honorable, patriotic hero, nobler than the noblest of noble savages. In effect, Irving reversed the version of King Philip's War that had been popular during the American Revolution. In 1775 Americans had been asked to think of the British as simply "more distant savages" than the Indian neighbors their forefathers had fought in 1675. They had seen King Philip's War (American colonists vs. redskins) as a crude rehearsal for the American Revolution (American colonists vs. redcoats).[22] Washington Irving disagreed. He asked Americans to identify less with Mather, Church, and Hubbard and more with Metacom and his warriors. Philip, in Irving's estimation, was a courageous leader struggling to free his people from the foreign tyranny embodied by colonial authorities.[23]

Both Edwin Forrest and the playwright John Augustus Stone seem to have been influenced by Irving's "Philip of Pokanoket." Their *Metamora* quite literally enacted Irving's reversal of the Revolutionary-era version of the war. In Stone's script Metamora himself was even made to echo Patrick Henry: "Our lands! Our nation's freedom! Or the grave!"[24] And, not long after the play's stunning debut, a writer for the prominent *North American Review* praised Philip as a leader who "did and endured enough to immortalize him as a warrior, a statesman, and we may add, as a high-minded and noble patriot."[25]

In addition to Irving's *Sketchbook,* Edwin Forrest's library also included copies of two epic poems about King Philip's War: Robert Southey's unfinished "Oliver Newman, A New-England Tale" (begun in 1815) and James Eastburn and Robert Charles Sands' *Yamoyden: A Tale of the Wars of King Philip* (published in 1820).[26] Although Irving's essay partly inspired these endeavors, the original seventeenth-century chronicles remained their chief source of information. Recalling how he and Eastburn came to write *Yamoyden,* Sands explained, "We had then read nothing of the subject; and our plot was formed from a hasty glance into a few pages of Hubbard's Narrative."[27] Finally, Forrest owned a copy of Benjamin Church's original history of the war in an 1827 reprint edition. How this book's text might have influenced Forrest is unclear, but its chief illustration, a copy of Paul Revere's 1772 engraving of Philip, seems to have caught Forrest's eye.[28] That Revere's engraving influenced Forrest's costuming is powerfully suggested by comparing it to Mathew Brady's photograph of Forrest as Metamora. Forrest's "Last of the Wampa-

LEFT: Paul Revere's King Philip. *Courtesy of the American Antiquarian Society*
RIGHT: Edwin Forrest as Metamora, from a photograph by Matthew Brady.
Courtesy of the Harvard Theatre Collection, Harvard University

noags"—his belt, moccasins, headband, and even posture—all seem to echo Revere's "Philip. King of Mount Hope."

To portray Philip, then, Edwin Forrest borrowed from Washington Irving, who borrowed (if grudgingly) from Increase Mather; from Eastburn and Sands, who borrowed from William Hubbard; and from Paul Revere (who had himself copied his Philip from John Simon's 1710 engraving of Mohawk chief Joseph Brant).[29] Metamora was a strange hybrid indeed. Clearly, while Forrest's Metamora flowered in the nineteenth century, he was nonetheless rooted in the rich soil of myth, memory, and history.

EDWIN FORREST LOVED history, and he loved the idea of America. In soliciting and performing a play about "an aboriginal of this country," he saw himself as embracing his nation's past and, more specifically, advancing the cause of American literary independence from England. At the debut performance of *Metamora* in 1829, a poetic epilogue celebrated Stone as the "native bard" who, along with Forrest, "a native actor too, / Have drawn a native picture to your view."[30] Riding on the success of *Metamora*, Forrest later publicly boasted of his efforts "to give to my country, by fostering the exertions of our literary friends, something like what might be called an American national drama."[31] In 1837 Ralph Waldo Emerson declared, "We will walk with our own feet; we will work with our own hands; we will speak our own minds," but three years earlier, Edwin Forrest had insisted, rather more prosaically, "Our literature should be independent."[32]

America's most prominent actor saw himself as uniquely suited to inaugurate an "American national drama," and many observers agreed. A critic for the *Albion* wrote of Forrest in 1848, "He has created a school in his art, *strictly American*, and *he stands forth as the very embodiment, as it were, of the masses of American character.*"[33] If national identity can indeed be embodied and even performed; if one's political allegiances and cultural inheritances are expressed, in part, in one's way of moving, talking, walking, and eating, then Edwin Forrest embodied Americanness. In the early decades of the newly minted nation, an age obsessed with a search for American identity, Forrest's theatrical performances were, in a sense, at the vanguard of establishing what it was to be American. His expansive acting style was itself based on an explicit contrast with the more reserved style of English actors, a contrast that was obvious to everyone. To American eyes Forrest was forceful and passionate; to English eyes he was vulgar and bombastic. In England, Forrest was often poorly received (especially in the role of Metamora), and his English counterpart, Charles Macready, did not always fare well in the States. A rivalry soon developed between the two actors. During the 1840s Forrest, who grew more rancorous with age, came to believe that Macready was actually sabotaging his career.[34] Yet it was Forrest who hissed from the balcony when Macready was onstage, disgusted at Macready's effete acting style. When Macready came to New York in 1849, Forrest's fans brought the two actors' feud to a head by staging a protest outside the Astor Place Opera House, where Macready was performing. There, what began as protest ended as mayhem; at least 22 people were killed and 150 wounded in the infamous Astor Place Riot.[35]

The Astor Place Riot was undoubtedly a product of class antagonisms symbolized by the contrasting styles of Forrest (the hardy common man) and Macready (the delicate aristocrat). Within these class antagonisms, however, lay a broader concern with national identity, a concern with defining what it meant to be "American." To his supporters, Forrest's style represented all that was good about America, Macready's all that was bad about England. As one of the Astor Place protesters later explained, "I was not hostile to Mr. Macready because he was an Englishman, but because he was full of his country's prejudices from the top of his head to his feet."[36] If Macready's body, from the top of his head to the bottom of his feet, was filled with Englishness, then Forrest's was filled with Americanness. Yet, ironically, Forrest was most American when he played an *Indian*.[37] Only by appropriating Indianness did Forrest most effectively distinguish himself from all that was English. Without its aboriginal heritage, America was only a more vulgar England, but with it, America was its own nation, with a unique culture and its own ancestral past.[38]

Critics called Edwin Forrest the "very embodiment . . . of the masses of American character" even as they called him, as Metamora, "the complete embodiment of our idea of King Phillip." Forrest was at once "strictly American" and "wholly Indian."[39] "For the portraying of such personages, we say again Mr. F is peculiarly suited," a critic for the *New York Morning Herald* insisted in 1837:

> His hoarse voice, uncontrolled by art—his sullen features, his dogged walk, his athletic frame, and his admirable personations of the transitions of the mind from calmness to passion, are lofty and enviable qualifications for the attainment of excellence in this range of the drama.[40]

William Alger, a friend of Forrest as well as his earliest biographer, claimed that Forrest as an Indian

> appeared the human lord of the dark wood and the rocky shore, and the natural ruler of their untutored tenants; the soul of the eloquent recital, the noble appeal, and the fiery harangue; the embodiment of a rude magnanimity, a deep domestic love, an unquivering courage and fortitude, an instinctive patriotism and sense of justice, and a relentless revenge.[41]

Forrest became "wholly Indian" by careful study of the sources in his library—Cooper, Irving, Revere, Church—and also by undergoing a profound physical transformation. He literally metamorphosed into Metamora. "Never did an actor more thoroughly identify and merge himself with his part than Forrest did in Metamora. . . . The carriage of his body, the inflections of his voice, his facial expressions, the very pose of his head and neck and shoulders, were new."[42] He took on not only the costuming but also the bearing and accents of an Indian (or, rather, of his idea of an Indian). "So accurate had been his observations that he caught the very manner of their breathing. . . . Everything that could be absorbed by one nature from another was absorbed and embodied and represented."[43] (Forrest himself apparently identified with

Metamora on a more intimate level as well: in personal correspondence he referred to his mistress as "Nahmeokee.")[44]

Forrest often attributed his success in the role of Metamora to time allegedly spent with a close friend, a Choctaw Indian named Push-ma-ta-ha. The two men shared a curiously physical and romantic if not sexual relationship. As William Alger himself admitted, "A genuine friendship grew up between this chief and Forrest, not without some touch of simple romance." Forrest's love for Push-ma-ta-ha was based on admiration (Push-ma-ta-ha was "a natural orator of a high order") and on physical attraction. During the mid-1820s, when Forrest briefly lived with Push-ma-ta-ha, the two men are said to have been lying around a campfire, far from the Choctaw village, when "Forrest asked [Push-ma-ta-ha] to strip himself and walk to and fro before him between the moonlight and the firelight, that he might feast his eyes and his soul on so complete a physical type of what man should be. The young chief, without a word, cast aside his Choctaw garb and stepped forth with a dainty tread, a living statue of Apollo in glowing bronze." (Alger claims Forrest later recalled, "My God, what a contrast he was to some fashionable men I have since seen, half made up of false teeth, false hair, padding, gloves, and spectacles!")[45]

A trifle uncomfortable with Forrest's longing for Push-ma-ta-ha's body, Alger (biographer-cum-hagiographer) felt compelled to explain, "Like an artist, or like an antique Greek, Forrest had a keen delight in the naked form of man, feeling that the best image of God we have is nude humanity in its perfection, which our fashionable dresses so travesty and degrade."[46] But the "simple romance" between Forrest and Push-ma-ta-ha is, it would seem, far more complicated; at the very least, it speaks to the broader attraction the idealized Indian held for Americans in the first half of the nineteenth century. Forrest admired Push-ma-ta-ha for his primitiveness but also for his unfettered masculinity. The nakedness that, in the seventeenth century, signaled depravity and disorder now signaled virility and liberty. In the spirit of the writings of James Fenimore Cooper, Forrest saw Push-ma-ta-ha as a man uncompromised by the feminizing (European-derived) forces in American life—the constraints of living in a city, the dictates of (European) fashion, the etiquette of civilized society.[47] In contemplating Philip's life, Washington Irving had himself reflected on the opposition between the artifices of civilized man and the naturalness of the Indian, "free from the restraints and refinements of polished life."[48] Now, in the fine form of Push-ma-ta-ha's body, Forrest and others like him saw a new way for Americans to define themselves, to forge a national identity by taking on the unique Americanness of America's indigenous inhabitants. In performing Indianness, Forrest, in a sense, "imagined" himself into a new national identity; he performed "Americanness."[49]

Forrest became Metamora in the same way he wished for Americans to become Indian, to take on their unique American inheritance, thereby distinguishing themselves from Europeans and European culture, and particularly from all that was English, to become American by becoming Indian.[50] This was a far cry from what Increase Mather had had in mind when he had admonished, "Christians in this Land have become too like unto the Indians."[51]

II

Metamora made money but it drew fire. Most often, reviewers objected to the play's whitewashing (so to speak) of Philip. Writing in 1830, the critic for the *American Quarterly Review* proposed that perhaps Edwin Forrest's fame gave the role of Metamora—and the character of Philip—a legitimacy it did not otherwise deserve:

> Mr. Forrest, by virtue of some considerable reputation as an actor, carried this heavy play on his shoulders from one end of the Union to the other; and its performance is nightly witnessed by crowded theaters, applauding with strange enthusiasm the reckless cruelties of a bloody barbarian, who stabs his subjects like pigs, and delights the white men of the present day, by burning the villages of their forefathers, and involving women and children in one indiscriminate massacre. Let us hope, for the honour of humanity, that this applause is bestowed on Mr. Forrest, rather than the ferocious savage whom he impersonates.[52]

Similar alarm at the conflation of a fictionalized Philip with the historical Philip had greeted reviews of *Yamoyden* a decade earlier. In the *North American Review,* John Gordon Palfrey complained, "we doubt whether poetically, and we do not doubt whether historically speaking, it was best to represent the settlers as entirely in the wrong, and the Indians as wholly in the right." Attempting to distinguish between artistic license and historical accuracy, Palfrey continued, "If the authors found that this representation of the conduct of the English settlers towards the native tribes answered best the purposes of their plan, they are chargeable with no transgression of poetical rules. But when they adhere to it in the notes, we are obliged to suppose that such was in reality their view of the subject."[53]

Palfrey might compare *Yamoyden*'s text to its footnotes, but critics of *Metamora* found themselves considerably more confused about the real meaning of the play. Even the applause was ambiguous. The *American Quarterly Review* critic was uncertain whether audiences were cheering Forrest or "the ferocious savage whom he impersonates." The risk of playing Indian to become American was playing Indian too convincingly. The more authentic Forrest's Indian, the more worrisome the applause. If spectators were seduced by the tragedian's seamless acting into believing that he really was an Indian, then they were applauding a "bloody barbarian." If, on the other hand, they were keenly aware that he was only a stage Indian, albeit an engaging one, enthusiastic audiences were simply acknowledging Forrest's quite considerable talents and joining in his appreciation for America's Indian heritage. Either way, Forrest's Indian authenticity was at the heart of the dilemma. William Alger claimed that "when [Forrest] came to impersonate Metamora it was the genuine Indian who was brought upon the stage, merely idealized a little in some of his moral features."[54] Other critics insisted rather more honestly that Forrest was only "the impersonation of the Indian of romance. The Indian in his *true* character never *can* find a representative among the whites. Disgust, rather than admiration, would ensue, but if the author made him successful, our prejudices would revolt at the scene."[55]

One test of whether white audiences applauded Forrest's impressive acting or Philip's bloody barbarism is to be found in just such a revolt. When Forrest's portrayal seemed, to some white audiences, too true, too authentic, disgust was indeed forthcoming. In Augusta, Georgia, in 1831, a full house turned tempestuous during the "council-scene" of Act Two when, after being interrogated by a colony officials regarding "Sassamond"'s death, Metamora delivers perhaps the most belligerent speech of the play:

> White man, beware! The mighty spirits of the Wampanoag race are hovering o'er our heads; they stretch out their shadowy arms to me and ask for vengeance; they shall have it. The wrath of the wronged Indian shall fall upon you like a cataract that dashes the uprooted oak down the mighty chasms. The war whoop shall start you from your dreams at night, and the red hatchet gleam in the blaze of your burning dwellings! From the east to the west, in the north and in the south shall cry of vengeance burst, till the lands you have stolen groan under your feet no more!

After delivering this speech, Metamora throws his hatchet into the stage, gives a war whoop, and disappears. The crowd in Augusta was not pleased. An actor in the audience recalled,

> Evident dissatisfaction had begun to find expression long before the climax was reached, and as the chief rushed from the stage he was followed by loud yells and a perfect storm of hisses from the excited audience, who seemed in

their fury to tear everything to pieces. Order was with difficulty restored, and the performance continued till the curtain fell upon the dying chief amid unqualified evidences of disapprobation.[56]

The following day a local judge declared,

Any actor who could utter such scathing language, and with such vehemence, must have the whole matter at heart. Why, his eyes shot fire and his breath was hot with the hissing of his ferocious declamation. I insist upon it, Forrest believed in that d——d Indian speech, and it is an insult to the whole community.[57]

No one showed up for the next night's performance, and the play's run in Augusta was eventually canceled.[58]

Evidently the people of Augusta had taken Forrest's "d——d Indian speech" as a personal attack, a direct indictment of their own treatment of Indians. When Edwin Forrest shouted, "From the east to the west, in the north and in the south shall cry of vengeance burst, till the lands you have stolen groan under your feet no more!" Georgians ran riot. They, at least, were unwilling to applaud Forrest's Philip, who was either too real or too insulting or both.

If *Metamora* insulted Georgians in 1831, does that mean the play was meant as an indictment of Indian removal? Not necessarily. To understand the Georgians' reaction it may be wise to drop the curtain on *Metamora* for the moment and consider the broader debate over Indian removal and the places of other stories about Philip within it.

GEORGIA HAD much to gain by "removing" its Indians. Land. Lots of it. With Andrew Jackson's support, Georgians hoped to drive the Cherokee Indians out of the state and to claim more than seven thousand square miles of tribal territory. But the Cherokees, one of the "Five Civilized Tribes," had formed a powerful resistance movement and had unified their self-defined "nation" with a bicameral legislature, courts, and other trappings of bureaucracy and democracy. And, beginning in 1821, large numbers of Cherokees had learned to read and write when a leader named Sequoyah devised a syllabic writing system. Cherokee resistance to forced relocation was strong and strategic, and greatly aided by the tribe's newspaper, the *Cherokee Phoenix*, printed in both English and the Cherokee syllabary.[59] The cultural solidarity that resulted from widespread Cherokee literacy helped Cherokees bring their case against Georgia to the highest court in the United States. In 1831, just as *Metamora* came to Augusta, the state of Georgia was defending its case against the Cherokees in the halls of the U.S. Supreme Court in the landmark *Cherokee Nation v. Georgia.*

Many Americans, especially New Englanders, were sympathetic with the Cherokee protest, largely because of the Cherokees' advanced state of "civilization," measured by their democratic government and their high level of literacy. Cherokees *seemed* like white Americans. Most were settled farmers who adopted European dress and even the peculiarly American institution of slavery (about fifteen thousand Cherokees held about fifteen hundred Africans as chattel slaves). Because the Cherokees were so obviously "civilized," Indian rights activists asked Americans to take the Cherokees to stand for all Indian peoples. Since "nearly the same principles are involved in the claims of all the Indian nations," Jeremiah Evarts argued, "let the case of a single tribe or nation be considered."[60] In Evarts' eyes, the Cherokee Nation was a best-case scenario. As Supreme Court chief justice John Marshall declared, "if courts were permitted to indulge their sympathies, a case better calculated to excite them can scarcely be imagined."[61]

Such sympathy had surely been excited in Lydia Maria Child, an ardent advocate of Indian rights.[62] Yet she chose to further that cause, in part, by writing a history of King Philip's War, implying that if the colonists had no right to take lands from Wampanoags, the U.S. government had less right to do the same to the Cherokees. In an 1829 history of the war, Child explicitly attacked Puritan historian William Hubbard while applauding Washington Irving's portrait of Philip. She concluded that the "heroism of the Indians," as demonstrated in King Philip's War, showed that all that contemporary Indians required was a chance to become civilized.[63] Sarah Savage took the same approach, writing a "Life of Philip" that, in heroizing Metacom, argued against Indian removal. "Be the *friend* of Indians," she advised. "Our sympathy should result in active exertions to introduce Christianity, and the arts of civilized life; to secure to them a permanent local habitation, and in uniformly making their happiness, virtue and respectability, the subject of our deep and solicitous concern."[64]

Reformers like Child and Savage urged that Indians be civilized, Christianized, and ultimately assimilated. They also opposed Indian removal (Savage wished instead to secure Indians a "local habitation") on the theory that they would be better served by remaining nearer to whites. This attitude was common in liberal and especially in abolitionist circles, constituencies who generally opposed Indian removal in favor of assimilation—in favor, that is, of making Indians Americans.

Not all opponents of Indian removal who had occasion to discuss King Philip's War, however, felt compelled to heroize Philip or to draw a simple analogy between the plight of seventeenth-century Wampanoags and nineteenth-century Cherokees. In 1835 Edward Everett, a Massachusetts legislator who led the fight against Indian removal in Congress, delivered a speech dedicating a monument to King Philip's War. Everett swam against the tide of popular romantic sentiment when he defended the *colonists'* conduct in the war, asking rhetorically, "Is the blame all on one side? Does reason require us to trace all the evils to the corruption of the civilized race; to suppose that no malignant feelings, no acts of barbarity, no outbreakings of savage race or savage fraud are to be laid to the account of the untutored child of nature?" In explaining his vindication of the colonists, Everett hit on the main contradiction in the romantic portrait of Philip:

> I dwell the more on this point, because it is one of vague reproach to the memory of our fathers, and yet I am not sure that, unless we deny altogether the rightfulness of settling the continent,—unless we maintain that it was from the origin unjust and wrong to introduce the civilized race into America, and that the whole of what is now our happy and prosperous country ought to have been left as it was found, the abode of barbarity and heathenism,—I am not sure, that any different result could have taken place.[65]

Everett was, alas, almost entirely alone in pointing out this particular hypocrisy. Most white Americans, including New Englanders, were quite comfortable celebrating Philip as a hero (and as an ancestor) without questioning their own right to the land they lived on, or, even more basically, "the rightfulness of settling the continent." One of the baldest statements of this contradiction was offered in 1831, by the members of the Worcester Historical Society who offered a two-part toast to "*Philip of Pokanoket*—Had we lived in the days of our forefathers, as an enemy we would have slain him." Yet "the *present* generation may safely express their respect for his sagacity and patriotism."[66]

What allowed these well-heeled Worcester men to admire Philip "safely" was their assumption that there were essentially no more Indians left alive in New England, an assumption that became commonplace in the first half of the nineteenth century. As Ralph Waldo Emerson would write in 1845, "We in Massachusetts see the Indians only as a picturesque antiquity. Massachusetts, Shawmut, Samoset, Squantum, Nantasket, Narragansett, Assabet, Musketaquid. But where are the men?"[67] To many New Englanders, the Indians seemed to have vanished as early as the 1810s. In a letter to Thomas Jefferson in 1812, for instance, John Adams wrote from Massachusetts, "We scarcely see an Indian in a year. I remember the Time when Indian Murders, Scalpings, Depredations and conflagrations were as frequent on the Eastern and Northern Frontier of Massachusetts as they are now in Indiana, and spread as much terror." [68] Adams, clearly, had little nostalgia for New England's Indians and the violence he associated with them, but by the 1820s and 1830s many New England writers expressed only sorrow at the Indians' disappearance. In 1828 Joseph Story noted the disappearance of New England's Indians with more regret than relief: "We hear the rustling of their footsteps, like that of the withered leaves of autumn, and they are gone forever." And while lamenting the fate of northeastern Indians had become a cliché by the 1820s, Story and others applied their remarks not just to New England's Indians but to Indians all along the eastern seaboard. "Two centuries ago," Story declared, "the smoke of their wigwams and the fires of their councils rose in every valley, from Hudson's Bay to the farthest Florida," while today, "The winds of the Atlantic fan not a single region, which they may now call their own. *Already the last feeble remnants of the race are preparing for their journey beyond the Mississippi.*" [69] The Cherokees, Choctaws, and Chickasaws, that is, would vanish as surely as had the Wampanoags, Nipmucks, and Narragansetts.

Joseph Story was no idle observer. He was a U.S. Supreme Court justice. After making these remarks (in a speech given in Salem, Massachusetts), Story sent a copy of them to John Marshall, the Supreme Court's chief justice, and Marshall made the same connection Story had, between the vanished Indians of New England and the vanishing Indians of the Southeast: "The conduct of our forefathers in expelling the original occupants of the soil grew out of so many mixed motives that any censure which philanthropy may bestow upon it ought to be qualified," Marshall remarked. And yet, he continued, "I often think with indignation on our disreputable conduct . . . in the affair of the Cherokees in Georgia." [70] When John Marshall wasn't behind the bench, he was an armchair historian. He knew a thing or two about King Philip's War and had even written a brief and, all things considered, relatively balanced account of it in his *History of the Colonies,* published in 1824. Perhaps his acquaintance with the cruelties of the conflict ("a war so bloody as to threaten the very existence of New England") led him to qualify his censure of the colonists. [71] Whatever its origin, Marshall's position, as revealed in his letter to Story, made the fine distinction of exonerating the conduct of seventeenth-century New England Puritans while criticizing contemporary Indian policy. Such a distinction was as uncommon in the debate about Indian removal as was Everett's acknowledgment of the hypocrisy of New Englanders romanticizing Philip.

* * *

FOR LYDIA MARIA CHILD and Sarah Savage, the story of King Philip's War was a parable about white greed, a cautionary tale told to raise support for the Cherokees in their struggle with land-hungry Georgians. For Edward Everett and John Marshall, King Philip's War was a horrible, complicated, and perhaps not altogether regrettable tragedy whose similarities to the Cherokee case were mostly superficial but whose memory should inspire all men of integrity to consider their consciences in dealing with the Indian question. Jeremiah Evarts took this position a step farther. For him, the Cherokee case bore no relation to earlier events; it was a radical break with history. "Nothing of this kind has ever yet been done," Evarts wrote in 1829. "To us, as a nation, it will be a new thing under the sun."[72]

Andrew Jackson, of course, frowned at each of these faces of the past, but most of all he frowned at Evarts'. To Jackson, Indian removal was entirely consistent with the past and entirely consistent with the (justifiable) conduct of America's earliest colonists. "The present policy of the Government," he wrote, "is but a continuation of the same change by a milder process."[73] In his first annual address on December 8, 1829, when Jackson first articulated his Indian removal policy, he himself compared the contemporary Indians of the Southeast to the historical Indians of the Northeast: "Surrounded by the whites with their arts of civilization, which by destroying the resources of the savage doom him to weakness and decay, the fate of the Mohegan, the Narragansett, and the Delaware is fast overtaking the Choctaw, the Cherokee, and the Creek."[74] What Jackson's address underscores is that both advocates and opponents of Indian removal looked to earlier Indian conflicts—especially the much-memorialized conflicts of the seventeenth-century colonies—to bolster their arguments. Whether they (like Child and Savage) characterized the Cherokee case as history repeating itself or (like Evarts) as a radical break with the past or simply (like Jackson) as another small step toward America's date with its manifest destiny, all commentators on Indian removal related it to older policies. They differed only in the uses to which they put the past.

Perhaps no one understood this better than Old Hickory himself. In that first annual address, Jackson attempted to collapse the past into the present to challenge those Americans who supported the Cherokees by exposing their hypocrisy. Opposition to Indian removal was strongest in New England, and in an adroit attempt to garner the support of northern congressmen, Jackson posed what he believed to be an absurd set of questions:

> Would the people of Maine permit the Penobscot tribe to erect an independent government within their State? And unless they did would it not be

the duty of the General Government to support them in resisting such a measure?[75]

These were provocative questions, but, in his attempt to recruit New England congressmen to his side, Jackson ultimately failed entirely. In the vote on the Indian Removal Bill in 1830, New England senators voted 11 to 1 against the bill, while Southerners voted 18 to 0 in favor; in the House, New Englanders voted 28 to 9 against, Southerners 60 to 15 in favor. New Englanders' opposition, of course, counted for little in the end. The Indian Removal Act passed. And while Marshall ruled in *Cherokee Nation v. Georgia* that "the laws of Georgia can have no force" over the Cherokee Nation, Jackson simply ignored the ruling, since it did not prevent the federal government from acting on Georgia's behalf. The president was even rumored to have remarked, "John Marshall has made his decision: now let him enforce it."[76]

Andrew Jackson believed that no real American could ever truly mourn the fate of America's Indians:

> What good man would prefer a country covered with forests and ranged by a few thousand savages to our extensive Republic, studded with cities, towns, and prosperous farms, embellished with all the improvements which art can devise or industry execute, occupied by more than 12,000,000 happy people, and filled with all the blessings of liberty, civilization, and religion?[77]

What good man indeed? Of all the participants in the debate, only Edward Everett went so far as to admit, "unless we maintain that it was from the origin unjust and wrong to introduce the civilized race into America . . . I am not sure, that any different result could have taken place."[78] Yet Everett and other opponents of Indian removal also understood that supporting the Cherokees did not necessarily mean turning back the clock to October 11, 1492. When carried to its logical conclusion, the Cherokees' case did indeed undermine Americans' earliest territorial claims, but as Everett knew, such retroactivity would not have been the practical consequence of a Cherokee victory in the Supreme Court (although it would have strengthened Indian tribes' *subsequent* resistance to white encroachment and treaty violation). Andrew Jackson believed that "the fate of the Mohegan, the Narragansett, and the Delaware is fast overtaking the Choctaw, the Cherokee, and the Creek" and that this fate was inevitable. Edward Everett believed that these were different matters entirely and that the fate of the southeastern Indians could, and should, be different. Between Jackson and Everett a vast horizon of opinion stretched over the nation—but the majority of Americans supported removal.

* * *

HAVING SURVEYED the debate over Indian removal and the place of history in it, it is time to raise the curtain on *Metamora* once again. Act V, Scene 5: *"Metamora's stronghold. Rocks, bridge, and waterfall."* Nahmeokee waits for her husband ("He comes not, yet the sound of the battle has died away like the last breath of a storm!"). The Wampanoags have lost. When Metamora arrives, Nahmeokee shows him their son's body ("Ha! Dead! Dead! Cold!"). To save his wife from bondage, Metamora stabs and kills her ("In smiles she died!"). Benjamin Church and his soldiers arrive ("Fire upon him!") and Metamora is shot. Dying, the last of the Wampanoags issues his final curse ("Spirits of the grave, I come! But the curse of Metamora stays with the white man! I die!"). According to the final stage direction, Metamora *Falls and dies; a tableau is formed. Drums and trumpet sound a retreat till curtain. Slow curtain."*[79]

THE END. The end of the play and the end of the race. The audience rises in rapturous applause. Recall the words of the critic for the *American Quarterly Review*: "Let us hope, for the honour of humanity, that this applause is bestowed on Mr. Forrest, rather than the ferocious savage whom he impersonates."[80] He need not have worried. *Metamora* might be full of ambiguities and might be seen by at least one audience in Augusta as condemning Georgians, but in the end, quite literally *at* the end, *Metamora* spotlighted Philip's death. A tragic death, yes, but a necessary one. *Metamora* mourned the passing of Philip and the disappearance of New England's Indians but it mourned these losses as inevitable and right. In this, *Metamora; or the Last of the Wampanoags* had much in common with the fiction, verse, and painting of its day, including, most famously, Cooper's *Last of the Mohicans*.[81] *Yamoyden*, for example, mourned "a departed race,— / Long vanished hence,"[82] and in John Greenleaf Whittier's 1830 poem "Metacom," the dying chief moans about his tribe's decay:

> The scorched earth—the blackened log—
> The naked bones of warriors slain,
> Be the sole relics which remain
> Of the once mighty Wampanoag.[83]

Philip's death is also the most commonly depicted scene of the war, and most illustrations, like G. I. Brown's painting *The Last of the Wampanoags*, show him falling or fallen, alone in the wilderness. Here, as in the final scene of *Metamora* ("Rocks, bridge, and waterfall"), Philip is closely associated with the

The Last of the Wampanoags by G. I. Brown. Engraved by G. E. Ellis, c. 1850.
Courtesy of the Harvard College Library

wilderness and with a rocky landscape. Most critics supposed that "Metamora" was simply a poetic rendering of "Metacom"; in fact it is bad Greek for "big rock."[84] And by the end of the play, Metamora *is* a rock, a speechless, motionless memorial. In paintings, plays, poems, and prose, Philip is similarly petrified—dead but symbolically transformed into a mute rock, a stage prop. (A popular engraving of Forrest in the role of Metamora pictured him leaning on a massive boulder.)

At the end of Forrest's performance, white audiences applauded Metamora's death, and the death of his race. But what of his curse? The irate judge in Augusta, Georgia, believed that "Any actor who could utter such scathing language, and with such vehemence, must have the whole matter at heart."[85] Yet Forrest was an ardent supporter of Andrew Jackson and most likely shared his views on Indian removal. It is probable that for Forrest, if the fate of the Wampanoags was tragic, inevitable, and right, so was the fate of the Cherokees. As the historian Brian Dippie has astutely observed, "the belief in the Vanishing Indian was the ultimate cause of the Indian's vanishing."[86] *Metamora* was just one of dozens if not hundreds of literary productions by which the fate of the Cherokees, Choctaws, Seminoles, Creeks, and Chickasaws was made acceptable to the American public by virtue of its very inevitability, an inevitability embodied, for many readers and theatergoers, in the story of King Philip's War. In the end, Metamora was dead, and Forrest was only a stage Indian who did not, after all, believe in "that d——d Indian speech." And, outside of the people of Augusta, Georgia, neither did most of his audience.

But only most.

III

ON THE NIGHT of November 6, 1833, *Metamora* played to a crowded house at the Tremont Street Theater in Boston. Edwin Forrest was no doubt in fine form, in full costume. It was a performance like any other, but for the eagerly awaited and much-honored guests: a delegation of Penobscot Indians from Maine. They were late, and the restless audience worried. As the *Boston Morning Post* reported, "It was thought that when their box remained so long empty they did not intend coming"[87] Unfortunately, when the Penobscots did arrive, they proved to be not nearly as entertaining as the proprietors of the Tremont Street Theater had hoped. According to the *Post,* the Indians "doubtless do not wish to peril their popularity and consequently made no speeches."[88] Years later, William Alger would tell a slightly different story. In Alger's account of this same night, probably told to him by Forrest, the Penobscots were "so excited by the performance that in the closing scene they rose and chanted a dirge in honor of the death of the great chief."[89]

On the face of it, the *Post* report and Alger's anecdote about this very intriguing evening seem contradictory. If the Penobscots "made no speeches," can they still be said to have "chanted a dirge"? Is a dirge speech? These will prove to be tricky questions. Perhaps it would be better to begin by asking why the Penobscots were at the Tremont Street Theater in the first place, and why they were delayed.

Indian attendance at performances of *Metamora* was not uncommon. As Alger remarked,

> many a time delegations of Indian tribes who chanced to be visiting the cities where [Forrest] acted this character—Boston, New York, Washington, Baltimore, Cincinnati, New Orleans—attended the performance, adding a most picturesque feature by their presence, and their pleasure and approval were unqualified.[90]

Pleasure, approval, and enhanced ticket sales. Real Indians could pack a house (and line Forrest's pockets).

Because the reason for the Penobscots' attendance was obvious, the reporter for the *Boston Morning Post* failed to remark on it. He did, however, comment on why they were late: "The motives attributed to their absence was that their presence might have some bias on the present difficulties between Alabama and the Government!" Those "present difficulties" consisted of Alabama's attempt to force Cherokees and Creeks out of their state, following the lead of their Georgia neighbors. If the Penobscots feared that their presence at a performance of *Metamora* in Boston might adversely affect Cherokees and Creeks struggling to hold on to their land in Alabama, they were indeed keen observers of the national scene. Did they suspect that white New Englanders' valuable opposition to Indian removal depended on the illusion that there were no more Indians in New England? Possibly. Certainly they remained, at the very least, rather quiet at the performance. As the *Boston Morning Post* reporter suggested, the Penobscots made no speeches because they "doubtless do not wish to peril their popularity." [91] Maybe the Indians in the audience believed that if they could not disappear into the romantic mist in the forest they could at least be mute, silent as a rock. As Justice Joseph Story had declared in 1828, New England's Indians "shed no tears; they utter no cries; they heave no groans. There is something in their hearts, which passes speech." [92]

Maybe the Penobscots sensed that their reception at the Tremont Street Theater depended on their "passing speech." But they were not expected to be entirely silent. As anyone who had heard Edwin Forrest knew, Indians were *LOUD.* One of the most distinctive features of Forrest's Indian/American was the strength of his voice. Truth be told, he positively bellowed. English actor George Vandenhoff saw Forrest perform the role of Metamora in 1842 and noted: "His voice surged and roared like the angry sea, lashed into fury by a storm; till, as it reached its boiling, seething climax, . . . it was like the falls of Niagara." [93] But if Forrest was widely known for his trademark hollering, he was almost as often mocked for it (one parody of *Metamora* went by the name *Metaroarer*). [94] Yet some criticism of Forrest's high-decibel performance was clearly aimed, at least in part, at the barbarity of the character—and the race—he portrayed. A particularly vituperative attack likened Metamora's speeches to the noises made by primates:

> The *Metamora* of Mr. Forrest is as much like a gorilla as an Indian, and in fact more like a dignified monkey than a man. . . . We are told by that celebrated traveller that upon the approach of an enemy this ferocious baboon, standing upright on his hind legs, his eyes dilated, his teeth gritting and grinding, gives vent to divers snorts and grunts, and then, beating his breast fiercely with his hands till it sounds like a muffled drum, utters a loud roar. What a singular coincidence. The similarity needs scarcely be pointed out.

Substitute the words "great tragedian" for "ferocious baboon," omit the word "hind," and you have as accurate a description of Mr. Forrest in *Metamora* as any reasonable man can wish.[95]

What such criticism reveals is a congeries of deeply racist attitudes about Indians and their capacity for language and intelligence, attitudes that lay just beneath the surface of the image of the noble savage. Well before such attitudes were articulated in any elaborate or scientific way (as they would be later in the century), the Penobscots at the Tremont Street Theater were nonetheless expected to roar. Forrest was loud, Forrest was an Indian, Indians were loud. How else could the audience enjoy the Penobscots if they failed to whoop, grunt, or chant? "Real" Indians singing a dirge at Metamora's death scene was the perfect coda to Forrest's own performance, especially since it also met white audiences' expectations of Indians' alleged credulity: Forrest's promoters were fond of claiming that his portrayal of Metamora was so authentic "it might have deceived nature herself"—in other words, bona fide Indians might be deceived by Forrest's performance and believe that an actual war was being waged before their own eyes—ending with an actual death. (No matter that white audiences, like the one in Augusta, Georgia, in 1831, were perhaps more likely to be tricked by Forrest's acting.) When Alger claimed that the Penobscots at the Tremont Street Theater "chanted a dirge" to mourn Metamora's passing, he mocked their naïveté while celebrating Forrest's talent. But he didn't necessarily make it up, and his version of the performance does not necessarily contradict that in the *Boston Morning Post*. The Penobscots might have "made no speeches" and still "chanted a dirge." That is to say, a dirge is not speech if an Indian utters it.

"Speech" or no speech, if Alger was right and the Penobscots did chant a dirge after Metamora issued his dying curse, they had reasons of their own to do it. Recall that in an effort to recruit the support of New England congressmen for Indian removal in 1829 Andrew Jackson had asked hypothetically, "Would the people of Maine permit the Penobscot tribe to erect an independent government within their State?"[96] To the Penobscots, this question apparently did not sound as absurd as it did to Maine and Massachusetts legislators. (Maine had been part of Massachusetts until 1820, and many of the Penobscots' treaties fell under Massachusetts jurisdiction.) In November 1833 a delegation of Penobscots traveled to Boston and petitioned to do more or less what Jackson had threatened, "to erect an independent government," to regain territory and political autonomy that had eroded in the first third of the century. The Penobscots' claims were largely ignored, but while the delegation was spurned at the State House, it was welcomed in the theater district. Instead of regaining their land, the Penobscots were sent on a short walk across Boston Common to attend a performance of *Metamora* at the Tremont Street Theater.

THE PENOBSCOTS MAY HAVE failed, but other New England Indians were more successful in pressing their claims for land and autonomy during the era of Indian removal. The same year the Penobscots traveled to Boston, Wampanoag Indians living in Mashpee, Massachusetts, also filed claims against the Massachusetts government. (The Mashpees had been relatively isolated from the battles of King Philip's War and, in the aftermath of the war, had absorbed many Wampanoag and other Indian refugees. In 1833 the Mashpee community was the largest single group of Indians living in Massachusetts.)[97] In May 1833 William Apess, a Pequot Indian and Methodist minister, traveled to Mashpee and found there a community of Indians dispossessed of their own meetinghouse. Phineas Fish, a minister paid by Harvard to convert

William Apess. *Courtesy of the Harvard College Library*

the Mashpees to Christianity, used the Mashpee meetinghouse to preach to a congregation almost entirely made up of white parishioners. Meanwhile, neighboring whites made liberal use of Mashpee Indian land. Appalled at this treatment, Apess, after being formally adopted into the tribe, led the Mashpees in sending a petition to the governor and Council of Massachusetts, demanding that the tribe be allowed to govern itself and to protect its property. The Mashpees declared "That we as a tribe will rule ourselves and have the rights so to do for all men are born free. . . . That we will not permit any white man to come upon our Plantation to cut . . . wood . . . hay or any other article. . . . That we will have our own Meeting House, and place in the pulpit whom we please." [98] In July Apess and several Mashpees prevented a white man from taking wood from Mashpee land and were later arrested for inciting riot.

Apess' trial brought the Mashpee case into the public eye, and in the weeks and months to follow, the "Mashpee Revolt" generated a host of petitions, newspaper editorials, and court pronouncements, many of which countered anti-Mashpee sentiment by raising the specter of Georgia's treatment of the Cherokees and by pointing out Massachusetts' hypocrisy in much the same way as Andrew Jackson had attempted to do five years earlier. (Jackson might well have asked, "Would the people of Massachusetts permit the Mashpee tribe to erect an independent government within their State?") When Apess was sentenced to thirty days in prison, Benjamin Franklin Hallett, editor of the *Boston Daily Advocate,* asked pointedly, "Where are all our Cherokee philanthropists at this time?" [99] Playing on New Englanders' knowledge that the Mashpees, like the Penobscots, had fought alongside the colonists against the British in the American Revolution, Hallett also employed the Irvingesque image of Philip's descendants as Revolutionary patriots, comparing the Mashpee Revolt to the Boston Tea Party: "The persons concerned in the riot, as it was called, and imprisoned for it, I think were as justifiable in what they did, as our fathers were, who threw the tea overboard." [100] Much of Hallett's rhetoric seems to have been inspired by *Metamora* itself. In February 1834, during or soon after the run of *Metamora* at the Tremont Street Theater, Hallett (a Bostonian) editorialized on behalf of the Mashpees in phrases that echo Metamora's dying curse: "O white man! white man! the blood of our fathers, spilt in the Revolutionary War, cries from the ground of our native soil to break the chains of oppression and let our children go free." [101]

Meanwhile, the Mashpees themselves were quick to employ the rhetoric of anti-Indian removal sentiment to further their own political goals. In a petition complaining about Fish's negligence, for instance, the tribe's repre-

sentatives wrote, "Perhaps you have heard of the oppression of the Cherokees and lamented over them much, and thought the Georgians were hard
and cruel creatures; but did you ever hear of the poor, oppressed and de-
graded Marshpee Indians in Massachusetts, and lament over them?" Similarly, on December 19, well after Apess had been released, and just a few
weeks after the Penobscots sat through a performance of *Metamora,* the
Mashpees presented an "Appeal to the White Men of Massachusetts":

> As our brethren, the white men of Massachusetts, have recently manifested
> much sympathy for the red men of the Cherokee nation, who have suffered
> much from their white brethren; as it is contended in this State, that our red
> brethren, the Cherokees, should be an independent people, having the priv-
> ileges of the white men; we, the red men of the Marshpee tribe, consider it
> a favorable time to speak. We are not free. We wish to be so, as much as the
> red men of Georgia. How will the white man of Massachusetts ask favor for
> the red men of the South, while the poor Marshpee red men, his near neigh-
> bors, sigh in bondage? Will not your white brothers of Georgia tell you to
> look at home, and clear your own borders of oppression, before you trouble
> them? Will you think of this? What would be benevolence in Georgia, the
> red man thinks would be so in Massachusetts. You plead for the Cherokees,
> will you not raise your voice for the red man of Marshpee? [102]

No doubt largely due to the poignancy of such rhetoric (and Hallett's
prominent support), the Mashpees were eventually rewarded with a type of
self-government: their land was redefined as an independent district.[103] The
coincidence of *Metamora*'s run at the Tremont Street Theater in Boston and
the revolt in Mashpee (about sixty miles away) suggests any number of associations—that Apess attended the play, that Hallett attended the play, that the
Penobscots visited the Mashpees after they attended the play, that the Mashpees attended the play. . . . Unfortunately, none of these associations can be
positively demonstrated, yet it seems likely that *Metamora*'s successful run in
Boston may have in some way bolstered the Mashpees' cause.

The case for William Apess' familiarity with *Metamora,* at least, is somewhat strengthened by his subsequent fascination with Philip. In 1836 Apess
appeared in Boston to deliver a popular lecture titled *Eulogy on King Philip* at
the Odeon, just a few blocks away from the Tremont Street Theater (where
Forrest returned to revive the role of Metamora regularly, possibly each November).[104] Like Forrest, Apess borrowed from the conventions established in
the writings of men like Washington Irving. He declared King Philip's War
"as glorious as the *American* Revolution," compared Philip to George Washington, and pronounced him unequivocally "the greatest man that was ever

Frontispiece of Apess, *Eulogy on King Philip.* This illustration, labeled "King Philip Dying for His Country," shows two *colonists* killing a helpless Philip—only a tiny errata notice on the bottom of the very last page of the pamphlet issues the following correction: "In the Frontispiece, the man at the head of Philip, should be an Indian." *Courtesy of the Harvard College Library*

in America."[105] Like *Metamora*, Apess' address, his *eulogy*, also fetishized Philip's dire end; the frontispiece engraving of the pamphlet version of his speech depicted Philip's death scene.

More than any other early nineteenth-century commentator, William Apess collapsed the century-and-a-half divide between King Philip's War and Indian removal. By his mere existence, Apess (although a Pequot, not a Wampanoag) gave the lie to *Metamora*'s subtitle, "Last of the Wampanoags." Standing in front of the Odeon before, presumably, a largely white audience, Apess was himself, in his physical presence, evidence that New England's Indians did not die out with Philip in August 1676. (In his autobiography, Apess recalled that when he held revival meetings, "crowds flocked out, some to *hear* the truth and others to *see* the 'Indian.'")[106] Unlike the Penobscots attending *Metamora*, Apess did not decline to make speeches. And unlike Edwin Forrest, Apess was an "authentic" Indian, as he made clear in his *Eulogy*, again and again referring to Indians as "we." Also unlike Forrest, Apess directly addressed contemporary political issues. After citing the prejudice he had faced in his own life and the unjust legislation Indians were subject to, Apess offered an ultimatum: "Give the Indian his rights, and you may be assured war will cease." Moreover, Apess proposed a radical legacy for King Philip's War. Quoting "Dr. Mather," who had called Philip a man "of cursed memory," Apess addressed the possibility that in vindicating Philip's memory his Indian descendants might seek vengeance through attacks on Mather's progeny. "Now we wonder if the sons of the pilgrims would have us, poor Indians, come out and curse the doctor, and all their sons, as we have been, by many of them."[107]

William Apess, standing at the Odeon, *threatened* to curse "the sons of the pilgrims," but he resisted the temptation. Such a curse, he believed, was itself vindictive, and, as Apess remarked, "we sincerely hope there is more humanity in us, than that."[108] Perhaps Apess was unwilling to utter a curse because he knew well that, within the conventions of the romanticized and vanished Indian, the curse was all that survived. In Whittier's "Metacom," as in *Metamora*, Philip dies but "The dying curse of Metacom, / Shall linger, with abiding power."[109] While Apess refused to offer a curse, he did offer two very special "authentic" Indian speeches. He claimed that before the outbreak of war, Philip had roused his warriors and explained his reasons for fighting against the English. In the voice of Philip, Apess began,

> BROTHERS,—You see this vast country before us, which the great spirit gave to our fathers and us; you see the buffalo and deer that now are our support.

But wait . . . buffalo in New England? Like every other "authentic" speech by Philip, Apess' is a fiction. Not a few historians and writers have dearly wished that Philip had left a speech. (In *Metamora*, Philip's counselors even urged him, "Speak, Metamora, speak!")[110] But no such speech survives. Indeed, very little of what Philip actually said in his life survives in the written historical record. As a result, the passion for inventing a speech by Philip has found expression in nearly everything that has been written about him, beginning with the fictitious speech John Eliot included in his *Indian Dialogues* in 1671, in which "Philip" humbly accepts Christianity, and continuing, in 1676, with Benjamin Tompson's version of Philip's call to arms ("My friends, our fathers were not half so wise / As we ourselves who see with younger eyes / They sell our land to Englishmen who teach / Our nation all so fast to pray and preach").[111] Following in Eliot's and Tompson's footsteps, nineteenth-century writers—including Apess—found inventing a speech for Philip an irresistible temptation.[112]

Perhaps uncomfortable with his own fictitious Philip speech, however, William Apess decided to provide a second, even more "authentic" speech. At the end of his public oration eulogizing Metacom, Apess offered "a specimen of Philip's language," reciting the Lord's Prayer in the Massachusett language (as translated by John Eliot and John Sassamon). Such a recital had probably not been offered, even privately, for more than a century. It must have been a strange day at the Odeon indeed, when Apess began, "Noo-chun kes-uk-qut-tiam-at-am unch koo-we-suonk, kuk-ket-as-soo-tam-oonk pey-au-moo-utch, keet-te-nan-tam-oo-onk ne nai. . . ."[113] Tellingly, the prayer was expected to be a crowd-pleaser; it was the one feature of Apess' "performance" that was mentioned in a newspaper advertisement for the event: "At the close he will give a specimen of Philip's language."[114]

It could be said that if Edwin Forrest "played Indian," so, too, did William Apess. Forrest's rendering of Indian speech was an invented fiction, but so was Apess'. His buffalo speech was certainly as spurious as anything Forrest ever uttered. Yet Apess also subtly played with the conventions of the stage Indian, and with the expectations of his white audience. Forrest was considered "wholly Indian" because he took on the bearings and posture of an Indian; he embodied Indianness. Attempting to distinguish himself from this stage Indian, to out-Indian him, Apess fell back on the most authentic Indian speech recoverable to him in 1836—the Lord's Prayer in Massachusett. Edwin Forrest could talk the talk. William Apess could talk the language.

IV

ONE FINAL PERFORMANCE. On the evening of November 29, 1847, on the stage of the Adelphi Theater in Boston, "Philip" died again. But this time Philip (here, too, known as "Metamora") did not die silently. This time Philip would not stay dead. On this, the opening night of John Brougham's brilliant burlesque *Metamora; or, the Last of the Pollywogs*, three English colonists ("Badenough," "Worser," and "Vaughan") shoot the Pollywog leader with popguns. *("At each shot, METAMORA jumps and staggers as if shot.")* Finally, and with great flailing, Metamora falls, moaning:

> I feel it's almost time for me to slope.
> The red man's fading out, and in his place
> There comes a bigger, not a better race.
> Just as you've seen the squirming Pollywog
> In course of time become a bloated frog.   *(Dies.)*

But the curtain does not yet fall. The trumpets do not yet sound their mournful note. The audience does not here rise in rapturous applause. Instead, the chorus sings,

> We're all dying, die, die, dying,
> We're all dying just like a flock of sheep.

To which Metamora replies,

> You're all lying, lie, lie, lying
> You're all lying; I wouldn't die so cheap.

Brougham's Metamora will not play dead. Instead he rises in a sprightly manner and, turning to the audience, harrumphs, "Confound your skins, I will not die to please you." On hearing Metamora's final speech, the audience at the Adelphi Theater was no doubt doubled over in rapturous laughter.[115]

Nearly two decades after Forrest's original *Metamora* debuted and a decade after Apess offered his *Eulogy on King Philip*, the ubiquitous Indian speechifying in *Metamora*, delivered in Forrest's uniquely ear-piercing style, had become the subject of parody. John Brougham's wonderfully titled *Metamora; or, the Last of the Pollywogs* exploited the conventions of the costume Indian: "With rifle, belt, plume, moccasin, and all, / Just as you would see them at a fancy ball." And Brougham employed a different kind of "Indian speak" to mock Forrest's bellowing style: "Ugh" is one of Brougham's Metamora's more frequent lines. But this Metamora, and his witless wife "Tapiokee," also mock the melodramatic conventions of Forrest's soliloquies and the trope of the dying Indian. When the Pollywog warriors leave the stage to fight the English, Brougham's Metamora stays behind to address the audience and appease their demand for a rousing war cry and impassioned explanation of Philip's motives:

> It's very probable you'd like to know
> The reason why the Pollywog don't go
> With his red brethren. Pray take notice, each,
> He stops behind to have an exit speech. And here it is:— *(Takes stage . . .)*
> Into the foe a feet or two I'll walk!
> Death or my nation's glory! That's the talk. *(Exit.)*

And that is, after all, the talk.

In *The Last of the Pollywogs*, John Brougham parodied more than a few elements of the stage Indian, and, perhaps most powerfully, he resisted the vanishing-Indian theme prevalent in nineteenth-century Indian drama by simply refusing to kill off his protagonist. In its final lines ("I will not die to please you") Brougham's parody acknowledged the cultural importance of the

A HISTRIONIC SAVAGE.

Parody of Forrest's Metamora. *Courtesy of the Harvard Theatre Collection*

dead stage Indian in placating whites' fears of real-life Indians. But while *The Last of the Pollywogs* mocked the conventions of early Indian dramas, it also expressed bitter scorn for Indian peoples, an attitude that was becoming increasingly widespread at midcentury.[116] In 1852, at the height of Brougham's parody's popularity, Massachusetts governor George Boutwell delivered a speech at the dedication of a King Philip's War monument whose tone suggests the pervasiveness of this diminishing regard. Boutwell made a point of distinguishing between the Indians of King Philip's time, who, he admitted, may have been unjustly treated, and the Indians of 1852, who deserved little sympathy. While acknowledging that New England Indians had not become extinct, the governor expressed nothing but contempt for Philip's descendants:

> The human family has ever been subject to one great law. It is this. Inferior races disappear in the presence of their superiors, or become dependent upon them. Now, while this law shall not stand as a defence for our fathers, it is satisfactory to feel that no policy could have civilized or even saved the In-

dian tribes of Massachusetts. The remnants that linger in our midst are not the representatives of the native nobility of the forest of two centuries ago.

(Boutwell even attempted, albeit halfheartedly, to vindicate the sullied reputations of the Puritan historians of the war. "It is just to say that our ancestors made no concealment of the facts, although the comments of Mather and Hubbard are often strangely barbarous in spirit.")[117]

As the nineteenth century progressed, Edwin Forrest's *Metamora*, the victim of changing attitudes and a brilliant burlesque, became less and less popular.[118] It met with bad reviews throughout the 1860s largely because, as one reviewer remarked, "the Indian has become a nuisance."[119] After Forrest's death in 1872, the play lay dormant until it was resurrected in 1877 (possibly occasioned by the bicentennial anniversary of King Philip's War), with the title role performed by D. H. Harkins. By then *Metamora* had clearly become a stark anachronism. A *New York Times* review found Harkins inferior to Forrest while conceding that "Mr. Harkins could scarcely have hoped to awake any interest in the piece itself, which is about as stupid as a piece can be, but the character of *King Philip*, who prefers to be called *Metamora*, can be made entertaining by a suffusion of robust manhood."[120] Ten years later, when yet another production of the play premiered, its datedness was even more poignant. This time the *Times* theater critic dismissed *Metamora* entirely.

> The play met with favor while such a popular actor as Forrest played the title rôle. But this was years ago, before the present conception of the Indian began to prevail. A longer experience with the red man has changed the ideal in the popular mind, as the corrupting influences of border civilization have changed the savage himself. Neither change has served to increase the popular sympathy in his behalf. An actor therefore who in these days strives to touch an audience by a recital of the Indian's woes has a much harder task than was the case in Forrest's time.

The sole redeeming element of this performance, it seems, was the supporting cast, which included "a detachment of real Indians from Buffalo Bill's party," who "helped to make the play go well."[121]

By the 1880s Buffalo Bill's Indians, and the idea of the Indian as an exhibit piece, had gained ascendancy. No longer did occasional Indians in the audience at Indian plays provide entertainment; now they were themselves on the stage, living relics of an earlier age. The long-winded speeches that Forrest uttered as Metamora were no longer popular; now a new kind of "Indian talk" prevailed. A dreadful play about King Philip's War written in 1884 contains no virtuous speeches or scathing curses, only ludicrous constructions and bad syntax. (It is possible that experience with the western Sioux and other tribes—who were unfamiliar with English and whose languages whites generally did not bother to learn—had convinced white Americans that Indians were incapable of grammatical speech.)[122] Sassamon's warning to the English, for instance, reads bizarrely: "Me have strong surmises that King Philip's treaty, recently ratified, will not restrain him from hostile invasions." And, during Sassamon's murder trial, the three accused Indians provide dunderheaded comic relief. The following excerpt is from the scene in which Wampapaquan, Mattashunannamo, and Tobias are asked if they have any objections:

> WAMPAPAQUAN. Me no lawyer, me no object.
> MAT. Me no lawyer, but me object.
> TOBIAS. Me object to um all.[123]

IN THE 1830S AND 1840S Edwin Forrest's *Metamora* served as an important vehicle by which white Americans came to understand Indian removal as inevitable, and Philip, newly heroized, became a central figure in the search for an American identity and an American past. An American identity founded on a romanticized Indian required that Indians themselves be "long vanished hence," and Metacom was, in this regard, an ideal candidate for canonization. For Indians' role in American history (even as wartime enemies) to be cherished, romanticized, and fetishized, Indians themselves must exist only in the past, mute memorials, silent as a rock. Either that or else they could be far, far away—exiled west of the Mississippi. By itself, *Metamora* neither advocated nor condemned Indian removal—the text of the play is deeply ambiguous. But if theater audiences are any reflection of the general population, most Americans who applauded Metamora's curse supported Indian removal. And in the end, and especially in its ending, *Metamora* made Indian removal palatable to the American public by insisting that Indians look best from a distance.

By the latter half of the nineteenth century, when the Indian had "become a nuisance," *Metamora* became an unprofitable throwback, utterly inconsistent with mainstream American culture's more thorough denigration of Indian culture and, especially, of Indian oratory. By then, "real," present-day, nearby Indians were once again a problem as Plains warfare raged in the West. And after the Civil War, white Americans became less interested in their imagined Indian ancestry and more interested in their Anglo-Saxon past. The nation was old enough to have its own history, and Indians were no longer necessary to Americans' understanding of themselves as a nation. Forrest's *Metamora* flopped; Brougham's *Metamora* triumphed, and white hatred of Indians was freed from the restraints of nationalistic nostalgia.

For Edwin Forrest, reenacting King Philip's War was a step on the path toward an American national drama. Like so many other artists of his generation, Forrest appropriated Indianness and Indian ancestors to make himself American, to distance himself from all that was English. In this he exactly reversed what writers like Mather and Hubbard had tried to do so furiously—and so prolifically—a century and a half earlier. Late-seventeenth-century colonists had tried to purify themselves of the contamination of America's indigenous inhabitants and make themselves more English. Early-nineteenth-century Americans tried to take on the attributes of Indianness to make themselves less English. Language was central to both endeavors. In the 1670s the colonists defined themselves through what they wrote and printed, and speech was itself a marker of Englishness: English captives were recognized by their ability to speak English, and Indian languages were considered by many to be babble. In the 1830s a certain kind of public performance of Indian speech—epitomized by Metamora's curse—came to be embraced by whites, and even applauded. Oratory was central to Forrest's performance ("Speak, Metamora, Speak!"), to Brougham's and other parodies ("Death or my nation's glory, that's the talk"), and to Apess' *Eulogy* (complete with spurious Philip speech). In the 1670s colonists silenced New England's Indians at every turn. In the 1830s Americans listened to them, but only if they were dead (Metamora) or if they were speaking about dead Indians (Apess' *Eulogy*) or if they were speaking in a dead Indian language (Apess' Lord's Prayer).

William Apess used the fascination with Indian speech to find a broader audience for his unapologetically political addresses while the Mashpees learned the lesson of *Metamora* and effectively targeted New Englanders' consciences in comparing their plight to that of the Cherokees. While the romantic Indian remained popular, men like William Apess and groups like the Mashpees used that image to their advantage. If whites were willing to say Indians fighting for their land were patriotic heroes, the Mashpees were willing to take them at their word and press their own claims. (The heroic Philip may have even inspired a Seminole resistance leader in Florida to take the name "King Philip.")[124] In these Indians' protests they took Indianness back from performers like Forrest and laid the foundation for new generations of Indian activists in New England. Just when the noble savage was falling out of favor and Philip was becoming less useful as an American hero, Indians in New England, especially Wampanoags and Narragansetts, began embarking on a road toward cultural renewal and revival, a road that would eventually lead them to their own public and private commemorations of the events of King Philip's War.

Tracing the history of New England's Native Americans throughout the course of the nineteenth century is an extraordinarily difficult project. Most white New Englanders believed Indians no longer existed in their midst, making them difficult to trace in historical records. Native people and communities, some of whom had remained in hiding since King Philip's War and had "passed" as either white or black, began to build a collective identity, to reassert their tribal identities, and, increasingly, to think of themselves as "Indians."[125] If tracing those communities is difficult, linking their sense of themselves to productions like Edwin Forrest's famous Indian play is an even more daunting task. Penobscot attendance at a performance of *Metamora* at the Tremont Street Theater is about as close as one might expect to come to demonstrating a connection between the play and New England Indian protests of the 1830s and subsequent tribal and pan-Indian consciousness. Yet one final tantalizing clue remains to suggest that memories of Metamora may have survived among New England Indians for more than a century. In 1935 a Narragansett lawyer living in Providence, Rhode Island, placed an ad for his services in the Narragansett newspaper *Narragansett Dawn*. His name was James Stockett, Jr., but his middle name was Matamora.[126]

Epilogue

The Rock

S outh of the Kickamuit River, on the shore of Mount Hope Bay in Bristol, Rhode Island, a large, graywacke rock sits at the tide line. Its surface is low and flat and worn and scarred and, much of the time, underwater. But when the tide is low and the sun is high, the rock's surface reveals the shallow, faded marks of an inscrutable inscription: vague outlines of a boat above a row of mysterious, narrowly carved characters. In 1845 a Bristol historian proposed that the inscription had been made by Norsemen in the eleventh century, and even though he refuted his attribution in decades to come, when the American infatuation with Viking visitors began to wane, the rock soon became widely known as "Northmen's Rock." In 1919 the Rhode Island Historical Society even held a ceremony to christen it with corn, wine, and oil, taking the occasion to rename it "Lief's Rock," an act that so galled a Brown psychology professor and inscribed-rock enthusiast named Edmund Delabarre that he set about to disprove the theory of the inscription's Norse origins.[1]

Delabarre began by pointing out that the inscription had not been observed or described before about 1835 and, as he claimed, there is no reason to believe it was made much before then, the "ancient" appearance of its characters being due to their shallowness when first carved rather than to centuries of erosion. The theory of the inscription's Norse origins, Delabarre concluded, was an elaborate myth, built on the equally mythical, unsound, and improbable assertion that Vikings visited southern New England in the year 1007. In

The Mount Hope Rock, Bristol, Rhode Island. *Photograph by the author*

place of the Norse myth, Delabarre offered a new theory, one that, on the surface of things, seems even more improbable and wildly fanciful than its predecessor. Delabarre proposed that the inscription's characters belonged not to the ancient runic alphabet but to the Cherokee syllabary. Not only that, but the inscription could be read. According to Delabarre's reconstruction, when the row of characters is correlated with Cherokee syllabic symbols it produces a combination of sounds that is pure nonsense, but if it is taken to be a Cherokee transcription of spoken Algonquian in the Wampanoag dialect and then translated into English, it reads: "Metacomet, Great Sachem."[2] And Metacom, of course, is the Wampanoag name for King Philip.

The inscription, then, had to have been made after 1821, when the Cherokee syllabary was invented, but before 1835, when the curious rock was first noticed.[3] This window of time, intriguingly, coincides not only with a peak of interest in King Philip's War—ushered in by Washington Irving's 1814 essay and sustained, after 1829, by Edwin Forrest's *Metamora*—but also with Cherokee resistance to Indian removal (itself made possible by the invention of the syllabary). Whoever carved an inscription in the Cherokee syllabary on a rock in Rhode Island to praise Philip may perhaps have been spelling out the links between Cherokee and Wampanoag resistance. Still, one very tricky question remains: Who could have done it?

The inscription on Mount Hope Rock, Bristol, Rhode Island. Photograph
by John R. Hess, 1919. *Courtesy of the Harvard College Library*

	1	2,3	4	5	6	7	8	9	
1. Miller	Y	⋏ᷓ	⅂ᷓ	.	⅂	Y	⋀	⊢	⋰
2. Munro	Y	⋀⋀	⅂ᷓ	∷	⅂	Y	A	⊢	
3. Bacon	✓	⋀⋀	⅂ᷓ	⊤	\	Y	R	⊢	
4. Chapin		⋀	⅂ᷓ	‒	⅂	⋗	R	⊢	
5. Delabarre	/	⋏ᷓ	⊿		⅂	>	⋀	⊢	
6. Cherokee	Ɣ	⅄Ϝɦ	O⫯	λ	Ɏ	R	Ɛ		
7. Photograph	Ɏ	⅄Ϝ⅄	⋋	Φ⎪	⅂	Ɏ	R	Ɛ	
8. Warren	⊣		⊢		▷	Þ			
9. New Jersey	Ɏ	⋌Ɫ	⋎Ɫ		⅂	ʃ	⅀	⟨	⫻×
10. Tennessee	±	⌁	7		⅂	⌣	⋪	Ɛ	⋋

A chart of various recordings of the inscription on Mount Hope Rock,
matched against a row of Cherokee syllabics (line 6). *Courtesy of the
Harvard College Library*

There is, of course, the distinct possibility that Delabarre's rendering was flawed; perhaps the inscription is not in fact in the Cherokee syllabary, or maybe, if it is, it says something other than "Metacomet, Great Sachem." Since the inscription has now faded almost to invisibility, Delabarre's transcription cannot itself be checked for accuracy, and the best that can be said is that Delabarre, who cannot be proved wrong, might have been right (his transcriptions, based on early photographs, seem plausible enough, and, according to Cherokee syllabary scholar Willard Walker, "it seems possible that Delabarre's inscription is a sequence of badly executed Cherokee syllabics").[4] Yet even while granting, for the moment, that Delabarre's basic premise about the inscription was correct, the question of authenticity nonetheless remains.

Mysterious rocks were not unprecedented in New England. In the seventeenth century, prominent colonists, including Samuel Sewall, John Danforth, and Increase Mather, all became intrigued by a series of inscriptions on Dighton Rock near the Taunton River in Plymouth. (The inscriptions had been observed since the Pilgrims' first landing in 1620, and it was to Dighton Rock that Cotton Mather referred when he wrote of the Indians, "Reading and Writing is altogether unknown to them, tho there is a Rock or two in the Country that has unaccountable Characters engrav'd upon it.")[5] Interest in Dighton Rock was renewed in the early part of the nineteenth century, and in 1839, ethnologist and explorer Henry Schoolcraft showed a picture of the carvings to an Algonquin religious leader from Saulte Ste. Marie named Chingwauk. After careful study, Chingwauk told Schoolcraft that the carvings were ideographs relating the ancient battles of two native peoples. (Parts of the inscription have since been attributed to visiting Vikings, as well as to Portuguese explorers, though little has been definitively proved.)[6]

What had been curiosities to men like Sewall and Mather in the seventeenth century became a quest to ethnologists like Schoolcraft in the early nineteenth century. But Schoolcraft, who traveled across America looking for authentic Indian writings, was joined by many less-careful hobbyists. It was in the early years of this faddish fascination that the inscription on Mount Hope rock was first noticed, circa 1835. As a result it has been suggested that, like the notorious "Bat Creek Stone" planted in a Tennessee burial mound or the supposed "runic" marks of "Leif Ericson 1001" on No-Man's-Land, the Mount Hope Rock's "Metacomet, Great Sachem," might have been a hoax perpetrated by mischievous antiquarians or amateur archaeologists.[7]

But if the inscription was not a hoax, and if Delabarre's reading was not flawed, there are at least two likely attributions, both proposed by Delabarre himself. First, Delabarre suggested that the inscription might have been carved in 1833, when a group of Penobscot Indians from Maine visited southern New England to negotiate land claims and, having already traveled so far south, might possibly have made a pilgrimage to Mount Hope, Philip's former home. There, Delabarre proposed, one of them made the inscription on the rock, memorializing Philip as "Metacomet, Great Sachem."[8] What Edmund Delabarre did not know, of course, is that the Penobscots who visited southern New England in 1833 had other memorial activities on their itinerary: on November 6 they spent the evening at the Tremont Street Theater in Boston, attending a performance of *Metamora*. If a Penobscot Indian really did carve an inscription on the Mount Hope Rock, it may well have been in response to the passionate performance of *Metamora*. Perhaps whoever wrote the inscription chose to use the Cherokee syllabary rather than English as a means of establishing the inscription's Indian authenticity, and of spelling out the links between Cherokee removal and King Philip's War.[9] To Delabarre's first theory, I would add the possibility that the inscription might have been made in 1833 not by Penobscots, but by Mashpee Wampanoags involved in the Mashpee Revolt (or even by Pequot William Apess himself), especially since the Mashpees' appeals to the Massachusetts government almost always included exploiting the sympathy of northern whites for Georgian Cherokees ("You plead for the Cherokees, will you not raise your voice for the red man of Marshpee?")[10] How a Penobscot or Mashpee Indian might have come by a knowledge of the Cherokee syllabary is more difficult to explain, but it is possible that, since a Cherokee printing press was itself built in Boston in 1827, someone among the Mashpees or among the Penobscot delegation might have visited there and picked up a copy of the Cherokee syllabary (again, Apess seems a likely candidate). The inscription, after all, is formed, at best, of "badly executed" Cherokee syllabics and might have been made by a novice.

The problem of knowledge of the syllabary does not plague Edmund Delabarre's second conjectural explanation for the inscription's origins. If not by the Penobscots, Delabarre proposed, the inscription on the Mount Hope Rock might have been carved by a Cherokee Indian named Thomas Mitchell and his Wampanoag wife, Zerviah Gould, who herself claimed to be a direct descendant of Massasoit, Philip's father (and also, ironically, of John Sassamon, through his granddaughter, Mercy Felix, who married Massasoit's great-grandson, Benjamin Tuspaquin; their daughter, Lydia Tuspaquin—Zerviah's grandmother—drowned in Assowampset Pond in 1812).[11] Gould and Mitchell married in 1824 and lived for the next several decades outside Boston, where they would have had the means, the opportunity, and, one might imagine, the motive to carve an inscription on the rock in nearby Rhode Island, thus memorializing Zerviah's Wampanoag ancestors in Thomas' Cherokee language.

Zerviah G. Mitchell. *Courtesy of the Harvard College Library*

The image of Zerviah Gould and Thomas Mitchell standing on the rocky beach of Mount Hope Bay, peering over each other's shoulders the better to view their handiwork, is a tempting image indeed. In a contest for meaning that began with the earliest reports of John Sassamon's death and included gestures as powerful and bizarre as Josiah Winslow sending Philip's "crowne" to the king of England, James Printer setting the type for Mary Rowlandson's captivity narrative, Cotton Mather pulling the jaw off Philip's decaying skull, and Edwin Forrest bellowing out Metamora's curse, a Cherokee man and a Wampanoag woman carving "Metacomet, Great Sachem" on a rock near Philip's home seems a sublimely suitable coda. The consequences of literacy, the power of print, the negotiation of identity, the suppleness of memory, all are here. And here, too, for extra measure, is a bit of romance, in the marriage of two Indian cultures, and in the mysteriousness of the inscription—for who, other than Zerviah and Thomas, would ever be able to read it?

Tempting as it is to end here, with this romantic and mysterious fantasy (for fantasy it must remain, since there seems no way of proving it), there are good reasons to take this story a few steps farther and to carry it, even, all the way up to the present. In her youth, Zerviah Gould Mitchell may or may not have been involved in carving the inscription on Mount Hope Rock with a chisel or a sharp stone, but at a later age she most certainly did have other tools at her disposal. In 1878 Gould Mitchell, at age seventy-one, published a book on the history of the Wampanoag Indians, with particular reference to the story of King Philip's War. As she wrote in the preface, "I now, through the medium of the printing press, and in book form, speak to the understanding and sense of justice of the reading public." (Now, what might have been read by Zerviah and Thomas alone was made legible to all.) Sometime in the 1870s Gould Mitchell hired a genealogist named Ebenezer Peirce to research and write a book whose publication she would fund, partly, no doubt, with her own savings, and partly by advance subscriptions solicited by two of her children, Charlotte (Wootonekanuske) and Melinda (Teweelema).[12] *Indian History, Biography, and Genealogy: Pertaining to the Good Sachem Massasoit of the Wampanoag Tribe, and His Descendants* appeared in 1878, with "Zerviah G. Mitchell" listed as publisher. As Gould Mitchell explained,

> My object in bringing this work before the public is not only to show that I am a lineal descendant, in the seventh generation, from the great and good Massasoit, whom both the red and white man now venerate and honor, but also to make record of the wrongs which during all these generations have been endured by my race.[13]

Gould Mitchell's motives for establishing her descendance from Massasoit were also practical. In the 1850s she had placed a series of petitions before the Massachusetts legislature, attempting to regain control of Indian property near Fall River and to receive compensation from a white neighbor, Benjamin F. Winslow (himself possibly a descendant of Josiah Winslow, who had proclaimed in 1676, "I think I can clearly say, that before these present troubles broke out, the English did not possess one foot of Land in this Colony, but what was fairly obtained by honest purchase of the Indian Proprietors").[14] Benjamin Winslow admitted to harvesting lumber from the Indian property, but pleaded that no Indian heirs existed who might warrant compensation. Zerviah Gould Mitchell aimed to confound Winslow's plans for the Indian land: "It seemed as though, when it was thought by him that all the Indians were dead, one was dug right up out of the grave." Gould Mitchell, however, was unable to receive satisfaction in court ("there seems to be no law for the Indian," she wrote bitterly), and decided instead to seek public, historical vindication.[15]

Gould Mitchell's hiring of Ebenezer Peirce to write *Indian History, Biography, and Genealogy* may also have been inspired by the bicentennial anniversary of King Philip's War, celebrated in 1875 and 1876. (While the actual genealogy of Massasoit and his family is crowded into a brief appendix of the book, the great bulk of it is devoted to a detailed history of King Philip's War.)[16] The bicentennial of King Philip's War was celebrated largely by white New Englanders making speeches and dedicating monuments, but Zerviah's own family attended at least one of these public commemorations. In August 1876, on the two hundredth anniversary of Philip's death, Charlotte and Melinda Mitchell were invited to participate in "King Philip's Day" in Bristol.[17] The Rhode Island Historical Society, which had organized the festivities, oversaw the delivery of numerous addresses detailing the horrors of King Philip's War, but the keynote address was made by the governor of Rhode Island. True to the nineteenth century's ambivalent embrace of the noble but vanished savage, the governor passionately defended Philip—"Hadn't he a right to fight? Would any of us have had him do differently?"—at the same time as he relished the colonists' victory over him: "That he must fail every one felt assured. And we know that he did fail; and of course we thank God that he did." Finally, the governor gladly conceded the extinction of the Indian: "Within a few years the red man will be practically wiped out. We cannot help it. There is no use in wailing about it, because it is one of the things that are inevitable. It has been proven many times that the two races cannot live together."[18]

On King Philip's Day in 1876, the governor of Rhode Island and his largely white audience celebrated not only their own Americanness (for Philip's story "must necessarily excite the interest of every American citizen") but also the obsolescence of Indianness (on exhibit were a kettle and a belt supposedly owned by Philip, along with several other Indian "relics"). Meanwhile, no doubt just a few yards away from the governor's podium, Charlotte and Melinda Mitchell stood dressed in full Indian regalia, selling traditional Wampanoag baskets and perhaps taking subscriptions for their mother's soon-to-be-published history of Massasoit's descendants.[19] Charlotte, Melinda, and Zerviah Mitchell would not be made relics and, contrary to the governor's words, "the red man" would not be "wiped out."

EVEN AS Zerviah Gould Mitchell and her daughters staged a revival of Wampanoag heritage in the latter half of the nineteenth century, nearby Narragansetts were engaged in extraordinary attempts to preserve their own cultural identity and tribal lands. After a protracted struggle, Narragansett representatives finally agreed to detribalization legislation proposed by the Rhode Island Assembly in 1880.[20] Yet the loss of their lands and tribal status did not diminish Narragansetts' sense of identity; as one Narragansett said in

Melinda Mitchell. *Courtesy of the Harvard College Library*

1883, "We have the same blood running through our veins that we had before we sold the lands."[21] The tenacity of Narragansett identity led ultimately to a dramatic Narragansett cultural revival that can best be dated to the 1930s, when a woman named Princess Red Wing began publishing a tribal newspaper, *Narragansett Dawn,* to tell her people about their history and to teach them the Narragansett language.[22]

Red Wing was actually both Narragansett and Wampanoag, and she claimed to be the direct descendant of a man named Simeon Simons, who, as tradition has it, was the grandson of Philip, the son of the long-lost son of Philip who had been sold into slavery in 1677. According to this tradition, Philip's grandson escaped the West Indies, returned to the colonies, and served as a close aide to George Washington during the Revolutionary War. Many of Red Wing's descendants, calling themselves the "Royal House of Pokanoket," continue to embrace this tradition of direct descendance from Philip.[23] (Members of the Pokanoket royal family call Philip's son by the name "Metom," which I suspect may be a corruption of "Metamora.")[24]

Led by men and women like Zerviah Gould Mitchell and Princess Red Wing, similar revivals took place among other New England Indian groups at about the turn of the century. In the early twentieth century, such revivals were further fueled by a new spirit of pan-Indianism as well as by the continuing patronage of white historians and antiquarians. In 1923 the "Indian Council of New England" was formed to cultivate interest in Indian heritage and to ensure cultural survival (the Council's motto was "Algonquin 'I still live' "). A coalition of New England Indians and white amateur historians and other nonacademics, the Council was often subject to its white members' romanticism, yet it nonetheless greatly increased native regional consciousness among Algonquians in New England.[25] That consciousness, in turn, laid the foundation for renewed efforts at political mobilization, especially during the American Indian Movement. In the 1970s and 1980s Narragansetts, Mashpee Wampanoags, Pequots, Mohegans, and Penobscots all began pressing for federal recognition and for the return of lost tribal lands. Since that time, groups that have succeeded in establishing economic and political autonomy (and often in accumulating massive wealth, due to the success of tribal-run casinos) have also become passionately involved in researching and documenting their heritage.[26] Among some groups, interest in commemorating the events of King Philip's War and understanding its legacy has become a powerful concern. Yet, for other New England Indians, the importance of Philip and his war has been exaggerated; the Mashpee Wampanoags, especially (most of whose ancestors were not actually involved in the war), are not particularly interested in Philip and some even consider him a "renegade."[27]

Much of the contestation over King Philip's War today concerns public commemoration of the war. In the nineteenth and early twentieth centuries, monuments to the war were erected all over New England, many by the Society of Colonial Wars, a group whose members trace their ancestry to colonial soldiers.[28] Markers at sites with names such as Bloody Brook, Redemption Rock, and Nine Men's Misery celebrate the deeds and mourn the sufferings of the colonists, not their enemies, while sites of special significance to Indians have rarely been preserved.[29] Recently native groups have attempted to change all that. In 1991, when the Massachusetts Water Resource Authority proposed constructing a sewage-treatment plant on Deer Island, a coalition of Indians from New England and elsewhere, calling themselves the Muhheconneuk Intertribal Committee, staged a series of protests and demonstrations, including annual marches retracing the steps of Natick Indians forced to remove to the island in October 1675.[30] But no protest has been more sustained, or more deeply symbolic, than the Narragansetts' efforts to reclaim the monument at the Great Swamp.

The Great Swamp Fight Monument was first unveiled at a dedication ceremony in October 1906. About a hundred people, including "three lineal descendants of the noble but now almost vanished Narragansett Tribe," gathered at the Great Swamp in South Kingston, Rhode Island, for the dedication, hosted by the Society of Colonial Wars. Soon after the ceremony began, rain began to fall, and it seemed to some "as if the clouds shed tears over the memory of the bloody scene recalled by the memorial about to be unveiled." Squinting against the heavy rain, the three Narragansetts drew the veil from the monument, revealing four massive boulders, one for each of the United Colonies, planted around a granite obelisk, signaling "a perpetual memorial of the stern purpose and high valour of our forefathers." Next, the chaplain delivered a dedicatory address, placed a wreath and an American flag at the base of the shaft, and called the exercises to a close.[31]

In September 1992, some fifty people gathered at the same site, in a circle around those same four boulders and solitary granite shaft in South Kingston. But this time, several dozen members of the Narragansett Nation led the ceremonies. (Narragansetts had achieved federal recognition as a "nation" in 1983.) They commemorated not the "Great Swamp fight" but the "Great Swamp massacre." Many wore full regalia—fringed leather dresses and vests,

The Great Swamp Monument, South Kingstown, Rhode Island.
Photograph by the author

or pants, and also moccasins and beaded headbands. Strong Horse (Kenneth Smith), the subsachem of the Narragansett Nation, began the ceremonies, asking those present to honor the dead and pray for peace. Next, Lloyd Wilcox, a medicine man, cleansed the circle of evil spirits and lit fires. A peace pipe ritual followed, and the women of the tribe conducted a mourning ceremony, wailing for the dead. John Brown, a tribal councilman, also spoke:

> I'm not sure that they thought we'd be walking here in the twentieth century or in the forthcoming twenty-first century. Because, you see this place here was built not as a memory to us, but as a memory to our slaughter.

Next, Brown looked to the monument, erected by the Society of Colonial Wars in 1906, and pointed to the four massive boulders, explaining that they represent the four colonies: "The state of Rhode Island, over there, the state of Connecticut, the state of Massachusetts, and Plymouth Colony." Finally, he pointed to the granite shaft, which, in 1906, was erected to represent the colonists' "stern purpose and high valour," but as Brown interpreted it, "that spire means that that's the Narragansetts, we are again sitting in the middle, looking out at all of them." Finally, the Narragansetts and their guests formed a circle, hands together, and danced a round dance.

To me, watching that dance around that circle during a research trip, the scene powerfully echoed a passage in William Hubbard's 1677 *Narrative,* of the torture of a Narragansett man, circled by Mohegans and English soldiers. In Hubbard's account, English soldiers stood in a circle and watched the man in the middle being tortured to death, and, as I read it (and relate in this work's Prologue), the scene serves as a metaphor for the elaborate maneuverings by which seventeenth-century English colonists preserved their Englishness while engaging in a cruel war against their Indian neighbors. But at the Great Swamp in September 1992, the Narragansetts themselves formed the circle, along with their guests, and there was no tormented man in the middle; instead, they danced around a granite shaft, a memorial that for the Society of Colonial Wars had celebrated seventeenth-century colonists (of "stern purpose and high valour"), but that, for twentieth-century Narragansetts, towers as a testament to their own survival ("sitting in the middle, looking out at all of them"). Here was yet another metaphor, suggesting the still more subtle maneuverings of language and memory.

TO GET to the rocky beach where the Mount Hope Rock sits, Edmund Delabarre had to travel down Metacom Avenue in Bristol, Rhode Island. Taking the same road today, we would pass by the King Philip Inn, at 400 Metacom Avenue. "King Philip" is a popular theme in Bristol, the name of streets, schools, and automotive repair shops. But Delabarre's theory about the rock's inscription has gone unnoticed; people in town call it "Viking's Rock," and, though everyone has heard of it, no one seems to remember exactly where it is. And almost no one, of course, remembers Edmund Delabarre, a young psychology professor who arrived at Brown University in 1892, just a year before Frederick Jackson Turner delivered his address "The Significance of the Frontier in American History." Delabarre had trained at Harvard with William James, and though his interests shifted from rapid movement, the subject of his dissertation, to inscribed rocks, his newfound New England hobby, he remained true to his Jamesian education. That is, he prided himself on his rigor in debunking romantic Victorian myths; he considered his investigation of inscribed rocks "an exceedingly valuable discipline in scientific method and an enlightening commentary on the psychology of . . . the differing ways in which the same object may be seen by different observers."[32]

King Philip Inn, Bristol, Rhode Island. *Photograph by the author*

For the same reason, Edmund Delabarre would have been fascinated by the waging, writing, and remembering of King Philip's War. Or at least I would like to think so. The story of King Philip's War, as I have tried to tell it, is the story of how English colonists became Americans, and of the sometimes graceful, sometimes awkward, sometimes brutal posturing by which they positioned themselves in relation to the indigenous people of America and of Europe. It is a story of words and of wounds and of resurrections. Behind that story, however, is yet another tale. King Philip's War, in all its reincarnations, also traces shifting conceptions of Indian identity—from tribal allegiances to campaigns for political sovereignty to pan-Indianism, and, today, to struggles for cultural survival and political recognition. In the 1830s, Penobscots attended performances of *Metamora* and turned its sympathy for "vanished" Indians to their own political ends; and by the end of the nineteenth century, the story of King Philip's War had gained an important place within New England Algonquian folklore. By the early twentieth century, white and Indian traditions merged with, competed with, and borrowed from one another. Finally, today, the meaning of King Philip's War has become, once again, hotly contested, especially in the struggles for renaming the site at the Great Swamp and preserving the sacredness of Deer Island. During the 1993 celebration at the Great Swamp Memorial, Ella Sekatau, a Narragansett tribal historian, proclaimed, "We are Narragansetts first, and we are Americans when it is convenient."[33] Ella Sekatu's words, like John Brown's interpretation of the Great Swamp monument, suggest that Indians in New England in the latter part of the twentieth century are attempting, in effect, to preserve their Indianness as passionately as seventeenth-century colonists once struggled to preserve their Englishness. They want to stand in a circle, they want to mark the rock.

Abbreviations

tion Residing in London, Appointed by the King's Most Excellent Majesty for Promoting the Gospel among the Indians in America" [1677], in *Collections of the American Antiquarian Society* 2 (1836): 423–534.

Harris, *A Rhode Islander Reports*
William Harris to Sir Joseph Williamson, August 12, 1676, as edited and transcribed by Douglas Leach in *A Rhode Islander Reports on King Philip's War: The Second William Harris Letter of August, 1676* (Providence: Rhode Island Historical Society, 1963).

Hubbard, *Narrative*
William Hubbard, *A Narrative of the Troubles with the Indians in New-England, from the first planting thereof in the year 1607. to this present year 1677. But chiefly of the late Troubles in the two last years, 1675. and 1676. To which is added a Discourse about the Warre with the Pequods In the year 1637* (Boston, 1677); reprinted in *The History of the Indian Wars in New England,* ed. Samuel Gardner Drake (New York: Burt Franklin, 1865; Bowie, Md.: Heritage Books, 1990).

Hutchinson, *Warr in New-England Visibly Ended*
R[ichard] H[utchinson], *The Warr in New-England Visibly Ended. King Philip that barbarous Indian now Beheaded, and most of his Bloudy Adherents submitted to Mercy, the Rest fled far up into the Countrey, which hath given the Inhabitants Encouragement to prepare for their Settlement, Being a True and Perfect Account brought in by Caleb More, Master of a Vessel newly Arrived from Rhode Island, And Published for general Satisfaction* (London, 1677); reprinted in Lincoln, *Narratives of the Indian Wars,* 103–6.

Massachusetts Council, *To Our Brethren*
Massachusetts Council, *To Our Brethren and Friends the Inhabitants of the Colony of the Mattachusets* (Cambridge, 1675), brs.

Mather, *Brief History*
Increase Mather, *A Brief History of the Warr with the Indians in New-England. From June 24. 1675. (when the first Englishman was Murdered by the Indians) to August 12. 1676. when Philip, alias Metacomet, the principal Author and Beginner of the War was slain. Wherein the Grounds, beginning, and Progress of the War, is summarily expressed* (London, 1676); reprinted in *The History of King Philip's War,* ed. Samuel Gardner Drake (Albany, N.Y.: J. Munsell, 1862; Bowie, Md.: Heritage Books, 1990).

Mather, *Exhortation*
Increase Mather, *An Earnest Exhortation To the Inhabitants of New-England, To hearken to the voice of God in his late and present Dispensations As ever they desire to escape another Judgement, seven times greater then any thing which as yet hath been* (Boston, 1676); reprinted in Richard Slotkin and James Folsom, eds., *So Dreadfull a Judgment: Puritan Responses to King Philip's War* (Middletown, Conn.: Wesleyan University Press, 1978), 165–206.

Mather, *Historical Discourse*
Increase Mather, *An Historical Discourse Concerning the Prevalency of Prayer Wherein is shewed that New-Englands late Deliverance from the Rage of the Heathen, is an eminent Answer of Prayer* (Boston, 1677).

Mather, *Relation*
Increase Mather, *A Relation of the Troubles which have hapned in New-England, By reason of the Indians there: From the Year 1614 to the Year 1675. Wherein the frequent Conspiracyes of the Indians to cutt off the English, and the wonderfull providence of God, in disappointing their devices, is declared.* (Boston, 1677).

Mather, C., *Magnalia*
Cotton Mather, *Magnalia Christi Americana* (1702; Hartford, Conn., 1840).

News from New-England
Anonymous. *News from New-England, Being A True and last Account of the present Bloody Wars carried on betwixt the Infidels, Natives, and the English Christians, and Converted Indians of* New-England, *declaring the many Dreadful battles Fought betwixt them: As also the many Towns and Villages burnt by the merciless Heathens. And also the true Number of all the Christians slain since the beginning of that War, as it was sent over by a Factor of* New-England *to a Merchant in* London (London, 1676).

Nowell, *Abraham in Arms*
S[amuel] N[owell], *Abraham in Arms: Or The first Religious General with his Army Engaging in a War For which he had wisely prepared, and by which, not only an eminent Victory Was obtained, but A Blessing gained also. Delivered in an Artillery-Election Sermon, June, 3, 1678* (Boston, 1678); reprinted in Slotkin and Folsom, *So Dreadfull a Judgment,* 271–300.

Randolph, "Short Narrative"
Edmund Randolph, "A short narrative of my Proceedings an Several Voyages to and from New England to White Hall to the Lords of the Privvy Council. [London, October 12, 1676]," in *Hutchinson Papers* (Albany: Prince Society, 1865), 2:226.

Rowlandson, *Soveraignty*
Mary Rowlandson, *The Soveraignty & Goodness of God, Together, With the Faithfulness of His Promises Displayed; Being a Narrative of the Captivity and Restauration of Mrs. Mary Rowlandson. Commended by her, to all that desires to know the Lords doings to, and dealings with Her. Especially to her dear Children and Relations* (Cambridge, 1682); reprinted in Slotkin and Folsom, *So Dreadfull a Judgment,* 315–69.

Saltonstall, *Continuation*
N[athaniel] S[altonstall], *A Continuation of the State of New-England; Being a Farther Account of the Indian Warr, And of the Engagement betwixt the Joynt Forces of the United English Collonies and the Indians, on the 19th of December, 1675, With the true Number of the Slain and Wounded, and the Transactions of the English Army since the said Fight. With all other Passages that have there Hapned from the 10th of November, 1675, to the 8th of February 1675/6. Together with an Account of the Intended Rebellion of the Negroes in Barbadoes* (London, 1676); reprinted in Lincoln, *Narratives of the Indian Wars,* 53–74.

Saltonstall, *New and Further Narrative*
N[athaniel] S[altonstall], *A New and Further Narrative of the State of New-England; being a Continued Account of the Bloudy Indian War. From March till August 1676, Giving a Perfect Relation of the Several Devastations, Engagements, and Transactions there; As also the Great Successes Lately obtained against the Barbarous Indians, The Reducing of King Philip, and the Killing of one of the Queens, etc., Together with a Catalogue of the Losses in the whole, sustained on either Side since the said War began, as near as can be collected* (London, 1676); reprinted in Lincoln, *Narratives of the Indian Wars,* 77–99.

Saltonstall, *Present State*
N[athaniel] S[altonstall], *The Present State of New-England with Respect to the Indian War, Wherein is an Account of the true Reason thereof, (as far as can be judged by Men), Together with most of the Remarkable Passages that have happened from the 20th of June, till the 10th of November, 1675. Faithfully Composed by a Merchant of Boston and Communicated to his Friend in London* (London, 1675); reprinted in Lincoln, *Narratives of the Indian Wars,* 24–50.

Tompson, *New England's Crisis*
> Benjamin Tompson, *New Englands Crisis. Or a Brief Narrative, of New-Englands Lamentable Estate at present, compar'd with the former (but few) years of Prosperity. Occasioned by many unheard of Crueltyes practised upon the Persons and Estates of its united Colonyes, without respect of Sex, Age or Quality of Persons, by the Barbarous Heathen thereof. Poetically Described. By a Well-wisher to his Countrey* (Boston, 1676); reprinted in Slotkin and Folsom, *So Dreadfull a Judgment*, 213–33.

True Account
> Anonymous. *A true Account Of the Most Considerable Occurrences That have hapned in the Warre Between The English and the Indians in New-England, From the Fifth of May, 1676, to the Fourth of August last; as also of the Successes it hath pleased God to give the English against them: As it hath been communicated by Letters to a Friend in London* (London, 1676).

Walker, "Captan Perse"
> Philip Walker, "Captan Perse & his coragios Company," edited and with an introduction by Diane Bornstein in *AAS Proceedings* 83 (1973): 67–102.

Wharton, *New-England's Present Sufferings*
> [Edward Wharton], *New-England's Present Sufferings under Their Cruel Neighboring Indians. Represented in two Letters, lately Written from Boston to London* (London, 1675).

Wheeler, *Thankefull Remembrance*
> Thomas Wheeler, *A Thankefull Remembrance of Gods Mercy To Several Persons at Quabaug or Brookfield: Partly in a Collection of Providences about them, and Gracious Appearances for them: And partly in a Sermon Preached by Mr. Edward Bulkley, Pastor of the Church of Christ at Concord, upon a day of Thanksgiving, kept by divers for their Wonderfull Deliverance there* (Cambridge, 1676); reprinted in Slotkin and Folsom, *So Dreadfull a Judgment*, 227–57.

Winslow and Hinckley, "Narrative"
> Josiah Winslow and Thomas Hinckley, "Narrative shewing the manor of the beginning of the present Warr with the Indians of Mount hope and Pocassett," *PCR* 10:362–64.

Winthrop, *Some Meditations*
> W[ait] W[inthrop], *Some Meditations Concerning our Honourable Gentlemen and Fellow-Souldiers, in Pursuit of those Barbarous Natives in the Narragansit Country; and Their Service there. Committed into Plain Verse for the Benefit of those that Read it* (n.p., 1675; New London, 1721).

ARCHIVES AND SERIALS

AAS	American Antiquarian Society, Worcester, Mass.
AHR	*American Historical Review*
AICRJ	*American Indian Culture and Research Journal*
AIQ	*American Indian Quarterly*
AQ	*American Quarterly*
CCR	J. Hammond Trumbull, ed., *The Public Records of the Colony of Connecticut* (Hartford: F. A. Brown, 1850–90)
CSP	W. Noel Sainsbury, ed., *Calendar of State Papers*, Colonial Series, America and the West Indies (London, 1893)

EAL	*Early American Literature*
HNAI	*Handbook of North American Indians,* vol. 15, *The Northeast,* ed. Bruce G. Trigger (Washington, D.C.: Smithsonian Institution Press, 1978)
IJAL	*International Journal of American Linguistics*
JAH	*Journal of American History*
JCB	John Carter Brown Library, Brown University, Providence
Mass. Arch.	The Massachusetts State Archives, State House, Boston
MCR	Nathaniel B. Shurtleff, ed., *Records of the Governor and Company of the Massachusetts Bay in New England* (New York: AMS Press, 1968).
MHS	Massachusetts Historical Society, Boston
MHSC	*Collections of the Massachusetts Historical Society*
MHSP	*Massachusetts Historical Society Proceedings*
NEHGR	*New England Historical and Genealogical Register*
NEQ	*New England Quarterly*
PCR	David Pulsifer, ed., *Records of the Colony of New Plymouth in New England* (Boston: William White, 1861; reprinted New York: AMS Press, 1968)
RICR	*Records of the Colony of Rhode Island and Providence Plantations in New England* (Providence, 1857)
RIHS	Rhode Island Historical Society, Providence
RIHSC	*Collections of the Rhode Island Historical Society*
RIHSP	*Rhode Island Historical Society Proceedings*
WMQ	*William and Mary Quarterly* (all references are to the third series, unless otherwise noted)

Notes

WHAT'S IN A NAME?

1. Michel de Montaigne, *The Complete Essays of Montaigne*, trans. Donald M. Frame (Stanford, Calif.: Stanford University Press, 1968), 152. Thomas Hobbes, *Leviathan*, ed. Richard Tuck (Cambridge: Cambridge University Press, 1991), 31.

2. Michael Walzer, *Just and Unjust Wars: A Moral Argument with Historical Illustrations* (New York: Basic Books, 1977), 16.

3. Elaine Scarry, *The Body in Pain: The Making and Unmaking of the World* (New York: Oxford University Press, 1985), 96. My discussion of the nature of war is more generally indebted to pp. 60–96 and 133–57 and to Walzer, *Just and Unjust Wars*, especially Chapters 1–3.

4. Some of these "War is . . ." quotes are more recognizable than others, but all can be found in most collections of familiar quotations. "War is hell" and "War is at best barbarism" are the words of William Tecumseh Sherman. "But war's a game, which, were their subjects wise / Kings would not play at" is from William Cowper's "The Wintry Morning Walk." Clausewitz, of course, said, "War is . . . politics by other means." "War is a contagion" are the words of Franklin Delano Roosevelt. "War is, after all, the universal perversion" is from John Rae, and "War seems to me a mean, contemptible thing" is the opinion of Albert Einstein.

5. Elaine Scarry calls this the "unmaking of the world" and the "verbal unanchoredness of war." "War," she writes, "is in the massive fact of itself a huge structure for the derealization of cultural constructs and, simultaneously, for their eventual reconstitution. The purpose of the war is to designate as an outcome which of the two competing cultural constructs will by both sides be allowed to become real" (*The Body in Pain*, 60–96). Scarry's analysis is invaluable to this study, but I should pause here to emphasize two of our differences. First, I believe that war's consequences for language are neither universal nor transhistorical, as Scarry's work implies. King Philip's War certainly transformed New England Indians' relationship to language, but in vastly different ways than it did for their English neighbors. Any discussion of the power of language in a particular society must necessarily involve a survey of how its people communicate: how they speak, read, and write. In this study, then, I investigate such matters as rates of literacy and bilingualism as well as the timely (or untimely) de-

livery of letters and the output of printing presses. Second, to the extent that an unmade world is reconstituted by language, this reconstitution, I believe (following Walzer), is largely accomplished by moral language.

6. The most comprehensive account of this conflict is still to be found in Douglas Leach, *Flintlock and Tomahawk: New England in King Philip's War* (New York: The Macmillan Company, 1958; reprint, East Orleans, Mass.: Parnassus Imprints, 1992). Detailed information about English participants and particular military engagements can be found in George Madison Bodge, *Soldiers in King Philip's War* (Leominster, Mass.: for the author, 1896). For accounts of the war within the broader context of late seventeenth-century colonial-Indian relations, see Alden T. Vaughan, *New England Frontier: Puritans and Indians, 1620–1675* (New York: W. W. Norton & Company, 1965; rev. ed., 1979), 309–38; Francis Jennings, *The Invasion of America: Indians, Colonialism, and the Cant of Conquest* (New York: W. W. Norton & Company, 1975), 298–326. (It is worth noting that Vaughan has been accused of being a Puritan apologist, while Jennings' work is occasionally dismissed as polemical.) Russell Bourne's *The Red King's Rebellion: Racial Politics in New England, 1675–1678* (New York: Oxford University Press, 1990) provides a lively retelling of some events of the war, though it makes no new broad analysis. James David Drake has recently examined the native perspective on the war in his "Severing the Ties That Bind Them: A Reconceptualization of King Philip's War" (Ph.D. diss., UCLA, 1995). A fine examination of the war's effect on a single community can be found in Richard I. Melvoin, *New England Outpost: War and Society in Colonial Deerfield* (New York: W. W. Norton & Company, 1989), 92–123. On the economic and political repercussions of King Philip's War see Michael J. Puglisi, *Puritans Besieged: The Legacies of King Philip's War in the Massachusetts Bay Colony* (Lanham, Md.: University Press of America, 1991) and Stephen Saunders Webb, *1676: The End of American Independence* (New York: Alfred A. Knopf, 1984), especially 221–44, 411–12. On Algonquian-English relations see Neal Salisbury, *Manitou and Providence: Indians, Europeans, and the Making of New England, 1500–1643* (New York: Oxford University Press, 1982); Robert F. Trent, "Coastal Algonkian Culture, 1500–1680: Conquest and Resistance," in Jonathan Fairbanks, ed., *New England Begins: The Seventeenth Century* (Boston: Museum of Fine Arts, 1982), 1:66–71; Karen H. Dacey, *In the Shadow of the Great Blue Hill* (Lanham, Md.: University Press of America, 1995); Karen Kupperman, *Settling with the Indians: The Meeting of English and Indian Cultures in America, 1580–1640* (Totowa, N.J.: Rowman & Littlefield, 1980; and Vaughan, *New England Frontier*. On the native peoples of seventeenth-century southeastern New England see Kathleen J. Bragdon, *Native People of Southern New England, 1500–1650* (Norman: University of Oklahoma Press, 1996), as well as the important essays in *HNAI* 15:58–197.

7. Samuel Green, ed., *Diary of Increase Mather, March, 1675–December, 1676* (Cambridge, Mass.: John Wilson & Son, 1900), 18.

8. Whenever it is possible to identify the native people involved in a particular event I will refer to individuals by name and to groups by affiliation—Wampanoag, Narragansett, Pequot, Mohawk, etc. Unfortunately, the sources do not always provide that information, and in its absence, I will generally use "Algonquians," "Indians," and "natives." (I have tried to avoid using "tribe," since it remains a contested term.) To avoid confusion, I have generally not used the names of smaller groups if they are more easily identified as members, usually both ethnically and politically, of larger ones (e.g., "Pokanokets" refers to Wampanoags living in the Mount Hope area, but I use simply "Wampanoags"). Since most coastal populations were devastated by diseases early in the seventeenth century, evidence about prewar groups is varied, and since some smaller groups either died out or merged with others in the early decades of contact, reconstructing political divisions on the eve of King Philip's War is

tentative. By far the best source for further information is Bert Salwen, "Indians of Southern New England and Long Island: Early Period," *HNAI* 15:160–76. Readers may benefit from a few clarifications: some scholars have used "Nipmuck" and "Massachusett" interchangeably, though possibly without cause; Niantics are closely related to Narragansetts, though the former remained largely neutral during the war; Pawtuckets are also called Penacooks and are occasionally subsumed under the broader group, Massachusett, as are the more western Pocumtucks; "Christian Indians" is the term used to refer to Algonquian converts, the great majority of whom were Massachusett or Pawtucket; and "Penobscots" refers to eastern Abenakis who remained in their homelands after King Philip's War.

9. Melvoin has convincingly argued that moving the line of English settlement toward the coast was, in fact, the Algonquian strategy (*New England Outpost*, 108–11). Webb argues that "Per-capita incomes in New England did not recover their 1675 levels until 1775. . . . A century of dependence on England would be required to recover the physical basis of New England's independence" (*1676*, 243).

10. Scholarship on colonial writings about King Philip's War includes, most notably, Richard Slotkin, *Regeneration through Violence: The Mythology of the American Frontier, 1600–1860* (Middletown, Conn.: Wesleyan University Press, 1973), 78–93.

11. The most valuable recent works on colonial identity are John Canup, *Out of the Wilderness: The Emergence of an American Identity in Colonial New England* (Middletown, Conn.: Wesleyan University Press, 1990); the essays in *Colonial Identity in the Atlantic World, 1500–1800*, ed. Nicholas Canny and Anthony Pagden (Princeton, N.J.: Princeton University Press, 1987); and Jack P. Greene's important collection of essays, *Imperatives, Behaviors, and Identities: Essays in Early American Cultural History* (Charlottesville: University Press of Virginia, 1992). The idea that colonists in America defined themselves in opposition to the Indians they met there, however, has a history that predates the more recent interpretations of scholars such as Canup. Among the most influential of these earlier works are Roy Harvey Pearce, *The Savages of America: A Study of the Indian and the Idea of Civilization* (Baltimore: The Johns Hopkins Press, 1965); Robert F. Berkhofer, Jr., *The White Man's Indian: Images of the American Indian from Columbus to the Present* (New York: Vintage Books, 1979); and Richard Drinnon, *Facing West: The Metaphysics of Indian-Hating and Empire-Building* (Minneapolis: University of Minnesota Press, 1980). Powerful earlier works on the relationship between Puritan and American identity include Perry Miller, *The New England Mind: The Seventeenth Century* (Cambridge: Harvard University Press, 1939) and Sacvan Berkovitch, *The Puritan Origins of the American Self* (New Haven, Conn.: Yale University Press, 1975). Recent scholarship has placed this development within the broader context of the Atlantic world and ideas about language. As Eric Cheyfitz has written,

> For England, the initial period of expansion into the Atlantic and Caribbean regions . . . corresponds, as it did for England's European competitors, with a powerful surge in the formation of a national identity. The formation of this identity, as writers of the time instruct us, was particularly dependent on the formation of a national language. The articulation of ideas about such a language registers acutely how volatile definitions of the native and the foreign were at the time, when the line between internal and external frontiers was not nearly as clear-cut as it is in the political schemes of today (*The Poetics of Imperialism: Translation and Colonization from* The Tempest *to* Tarzan [New York: Oxford University Press, 1991], 95–96).

12. Bernard Bailyn has called the British North American colonies "the exotic far western periphery, a marchland of the metropolitan European culture system" (*The Peopling of British North America: An Introduction* [New York: Alfred A. Knopf, 1986], 112–31), a perspec-

tive I have found useful to understanding the colonists' keen sense of their distance from Europe, but my discussion of seventeenth-century New England is also informed by Richard White's persuasive arguments about a frontier space he calls "the middle ground." "The middle ground is the place in between: in between cultures, peoples, and in between empires and the nonstate world of villages. It is a place where many of the North American subjects and allies of empires lived. It is the area between the historical foreground of European invasion and occupation and the background of Indian defeat and retreat" (*The Middle Ground: Indians, Empires, and Republics in the Great Lakes Region, 1650–1815* [Cambridge: Cambridge University Press, 1991], x).

13. William Cronon, George Miles, and Jay Gitlin, "Becoming West: Toward a New Meaning for Western History," in *Under an Open Sky: Rethinking America's Western Past*, ed. Cronon, Miles, and Gitlin (New York: W. W. Norton & Company, 1992), 15.

14. Andrew Knaut, *The Pueblo Revolt of 1680: Conquest and Resistance in Seventeenth-Century New Mexico* (Norman: University of Oklahoma Press, 1995).

15. According to Frederick Jackson Turner,

> At the Atlantic frontier one can study the germs of processes repeated at each successive frontier. . . . The first frontier had to meet its Indian question, its question of the disposition of the public domain, of the means of intercourse with older settlements, of the extension of political organization, of religious and educational activity. And the settlement of these and similar questions for one frontier served as a guide for the next ("The Significance of the Frontier in American History," in *The Frontier in American History* [New York: Henry Holt & Company, 1920], 1–38).

Cronon, Miles, and Gitlin argue that Turner's "most compelling argument about the frontier was that *it repeated itself* " ("Becoming West," 6).

16. At the most literal level, Russell Bourne has recently argued that the most commonly accepted end point for the war, Philip's death in August 1676, is inaccurate, since the war continued in Maine and western New England (Bourne, *Red King's Rebellion*, 205–9). Richard Slotkin has argued that "the Indian wars proved to be the most acceptable metaphor for the American experience" and that King Philip's War was "an archetype of all the wars which followed" (Slotkin, *Regeneration through Violence*, 68, 79).

17. Patricia Nelson Limerick, "Making the Most of Words: Verbal Activity and Western Americana," in *Under an Open Sky*, 168. Limerick further argues, "Filled with people using written words to justify, promote, sell, entice, cover up, evade, defend, deny, congratulate, persuade, and reassure, western history puts a premium on the critical evaluation of words."

18. "From its beginnings the imperialist mission is, in short, one of translation: the translation of the 'other' into the terms of the empire, the prime term of which is 'barbarian,' or one of its variations such as 'savage,' which, ironically, but not without a precise politics, also alienates the other from the empire" (Cheyfitz, *The Poetics of Imperialism*, 112). Other important literature on the intellectual and linguistic consequences of the encounter includes Stephen Greenblatt, *Marvelous Possessions: The Wonder of the New World* (Chicago: The University of Chicago Press, 1991); Greenblatt, ed., *New World Encounters* (Berkeley: University of California Press, 1993); Peter Hulme, *Colonial Encounters: Europe and the Native Caribbean, 1492–1797* (London: Methuen, 1986); Karen Kupperman, ed., *America in European Consciousness, 1493–1750* (Chapel Hill: University of North Carolina Press, 1995); Anthony Pagden, *European Encounters with the New World* (New Haven, Conn.: Yale University Press, 1993); and

Tzvetan Todorov, *The Conquest of America*, trans. Richard Howard (New York: Harper & Row, 1987).

19. Quoted in Hulme, *Colonial Encounters*, 1. Hulme writes that language is indeed the "perfect instrument of empire" because it masks economic exploitation with a colonial discourse of difference: "The topic of land is dissimulated by the topic of savagery, this move being characteristic of all narratives of the colonial encounter." He defines "colonial discourse" as "an ensemble of linguistically-based practices unified by their common deployment and management of colonial relationships, an ensemble that could combine the most formulaic and bureaucratic of official documents . . . with the most non-functional and unprepossessing of romantic novels" (2–3).

20. Perry Miller argued that New England's colonists measured themselves against England and that their failure to measure up constituted their chief crisis of identity (*Errand into the Wilderness* [Cambridge: The Belknap Press, 1956, 1984], ch. 1), but I am here arguing that the colonists also measured themselves against the colonial ventures of other European countries, following scholars such as Canny and Pagden.

21. See William S. Maltby, *The Black Legend in England: The Development of Anti-Spanish Sentiment, 1558–1660* (Durham, N.C.: Duke University Press, 1971); and Peter Lake, "Anti-popery: The Structure of a Prejudice," in *Conflict in Early Stuart England: Studies in Religion and Politics, 1603–1642*, ed. Richard Cust and Ann Hughes (London: Longman, 1989), 72–106.

22. Stephen Greenblatt, "Learning to Curse: Aspects of Linguistic Colonialism in the Sixteenth Century," in *First Images of America: The Impact of the New World on the Old*, ed. Fredi Chiappelli, 2 vols. (Berkeley: University of California Press, 1976), 566–68.

23. Benedict Anderson has argued that national identity is best understood as an "imagined community" of people sharing traditions and territory. For Anderson, the printed word is central to the construction of imagined communities (*Imagined Communities: Reflections on the Origin and Spread of Nationalism* [London: Verso, 1983]). My understanding of nationalism and national identity is also informed by Anthony D. Smith, *National Identity* (Reno: University of Nevada Press, 1991).

24. Hubbard, *Narrative*, 1:15. Discussions of this naming controversy can be found in Drake, "Severing the Ties That Bind Them," 3–13; and Philip Ranlet, "Another Look at the Causes of King Philip's War," *NEQ* 61 (1988): 80–81, especially n. 3.

25. Francis Jennings was the first to suggest "Puritan Conquest" (*Invasion of America*, 298). Bourne, among others, has suggested "rebellion" (*Red King's Rebellion*). James Drake and Harold W. Van Lonkhuyzen have both suggested that King Philip's War is better understood as an Indian civil war, and Drake proposes "Northeast Civil War" as a new name (Drake, "Severing the Ties that Bind Them," 9; Lonkhuyzen, "A Reappraisal of the Praying Indians: Acculturation, Conversion, and Identity at Natick, Massachusetts, 1646–1730," *NEQ* 63 [1990]: 420). While each of these critiques, Drake and Lonkhuyzen especially, offers useful correctives to our understanding of the war, my position is closest to that of Philip Ranlet, who argues in favor of "King Philip's War," though our reasoning differs ("Another Look at the Causes," 80–81).

26. "Att the ernest request of Wamsitta, desiring that in regard his father is lately deceased, and hee being desirouse, according to the custome of the natives, to change his name, that the Court would confer an English name upon him, which accordingly they did, and therefore ordered, that for the future hee shalbee called by the name of Allexander

Pokanokett; and desireing the same in the behalfe of his brother, they have named him Phillip" (*PCR* 3:192).

27. Hubbard, *Narrative*, 1:52.

28. This connection is corroborated in *Farther Brief and True Narration*, 4, and Mather, *Exhortation*, 190.

29. Hubbard, *Narrative*, 1:15–16. (Meanwhile, in a poetic prologue, Benjamin Tompson said Hubbard's *Narrative* was "Wrote by exacter Hand than ever took / Historians Pen since Europe we forsook" [*Narrative*, 1:24].)

30. Mather, *Brief History*, 36.

31. Samuel Purchas, *Hakluytus Posthumus or Purchas His Pilgrimes* (Glasgow: James MacLehose and Sons; reprint, New York: The Macmillan Company, 1905), 486–87.

32. Ninigret, possibly the most powerful sachem in southern New England, actually became an important ally of the English during the war, even offering to persuade the Mohawks not to ally with Philip. See Leach, *Flintlock and Tomahawk*, 112–16; and, more broadly, Timothy J. Sehr, "Ninigret's Tactics of Accommodation—Indian Diplomacy in New England, 1637–1675," *Rhode Island History* 36:1 (May 1977): 43–53. His service may partly explain why his portrait came to be painted. In 1669, however, Ninigret may have plotted with Philip to plan the war (*RICR* 2:266), and some evidence indicates that he was sympathetic with Algonquians who fought against the English.

33. The note read, in part, "we care not though we have war with you this 21 years." Noah Newman copied the note out in his letter to John Cotton, March 14, 1676, Curwen Papers, AAS.

34. Philip to Governor Prince, n.d., *MHSC*, ser. 1, 2:40.

35. For Philip's mark, see, e.g., *PCR* 12:237; 4:26; 5:79. Philip's brother Alexander at times signed with an "A" and at other times signed with an "M" (possibly an upside-down "W"), favoring his Algonquian name "Wamsutta," or an earlier Algonquian name, "Moonanam" (Ebenezer Peirce, *Indian Biography and Genealogy* [1878; reprint, Freeport, N.Y.: Books for Libraries Press, 1972], 240, 210, *Early Records of the Town of Providence* [Providence, 1892]:5:283). My contention that Philip probably knew the alphabet is based on evidence that John Sassamon attempted to teach him to read, as I discuss in Chapter 1.

36. Quoted in Hugh Amory, *First Impressions: Printing in Cambridge, 1639–1989* (Cambridge, Mass.: Harvard University Press, 1989), 41. On Algonquian naming practices, see also William Simmons, *Spirit of the New England Tribes: Indian History and Folklore, 1620–1984* (Hanover, N.H.: University Press of New England, 1986), 46; Bragdon, *Native Peoples*, 170.

37. William Scranton Simmons, *Cautantowwit's House: An Indian Burial Ground on the Island of Conanicut in Narragansett Bay* (Providence: Brown University Press, 1970), 58. The recent claim that Philip was actually Massasoit's grandson, not his son (Betty Groff Schroeder, "The True Lineage of King Philip [Sachem Metacom]" *NEHGR* 144 [1990]: 211–14), appears to be mistaken, and based primarily on Nathaniel Saltonstall's own error (*Present State*, 26).

38. In the summer of 1676 the Christian Indian Jacob Muttamakoog wrote to John Eliot and others, "my wonder concerning *Philip*, but his name is ——— *Wewesawamit*" (emphasis in original; the letter is printed in *True Account*, 6). Philip was also occasionally referred to as "Philip Keitasscot," but James Drake has astutely argued that " 'Keitasscot' is simply a variation on the Massachusett word 'ketahsoot,' meaning king or sachem." ("Severing the

Ties That Bind Them," 8). Drake has further suggested that Wewesawamit, or Wewa-sowannett, may also be a title rather than a name, though I have found no evidence to that effect. Ranlet rejects renaming the conflict "Wewesawamit's (or Wewasowannett's) War" for other reasons ("Another Look at the Causes," 80).

39. This romantic image of Philip is discussed in Chapter 8. But see, for example, John Greenleaf Whittier's poem "Metacom," *The Ladies Magazine* 3 (1830): 58; or John August Stone's 1829 play about King Philip's War, in which Philip is called "Metamora." When an English ambassador addresses Metamora as "Philip," he fiercely corrects him, "Philip! I am the Wampanoag chief, Metamora" (Stone, "Metamora; or, the Last of the Wampanoags: An Indian Tragedy in Five Acts as played by Edwin Forrest," in *Metamora and Other Plays,* ed. Eugene R. Page [Princeton, N.J.: Princeton University Press, 1941], 17). In John Brougham's parody of Stone's play, Metamora's reply to being called "Philip" is "What mean ye by Philip, you rude dogs? I'm Metamora, chief of the Pollywogs" (*Metamora; or, the Last of the Pollywogs* [New York: Samuel French, n.d.], 8).

40. Walzer, *Just and Unjust Wars,* xxv.

41. Scarry, *The Body in Pain,* 61.

42. When quoting from other scholars' edited reprints of seventeenth- or eighteenth-century narratives of King Philip's War, however, I have generally deferred to their editorial standards, which, on the whole, tend to modernize the text more thoroughly than my own. This is especially true of one of the major modern collections of such narratives, *So Dreadfull a Judgment: Puritan Responses to King Philip's War, 1676–1677,* ed. Richard Slotkin and James Folsom (Middletown, Conn.: Wesleyan University Press, 1978) but since it is also the most easily available to readers, I have chosen to cite from it directly.

43. Hubbard, *Narrative,* 1:15.

Prologue · THE CIRCLE

1. Hubbard, *Narrative,* 2:63–64. This scene is briefly analyzed in John Canup's important monograph *Out of the Wilderness: The Emergence of an American Identity in Colonial New England* (Middletown, Conn.: Wesleyan University Press, 1990), 192–93. For a very similar account of an Indian torture scene before the war see John Josselyn, *An Account of Two Voyages to New-England, Made during the Years 1638, 1663* (London, 1675), 148–49.

2. William Ames, *Conscience, with the Power and Cases Thereof* (London, 1643), 184. Ames also warned against the excesses of vengeance: "Those that are guilty, are not to bee hurt any further then the compassing the just end of the Warre doth require, that is so farre, that they make a faire restitution of the thing taken away, or that the injury bee sufficiently revenged, or a peace established" (190–91).

3. Thomas Aquinas, *Summa Theologica,* part 3, question 159, article 2.

4. Michael Zuckerman has argued that "descendants of the original pioneers did their best to recover the culture their parents had left behind, but the pioneers themselves often embarked upon the ocean passage in a willful rejection of the emerging English modes" ("Identity in British America: Unease in Eden," in *Colonial Identity in the Atlantic World, 1500–1800,* ed. Nicholas Canny and Anthony Pagden [Princeton, N.J.: Princeton University Press, 1987], 115). While I agree that the yearning for English ways intensified with each generation, I am arguing here that even the pioneering colonists, while they rejected much in England, never fundamentally rejected an English cultural identity.

5. Edward Winslow, in *Hypocrisie Unmasked* (1646), as quoted in John Canup, *Out of the Wilderness,* 58. Or, as William Bradford reported, "they heard a strange and uncouth language, and beheld the different manners and customs of the people, with their strange fashions and attires; all so far differing from that of their plain country villages, wherein they were bred and born and had so long lived, as it seemed they were come into a new world" (*Chronicles of the Pilgrim Fathers,* ed. Alexander Young [Boston, 1841], 33).

6. David Cressy, *Coming Over: Migration and Communication between England and New England in the Seventeenth Century* (Cambridge: Cambridge University Press, 1987), 192; see also ch. 8.

7. Roger Williams, *A Key into the Language of America,* ed. John J. Teunissen and Evelyn J. Hinz (Detroit: Wayne State University Press, 1973), 85.

8. Daniel Gookin, "Historical Collections of the Indians of New England," *MHSC,* 3rd ser., 1:223.

9. Canup, *Out of the Wilderness,* 60–64; Zuckerman, "Identity in British America," 137–38. Zuckerman, summarizing the paradox articulated by Michael Kammen, writes, "The colonists emphasized the heathenism of other races in the New World in order to reassure themselves of their own Christian character in the wilderness. But their Christian identity constrained them to convert the heathen and risk eradicating the very contrast on which they had predicated their religious conception of themselves" (153). See Michael Kammen, *People of Paradox: An Inquiry Concerning the Origins of American Civilization* (New York: Alfred A. Knopf, 1972), and also earlier scholarship on the construction of American "savages," e.g., Roderick Nash, *Wilderness and the American Mind* (New Haven, Conn.: Yale University Press, 1967; rev. ed., 1973), especially ch. 2; Peter N. Carroll, *Puritanism and the Wilderness: The Intellectual Significance of the New England Frontier, 1629–1700* (New York: Columbia University Press, 1969); and Roy Harvey Pearce, *The Savages of America: A Study of the Indian and the Idea of Civilization* (Baltimore: The Johns Hopkins Press, 1965), especially 4–7, 19–35.

10. Increase Mather, *The Day of Trouble is Near* (Cambridge, Mass., 1674), 21–23.

11. Samuel Danforth, *The Cry of Sodom Enquired Into* (Cambridge, Mass., 1674), 5.

12. Quoted in James Muldoon, "The Indian as Irishman," *Essex Institute Historical Collections* 11 (1975): 275–76.

13. James Axtell, "The White Indians," in *The Invasion Within: The Contest of Cultures in Colonial North America* (New York: Oxford University Press, 1985), 302–27. On the similarities between English ideas about the Irish and about Indians, see Muldoon, "The Indian as Irishman," 267–89; David B. Quinn, *England and the Discovery of America* (New York: Alfred A. Knopf, 1974); and Nicholas Canny, "The Ideology of English Colonization: From Ireland to America," *WMQ* 30 (1973): 575–98.

14. Gabriel Sagard-Théodat, *Histoire du Canada et Voyages que les frères Mineurs Recollects y ont faicts pour la Conversion des Infidèlles depuis l'an 1615* (Paris: Sonnius, 1636), 166. Quoted in Olive Patricia Dickason, "From 'One Nation' in the Northeast to 'New Nation' in the Northwest: A Look at the Emergence of the Métis," in Jacqueline Peterson and Jennifer S. H. Brown, eds., *The New Peoples: Being and Becoming Métis* (Lincoln: University of Nebraska Press, 1985), 23.

15. And, as Michael Zuckerman has argued, "The more the colonists fell short of their own standards of civility, the more vehemently they inveighed against the savagery of others" ("Identity in British America," 152).

16. Quoted in William Simmons, *Spirit of the New England Tribes: Indian History and Folklore, 1620–1984* (Hanover, N.H.: University Press of New England, 1986), 63.

17. Easton, "Relacion," 10.

18. Increase Mather, *The Necessity of Reformation* (Boston, 1679), 5.

19. The colonists were unconcerned about sparing their Indian allies because these were either members of very weakened tribes or individuals who had already subjected themselves politically to the English. Also, according to English Puritan thought, Christians could enlist the aid of infidels in war, since "as it is lawfull to use the helpe of beasts, as of Elephants, Horses, &c. So also is it lawfull to use the aid of beastlike men" (Ames, *Conscience*, 188–89).

20. The full stanza reads: "Wee Came to wild America / whos native brood to divels pray / a savig race for blud that thirst / off all the nations most acurst / ffrom ffamin, scurvi, feare they past / and yit for all god did at last / as he in wisdom most devine / purg ther dros from purer Coyne" (Walker, "Captan Perse," 86).

21. Benedict Anderson, *Imagined Communities: Reflections on the Origins and Spread of Nationalism* (London: Verso, 1983), 47–49. Peter Furtado has argued that "the later seventeenth century was the time when the language of patriotism became firmly established in the repertoire of English political rhetoric" ("National Pride in Seventeenth-Century England," in *Patriotism: The Making and Unmaking of British National Identity*, ed. Raphael Samuel, vol. 1: History and Politics [London: Routledge, 1989], 44).

22. John Eliot to the Massachusetts governor and Council in Boston, August 13, 1675, *PCR* 10:451–52.

23. As Myron Gilmore has argued, "The literature on the New World furnished material for religious and national polemics: condemnation of Spanish colonialism and of forced conversion, praise for French and English motives and for their treatment of Indians" ("The New World in French and English Historians of the Sixteenth Century," in *First Images of America: The Impact of the New World on the Old*, ed. Fredi Chiappelli [Berkeley: University of California Press, 1976], 525).

24. Richard Hakluyt, "Discourse on Western Planting" (1584), in Jack P. Greene, ed., *S ettlements to Society, 1607–1763: A Documentary History of Colonial America* (New York: W. W. Norton & Company, 1975), 7–8.

25. Sir Walter Ralegh, "Of the Voyage for Guiana," in Robert H. Schomburgk, ed., *The Discovery of the Large, Rich, and Beautiful Empire of Guiana . . . by Sir W. Ralegh*, Works Issued by the Hakluyt Society, no. 3 (n.d.; reprint, New York: Burt Franklin, 1970), 143.

26. Mather, *Brief History*, 41.

27. The one interruption to peaceful relations, the Pequot War of 1637, was given brief treatment as a just and entirely defensive war. See John Mason, *A Brief History of the Pequot War* (Boston, 1736; reprinted in *MHSC*, 2nd ser., 8 [1826]); Philip Vincent, *A True Relation of the Late Battell fought in New-England* (London, 1638; reprinted in *MHSC*, 3rd ser., 6 [1837]); John Underhill, *News from America; or, a New and Experimentall Discoverie of New England* (London, 1638); reprinted in *MHSC*, 3rd ser., 6 [1837]). For a recent scholarly history of that conflict see Alfred A. Cave, *The Pequot War* (Amherst: University of Massachusetts Press, 1996).

28. Roger Williams to the Commissioners of the United Colonies, October 5, 1654, *PCR* 10:439–40.

29. Bartolomé de Las Casas, *The Tears of the Indians: Being An Historical and true Account of the Cruel Massacres and Slaughters of above Twenty Millions of innocent People* (London, 1656), trans. J. P., Preface.

30. Canup makes a related argument in *Out of the Wilderness,* in a chapter aptly titled "The Triumph of Indianism" (149–97).

31. See, e.g., James Cranford, *The Teares of Ireland* (London, 1642), and Samuel Clarke, *A Generall Martryologie* (London, 1651). Germany's atrocities were publicized most notably in *The Lamentations of Germany,* printed in London in 1638, after being translated into English by Philip Vincent, probably the same Philip Vincent who had authored an account of the Pequot War. James D. Drake has observed and explored the coincidence of Vincent's probable authorship of both tracts ("Restraining Atrocity: The Puritan Conduct of King Philip's War," paper delivered at the Institute for Early American History and Culture Second Annual Conference, June 1996). This entire propaganda literature is powerfully analyzed in Barbara Donagan, "Atrocity, War Crime, and Treason in the English Civil War," *AHR* 99 (1994): 1137–66. On the traditions of Protestant martyrdom see John Knott, *Discourses of Martyrdom in English Literature* (Cambridge: Cambridge University Press, 1993).

32. Tompson, *New England's Crisis,* 230.

33. As Stephen J. Greenblatt has written, "the very conception that a culture is alien rests upon the perceived difference of that culture from one's own behavioral codes, and it is precisely at the points of perceived difference that the individual is conditioned, as a founding principle of personal and group identity, to experience disgust" ("Filthy Rites," in *Learning to Curse: Essays in Early Modern Culture* [New York: Routledge, 1990], 61). See also Peter Stallybrass and Allon White, *The Politics and Poetics of Transgression* (Ithaca, N.Y.: Cornell University Press, 1986), 191.

On the necessity of viewing an enemy's conduct during war as "savage," see Thomas S. Abler, "Scalping, Torture, Cannibalism and Rape: An Ethnohistorical Analysis of Conflicting Values in War," *Anthropologica* 34 (1992): 3–20.

34. Mather, *Brief History,* 136–38.

35. Nathaniel Knowles, "The Torture of Captives by the Indians of Eastern North America," *American Philosophical Society Proceedings* 82 (1940): 151–225; Anthony F. C. Wallace, *The Death and Rebirth of the Seneca* (New York: Vintage Books, 1979), 103–7; Daniel K. Richter, *The Ordeal of the Longhouse: The Peoples of the Iroquois League in the Era of European Colonization* (Chapel Hill: University of North Carolina Press, 1992), 66–71; Richter, "War and Culture: The Iroquois Experience," *WMQ* 40 (1983): 530–34; and Adam J. Hirsch, "The Collision of Military Cultures in Seventeenth-Century New England," *JAH* 74 (1988): 1192. On the cultural differences (and similarities) between European and Indian torture see Jennings, *Invasion of America,* 161–65.

36. Stonewall John (who was also known as "Stonelayer John" and "John Wall Maker") was reported killed during the two-day campaign during which this torture/execution took place; others who were captured with him were taken to English towns for trial, public execution, or sale (Saltonstall, *New and Further Narrative,* 96; Samuel Gardner Drake, *Book of the Indians* [Boston, 1841], 3:77–78). As Patrick M. Malone has pointed out, earlier historians, skeptical that an Indian could have considerable construction and craft skills, made the error of believing Stonewall John must have been a renegade colonist (*The Skulking Way of War: Technology and Tactics Among the New England Indians* [Lanham, Md.: Madison Books, 1991], 75).

37. Roger Williams to [Robert Williams?], April 1, 1676, *The Correspondence of Roger Williams,* ed. Glenn W. LaFantasie (Providence: Brown University Press, 1988), 2:723.

38. Harris, *A Rhode Islander Reports*, 76.

39. Hubbard, *Narrative*, 1:16.

40. Hubbard, *Narrative*, 1:244. See also Major John Talcott to the Connecticut War Council, Hartford, July 4, 1676, *CCR* 2:458. Talcott summarized the expedition but did not relate the story of the torture of the captured Narragansett man. On Talcott's campaign see Douglas Leach, *Flintlock and Tomahawk: New England in King Philip's War* (New York: The Macmillan Company, 1958; reprint, East Orleans, Mass.: Parnassus Imprints, 1992), 211–12.

41. Connecticut War Council, Hartford, to Governor Andros, New York, August 19, 1676, *CCR* 2:469. Emphasis mine.

42. Francis Bland, *The Souldiers March to Salvation* (Yorke, 1647), 30.

43. On this paradox more generally, see Hayden White, "The Noble Savage Theme as Fetish," in *First Images of America*, 121–35, especially 132.

44. Hubbard, *Narrative*, 2:64.

45. Church, *Entertaining History*, 65–67. Church, however, ended up fighting the man whose execution he refused to watch, after the Nipmuck tried to escape. Although the published account was actually written by Benjamin Church's son Thomas, it followed Church's own papers and recollections. But because Church's narrative was written so much later than the others, and secondhand, I rely on it very little in the first three parts of this study. On the question of the authorship of *Entertaining History* (first published under the title *Entertaining Passages*), see Richard Slotkin and James K. Folsom, eds., *So Dreadfull a Judgment: Puritan Responses to King Philip's War, 1676–1677* (Middletown, Conn.: Wesleyan University Press, 1978), 376, and Slotkin, *Regeneration through Violence: The Mythology of the American Frontier, 1600–1860* (Middletown, Conn.: Wesleyan University Press, 1973), 577n.

46. Church, *Entertaining History*, 147–49.

47. On the perils of writing about cruelty see Judith N. Shklar, *Ordinary Vices* (Cambridge: The Belknap Press, 1984), ch. 1: "Putting Cruelty First," 7–44. On the perilous position the historian occupies in resurrecting and retelling scenes of cruelty see Stephen J. Greenblatt, "Learning to Curse," in *Learning to Curse*, 13.

Chapter 1 · BEWARE OF ANY LINGUIST

1. Winslow and Hinckley, "Narrative," 362. Mather, *Relation*, 74–75. Variant spellings of John Sassamon's last name include Sausiman, Sossiman, Sosoman, Sausimun, Sausaman, Sosoman, Sosaman, Sasamand, Wussasoman, and Wussasamon.

2. Winslow and Hinckley, "Narrative," 363.

3. *PCR* 5:167. Variant spellings of Mattashunannamo's name include Mattashunnamo, Mattashanamo, Mattushamama, and Mattashinnamy. Wampapaquan is also rendered as Wampapaum.

4. Mather, *Brief History*, 48. Variant spellings of William Nahauton's last name include Ahaton, Ahatton, Ahawton, Hahaton, and Nahaton.

5. Mather, *Relation*, 74–75; C. Mather, *Magnalia*, 559–60. For the official account of the trial see *PCR* 5:159, 167–68. Contemporary accounts of Sassamon's death and of the subsequent trial of his alleged murderers also include Hubbard, *Narrative*, 1:60–64; Mather, *Brief History*, 47–53; Saltonstall, *Present State*, 24–25; Saltonstall, *Continuation*, 54–55. Scholarly discussions of the trial include James Drake, "Symbol of a Failed Strategy: The Sassamon Trial, Political Culture, and the Outbreak of King Philip's War," *AICRJ* 19 (1995): 111–41; James P.

and Jeanne Ronda, "The Death of John Sassamon: An Exploration in Writing New England Indian History," *American Indian Quarterly* 1 (1974): 91–102; David Bushnell, "The Treatment of the Indians in Plymouth Colony," *NEQ* 26 (1953): 214–15; and Yasuhide Kawashima, *Puritan Justice and the Indian: White Man's Law in Massachusetts, 1630–1763* (Middletown, Conn.: Wesleyan University Press, 1986), 129, 131, 232–33.

6. *PCR* 5:167.

7. Saltonstall, *Present State*, 25.

8. On Philip's men arming outside Plymouth see John Brown to Josiah Winslow, June 11, 1675, Winslow Papers, MHS. English accounts of the beginning of the war are varied, and some contradict one another, but most concur in dating the outbreak of fighting to June 24 (e.g., *Brief and True Narration*, 5; Hubbard, *Narrative*, 1:64–65; Mather, *Brief History*, 54). John Easton's "Relacion" differs from most in telling the story of a young English boy firing the first shot on June 23, killing an Indian who was looting English houses ("Relacion," 8–12). And Nathaniel Saltonstall reported that two colonists were killed at Swansea on June 23 (*Present State*, 26–29). See also Josiah Winslow to John Leverett, June 21, 1675, Mass. Arch. 67:202. There is some evidence that Philip, while he had intended to wage war against the English, had not wanted the war to begin when it did, and that his preparations were incomplete (see Hubbard, *Narrative*, 1:48; Harris, *A Rhode Islander Reports*, 20–22, 64).

9. Hubbard, *Narrative*, 1:67–68. On the colonists' penchant for such interpretations see Jon Butler, "Magic, Astrology, and the Early American Religious Heritage, 1600–1760," *AHR* 84 (1979): 317–46; and David Hall, *Words of Wonder, Days of Judgment: Popular Religious Belief in Early New England* (New York: Alfred A. Knopf, 1989), 76–94. On other omens forecasting the course of the war see William Simmons, *Spirit of the New England Tribes: Indian History and Folklore, 1620–1984* (Hanover, N.H.: University Press of New England, 1986), 271.

10. Roger Williams, June 25, 1675, Roger Williams Papers, AAS. Easton, "Relacion," 7.

11. *PCR* 5:167–68. Mather, *Relation*, 74–75. C. Mather, *Magnalia*, 559–60.

12. Easton, "Relacion," 7–8.

13. Massachusetts Council to Josiah Winslow, April 21, 1676, Mass. Arch. 68:200; reprint, *NEHGR* 41 (1887): 400–401. William Nahauton's credibility is indeed somewhat compromised by his extraordinary allegiance to the English, a loyalty that will be demonstrated in subsequent chapters; before the war he worked with Eliot at converting Philip, and after the war he petitioned the Massachusetts Council for several favors he believed owed him due to his service. His relationship with John Sassamon was probably a close one; in 1679 he petitioned the authorities of Plymouth Colony for the release of John Sassamon's sister from servitude (*PCR* 10:366).

14. Easton, "Relacion," 7. Just months after Sassamon's trial the Plymouth court had investigated a similar death, and in that case they did determine that one John Fallowell had indeed been "accessary to his owne death" by drowning himself (*PCR* 5:182).

15. For example, the contrived basis for the Pequot War in 1637, the best account of which can be found in Alfred A. Cave, *The Pequot War* (Amherst: University of Massachusetts Press, 1996), ch. 3.

16. Since I once nearly drowned after falling through the ice on a frozen pond, I can attest personally to the nature of the injuries sustained in such an accident. For corroboration I checked with a pathologist, who confirmed that injuries and bruises to the neck strongly suggest strangulation and that the neck and throat are extremely unlikely to sustain injuries in a frozen pond drowning since those areas are, relatively speaking, protected; instead, the

hands and arms are most vulnerable (James Connolly, M.D., pathologist, Beth Israel Hospital, Boston, personal communication, November 4, 1996).

17. Josiah Winslow to John Winthrop, Jr., July 29, 1675, *MHSC*, 5th ser., 1 (1871): 429. Cotton Mather wrote that "though they were all successively turned off the ladder at the gallows, utterly denying the fact, yet the last of them happening to break or slip the rope, did, before his going off the ladder again, confess that the other Indians did really murder John Sausaman, and that he himself, though no actor in it, yet a looker on" (*Magnalia*, 560). In any event, Wampapaquan was "afterwards shott to death within the said month" (*PCR* 5:167).

18. Saltonstall, *Continuation*, 54–55. Mather, *Brief History*, 49. Easton, "Relacion," 8. This version of the story is by far the most common; see, for example, *Brief and True Narration*, 4.

19. Mather, *Brief History*, 48. Saltonstall, *Present State*, 24–25. Philip Walker also voiced this interpretation: "To send a ffelow of so low degree / that woss subservil as wee know wos hee / put ffrom his master upon Ielose / To prate & preach give lawes & teach / to men above his spher & reach" ("Captan Perse," 90).

20. Easton, "Relacion," 7. This "will," if it existed, was more likely a land deed; Sassamon served as scribe for many.

21. The Indian interpreter, or "cultural broker," has been the subject of considerable recent scholarship. See, for example, Nancy L. Hagedorn, " 'A Friend to Go Between Them': The Interpreter as Cultural Broker during Anglo-Iroquois Councils, 1740–70," *Ethnohistory* 35 (1988): 60–80; and Margaret Connell Szasz, ed., *Between Indian and White Worlds: The Cultural Broker* (Norman: University of Oklahoma Press, 1994).

22. Samuel Purchas, *Hakluytus Posthumus or Purchas His Pilgrimes* (Glasgow: James MacLehose & Sons; reprint, New York: The Macmillan Company, 1905), 486.

23. Jack Goody and Ian Watt, "The Consequences of Literacy," in *Literacy in Traditional Societies*, ed. Jack Goody (Cambridge: Cambridge University Press, 1968), 34; also M. I. Finley, "Myth, Memory, and History," *History and Theory* 4 (1965): 281–302; and Walter Ong, *Orality and Literacy: The Technologizing of the Word* (London: Methuen, 1982).

24. Anthropological works on notions of time and history in oral cultures include Joanne Rappaport, *The Politics of Memory: Native Historical Interpretation in the Colombian Andes* (Cambridge: Cambridge University Press, 1990); Richard Price, *First-Time: The Historical Vision of an Afro-American People* (Baltimore: The Johns Hopkins University Press, 1983); and Robert Borofsky, *Making History: Pukapukan and Anthropological Constructions of Knowledge* (Cambridge: Cambridge University Press, 1987). On the disappearing line between history and fiction see Dominick LaCapra, *History and Criticism* (Ithaca, N.Y.: Cornell University Press, 1985) and Hayden White, *Tropics of Discourse: Essays in Cultural Criticism* (Baltimore: The Johns Hopkins University Press, 1978). And on popular perceptions of history see David Lowenthal, *The Past is a Foreign Country* (Cambridge: Cambridge University Press, 1985). For a discussion of this convergence of anthropological and historical theory see Rappaport, *The Politics of Memory*, 10–14.

25. As Brian Street has argued, "faith in the power and qualities of literacy is itself socially learnt and is not an adequate tool with which to embark on a description of its practice" (*Literacy in Theory and Practice* [London: Cambridge University Press, 1984], 1). See also Harvey Graff, *The Legacies of Literacy: Continuities and Contradictions in Western Culture and Society* (Bloomington: University of Indiana Press, 1987), and Ruth Finnegan, *Literacy and Orality: Studies in the Technology of Communication* (Oxford: Blackwell, 1988).

26. Calvin Martin, ed., *The American Indian and the Problem of History* (New York: Oxford University Press, 1987), 3–26, 27–34. Martin identifies the "problem" as Western-bred historians' failure to fully understand Native Americans' intriguing "metaphysics," "their astounding ability to annul time, their remarkable capacity to repudiate systematically time and history." According to Martin, white historians writing Indian history have underestimated the importance of myth in Indian societies and have imposed their own Western perceptions of historical reality onto their Indian subjects.

27. *PCR* 10:362.

28. On such epidemics and their consequences see Neal Salisbury, *Manitou and Providence: Indians, Europeans, and the Making of New England, 1500–1643* (New York: Oxford University Press, 1982), especially 176 on the English settlers' reception at Dorchester.

29. Salisbury, *Manitou and Providence,* 191. While later chroniclers, such as Cotton Mather, would casually note that Sassamon "was the son of Christian Indians," earlier observers, such as Cotton's father, Increase, specified that Sassamon's "father and mother liv[ed] in Dorchester, and they both *died Christians.*" (C. Mather, *Magnalia,* 559–60; Mather, *Relation,* 74 [emphasis mine]). This may seem a minor distinction, but it provides an important clue: the elder Mather's implication is that Sassamon's parents converted *only at the time of their deaths.*

30. [John Eliot?], *New England's First Fruits* (London, 1643); reprinted in Samuel Eliot Morison, *The Founding of Harvard College* (Cambridge Mass.: Harvard University Press, 1935), 423.

31. My guess is that Sassamon was in his mid-teens when he participated in the Pequot War. In 1673 Sassamon had at least one daughter who was grown and married, and I would estimate he was in his mid-fifties the year he died. This estimate is not inconsistent with Samuel Eliot Morison's claim that Sassamon was "a man of forty-five to fifty years old" by 1670 (Morison, *Harvard College in the Seventeenth Century* [Cambridge Mass.: Harvard University Press, 1936], 353).

32. John Underhill, *News from America; or, a New and Experimentall Discoverie of New England* (London, 1638); reprinted in *MHSC,* 3rd ser., 6 (1837): 9.

33. Describing the Indian captives he was sending to Massachusetts, Captain Israel Stoughton wrote to the governor of the colony in 1637, "there is one . . . that is the fairest and largest that I saw amongst [the group of some fifty captives], to whom I have given a coate to cloathe her. It is my desire to have her for a servant. . . . There is a little squaw that steward Culacut desireth, to whom he hath given a coate. . . . Sosomon, the Indian, desireth a young little squaw, which I know not" (Samuel Gardner Drake, *Book of the Indians* [Boston, 1841], 2:107). Later Eliot would recall that Cockenoe was "a pregnant witted young man, who had been a servant in an English house, who pretty well understood his own language, and hath a clear pronunciation: Him I made my interpreter" (John Eliot, *The Indian Grammar Begun* [Cambridge, Mass., 1666], 66). See also William Wallace Tooker, *John Eliot's First Indian Teacher and Interpreter, Cockenoe-de-Long Island* (New York: F. P. Harper, 1896), 11; and Margaret Connell Szasz, *Indian Education in the American Colonies, 1607–1783* (Albuquerque: University of New Mexico Press, 1988), 111–13. Roger Williams, who negotiated with Callicott for Pequot captives, briefly hosted Sassamon at his house in Providence in August 1637 (Roger Williams to John Winthrop, Sr., August 20, 1637, and Williams to Winthrop, June 30, 1637, and September 9 and 12, 1637, *Correspondence of Roger Williams,* 113, 88, 119, 121). Although the editors claim that "it is doubtful that this Indian was John Sassamon," I have found no evidence to contradict my theory about Sassamon's age (see note 31, above). And in

the 1870s, John Sassamon's descendants claimed that "it is handed down traditionally that the Indian Sosomon, who aided the English in the Pequot War, was identical with John Sassamon, the educated and praying Indian, and that the 'young little squaw' he desired and was permitted from among the female captives to take, was a daughter of the Pequot chief Sasscus, which daughter, Sassamon made his wife" (Ebenezer W. Peirce, *Indian History, Biography, and Genealogy* [1878; reprint, Freeport, N.Y.: Books for Libraries Press, 1972], 215). On Williams hosting Stoughton and his troops, see Roger Williams to Major John Mason, June 22, 1670, in *MHSC*, 1st series, 1 (1792): 277. Sassamon may later have been present at a treaty signing in Boston in 1645 when "Serjeant Callicutt & an Indian his man being present" (*PCR* 9:49).

34. William Wood, *New England's Prospect* (London, 1634; reprint, Amherst: University of Massachusetts Press, 1977), 109–10. On Wood's linguistic work see George F. Aubin, "Towards the Linguistic History of an Algonquian Dialect: Observations on the Wood Vocabulary," *Papers of the Ninth Algonquian Conference*, ed. William Cowan (Ottawa: Carleton University, 1978), 127–37. On early English-Indian communication see Kathleen Bragdon, "Linguistic Acculturation in Massachusett: 1663–1771," *Papers of the Twelfth Algonquian Conference*, ed. William Cowan (Ottawa: Carleton University, 1981), 121–32; Ives Goddard, "Some Early Examples of American Indian Pidgin English from New England," *IJAL* 43 (1977): 37–41; Goddard, "A Further Note on Pidgin English," *IJAL* 44 (1978): 73.

35. Cotton Mather, *The Life and Death of the Renown'd Mr. John Eliot* (London, 1691), 76–78. For a powerful examination of European and American attitudes toward native tongues, see Edward Gray, "Indian Language in Anglo-American Thought, 1550–1820" (Ph.D. diss., Brown University, 1996).

36. John Eliot, "The Day Breaking, if not the Sun-Rising of the gospel with the Indians in New England" (London, 1647), reprint, *MHSC*, 3rd series, 4 (1834): 5.

37. Roger Williams, *A Key to the Language of America, or an Help to the Language of the Natives in that part of America called New-England* (London, 1643); reprinted in *RIHSC* 1 (1827): 17–166; on lying, see 63–64.

38. Cotton Mather's *Life and Death of . . . Eliot* is only the first in a long hagiographic tradition in which Eliot is revered by evangelicals and linguists alike. See, e.g., Stephen A. Guice, "Early New England Missionary Linguistics," *Papers in the History of Linguistics*, ed. Hans Aarsleff, Louis G. Kelly, et al. (Amsterdam: John Benjamins, 1987), 223–32. For a useful evaluation of the contributions of Wood, Williams, and Eliot see William Cowan, "Native Languages of North America: The European Response," *AICRJ* 1 (1974): 3–10. Guice, "Early New England Missionary Linguistics," 223–24, 228–29. James Constance Pilling remains the authority on works published in the Massachusett and other Algonquian languages. See Pilling, *Bibliography of the Algonquian Languages* (Washington, D.C.: U.S. Government Printing Office, 1891), but two linguists have recently published two extremely important volumes of translated manuscript writings in Massachusett: Ives Goddard and Kathleen Bragdon, *Native Writings in Massachusett* (Philadelphia: The American Philosophical Society, 1988), 2 vols. See also J. Hammond Trumbull, "The Indian Tongue and Its Literature as Fashioned by Eliot and Others," *The Memorial History of Boston . . . , 1630–1880*, ed. Justin Winsor (Boston: Ticknor & Company, 1880), 1: 465–80; George Littlefield, *Early Boston Booksellers 1642–1711* (Boston: The Club of Odd Volumes, 1900), 72–75. While my emphasis here is primarily on Eliot himself, other English colonists were also involved in missionary work, most notably the Mayhews of Martha's Vineyard, but also Abraham Peirce in Connecticut and Richard Bourne in Plymouth.

39. As James Axtell has shown, the Puritans' attempts at conversion were slowed because of their efforts to teach Indians to read. By contrast, Jesuits in New France used their own literacy as a magical tool of intimidation to gain converts. As Axtell argues, "The ability to read and write was awe-inspiring to the Indians largely because it duplicated a spiritual feat that only the greatest shamans could perform, namely, that of reading the mind of a person at a distance and thereby, in an oral context, foretelling the future. . . . every European who could read a handwritten note from a distant correspondent could, in effect, read the writer's mind. Small wonder that the natives who first witnessed this amazing feat regarded the literate Europeans as 'greater than all mankind.' " Puritans failed to capitalize on this mystical "power of print," according to Axtell, partly because by the time they began their missionary work the novelty of literacy had worn off. Moreover, Axtell argues, Puritan missionaries such as Eliot were "culturally inflexible" and unable to assume the role of shaman. Finally, "the Protestant belief in the priesthood of all believers and the need for each Christian to confront the scriptural message directly led the English missionaries to translate their religious writings into native languages as quickly as possible and to open schools to teach Indian children to read and write. This, of course, diminished the mystery of the foreign language and the exalted status of the priestly caste of literate guardians and interpreters of God's Word" (*After Columbus: Essays in the Ethnohistory of Colonial North America* [New York: Oxford University Press, 1988], 86–99).

40. Neal Salisbury, "Red Puritans: The 'Praying Indians' of Massachusetts Bay and John Eliot," *WMQ* 31 (1974): 43; Szasz, *Indian Education*, 114–15.

41. Hubbard, *Narrative*, 1:60; Mather, *Brief History*, 49; Saltonstall, *Continuation*, 54–55; "Rev. John Eliot's Records of the First Church in Roxbury, Mass.," *NEHGR* 33 (1879): 297.

42. On Long Island, Cockenoe served as an interpreter between the Montauk Indians and the English (Tooker, *John Eliot's First Indian Interpreter*, 18). One of Cockenoe's last entries in the historical record is his signature on a petition during King Philip's War, as counselor to a Long Island sachem, begging for the English to return guns taken during the war. The request was denied (54).

43. Goddard and Bragdon, *Native Writings in Massachusett*, 423.

44. [Eliot?], *New England's First Fruits*, 423.

45. Hubbard, *Narrative*, 1:60.

46. In 1649 Eliot recorded giving five pounds to the schoolmaster of Dorchester, where "the Children of those Indians that lived thereabout went, with a like good successe, if not better, because the children were bigger and more capable." Eliot himself visited the Dorchester school: "I take my constant course of catechising them every Lecture day." John Eliot, November 13, 1649, in Edward Winslow, "Glorious Progress of the gospel," *MHSC*, 3rd ser., 4(1834): 88.

47. Eliot, *Indian Grammar*, 4, 6.

48. While I am here suggesting that Sassamon's relationship with Eliot was reciprocal, I do not mean to discount the dramatic power imbalance between the two men. On this point see David Murray, who uses Eliot as a case study "to represent a characteristic white approach, which is to emphasize translation as an issue only when whites choose, or are forced, to do it, and to ignore it otherwise." Meanwhile, Indian converts "are doing something culturally more sophisticated than the whites can manage, but it is being used as evidence of their lack of civilization" (*Forked Tongues: Speech, Writing and Representation in North American Indian Texts* [London: Pinter Publishers, 1991], 7–8).

49. On Natick and other praying towns see Jean M. O'Brien, *Dispossession by Degrees: Indian Land and Identity in Natick, Massachusetts* (New York: Cambridge University Press, 1997); Sarah Jacobs, *Nonantum and Natick* (Boston: Massachusetts Sabbath School Society, 1853); Dane Morrison, *A Praying People: Massachuset Acculturation and the Failure of the Puritan Mission, 1600–1690* (New York: Peter Lang, 1995); Daniel Mandell, " 'To Live More Like my Christian English Neighbors': Natick Indians in the Eighteenth Century," *WMQ* 48 (1991): 552–79; Harold W. Van Lonkhuyzen, "A Reappraisal of the Praying Indians: Acculturation, Conversion, and Identity at Natick, Massachusetts, 1646–1730," *NEQ* 63 (1990): 396–428; Elise Brenner, "Strategies for Autonomy: An Analysis of Ethnic Mobilization in Seventeenth-Century Southern New England" (Ph.D. diss., University of Massachusetts, Amherst, 1984). On praying Indians more generally see Salisbury, "Red Puritans"; James P. Ronda, "Generations of Faith: The Christian Indians of Martha's Vineyard," *WMQ* 38 (1981): 369–94; James P. Ronda, " 'We Are Well As We Are': An Indian Critique of Seventeenth-Century Christian Missions," *WMQ* 34 (1977): 66–82; Robert James Naeher, "Dialogue in the Wilderness: John Eliot and the Indian Exploration of Puritanism as a Source of Meaning, Comfort, and Ethnic Survival," *NEQ* 62 (1989): 346–68; Elise M. Brenner, "To Pray or to Be Prey: That is the Question: Strategies for Cultural Autonomy of Massachusetts Praying Town Indians," *Ethnohistory* 27 (1980): 135–52; Kenneth M. Morrison, " 'That Art of Coyning Christians': John Eliot and the Praying Indians of Massachusetts," *Ethnohistory* 21 (1974): 77–92; William S. Simmons, "Conversion from Indian to Puritan," *NEQ* 52 (1979): 197–218.

50. John Eliot, "Letters of the Rev. John Eliot, the Apostle to the Indians," *NEHGR* 36 (1882): 298. Eliot, *Strength out of Weakness; or a Glorious Manifestation of the further Progress of the gospel among the Indians in New-England* (London, 1652); reprinted in *MHSC,* 3rd series, 4 (1834): 168. September 15, 1656, accounts of the New England Company in *PCR* 10:167. According to Daniel Gookin, Indians, rather than Englishmen, served as teachers because "learned English young men do not hitherto incline or endeavour to fit themselves for that service, by learning the Indian language" (Daniel Gookin, "Historical Collections of the Indians in New England [1674]," *MHSC,* 1st ser., 1 [1792]: 183). Or, as Eliot himself noted, "I find few English students willing to engage into so dim a work as this is. God hath in mercy raised up sundry among themselves to a competent ability to teach their countrymen" (*John Eliot's Indian Dialogues: A Study in Cultural Interaction* [1671], ed. Henry W. Bowden and James P. Ronda [Westport, Conn.: Greenwood Press, 1980], 59).

51. Eliot, *Strength out of Weakness,* 169–70.

52. Harvard historian Samuel Eliot Morison found this troubling indeed and noted that "one would be inclined to discount the story of Sassamon's Harvard affiliation" were it not for the conclusive records in the college steward's accounts. In the steward's accounts for 1653 there is an entry under the debits of John Eliot, Jr., that reads, "By Sasaman" in the amount of "7s 7d 1q" (*Publications of the Colonial Society of Massachusetts* 31 [1935]: 150). As Morison derisively writes, "Therein, it was hoped, Indian youths might acquire a university education, which (through some obscure workings of the academic mind) was confidently expected to qualify them as teachers and converters of their pagan brethren. Although the failure of this enterprise was so complete as to raise among modern readers the suspicion that it was merely a blind to get a new building for Harvard College, there is no reason to suppose it to have been anything but straightforward and sincere" (Morison, *Harvard College in the Seventeenth Century,* 341). Subsequent scholars have disagreed with Morison's defense of Harvard's intentions. Szasz has a more positive interpretation of Indian education, but most scholars follow Neal Salisbury's lead in arguing that Indian education was a last resort of impoverished

Indians. Bobby Wright, for example, argues that "only when war and disease had disintegrated tribal integrity and left Indian communities vulnerable to English domination did Indians embrace Christianity and European culture" (Bobby Wright, " 'For the Children of the Infidels?': American Indian Education in Colonial Colleges," *AICRJ* 12 [1988]: 2). See also Szasz, *Indian Education,* especially 126–28. On Sassamon at Harvard see Morison, *Harvard College in the Seventeenth Century,* 352–53. On Indian students at Harvard see Walter T. Meserve, "English Works of Seventeenth-Century Indians," *AQ* 8 (1956): 264–76.

53. John Eliot, July 8, 1649, in Henry Whitfield, *The Light appearing more and more towards the perfect Day . . .* (London, 1651); reprinted in *MHSC,* 3rd ser., 4 (1834): 121.

54. John Sibley, *Biographical Sketches of Graduates of Harvard University* (Cambridge, Mass.: Charles William Sever, 1873).

55. Morison, *Founding of Harvard College,* 161–62, and also Morison, *Harvard College in the Seventeenth Century,* 342–43.

56. Gookin, "Historical Collections," 173.

57. *A Late and Further Manifestation of the Progress of the gospel amongst the Indians in New England* (London, 1655); reprinted in *MHSC,* 3rd ser., 4 (1834): 274.

58. We can eliminate two other praying Indians who would otherwise seem likely candidates: Cockenoe had abandoned Eliot at least five years earlier, and the Natick schoolmaster Monequassum was ill at the time of examination (and would soon die). Job Nesuton, another Natick schoolmaster, could have participated in the scandal, but he, unlike Sassamon, seems to have been always loyal to Eliot. See *A Late and Further Manifestation,* 261–87.

59. Johnson was appointed to serve "in the Art of Printer for the printinge of the Bible in the Indian language and such other Books as he shall be directed to print for an duringe the terme of Three yeares" (Mass. Arch. 10:205). The Boston merchant and bookseller Hezekiah Usher traveled to London to secure the necessary fonts and paper for Eliot's Indian Bible (Littlefield, *Early Boston Booksellers,* 72). See also Robert F. Roden, *The Cambridge Press, 1638–1692* (New York: Burt Franklin, 19), 77–91; James Constance Pilling, *A Bibliography of the Algonquian Languages,* 127–84; J. Hammond Trumbull, "The Indian Tongue," 465–80.

60. Drake, *Book of the Indians,* 1:115.

61. John Eliot, *The Indian Primer* (Cambridge, Mass., 1669), 14.

62. Hugh Amory, *First Impressions: Printing in Cambridge, 1639–1989* (Cambridge, Mass.: Harvard University Press, 1989), 39.

63. John Eliot, "An Account of Indian Churches in New-England, in a letter written A.D. 1673," *MHSC,* 1st ser., 10 (1809): 127.

64. All data are from Daniel Gookin, "Historical Collections," 195–98. I have not here listed Gookin's partial data on praying towns in Connecticut, Martha's Vineyard, and Nantucket.

65. This survey of literacy rates can be found in a letter from Richard Bourne to Daniel Gookin dated September 1, 1664, and reprinted in Gookin's "Historical Collections," 197–98.

66. Kenneth A. Lockridge, *Literacy in Colonial New England* (New York, 1974), 13. These English literacy rates are in no way exact; what they measure is "signing literacy," the proportion of the population that signed documents with a written name rather than a mark. Since reading was taught before writing, some who signed with a mark may have been able

to read and, frustratingly, people who sign documents one year may use a mark the next, making such a measure even less reliable.

67. *Early Records of the Town of Providence* (Providence, 1892), 5:283. Alexander signed here with an "A."

68. Alexander died while being brought to be interrogated by the English, even though he claimed he was too ill to travel; rumor (reported by Easton, among others) was that he may have been poisoned by the English or treated harshly in the journey. There is no way of knowing whether Sassamon was with Alexander on this fateful journey, though it seems likely.

69. *PCR* 4:25–26.

70. Hubbard, *Narrative*, 1:60.

71. "When Philip and Wootonekanuske his wife, sold, in 1664, Mattapoisett to William Brenton, Sassamon was a witness and interpreter. The same year he was Philip's agent 'in settling the bounds of Acushenok, Coaksett, and places adjacent.' Again, in 1665, he witnessed the receipt of £10 paid to Philip on account of settling the bounds the year before" (Drake, *Book of the Indians*, 3:10). See also *PCR* 12:237; deed of Philip, June 9, 1665, mss. bound, MHS.

72. C. Mather, *Magnalia*, 559.

73. Gookin, "Historical Collections," 200.

74. C. Mather, *Magnalia*, 514.

75. John Eliot to the Commissioners of the United Colonies, August 25, 1664, *PCR* 10:383–84.

76. The events of 1671 are well summarized in Ranlet, "Another Look at the Causes," 89–95.

77. "Instructions from the Church at Natick to William and Anthony," August 1, 1671, *MHSC*, 1st ser., 6 (1799): 201–3.

78. James Walker to Governor Prince, September 1, 1671, *MHSC*, 1st ser., 6 (1799): 197–98.

79. Eliot, *Indian Dialogues*, 61.

80. *PCR* 12:230. On March 11, 1674, "old Tuspaquin and William Watuspaquin" allotted Felix, John Sassamon's son-in-law, 58½ acres in Assawampsett. The same year, "old Watuspaquin" granted "John Sassamon; allies Wussasoman twenty seaven acrees of land for a home lott; att Assowamsett Necke," which Sassamon in turn deeded to his daughter and son-in-law: "This abovesaid land John Sassamon above Named Gave unto his son in law ffelix, in Marriage with his daughter Bettey, as appeers by a line or two rudely written; by the said John Sassamons owne hand but onely witnessed by the said old Watuspaquen." In 1673 Tuspaquin and William Tuspaquin had given a (separate?) tract of land to Betty, John Sassamon's daughter, and Tobias (who was later executed for Sassamon's murder) signed as a witness to the deed (*PCR* 12:235). The elder Tuspaquin (also known as the "Black Sachem") was a shaman (William Simmons, *Spirit of the New England Tribes: Indian History and Folklore, 1620–1984* [Hanover, N.H.: University of New England Press, 1986], 42–43).

81. Mather, *Brief History*, 49–50. Gookin, "Historical Account," 440. Saltonstall, *Present State*, 24–25.

82. Easton, "Relacion," 10. Easton's reporting of this complaint is, however, subject to some question, and may have been motivated by his own disagreement with Puritan missionary efforts. Easton's wording sounds very much like a report made by Quaker leader

George Fox when he visited Rhode Island in 1672. Fox wrote in his journal, "In New England there was an Indian king that said he saw that there were many of their people of the Indians turned to the New England professors. He said they were worse since than they were before they left their own religion; and of all religions he said the Quakers were the best" (John L. Nickalls, ed., *The Journal of George Fox* [Cambridge: Cambridge University Press, 1952], 524). Fox may have met with Philip (with Easton along as well), or he may simply have been told about Philip's rejection of Eliot's gestures. In either case it's worth recalling that while Easton's perspective on Philip's hostility to Massachusetts' missionaries and their converts is significantly corroborated, Easton did have his own motives in highlighting this hostility. It was, in effect, a Quaker party line.

83. Easton, "Relacion," 7. One historian has recently argued that from the natives' perspective, Christianity was a "new cult" that "created an alternate social structure, essentially a new path to power within and among bands" and that "threatened some of the most basic premises of native society" (Lonkhuyzen, "Reappraisal of the Praying Indians," 404, 419–21). On Sassamon, more generally, as a "sutl knave," see Walker, "Captan Perse," 90.

84. C. Mather, *Magnalia*, 559.

85. John Allyn to Fitz-John Winthrop, September 20, 1675, *MHSC*, 6th ser., 3 (1889): 449.

86. Hubbard, *Narrative*, 1:61.

87. As Neal Salisbury has remarked, "the war brought not only the defeat of the hostile Indians but the end of the missionary program as conceived by Eliot" (Salisbury, "Red Puritans," 53).

88. "Rev. John Eliot's Records of the First Church," 416.

89. Jasper Danckaerts and Peter Sluyter, *Journal of a Voyage to New York*, ed. Henry C. Murphy (Brooklyn, N.Y.: Long Island Historical Society, 1867), 383.

90. Edward Gray, on the other hand, has suggested that the English themselves destroyed Eliot's Indian Bibles ("Who Burned the Eliot Bibles?," paper presented at the University of Cambridge, July 5, 1997).

91. Quoted in Longkhuzen, "A Reappraisal," 424.

92. Goddard and Bragdon, *Native Writings in Massachusett*, 10–11, 20.

93. Quoted in Nehemiah Adams, *The Life of John Eliot* (Boston: Massachusetts Sabbath School Society, 1847), 242. The latest manuscript documents written in Massachusett date from the 1760s (Goddard and Ives, *Native Writings in Massachusett*). In this century Samuel Eliot Morison would call the Indian Library "the most notable—and least useful—production of the press in this period" (Morison, *Harvard College in the Seventeenth Century*, 345).

94. In 1698 the building was torn down and the press moved to a new location (Morison, *Harvard College in the Seventeenth Century*, 359).

95. "Rev. John Eliot's Records of the First Church," 297, 415.

96. Gookin, "Historical Account," 55. Douglas Leach, *Flintlock and Tomahawk: New England in King Philip's War* (New York: The Macmillan Company, 1958; reprint, East Orleans, Mass.: Parnassus Imprints, 1992), 151. Gookin's account was not published until 1836, when it was uncovered by antiquarians (Frederick William Gookin, *Daniel Gookin, 1612–1687* [Chicago: privately printed, 1912], 161). On the failure of Gookin's narrative to be printed see Canup, *Out of the Wilderness*, 185–86.

97. Gookin, "Historical Account," 431.

98. Tompson, in Hubbard, *Narrative*, 1:24.

99. On employing a hermeneutics of suspicion see David Carrasco, *Quetzalcoatl and the Irony of Empire: Myths and Prophecies in the Aztec Tradition* (Chicago: University of Chicago Press, 1982). On verisimilitude see Tzvetan Todorov, who argues that "when an author is mistaken, or lying, his text is no less significant than when he is speaking the truth; the important thing is that the text be 'receivable' by contemporaries, or that it has been regarded as such by its producer" (*The Conquest of America: The Question of the Other,* trans. Richard Howard [New York: Harper & Row, 1984], 54). On attempting to piece together an Indian-centered narrative see the important work of James Merrell, *The Indians' New World: Catawbas and their Neighbors from European Contact through the Era of Removal* (Chapel Hill: University of North Carolina Press, 1989).

100. Cotton Mather, *Life and Death of . . . Eliot,* 73.

101. Experience Mayhew, *Indian Converts: Or, Some Account of the Lives and Dying Speeches of a Considerable Number of Christianized Indians at Martha's Vineyard, in New-England* (London, 1727), xxiii. Even those Indians who could read and write were probably less skilled than Englishmen classified as "literate." Surviving documents in the Massachusett language consist largely of land deeds used to supplement verbal agreements. According to the two linguists who have translated them, these documents are most appropriately understood "as aids to memory, rather than as independent forms of communication" and thus suggest that most native literacy was of a "restricted" type, relying heavily on oral formulas and rhetorical styles (Goddard and Bragdon, *Native Writings,* 18–20). Very few native documents are narrative in a sense that would be familiar to us; a notable exception can be found in Goddard and Bragdon, *Native Writings,* 85, though this account seems to have been dictated to Mayhew rather than written down by a literate Massachusett-speaker.

102. Many literate Indians, like Sassamon, died in the war: Job Nesutan, who had also assisted Eliot in translating the Bible, died in July 1675, fighting alongside the English in the early days of King Philip's War.

103. Mather, *Exhortation,* 172.

104. Walker, "Captan Perse," 91.

Chapter 2 • The Story of It Printed

1. Samuel Green, ed., *Diary of Increase Mather, March 1675–December 1676* (Cambridge: John Wilson & Son, 1900), 43.

2. Mather, *Brief History,* 35–36.

3. How Mather obtained a copy (or the original) of Easton's manuscript remains uncertain; Richard LeBaron Bowen has suggested that "Relacion" must have been printed, though no copy survives today (*Early Rehoboth, Documented Historical Studies of Families and Events in this Plymouth Colony Township* [Rehoboth, Mass.: privately printed, 1945–50], 3:10). That the manuscript is today housed at the New York State Archives suggests that Easton sent his narrative to Governor Andros at the time he wrote it.

4. According to one historian, the annual election sermon was "probably the highest honor which could be bestowed upon a clergyman at any time, but to be thus singled out in the midst of the greatest trial New England had undergone would certainly be recognition of highest order" (Anne Kuesner Nelson, "King Philip's War and the Hubbard-Mather Rivalry," *WMQ* 27 [1976]: 619–20). On the two ministers' differing interpretations of the war see

also Kenneth B. Murdock, "William Hubbard and the Providential Interpretation of History," *AAS Proceedings,* new ser., 52 (1942): 34–35; Bowen, *Early Rehoboth,* 3:1–5; Francis Jennings, *The Invasion of America: Indians, Colonialism, and the Cant of Conquest* (New York: W. W. Norton & Company, 1975), 182–85; Perry Miller, *The New England Mind: From Colony to Province* (Cambridge, Mass.: Harvard University Press, 1953), 30–31; and Richard S. Dunn, "Seventeenth-Century English Historians of America," in *Seventeenth-Century America: Essays in Colonial History,* ed. James Morton Smith (Chapel Hill: University of North Carolina Press, 1959), 195–225. Dunn argues that Hubbard's belief in God's preordination of all events and his explanation of the "cause-and-effect pattern of events by man's daily actions, rather than by omens and prodigies" explain "why Hubbard's description of the war is strongly partisan, whereas Increase Mather sees both colonists and Indians as God's instruments." In the end, Hubbard's view of the war seems to have been more acceptable to the magistrates; in 1682 the Massachusetts Court voted to pay him £50 to write a general history of New England (*MCR* 5:378).

5. *Diary of Increase Mather,* 29–34. After completing his *Brief History* and *Exhortation,* Mather took a well-deserved break from writing about the war, and it was not until October 30 that he began the *Relation of the Troubles.*

6. Winthrop, *Some Meditations,* indicates an earlier printing, in 1675. On the publication of Folger's poem see Florence Bennett Anderson, *A Grandfather for Benjamin Franklin* (Boston: Meador Publishing Company, 1940), 302.

7. For full bibliographic information about all of these chronicles see the Abbreviations.

8. Richard Chiswell to Increase Mather, February 16, 1677, *MHSC,* 4th ser., 8 (1868): 575–76. On Chiswell's subsequent role in the New England book trade see Worthington Chauncy Ford, *The Boston Book Market, 1679–1700* (Boston: The Club of Odd Volumes, 1917), 17–19.

9. On the printing history of Rowlandson's captivity narrative see Chapter 5 and also Frank L. Mott, *Golden Multitudes: The Story of Bestsellers in the United States* (New York: Macmillan, 1947); R. W. G. Vail, *The Voice of the Old Frontier* (Philadelphia: University of Pennsylvania Press, 1949); and Kathryn Zabelle Derounian, "The Publication, Promotion, and Distribution of Mary Rowlandson's Indian Captivity Narrative in the Seventeenth Century," *EAL* 23 (1988): 239–61.

10. According to David Hall, "The situation in England and New England was one of small press runs and limited circulation for most items. Press runs for quartos and octavos could dip as low as 300 or 400 copies, and rarely went above a maximum of 1,500" ("The Uses of Literacy in New England, 1600–1850," in *Printing and Society in Early America,* ed. William L. Joyce et al. [Worcester, Mass.: American Antiquarian Society, 1983], 26). A small but significant literature had also emerged in the wake of the Virginia Massacre in 1622. See John Frederick Fausz, "The Powhatan Uprising of 1622: A Historical Study of Ethnocentrism and Cultural Conflict" (Ph.D. diss., The College of William and Mary, 1977), 404–443.

11. Tompson, *New England's Crisis,* 225.

12. "Simon Bradstreet's Journal," *NEHGR* 9 (1855): 47–48.

13. John Cotton to Increase Mather, March 19, 1677, Mather Family Papers, AAS. Unfortunately for Cotton, Mather, hoping to discourage the Massachusetts authorities from endorsing Hubbard's narrative, read Cotton's letter to two Massachusetts officials, who reported its contents to Hubbard. Enraged, Hubbard complained to Winslow, who, in turn, berated Cotton. Much wounded by Mather's lack of discretion, Cotton asked in his next letter "how

it comes to pass that you, my most intire friend, have endangered my losse of my best friends here." This time Cotton warned, "I hope my letter you keepe close" (John Cotton to Increase Mather, April 14, 1677, Mather Family Papers, AAS). In reply, Mather pleaded innocent, telling Cotton he had only shown the original letter to two men and "did not mention your Name, onely that I had received the letter from a minister in Plymouth Colony" (Increase Mather to John Cotton, April 22, 1677, Mather Family Papers, AAS). Still, despite the exposure of their machinations, Cotton and Mather continued to solicit bad reviews of Hubbard's history. In June Cotton wrote Mather that "Mr Shove was this day at my house . . . (for your booke he thankes you) & told me that in Mr H's history, things are strangely falsifyed." (This time, Cotton emphasized, "I use his own words.") Shove, he said, "much commends your History, & sayes had Mr H: followed your Narrative he had showed more truth." "My request to you," Cotton continued, "is, that you will prudently of your owne accord (unless you see weighty reason to the contrary) write a letter to Mr Shove, & desire him to acquaint you with the mistakes he knowes to be in that booke; I doubt not but he will readily grant your desires; for he freely asserts many things to be notorious, & if you had the particulars in writing, I believe it would be of good use" (John Cotton to Increase Mather, June 25, 1677, *MHSC*, 4th ser., 8 [1868]: 239).

14. Hubbard, *Narrative*, 1:4.

15. John Eliot, *The Christian Commonwealth* (1656), was suppressed by the Massachusetts Court in 1661 (*MCR* 4:5–6).

16. Mary Pray to James Oliver, January 1, 1676, Mass. Arch. 69:91–92, but also see the transcription in *Further Letters on King Philip's War* (Providence: Society of Colonial Wars, 1923), 22–25. John Kingsley to the Connecticut War Council, May 5, 1676, *CCR* 2:445.

17. Hubbard, *Narrative*, 1:16.

18. Hall, "The Uses of Literacy," 20–38; David Hall, *Words of Wonder, Days of Judgment: Popular Religious Belief in Early New England* (New York: Alfred A. Knopf, 1989), 5–7, 18–19; and Chapters 1 and 2. The story of the man who put his faith in his Bible is told in John Kingsley to the Connecticut War Council, May 5, 1676. For other examples and a fuller analysis of New Englanders' belief in the special powers of the Bible see Hall, *Words of Wonder*, 24–31. On the monopoly of information held by seaboard cosmopolitans see Richard D. Brown, *Knowledge Is Power: The Diffusion of Information in America, 1700–1865* (New York: Oxford University Press, 1989).

19. *Brief and True Narration*, 3.

20. For a sample of a manuscript newsletter see the unsigned newsletter dated December 22, 1675, in the Codex Collections of the John Carter Brown Library, Brown University. The reports in *The London Gazette* were a digest of two letters by Benjamin Batten to Sir John Allin dated June 29, 1675, and July 6, 1675 (Gay Transcripts, Plymouth Papers, 1:39–46, MHS). Summaries of Batten's letters were also entered into the *Calendar of State Papers* (*CSP* 9:251–53). For a detailed discussion of Batten's letters and an examination of the gazette's editorial methods see Douglas E. Leach, "Benjamin Batten and the *London Gazette*," *NEQ* 36 (1963): 502–17. As Stephen Saunders Webb has written, "London coffee consumers were as well informed about the origins and progress of the Algonquian uprising in New England as they were tardily and incompletely told of Virginia's Indian and civil wars. Even *The London Gazette* reported regularly and extensively on the war in New England" (*1676: The End of American Independence* [New York: Alfred A. Knopf, 1984], 222). On getting the news in Virginia see Wilcomb E. Washburn, "Governor Berkeley and King Philip's War," *NEQ* 30 (1957).

Meanwhile, a pamphlet encouraging migration to New Jersey boasted that while "in New England they are at Wars with the Indians . . . in this place the Lord is making way to exalt his name and truth" (Robert Wade to his wife, April 2, 1676, in *A Further Account of New Jersey, in an Abstract of Letters Lately Writ from thence, By several Inhabitants there Resident* [London, 1676], 6–7). On communications between New and Old England more generally see David Cressy, *Coming Over: Migration and Communication between England and New England in the Seventeenth Century* (Cambridge: Cambridge University Press, 1987), 213–34.

21. Mather, *Exhortation,* 170.

22. Webb, *1676,* 222, 240. Among those accounts printed as supplements to *The London Gazette* were Saltonstall's *Present State* (no. A1051); Saltonstall's *Continuation* (no. A1091); Saltonstall's *New and Further Narrative* (no. A1141, October 23–26, 1676); and Mather's *Brief History* (no. 1156, December 14–16, 1676).

23. Saltonstall, *Present State,* 49–50.

24. Edward Arber, ed., *The Term Catalogues, 1668–1709* (London: Edward Arber, 1903), 1:226, 235, 240, and 252.

25. On the popularity of gruesome literature among English readers see Marjorie Plant, *The English Book Trade: An Economic History of the Making and Sale of Books* (London: George Allen & Unwin, 1965), 47–49. On literacy and the book trade in seventeenth-century England more generally see H. S. Bennett, *English Books and Readers, 1603 to 1650* (Cambridge, England, 1970); Margaret Spufford, *Small Books and Pleasant Histories: Popular Fiction and its Readership in Seventeenth-century England* (London: Methuen, 1981); and David Cressy, *Literacy and the Social Order: Reading and Writing in Tudor and Stuart England* (Cambridge: Cambridge University Press, 1980).

26. Saltonstall, *Continuation,* 53; Saltonstall, *New and Further Narrative,* 77.

27. Tompson, *New England's Crisis,* 225–26.

28. Saltonstall, *New and Further Narrative,* 77. Though these accounts purported to have been "communicated by Letters to a Friend in London," some are much more self-consciously written. Thus the author of *A True Account* directly addresses his audience, apologizing to the reader for the abruptness of his narrative, and asking his indulgence when he includes some letters written by Indians, containing "Barbarisms" (1, 6).

29. Wharton, *New-England's Present Sufferings,* 5.

30. *News from New England,* 6.

31. The number of booksellers in Boston rose dramatically during the decades during and after King Philip's War. According to James Hart, "From 1642 to 1661 Boston had only one bookseller, but in the 1660s there were two, in the seventies there was a jump to nine, and in the eighties there was another great rise to seventeen. . . . The increase was out of proportion to the growth of New England's population which rose from some 18,000 to almost 100,000 during this period, and Boston, which had not yet got around to naming its streets, had far more than a normal share of book shops for its 1,500 inhabitants in 1640 or for its 7,000 at the end of the century" (James D. Hart, *The Popular Book: A History of America's Literary Taste* [Westport, Conn.: Greenwood Press, 1976]). For a more general portrait of book publication and circulation in colonial New England see Hall, *Words of Wonder,* 44–52.

32. Wheeler, *Thankefull Remembrance,* 240. Wheeler's sermon was probably named after George Carlton's own *Thankefull Remembrance of God's Mercy* (London, 1624). On the colonists' reasons for writing about the war see also Louis J. Kern, "Savagery, Captivity, and

Redemption: Historical Memory and National Myth in Puritan Representations of King Philip's War, 1675–1678," paper presented at "Collective Memory and Private Memory in Pre-Industrial America," University of Paris, February, 1992, 6–16.

33. *Term Catalogues* 1:266, 507. *The London Gazette,* December 14–16, 1676. David Hall writes that "the marketplace made room for two quite different understandings of the book, the one that moralists preferred and another that printers and hack writers made their own, a frank embracing of inventiveness and competition" (Hall, *Words of Wonder,* 55).

34. On narratives sent to the king see Massachusetts Council to the King of England, April 6, 1676, Mass. Arch. 68:199–201; Commissioners of the United Colonies to the King of England, August 25, 1679, *PCR* 10:407–9.

35. John Hull to Edward Hull, October 20, 1676, John Hull's Letterbook, AAS. Next Hull wrote to Burfoot, explaining, "Excuse my not former answering you[r] request about the war[.] I waited untill our first edition [was] printed" (John Hull to Samuel Burfoot, October 20, 1676, ibid.).

36. Samuel Sewall to Stephen Dummor, 1684–1685, and Sewall to Nathaniel Dummor, February 2, 1685, transcribed in Samuel Jennison, ed., "Letters of Chief Justice Sewall," *NEHGR* 9 (1855): 287–88.

37. Joseph Eliot to John Winthrop, Jr., August 16, 1675, *MHSC,* 5th ser., 1 (1871): 430.

38. On the circulation of books within New England and between New and Old England see Thomas Goddard Wright, *Literary Culture in Early New England, 1620–1730* (New Haven, Conn.: Yale University Press, 1920), 25–61, 110–36, and, more important, David Hall's arguments about the shared print culture of England and New England ("The World of Print and Collective Mentality in Seventeenth-Century New England," in *New Directions in American Intellectual History,* ed. John Higham and Paul K. Conkin [Baltimore: The Johns Hopkins University Press, 1979], 166–80).

39. "Yours I received & the bookes, 7 of those which came first are sold at Bridgewater; I will endeavour to sell as fast as I can" (John Cotton to Increase Mather, October 20, 1677, quoted in Wright, *Literary Culture in Early New England,* 219).

40. Richard Blinman to Increase Mather, August 24, 1677, *MHSC,* 4th ser., 8 (1868): 329. Jonathan Tuckney to Increase Mather, April 3, 1678, *MHSC,* 4th ser., 8 (1868): 351. James Forbes, in England, thanked Mather for sending him the narrative of the war, along with two sermons, "for which I return you heartie thanks, and I do interprete it as an expression of your friendlie respects to me, at so great a distance, and after so long a silence" (James Forbes to Increase Mather, *MHSC,* 4th ser., 8 [1868]: 581). "Yours I received with the book concerning the warr, but it was long before the book came to hand. I heartily thank you for it. . . . I shall be glad to hear that the warr with the Indians is at an end" (Samuel Petto to Increase Mather, August 31, 1677, *MHSC,* 4th ser., 8 [1868]: 341). "I thank you heartily for the History of the wars you sent to Mr Petto for me . . ." (John Westgate to Increase Mather, May 8, 1677, *MHSC,* 4th ser., 8 [1868]: 577). "i received from you, your Relation of the Troubles in New England from 1614 to 1675, & a sermon therewith which were very acceptable to me, & heartily thank you for them" (Samuel Petto to Increase Mather, May 4, 1678, *MHSC,* 4th ser., 8 [1868]: 342). See also Samuel Petto to Increase Mather, August 31, 1677.

41. John Bishop to Increase Mather, July 8, 1676, *MHSC,* 4th ser., 8 (1868): 299. Later, in April 1677, Bishop would write again, "I am glad to hear that the History of N.E. is on foot & processe been made so far" (John Bishop to Increase Mather, April 13, 1677, *MHSC,* 4th ser., 8 [1868]: 300).

42. William Goffe to Increase Mather, September 8, 1676, *MHSC,* 4th ser., 8 (1868): 156.

43. Nathaniel Mather to Increase Mather, February 26, 1677, *MHSC,* 4th ser., 8 (1868): 7–8.

44. For full titles of the narratives see the Abbreviations.

45. Saltonstall, *Present State,* 24. This "true account" of the war's origins he later revised: "In my Last I also gave you (at First) an Account of the Reasons of the Rise and Original of these unhappy Wars, in which, my Information was not so Perfect, but that there was some-what amiss; although at that Time, the Account thereof was generally receiv'd, an the Alter-ation is not much . . ." (Saltonstall, *Continuation,* 54).

46. *Brief and True Narration,* 3. Hubbard, *Narrative,* 1:16.

47. *True Account,* 1.

48. Wheeler, *Thankefull Remembrance,* 240

49. Harris, *A Rhode Islander Reports,* 18. Noah Newman to John Cotton, March 14, 1676, Curwen Papers, AAS. Tompson, *New England's Crisis,* 221. Harris echoed Saltonstall, who wrote, "The Dispensation we lay under was Cloudy and Affrighting, Fresh Messengers (like Job's Servants) howrly arriving to bring the Doleful Tidings of New Massacres, Slaughters and Devastations committed by the Brutish Heathens" (*New and Further Narrative,* 78).

50. Joseph Moody to John Cotton, May 1, 1676, Curwen Papers, AAS. Nathaniel Brew-ster to unknown, July 12, 1675, Winthrop Papers, MHS. Unknown to unknown, May 18, 1676, Gay Transcripts, Plymouth papers, MHS, 1:53.

51. John Winthrop, Jr., to Fitz-John Winthrop, July 9, 1675, *MHSC,* 5th ser., 8 (1882): 170. William Leete to John Winthrop, Jr., September 21, 1675, *MHSC,* 4th ser., 7 (1865): 577–78.

52. Samuel Gorton to John Winthrop, Jr., September 11, 1675, *MHSC,* 4th ser., 7 (1865): 627. John Pynchon to John Winthrop, Jr., July 2, 1675, *The Pynchon Papers,* ed. Carl Briden-baugh and Juliette Tomlinson (Boston: Colonial Society of Massachusetts, 1985), 1:136–37.

53. Harris, *A Rhode Islander Reports,* 16. John Pynchon to John Winthrop, Jr., August 12, 1675, *Pynchon Papers* 1:143–44. Daniel Witherell to John Winthrop, Jr., July 29, 1675 (but mis-dated as 1677), *MHSC,* 3rd ser., 10 (1849): 118. John Kingsley to the Connecticut War Coun-cil, May 5, 1676.

54. Samuel Hooker to Increase Mather, *MHSC,* 4th ser., 8 (1868): 337. Roger Williams to John Winthrop, June 27, 1675, Winthrop Papers, MHS.

55. Massachusetts Council to Indian Sagamores, March 31, 1676, Mass. Arch. 68:193.

56. Sam Namphow to Massachusetts Council, October 12, 1675, Mass. Arch. 30:182. On the reason for Namphow's mission see Douglas Leach, *Flintlock and Tomahawk: New Eng-land in King Philip's War* (New York: The Macmillan Company, 1958; reprint, East Orleans, Mass.: Parnassus Imprints, 1992), 83–84.

57. Saltonstall, *Present State,* 44; John Pynchon to the Massachusetts Council, Septem-ber 30, 1675, *NEHGR* 38 (1884): 431.

58. Saltonstall, *Present State,* 31. See also Roger Williams, *A Key into the Language of America,* ed. John J. Teunissen and Evelyn J. Hinz (Detroit: Wayne State University Press, 1973), ch. 32.

59. John Russell to Increase Mather, September 15, 1675, transcribed in Mather, *Brief History,* 74. On marking trees see "Narrative of the Captivity of Quentin Stockwell," in Samuel Gardner Drake, ed., *Tragedies of the Wilderness* (Boston, 1846), 61.

60. Richard Jacob to unknown, April 22, 1676, *NEHGR* 40 (1886): 391–92. Similarly, Mary Rowlandson reported the Indians returning to camp after burning Medfield and "by their noise and whooping they signified how many they had destroyed (which was at that time twenty-three)" (Rowlandson, *Sovereignty*, 330).

61. Mary Pray to James Oliver, January 1, 1676.

62. Thomas Whalley to John Cotton, July 18, 1676, Davis Papers, MHS. Thomas Whalley to John Cotton, October 9, 1676, Curwen Papers, AAS. John Freeman to Josiah Winslow, July 3, 1675, Winslow Papers, MHS. Connecticut Council to John Pynchon, August 9, 1675, *CCR* 2:349 (emphasis mine).

63. Nathaniel Brewster to unknown, July 12, 1675, Winthrop Papers, MHS. Noah Newman to John Cotton, March 14, 1676, Curwen Papers, AAS.

64. Jane Hook to Increase Mather, August 12, 1677, *MHSC*, 4th ser., 8 (1868): 261. Christopher Whichcot to Isaac Waldron, July 4, 1676, Jeffries Papers, MHS.

65. Stephen Dummor to Henry Sewall, May 24, 1676, Curwen Papers, AAS. John Hall to Rebeckah Byley Hall Worcester Symonds, March 16, 1676, John Hall Letters, 1663–85, AAS.

66. John Pynchon to John Russell, October 5, 1675, *Pynchon Papers* 1:156–57.

67. Rowlandson, *Sovereignty*, 326.

68. John Kingsley to the Connecticut War Council, May 5, 1676. Kingsley's letter was so moving that the Connecticut War Council responded by sending out a call for donations. See Connecticut War Council to "all Christian friends" (May 30, 1676, *CCR* 2:445).

69. Mary Pray to James Oliver, October 20, 1675, *MHSC*, 5th ser., 1 (1871): 105. Walker, "Captan Perse," 92. Tompson, *New England's Crisis*, 217. John Hall to Rebeckah Symonds, June 22, 1676, John Hall Letters, AAS.

70. Daniel Denison to unknown, October 28, 1675, Mass. Arch. 68:30; see also the transcription in *NEHGR* 23 (1969):327.

71. Elaine Scarry, *The Body in Pain: The Making and Unmaking of the World* (New York: Oxford University Press, 1985), especially 133–37. For a slightly different but related argument see Paul Fussell, *The Great War and Modern Memory* (New York: Oxford University Press, 1975), ch. 5. According to Fussell,

> One of the cruxes of the war, of course, is the collision between events and the language available—or thought appropriate—to describe them. To put it more accurately, the collision was one between events and the public language used for over a century to celebrate the idea of progress. Logically there is no reason why the English language could not perfectly well render the actuality of trench warfare: it is rich in terms like *blood, terror, agony, madness, shit, cruelty, murder, sell-out, pain* and *hoax*, as well as phrases like *legs blown off, intestines gushing out over his hands, screaming all night, bleeding to death from the rectum*, and the like. Logically, one supposes, there's no reason why a language devised by man should be inadequate to describe any of man's works. The difficulty was in admitting that the war had been made by men and was being continued *ad infinitum* by them. The problem was less one of "language" than of gentility and optimism; it was less a problem of "linguistics" than of rhetoric (*The Great War*, 169–70).

At the same time, Fussell argues that soldiers often wrote about the war in high-literary terms: "The point is this: finding the war 'indescribable' in any but the available language of traditional literature, those who recalled it had to do so in known literary terms. Joyce, Eliot,

Lawrence, Pound, Yeats were not present at the front to induct them into new idioms which might have done the job better. Inhibited by scruples of decency and believing in the historical continuity of styles, writers about the war had to appeal to the sympathy of readers by invoking the familiar and suggesting its resemblance to what many of them suspected was an unprecedented and (in their terms) an all-but-incommunicable reality" (ibid., 174). Elsewhere, writing about World War II, Fussell has written that "Most of those with firsthand experience of the war at its worst were relatively inarticulate and have remained silent" ("Hiroshima: A Soldier's View," *New Republic*, August 22 and 29, 1981).

72. Hubbard (*Narrative*, 1:16) remarks on the importance of "eye or ear Witnesses," but see also Noah Newman to John Cotton, December 10, 1675, Bowen, *Early Rehoboth*, 2:49.

73. Tompson, *New England's Crisis*, 220. James Oliver to unknown, January 26, 1676, *NEHGR* 39 (1885): 380.

74. Tompson, *New England's Crisis*, 230. Winthrop, *Some Meditations*.

75. Saltonstall, *New and Further Narrative*, 99. Mary Pray to James Oliver, October 20, 1675. Later in the same letter, however, Pray abbreviated her remarks, claiming "It is to[o] much to writ to troubl you to read our sad condition." William Leete to John Winthrop, Jr., September 21, 1675, *MHSC*, 4th ser., 7 (1865): 577–78.

76. *News from New-England*, 4. Saltonstall, *New and Further Narrative*, 78.

77. Scarry, *The Body in Pain*, 60.

78. John Foster, *An Almanack of Coelestial Motions for . . . 1676* (Boston, 1676), 2.

79. Harris, *A Rhode Islander Reports*, 18.

80. Tompson, *New England's Crisis*, 218.

81. Hubbard, *Narrative*, 1:144.

82. Ibid., 1:97.

Chapter 3 • HABITATIONS OF CRUELTY

1. Saltonstall, *New and Further Narrative*, 98–99.

2. A powerful discussion of such notions of order can be found in Robert Blair St. George, " 'Set Thine House in Order': The Domestication of the Yeomanry in Seventeenth-Century New England," in Jonathan L. Fairbanks, ed., *New England Begins: The Seventeenth Century* (Boston: Museum of Fine Arts, 1982), 2:159–87.

3. Wharton, *New-England's Present Sufferings*, 6–7. Thomas Whalley to John Cotton, April 17, 1676, Davis Papers, MHS. Saltonstall, *Continuation*, 78.

4. Noah Newman to John Cotton, April 19, 1676, Curwen Papers, AAS. John Kingsley to Connecticut War Council, May 5, 1676, *CCR* 2:445. Noah Newman to John Cotton, April 19, 1676. On Rehoboth's fate see also Hubbard, *Narrative*, 1:180, and Mather, *Brief History*, 131.

5. Walker, "Captan Perse," 91. Wharton, *New-England's Present Sufferings*, 7. Wharton was clearly borrowing from Isaiah 30:22: "Ye shall defile also the covering of thy graven images of silver, and the ornament of thy molten images of gold: thou shalt cast them away as a menstruous cloth; thou shallt say unto it, Get thee hence."

6. Tompson, *New England's Crisis*, 226–27. On this common poetic device see Mary Tom Osborne, *Advice-to-a-Painter Poems, 1633–1856: An Annotated List* (Austin: University of Texas Press, 1949). On Tompson's use of this device see Jane Donahue Eberwein, " '*Harvardine* Quil': Benjamin Tompson's Poems on King Philip's War," *EAL* 28 (1993): 1–20; Robert L. Pincus, "Pictures of New England's Apocalypse: Benjamin Tompson's Transfor-

mation of the British Advice-to-a-Painter Poem," *EAL* 19 (1984–85): 268–78; and Peter White, "Cannibals and Turks: Benjamin Tompson's Image of the Native American" in Peter White, ed., *Puritan Poets and Poetics: Seventeenth-Century American Poetry in Theory and Practice* (University Park: The Pennsylvania State University Press, 1985), 198–209. White argues that Tompson's "advice to a painter" may really be advice to the Boston printer and engraver John Foster ("Cannibals and Turks," 204–5). White also argues that Tompson's Indians bear a greater resemblance to those depicted in John White's paintings of Virginian Indians than New England's natives. For a complete survey of Tompson's work see Peter White, *Benjamin Tompson: Colonial Bard* (University Park: The Pennsylvania State University Press, 1980).

7. Rowlandson, *Soveraignty*, 324.

8. Tompson, *New England's Crisis*, 227–28.

9. Elaine Scarry, *The Body in Pain: The Making and Unmaking of the World* (New York: Oxford University Press, 1985), 113–14.

10. Mary Douglas, *Purity and Danger: An Analysis of Concepts of Pollution and Taboo* (New York: Praeger, 1966), 115. Douglas's work on the body is often cited, appropriately, with Norbert Elias's work on the civilizing process and Pierre Bourdieu on the body. Recent scholarship that draws on these three influential works and especially explores the idea of culture being inscribed on the body includes Catherine B. Burroughs and Jeffrey David Ehrenreich, *Reading the Social Body* (Iowa City: University of Iowa Press, 1993); Mike Featherstone et al., eds., *The Body: Social Process and Cultural Theory* (London: Sage, 1991); Linda Lomperis and Sarah Stanbury, eds., *Feminist Approaches to the Body in Medieval Literature* (Philadelphia: University of Pennsylvania Press, 1993); Francis E. Mascia-Lees and Patricia Sharpe, eds., *Tattoo, Torture, Mutilation, and Adornment: The Denaturalization of the Body in Culture and Text* (Albany: State University of New York Press, 1992); Sue Scott and David Morgan, eds., *Body Matters: Essays on the Sociology of the Body* (London: The Falmer Press, 1993); Chris Shilling, *The Body and Social Theory* (London: Sage, 1993); Anthony Synnott, *The Body Social: Symbolism, Self and Society* (London: Routledge, 1993); and Katharine Young, *Bodylore* (Knoxville: The University of Tennessee Press, 1993).

11. "Wee know that a Chirugion in dressing a wound, puts a man oft to greater paine, then the assassinate did who gave it," Ashcam continued. Still, "we know no evill which can bee cur'd, but by another" (Anthony Ashcam, *A Discourse wherein is examined, what is particularly lawfull during the confusions and revolutions of government* [London, 1648], 101).

12. Mass. Arch. 68:174–76, quoted in Frederick Jackson Turner, "The First Official Frontier of the Massachusetts Bay," in *The Frontier in American History* (New York: Henry Holt & Company, 1920), 40.

13. George Ingersol to Leif Augur, September 10, 1675, *NEHGR* 8 (1854): 239. See also Hubbard, *Narrative*, 2:103. Major Richard Waldron also mentions this attack in a letter to Daniel Denison, September 25, 1675: "On Saturday and Sabbath day last at Scarborough they killed an old man and woman and burnt their house" (*NEHGR* 23 [1869]: 325–27).

14. For more on Wakely and for the attack on Purchase see Hubbard, *Narrative*, 2:100–104, and Mather, *Brief History*, 89.

15. As Eric Cheyfitz has argued, "property became identity" in the West sometime in sixteenth-century England, when "the social recognition of kinship was losing ground rapidly to the recognition of property in the social sphere" (*The Poetics of Imperialism: Translation and Colonization from* The Tempest *to* Tarzan [New York: Oxford University Press, 1991], 50–58).

16. John Locke, *Two Treatises of Government* (1690).

17. Robert Cushman, "Reasons and Considerations Touching the Lawfulness of Removing Out of England Into the Parts of America," in Alexander Young, ed., *Chronicles of the Pilgrim Fathers of the Colony of Plymouth, From 1602 to 1625,* 2nd ed. (Boston, 1844), 243. William Bradford, *Of Plymouth Plantation, 1620–1647,* ed. Samuel Eliot Morison (New York: Alfred A. Knopf, 1952). Francis Higginson, *New-England's Plantation* (London, 1630); reprinted in Alexander Young, ed., *Chronicles of the First Planters of the Colony of Massachusetts Bay* (Boston, 1846), 256. Allyn B. Forbes et al., eds., *Winthrop Papers, 1498–1649,* 5 vols. (Boston: Massachusetts Historical Society, 1929–47), 2:120. John Josselyn, *An Account of Two Voyages to New-England, Made during the Years 1638, 1663* (London, 1675; reprinted Hanover, N.H.: University Press of New England, 1988), 91. The best discussion of the colonists' ideas about land and its uses can be found in William Cronon, *Changes in the Land: Indians, Colonists, and the Ecology of New England* (New York: Hill & Wang, 1983); but see also Alfred Crosby, *Ecological Imperialism: The Biological Expansion of Europe, 900–1900* (Cambridge: Cambridge University Press, 1986), especially 188–89; John H. Elliott, "Colonial Identity in the Atlantic World," in *Colonial Identity in the Atlantic World, 1500–1800,* ed. Nicholas Canny and Anthony Pagden (Princeton, N.J.: Princeton University Press, 1987), 9–11; Zuckerman, "Identity in British America," 138–39; David Grayson Allen, "*Vacuum Domicilium:* The Social and Cultural Landscape of Seventeenth-Century New England," in Fairbanks, ed., *New England Begins,* 1:1–10; and, on King Philip's War, Virginia DeJohn Anderson, "King Philip's Herds: Indians, Colonists, and the Problem of Livestock in Early New England," *WMQ* 51 (1994): 601–24.

18. Thomas More, *The Best State of a Commonwealth and the New Island of Utopia* (1516), in Edward Surtz and J. H. Hexter, eds., *The Complete Works of St. Thomas More* (New Haven, Conn.: Yale University Press, 1965), 4:137.

19. Quoted in Cary Carson et al., "Impermanent Architecture in the Southern American Colonies," in *Material Life in America, 1600–1860,* ed. Robert Blair St. George (Boston: Northeastern University Press, 1988), 135. On the arrangement of the English domestic landscape see Robert Blair St. George, " 'Set Thine House in Order.' "

20. *Brief and True Narration,* 3. "A Wilderness," according to Thomas Shepard, "is not hedged in, nor fenced about" (quoted in Steven D. Neuwirth, "The Images of Place: Puritans, Indians, and the Religious Significance of the New England Frontier," *The American Art Journal* 18 [1986]: 51).

21. Mather, *Exhortation,* 171. Saltonstall, *New and Further Narrative,* 78. Samuel Symonds to Sir Joseph Williamson, April 6, 1676, Gay Transcripts, MHS.

22. Saltonstall, *New and Further Narrative,* 97–98. *Brief and True Narration,* 5. "Diary of Increase Mather," 43. Saltonstall, *Present State,* 30. *Brief and True Narration,* 5. Edmund Randolph's reckoning of the losses is interesting in that it includes Indians as English losses (in the form of potential labor): "No advantage but many disadvantages have arisen to the English by the warre, for about 600 men have been slaine, and 12 captains, most of them brave and stout persons and of loyal principles, whilest the church members had liberty to stay at home and not hazard their persons in the wildernesse. The losse to the English in the severall colonies . . . is reckoned to amount to 150,000£. there having been about 1200 houses burned, 8000 head of cattle, great and small, killed, and many thousand bushels of wheat, pease, and other grain burned . . . and upward of 3000 Indians men women and children destroyed, who if well managed would have been very serviceable to the English, which makes all manner of labour dear" ("Short Narrative").

23. Harris, *A Rhode Islander Reports*, 16.

24. John Pynchon to John Russell, October 5, 1675, *The Pynchon Papers*, ed. Carl Bridenbaugh and Juliette Tomlinson (Boston: Colonial Society of Massachusetts, 1985), 1:156–57. John Russell to the Massachusetts Council, October 6, 1675, Mass. Arch. 67:288.

25. John Sharpe to Thomas Meekins, April 8, 1676, *NEHGR* 10 (1856): 65.

26. Samuel Gorton to John Winthrop, Jr., September 11, 1675. Walter Gendle was brought to court to testify that "ther is no place that the Ingins have com on them to fight that they [the soldiers] presently left the field and horses to them to doe what they like which is a sad case thear beinn so many men" (Walter Gendle to the Massachusetts Council, July 27, 1676, Mass. Arch. [MHS photostat file]).

27. Richard Lord to John Winthrop, October 7, 1676, Winthrop Papers, MHS.

28. John Pynchon to John Leverett, October 8, 1675, *Pynchon Papers* 1:157–60.

29. *CCR* 2:268. Similarly, one English colonist wrote that the land was "unused and undressed" (quoted in Zuckerman, "Identity in British America," 154).

30. Mary Rowlandson also described Indians wearing necklaces made of human fingers (*Soveraignty*, 353).

31. Robert Blair St. George has suggested that a series of related binarisms characterized the colonists' worldview:

Nature	unartificial	waste	unfenced	undressed
Culture	artificial	improved	fenced	dressed

(St. George, " 'Set Thine House in Order,' " 161). On nakedness see also Stephen Greenblatt's discussion in "Learning to Curse: Aspects of Linguistic Colonialism in the Sixteenth Century," in *First Images of America: The Impact of the New World on the Old*, ed. Fredi Chiapelli (Berkeley: University of California Press, 1976), especially 562, where he writes, "In the eyes of the Europeans, the Indians were culturally naked." On the significance of adornment see, for example, Terence S. Turner, "The Social Skin," in Catherine B. Burroughs and Jeffrey David Ehrenreich, *Reading the Social Body* (Iowa City: University of Iowa Press, 1993), 15–39. In the Christian West, "naked bodies gathered meanings that ranged from innocence to shame, from vulnerability to culpability, and from present worthlessness to future bliss in the resurrection of the body." Nakedness has a history of meanings, including the medieval one of proximity to God (in giving up all worldly possessions, including clothes, adopted by ascetics), but to the Puritans it signified immodesty and savagery (Margaret R. Miles, *Carnal Knowing: Female Nakedness and Religious Meaning in the Christian West* [Boston: Beacon Press, 1989], xi–xii). On how the Reformation "desacramentalized" the body see Benedict M. Ashley, O.P., *Theologies of the Body: Humanist and Christian* (Braintree, Mass.: Pope John Center, 1985), 172–80.

32. On New Englanders' clothing see John Demos, *A Little Commonwealth: Family Life in Plymouth Colony* (London: Oxford University Press, 1970), 52–58. The distinction of the English as clothed and the Indians as naked is a simplification that not all observers subscribed to; some, such as William Wood and Thomas Morton, observed that the Indians did dress; they just dressed differently. See Wood, *New England's Prospect*, ed. Alden Vaughan (Amherst: University of Massachusetts Press, 1977), 84–85; and Thomas Morton, *New English Canaan or New Canaan* (Boston: Prince Society, 1833), 141–45.

33. Glenn W. LaFantasie, ed., *The Correspondence of Roger Williams* (Providence: Brown University Press, 1988), 2:413.

34. Roger Williams, *A Key into the Language of America*, ed. John J. Teunissen and Evelyn J. Hinz (Detroit: Wayne State University Press, 1973), 133, 185–88.

35. Eliot told Christian Indians "you should have cloths, houses, cattle, riches as they have, God would give you them" (*MHSC*, 3rd ser., 4 [1834]: 57–58). Daniel Gookin reported,

> The Indians' clothing in former times was of the same matter as Adam's was, viz. skins or beasts, as deer, moose, beaver, otters, rackoons, foxes, and other wild creatures. Also, some had mantles of the feathers of birds, quilled artificially; and sundry of them continue to this day their old kind of clothing. But, for the most part, they sell the skins and furs to the English, Dutch, and French, and buy of them for clothing a kind of cloth, called duffils, or trucking cloth, about a yard and a half wide, and for matter, made of coarse wool, in that form as our ordinary bed blankets are made, only it is put into colours, as blue, red, purple, and some use them white. Of this sort of cloth two yards make a mantle, or coat, for men and women, less for children. This is all the garment they generally use, with this addition of some little pieces of the same, or of ordinary cotton, to cover their seret parts. It is rare to see any among them of the most barbarous, that are remiss or negligent in hiding those parts. But the christian and civilized Indians do endeavour, many of them, to follow the English mode in their habit. Their ornaments are, especially the women's, bracelets, necklaces, and head bands, of several sorts of beads, especially of black and white wompom, which is of most esteem among them, and is acounted their chief treasure ("Historical Collections of the Indians in New England [1674]," *MHSC*, 1st ser., 1 [1792], 152).

36. See, for example, the testimony of Manasses Molasses, who took the coat of an Englishman he had killed and traded it for ground nuts (*A Court Martial Held at Newport, Rhode Island, in August and September, 1676* [Albany, N.Y.: J. Munsell, 1858]). In Benjamin Tompson's fictious Philip speech he has Philip tell his people, "Now if you'll fight I'll get you English coats" (*New England's Crisis*, 218). The English also rewarded Indians in their employ with "coats" (a term that was also used to refer to blankets and cloth) in exchange for enemy heads and scalps (John Allyn to unknown, August 2, 1675, Winthrop Papers, MHS). As Saltonstall reported,

> The English made this Agreement with them, That for every Indians Head-Skin they brought, they should have a Coat, (i.e. two Yards of Trucking Cloth, worth five Shillings per Yard here) and for every one they bring alive two Coats; for King Philips Head, twenty Coats, and if taken alive, Forty Coats (*Present State*, 34).

37. Rowlandson, *Soveraignty*, 337. Josselyn, *An Account of Two Voyages*, 143.

38. Rowlandson, *Soveraignty*, 348.

39. Williams, *Key into the Language*, 185–88.

40. Quoted in Ronald Takaki, "The *Tempest* in the Wilderness: The Racialization of Savagery," *JAH* 79 (1992): 893–94.

41. Hubbard, *Narrative*, 1:116–17. Harris, *A Rhode Islander Reports*, 76. Saltonstall, *Present State*, 30. Wharton, *New-England's Present Sufferings*, 4, 6. Mather, *Brief History*, 60–61. Hubbard, *Narrative*, 1:193–94, 1:117–18.

42. Wood, *New England's Prospect*, 27.

43. Helkiah Crooke, *Micropocosmographia: A Description of the Body of Man* (London, 1651), 47, 56.

44. Mather, *Exhortation*, 179.

45. John Allyn to the Massachusetts Council, October 7, 1675, Mass. Arch. 67:285. Massachusetts Council to unknown, undated, Mass. Arch. 18. Tompson, *New England's Crisis*, 221.

46. Wheeler, *Thankefull Remembrance*, 247. Roger Williams to Robert Williams, April 1, 1676, *Correspondence of Roger Williams*, 2:720. Harris, *A Rhode Islander Reports*, 45–46.

47. Another story tells of how "On the Lords Day, the ――― of July, an Indian came to Dorchester . . . to the House of Mr. Minor, in Sermon Time, and there were then at Home the Maid Servant and two young Children, she keeping the Door shut for Safety; the Indian when he saw he could not come in at the Door, went about to come in at the Window, she perceiving his Resolution, took two Brass Kettles, under which she put the two Children, she ran up Stairs and charged a Musket and fired at the Indian (he having fired at her, once or twice and mist her, but struck the Top of one Kettle, under which a child was) and shot him into his Shoulder; then he let his Gun fall, and was just coming in at the Window, she made haste and got a Fire-shovel full of live Coles and applied them to his Face, which forced him to flie and escape: But one was found dead within five Miles of that Place afterwards, and was judged to be this by his scalded Face" (Saltonstall, *Present State*, 31). Still another: "One of the men perceiving a stirring among the leaves Major Phillips looked out of his chamber window that way and from thence was immediately shot at" (Richard Waldron to Daniel Denison, September 25, 1675, *NEHGR* 23 [1869]: 326).

48. Cheyfitz even argues that "not to have 'propertie' . . . is to lose, from a European perspective, a significant part of one's humanness" (*Poetics of Imperialism*, 59).

49. Tompson, *New England's Crisis*, 226.

50. English readers must have eagerly examined Foster's map, attempting to make sense of the accounts of the war they had read. Few other maps of New England were available, and as a result, some colonists provided English readers with maps of their own. In Dublin, Ireland, Nathaniel Mather was glad to receive a map of New England made by his nephew Cotton, remarking that "it helps mee much in understanding your & other narratives" (Nathaniel Mather to Increase Mather, February 26, 1678, *MHSC*, 4th ser., 8 [1868]: 9).

51. Tompson, *New England's Crisis*, 226. Tompson was not referring to modest, Edenic loincloths, but to deliberate, strategic camouflage, as when, for example, Major Richard Waldron reported, "no Indians as yet appeared but only creeping decked with fearnes and boughs" (Major Richard Waldron to Daniel Denison, September 25, 1675, *NEHGR* 23 [1869]: 326). See also Gookin, "Historical Account," 441.

52. Mary Pray to James Oliver, October 20, 1675, *MHSC*, 5th ser., 1:105.

53. Foster's depiction, reducing all that is English to the icons "house" and "church," and all that is Indian to the icon "tree," is entirely consistent with the colonists' perception of their world and its significance. As Richard White has argued, "Perhaps the most important decision Europeans made about American nature in the centuries following Columbus was that they were not part of it, but Indians were" ("Discovering Nature in North America," *JAH* 79 [1992], 882). On the colonists' ideas about the wilderness see Peter N. Carroll, *Puritanism and the Wilderness: The Intellectual Significance of the New England Frontier, 1629–1700* (New York: Columbia University Press, 1969), 1–4, 206–18. See also Roderick Nash, *Wilderness and the American Mind* (New Haven, Conn.: Yale University Press, 1967), especially chs. 1 and 2 and pp. 29–38; Steven D. Neuwirth, "The Images of Place: Puritans, Indians, and the Religious Significance of the New England Frontier," *The American Art Journal* 18 (1986): 43–53; Zuck-

erman, "Identity in British America," 137–38; and John Canup, *Out of the Wilderness: The Emergence of an American Identity in Colonial New England* (Middletown, Conn.: Wesleyan University Press, 1990).

54. Tompson, *New-England's Crisis,* 220.

55. Saltonstall, *Present State,* 31. Or, as Benjamin Tompson wrote:

> The swamps were courts of guard, thither retired
> The straggling blue-coats when their guns were fired,
> In dark meanders, and these winding groves,
> Where bears & panthers with their monarch moves

(*New England's Crisis,* 220–21).

56. *Brief and True Narration,* 5.

57. Mather, *Brief History,* 62.

58. Hubbard, *Narrative,* 1:87. In issuing his official orders to Captain Joseph Syll, Gookin instructed him, "You are carefully so to march your men in the woods so that if it be possible to avoide or shunne or well serch before you com to neare all thick places as swamps or thicketts wher the enimy uses with subtilty to lurke in Ambushments" (Daniel Gookin to Captain Joseph Syll, November 2, 1675, *NEHGR* 41 [1887]: 403).

59. Stephen Saunders Webb, *1676: The End of American Independence* (New York: Alfred A. Knopf, 1984), 239. On the significance of swamp imagery in later American culture, see David C. Miller, *Dark Eden: The Swamp in Nineteenth-Century American Culture* (Cambridge: Cambridge University Press, 1989). Unfortunately, Miller makes no acknowledgment of the seventeenth-century roots of Anglo-American fears of swamps.

60. Saltonstall, *New and Further Narrative,* 77. Harris, *A Rhode Islander Reports,* 30. Williams, *Key into the Language,* 150. Samuel Symonds to Sir Joseph Williamson, April 6, 1676. Swamps, another Englishman complained, are "so soft Ground, that an Englishman can neither go nor stand thereon, and yet these bloody Savages will run along over it, holding their Guns cross their Armes (and if Occasion be) discharge in that Posture" (Saltonstall, *Present State,* 31). In July 1675, for example, Philip and his men secreted themselves in Pocasset Swamp while Plymouth forces tried desperately to apprehend them. On July 20 James Cudworth reported to Josiah Winslow that his 120 men had been "fired upon out of the bushes, and in and out of swamps were fired at, and we had a hot dispute, especially when we were to go near to a swamp." When they finally succeeded in entering the "hideous dismal swamp," they found all the women and children had fled. "They fly before us," Cudworth complained, "from one swamp to another" (James Cudworth to Josiah Winslow, July 20, 1675, *MHSC,* 1st ser., 6 [1799]: 84). Nine days later Winslow reported to John Winthrop, Jr., "Our enemy keeping them selves cloase within the most hideouse swamps they can finde, wher in wee cannot ingage them but at extream disadvantage, it threatens a continuance of the war longer then wee some times hoped it might have beene" (Josiah Winslow to John Winthrop, Jr., July 29, 1675).

61. Noah Newman to Lieutenant Thomas, September 30, 1675, transcribed in Bowen, *Early Rehoboth,* 3:89–90. The *OED* erroneously claims the word "swamp" was not used as a verb until 1688.

62. Hubbard, *Narrative,* 1:252. (Psalm 74:20: "The dark places of the world are full of the habitations of cruelty.")

63. Williams, *Key into the Language,* 150. Samuel Symonds complained that English soldiers "cannot meet with any Body of [Indians], their manner being to move from place to

place almost every day, Leaving their Women and Children in hideous Swamps & obscure, unaccessable places, of which the Country is Full" (Samuel Symonds to Sir Joseph Williamson, April 6, 1676).

64. Mather, *Brief History*, 206–7.

65. Kathleen J. Bragdon, "The Material Culture of the Christian Indians of New England, 1650–1775," in Mary C. Beaudry, ed., *Documentary Archaeology in the New World* (Cambridge: Cambridge University Press, 1988), 128–29. Kathleen J. Bragdon, "Probate Records as a Source for Algonquian Ethnohistory," in William Cowan, ed., *Papers of the Tenth Algonquian Conference* (Ottawa: Carleton University, 1979), 136. Elise Brenner, "Strategies for Autonomy: An Analysis of Ethnic Mobilization in Seventeenth-Century Southern New England" (Ph.D. diss., University of Massachusetts, Amherst, 1984), 127–32.

66. A notable exception is Nathaniel Saltonstall's definition for English readers: "*Wigwams* are Indian Huts or Houses" (Saltonstall, *New and Further Narrative*, 77). Thomas Morton made a common analogy when he wrote, "The Natives of New England are accustome to build them houses much like the wild Irish" (*New English Canaan or New Canaan*, 134).

67. James Cudworth to Josiah Winslow, July 20, 1675, *MHSC*, 1st ser., 6 (1799): 84.

68. Tompson, *New England's Crisis*, 223.

69. Rowlandson, *Soveraignty*, 334.

70. Francis Bland, *The Souldiers March to Salvation* (Yorke, 1647), 15.

71. When the Plymouth forces found Philip's empty fort in Pocasset Swamp in July 1675, they found there "four English heads on poles." These the English took down and put "four Indian heads in their place" (*Brief and True Narrative*, 5).

72. Samuel Moseley to John Leverett, August 16, 1675, *NEHGR* 37 (1883): 177.

73. Harris, *A Rhode Islander Reports*, 36–38. This attack is quite similar to the English attack on the Pequots in Mystic, Connecticut, in 1637; see, for example, John Underhill, "News from America," *MHSC*, 3rd ser., 6 (1837): 1–28. Since nearly all contemporary chronicles include a description of the Great Swamp fight, I have not listed them here, except to observe that the most complete contemporary printed account can be found in *Farther Brief and True Narration* and that Wait Still Winthrop's poem *Some Meditations* is a reflection on the battle. A usefully detailed secondary account is in George M. Bodge, *The Narragansett Fort Fight* (Boston, 1886), and, most useful of all, Leach, *Flintlock and Tomahawk*, 123–35.

74. Ashcam, *A Discourse*, 100. Adam Hirsch has argued that the English adopted tactics of "total war" in fighting the Indians after the Pequot War, and while he does not cite it, no example supports his argument more powerfully than this attack (Adam J. Hirsch, "The Collision of Military Cultures in Seventeenth-Century New England," *JAH* 74 [1988]: 1204–9).

75. Mather, *Brief History*, 107–8. *News from New England*, 1. Joseph Dudley to unknown, December 21, 1675, *NEHGR* 40 (1886): 89. Tompson, *New England's Crisis*, 223–24. Or, as another Englishman admitted, "ours had now a Carnage rather than a Fight, for every one had their fill of Blood" (*News from New-England*, 1). The celebratory assessment has been shared by many early historians of the event. Bodge, for instance, writes, "By any candid student of history I believe this must be classed as one of the most glorious victories ever achieved in our history, and considering conditions, as displaying heroism, both in stubborn patient and dashing intrepidity, never excelled in American warfare" (Bodge, *The Narragansett Fort Fight*, 13).

76. Noah Newman to John Cotton, March 3, 1676, Curwen Papers, AAS. For another account of the attack on Medfield see John Wilson and others to the Massachusetts Council, February 21, 1676, Mass. Arch. 68:139, transcribed in George Ellis, *Exercises at the Bi-Centennial Commemoration of the Burning of Medfield* (Medfield, 1876), 24–25. See also Gookin, "Historical Account," 493–94. And see Leach, *Flintlock and Tomahawk*, 159–60.

77. Noah Newman to John Cotton, March 3, 1676.

78. John Wilson to the Massachusetts Council, February 14, 1676, transcribed in Ellis, *Exercises at the Bi-Centennial*, 14–15.

79. Gookin, "Historical Account," 493; *News from New-England*, 4. John Wilson and others to the Massachusetts Council, February 21, 1676.

80. Hubbard, *Narrative*, 1:169.

81. Richard Waldron to the Massachusetts Council, September 25, 1675, *NEHGR* 42 (1888): 190. Edmund Browne to John Leverett, September 26, 1676, *NEHGR* 7 (1853): 268. John Kingsley to the Connecticut Council, May 5, 1676. John Hull to Philip French, September 2, 1675, John Hull's Letterbook, AAS.

82. Rowlandson, *Soveraignty*, 324–26.

83. Hubbard, *Narrative*, 1:70.

84. Mather, *Exhortation*, 171. Mather, *Brief History*, 123–24.

85. Noah Newman to John Cotton, March 3, 1676.

86. Rowlandson, *Soveraignty*, 324.

87. Williams, *Key into the Language*, 131.

88. Mather, *Brief History*, 61.

89. Quoted in Peter Furtado, "National Pride in Seventeenth-Century England," in *Patriotism: The Making and Unmaking of British National Identity*, ed. Raphael Samuel, vol. 1: *History and Politics* (London: Routledge, 1989), 46. See also John Bulwer, *Anthropometamorphosis, man transform'd, or, The artificial changeling: historically presented in the mad and cruel gallantry, foolish bravery, ridiculous beauty, filthy finenesse, an loathsome lovelinesse of most nations . . . with a vindication of the regular beauty and honesty of nature and an appendix of the pedigree of the English gallant* (London, 1650).

90. See Bulwer, *Anthropometamorphosis*.

91. Thomas Hall, *Comarum akosmia the loathsomnesse of long haire* (London, 1654), especially 13, 45.

92. Harris, *A Rhode Islander Reports*, 84.

93. Noah Newman to John Cotton, March 14, 1676, Curwen Papers, AAS. During her captivity Rowlandson met "one Mary Thurston of Medfield," who was probably Goodwife Thurston's daughter (Rowlandson, *Soveraignty*, 338).

94. However distinctive an English body's appearance might be, darkness could always obscure its unique qualities. Again and again the colonists complained that it was impossible to tell who was English at night: "The darkness was such as an English man could not be discerned from an Indian," or, perhaps more tellingly, "it was so dark that an Indian could hardly be discerned from a better Man" (Mather, *Brief History*, 131. Hubbard, *Narrative*, 1:208).

95. Gookin, "Historical Account," 478. Wheeler, *Thankefull Remembrance*, 253. Captives who lost their ability to speak English were likely to remain among the Indians; this transi-

tion marked a dramatic departure from English culture. For a compelling account of one such captivity see John Demos, *The Unredeemed Captive: A Family Story from Early America* (New York: Alfred A. Knopf, 1994).

96. Retreating Nipmucks burned the bridge beyond Medfield, preventing English soldiers from following them across the Charles River. Once on the Sherborn side of the bridge, the Nipmucks taunted the English from the riverbank. The note was discovered afterward (Leach, *Flintlock and Tomahawk*, 160). Noah Newman copied the note out in his letter to John Cotton, March 14, 1676, and Hubbard recorded a somewhat modified version: "As they passed the Bridg, [the Indians] left a Wrighting behind them, expressing something to this Purpose, that we had provoked them to Wrath, and that they would fight with us this twenty Years (but they fell short of their Expectation by nineteen) adding also, that they had nothing to lose, whereas we had Houses, Barns, and Corn" (*Narrative*, 1:171). Captain Benjamin Gibbs took the note from the tree and brought it to the Massachusetts Council, and Daniel Gookin, having read it, commented that it suggested "the pride and insolence of these barbarians at this time" (Gookin, "Historical Account," 494–95). Several antiquarian researchers have attributed this note to James Printer, including Samuel Gardner Drake (in the footnotes of his edition of Hubbard's *Narrative*) and William S. Tilden, *History of the Town of Medfield, Massachusetts* (Boston, 1887); and circumstantial evidence also points to Printer (he was one of a very few highly literate Indians living among the Indians who attacked Medfield).

97. Anderson has observed, "During the two decades before King Philip's War, Plymouth officials approached local Indians at least twenty-three times to purchase land, often mentioning a specific need for pasture" ("King Philip's Herds," 620).

98. Roger Williams to [Robert Williams?], April 1, 1676. The Narragansett Indian who spoke these words to Williams may well have been Stonewall John and the man tortured to death by Mohegans as described in the Prologue (Samuel Gardner Drake, *Book of the Indians* [Boston, 1841], 3:78).

99. Anderson, "King Philip's Herds," 613–14.

100. Easton, "Relacion," 11.

101. Noah Newman to John Cotton, March 14, 1676.

102. Quanohit, Sam, and Kutquen to the Massachusetts Council, April 12, 1676, transcribed in Gookin, "Historical Account," 508.

103. *Farther Brief and True Narration*, 3–4.

104. Quoted in William Simmons, *Spirit of the New England Tribes: Indian History and Folklore, 1620–1984* (Hanover, N.H.: University Press of New England, 1986), 46. Wampanoags also practiced this ritual.

105. For instances of this nature see Captain Benjamin Newberry to John Allyn, May 26, 1676, *NEHGR* 25 (1871): 72; Saltonstall, *Continuation*, 79–80; Hubbard, *Narrative*, 164–65; Lieutenant Richard Jacob to unknown, April 22, 1676, *NEHGR* 40 (1886): 391–92; Harris, *A Rhode Islander Reports*, 44–46; Joseph Dudley to unknown, *NEHGR* 40 (1886): 87–88; Mary Pray to James Oliver, October 20, 1675, *MHSC*, 5th ser., 1 (1871): 105. For more Indian attacks on cattle see Anderson, "King Philip's Herds," 622–23.

106. Randolph, "Short Narrative," 266.

107. Mather, *Brief History*, 132.

108. See Anderson, "King Philip's Herds," and Cronon, *Changes in the Land*.

109. Roger Williams to John Leverett, January 14, 1676.

Chapter 4 · Where is Your O God?

1. Rowlandson, *Soveraignty,* 353. For a very similar ceremony to resolve to go to war see Church, *Entertaining History,* 91–92; and for a powwaw predicting a storm see "Narrative of the Captivity of Quentin Stockwell" in Samuel Gardner Drake, ed., *Tragedies of the Wilderness* (Boston, 1846), 64. On the role of powwaws and other religious practitioners see Kathleen J. Bragdon, *Native People of Southern New England, 1500–1650* (Norman: University of Oklahoma Press, 1996), 200–216.

2. Rowlandson, *Soveraignty,* 354.

3. On manitou and the Algonquian spirit world see Bragdon, *Native People,* 184–87.

4. Samuel Green, ed., *Diary of Increase Mather, March 1675–December 1676* (Cambridge, Mass.: John Wilson & Son, 1900), 26, 28; see also Mather, *Brief History,* 116.

5. See Douglas Leach, *Flintlock and Tomahawk: New England in King Philip's War* (New York: The Macmillan Company, 1958; reprint, East Orleans, Mass.: Parnassus Imprints, 1992), 172–75. See also Saltonstall, *New and Further Narrative,* 92–94.

6. *True Account,* 2.

7. Increase Mather, *The Day of Trouble is Near* (Cambridge, 1674), 6. John Kingsley to the Connecticut War Council, May 5, 1676, *CCR* 2:445. On the colonists' need to interpret the war see Michael J. Puglisi, *Puritans Besieged: The Legacies of King Philip's War in the Massachusetts Bay Colony* (Lanham, Md.: University Press of America, 1991), 14. Much of the colonists' providential interpretation of the war must be seen as part of a broader rhetoric of jeremiads; see Sacvan Bercovitch, *The American Jeremiad* (Madison: University of Wisconsin Press, 1978).

8. John Eliot to John Winthrop, Jr., July 24, 1675, *MHSC,* 5th ser., 1 (1871): 424. Walker, "Captan Perse," 87, 93.

9. See Jon Butler, "Magic, Astrology, and the Early American Religious Heritage, 1600–1760," *AHR* 84 (1979): 317–46; and David Hall, *Words of Wonder, Days of Judgment: Popular Religious Belief in Early New England* (New York: Alfred A. Knopf, 1989), 76–94.

10. Mary Pray to James Oliver, October 20, 1675, *MHSC,* 5th ser., 1 (1871): 105.

11. John Josselyn, *An Account of Two Voyages to New-England, Made during the Years 1638, 1663* (London, 1675; reprint, Hanover, N.H.: University Press of New England, 1988), 125.

12. As, for instance, when Edward Wharton said the Indians had made of the English settlements "a burdensome and menstruous cloth" that, having fouled, they might now cast out of the land (*New-England's Present Sufferings,* 7).

13. "The bleeding body signifies as a shameful token of uncontrol, as a failure of physical self-mastery particularly associated with woman in her monthly 'courses' " (Gail Kern Paster, *The Body Embarrassed: Drama and the Disciplines of Shame in Early Modern England* [Ithaca, N.Y.: Cornell University Press, 1993], 92).

14. "Some of the Ancient Writers have dignified the frame of Man's body with the name and title of *The Book of God*" (Helkiah Crooke, *Micropocosmographia: A Description of the Body of Man* [London, 1651], 11).

15. Ambrose Paré, *The Works of Ambrose Paré* (London, 1649), 254.

16. Mather, *Exhortation,* 172. Or again, "We have been brought into such a bleeding state," Mather declared, "to make a right improvement of this dreadful Dispensation" (170).

17. John Kingsley to the Connecticut War Council, May 5, 1676. Roger Williams to John Leverett, October 11, 1675, *PCR* 10:453–55. John Pynchon to John Leverett and the Assistants, October 8, 1675, *The Pynchon Papers,* ed. Carl Bridenbaugh and Juliette Tomlinson (Boston: Colonial Society of Massachusetts, 1985), 1:157–60.

18. Saltonstall, *Present State,* 44.

19. Hubbard, *Narrative,* 1:48–49. For more on Passaconaway see Gookin, "Historical Account," 463.

20. Quoted in William Simmons, *Spirit of the New England Tribes: Indian History and Folklore, 1620–1984* (Hanover, N.H.: University Press of New England, 1986), 38. See also Daniel Gookin, "Historical Collections of the Indians in New England [1674]," *MHSC,* 1st ser., 1 (1792): 154.

21. Walker, "Captan Perse," 84. Walker also expressed some of the greatest fury against what he believed to be the Indians' basic evil:

> As a corupt tre brings forth Evill fruigh[ts] & a corupt ffountayne corupt & noysom stre[ams] So doath owr hethen Enimis being Corupt in th[e] ffountayne & rote of the mater streme forth Poysned waters of death as Cayne the first Murtherer, as Nero, Diocletian, & Domitio, Thos Hethen murthring Emperours that wear su[ch] Monsters of nature whos mad rage agaynst the Christians as out of Hell fomd out ther veno[m] (ibid.).

22. C. Mather, *Magnalia* 2:479–80. On the Puritans' theory of a "Satan-Indian alliance" see Steven D. Neuwirth, "The Images of Place: Puritans, Indians, and the Religious Significance of the New England Frontier," *American Art Journal* 18 (1986): 47–51.

23. *Laws & Ordinancies of Warre, Pass'd by the General Court of the Massachusets* (Cambridge, 1675), 32.

24. Mather, *Brief History,* 58, 92, 119–20, 157–62.

25. Wharton, *New-England's Present Sufferings,* 4.

26. Hutchinson, *Warr in New-England Visibly Ended,* 103. The argument that the colonists were being punished for their persecution of Quakers and other dissenters is most fully elaborated in Folger's poem; for example, "Let us then search what is the sin / that God doth punish for / . . . Sure tis not chiefly for those sins that magistrats do name . . . but its for the saim cryinge sin / that writers will not owen . . . / the sin of persecution . . ." (Folger, "Looking Glasse," 307). See also Wharton, *New-England's Present Sufferings,* 6–7; S[amuel] G[roome], *A Glasse for the People of New-England* ([London], 1676), 16–17.

27. On the practice of days of fasting, humiliation, and thanksgiving see W. DeLoss Love, *The Fast and Thanksgiving Days of New England* (Boston, 1895), especially 192–204; Bercovitch, *The American Jeremiad,* 80–83. On Plymouth Church's days see John Cotton's Plymouth Church Records in *Publications of the Colonial Society of Massachusetts* 222 (1920): 147–55. In Massachusetts printed broadsides declaring such days were posted beginning in June 1675. See *At a Council held at Boston, September the seventeenth 1675* (Cambridge, 1675); *At a Council held at Boston the 25th of June, 1675* (Boston?, 1675); *At a Council Held at Charlestown, June the 20th, 1676* (Cambridge, 1676). John Eliot gives an intriguing summary of the debate in June 1676 over whether to declare a day of fasting or of thanksgiving ("Rev. John Eliot's Records of the First Church in Roxbury, Mass.," *NEHGR* 33 [1879]: 299).

28. Wharton, *New-England's Present Sufferings,* 4. Rowlandson, *Soveraignty,* 360. Mather, *Brief History,* 125. Wheeler, *Thankfull Remembrance,* 247, 249. *News from New Eng-*

land, 5, but see also Mather, *Brief History,* 128–29; Saltonstall, *New and Further Narrative,* 85; Hubbard, *Narrative,* 1:205–6. Many of these actions, and the taunts that accompanied them, are quite similar to the acts and taunts used by Catholics and Protestants in religious riots (see Natalie Zemon Davis, "The Rites of Violence," in *Society and Culture in Early Modern France* [Stanford, Calif.: Stanford University Press, 1975], 152–87). I believe much of this similarity can be explained by understanding that New England Indians were indeed attacking a particular brand of English Protestantism, with which they themselves (especially renegade Christian Indians) were quite familiar; many no doubt employed methods they may have heard or read about in learning about Protestant martyrs, while others simply identified at what points the religion was most vulnerable (the fickleness of God's favor, for instance). The similarity may also be explained, however, by the colonists' disposition in reporting the events of the war to portray themselves as Protestant martyrs; hence some of the reports may have been stylized inventions intended to provoke the sympathies of Protestant readers.

29. Saltonstall, *New and Further Narrative,* 86. Indians probably also commonly stole or destroyed Bibles they found. On their return from attacking Medfield, Mary Rowlandson asked one of her captors if he had a Bible, and he gave her one out of a basket of plunder (Rowlandson, *Soveraignty,* 330).

30. Daniel Henchman to John Leverett, June 30, 1676, transcribed in Bodge, *Soldiers in King Philip's War,* 57.

31. Hubbard, *Narrative,* 1:71. The English subsequently pulled down these body parts and threw them into a river (Massachusetts Council to John Pynchon, July 10, 1675, Winthrop Papers, MHS).

32. *Farther Brief and True Narration,* 4.

33. Mather, *Brief History,* 47, 212–13. Mather may well have been responding to a request from Josiah Winslow that he help vindicate Plymouth Colony; to that end Winslow sent Mather a copy of his own "Narrative" (Josiah Winslow to Increase Mather, May 1, 1676, transcribed in Mather, *Brief History*).

34. Mather, *Brief History,* 47, 56.

35. William Hubbard, *The Happiness of a People* (Boston, 1676), 46.

36. John Bishop to Increase Mather, July 8, 1676, *MHSC,* 4th ser., 8 (1868): 299. Harris, *A Rhode Islander Reports,* 18.

37. Josiah Winslow to John Leverett, July 6, 1675, Davis Papers, MHS.

38. Randolph, "Short Narrative." Randolph charged the Massachusetts magistrates with calling Philip to court, when in reality it was Plymouth. See the response by the Massachusetts Council to the Lords of the Privy Council, June 28, 1678, Stevens Transcripts, JCB.

39. *PCR* 10:439. Easton, "Relacion," 9. Josiah Winslow to Weetamo and her husband, July 15, 1675, Winslow Papers, MHS.

40. Josiah Winslow to John Winthrop, Jr., July 29, 1675, *MHSC,* 5th ser., 1 (1871): 429; John Bishop to Increase Mather, July 8, 1676, *MHSC,* 4th ser., 8 (1868): 229. John Eliot to John Winthrop, Jr., July 24, 1675, *MHSC,* 5th ser., 1 (1871): 424. *PCR* 10:362–64. John Pynchon to John Allyn, August 25, 1675, *Pynchon Papers* 1:149–50.

41. *PCR* 10:364–65.

42. Massachusetts Council, "To Our Brethren." Andros to the governor and Council of Massachusetts, January 24, 1676, *Hutchinson Papers* 2:209–10. *CSP* 9:317–19.

43. Roger Williams to John Winthrop, Jr., December 18, 1676, Winthrop Papers, MHS.

44. Perry Miller, *The New England Mind: The Seventeenth Century* (Cambridge, Mass.: Harvard University Press, 1954), 99; Arthur H. Buffinton, "The Puritan View of War," *Publications of the Colonial Society of Massachusetts* 28 (1931): 69, 76. Grotius was not the only influence on the colonists' notions about what constituted a just war. Scripture, classical philosophy, English Puritan theology, and folk wisdom were all mixed into the stew of colonial political theory. Miller identifies the four principal sources of New England's intellectual heritage as European Protestantism, seventeenth-century preoccupations and interests, humanism, and medieval scholasticism (Miller, *New England Mind,* 92–100).

45. Hugo Grotius, *De Jure Belli Et Pacis,* trans. Francis W. Kelsey (Oxford: Clarendon Press, 1925), 1:171.

46. Michael Walzer, *Just and Unjust Wars: A Moral Argument with Historical Illustrations* (New York: Basic Books, 1977), 21.

47. John Leverett to "All people," September 12, 1676, mss. bound, MHS.

48. Urian Oakes, *The Soveraign Efficacy of Divine Providence, Preached September 10, 1677* (1682), 26. John Richardson, *The Necessity of a Well Experienced Souldiery* (Cambridge: J. Richardson, 1679), 1. Anthony Ashcam warned, "For as Warre introduces the greatest of evils, viz. the taking away of mens lives, and that which is equivalent to life: so right reason and equity tells us, that it ought not to be undertaken without the greatest cause, which is the keeping of our lives, and that without which our lives cannot be kept, or if they could bee kept, yet they would not be any value to us, seeing there may be a life worse then death" (Anthony Ashcam, *A Discourse wherein is examined, what is particularly lawfull during the confusions and revolutions of government* [London, 1648], 98–99). Or, in William Ames' words, "every light and small injury is not a just cause of Warre, because Warre being such a thing which punisheth men with the most grievous punishments, it is not to bee undertaken, but upon some injury, which is great or heynous, either in it selfe, or in the consequences" (Ames, *Conscience,* 186).

49. Establishing that the war was strictly defensive was not necessary for it to be considered just; Grotius, after all, had made provisions for offensive wars. And in the original Articles of Confederation the commissioners of the United Colonies were given authority to pursue "all just warrs whether offensive or defensive," provided at least six of the nine commissioners consented to it (Articles of Confederation, *PCR,* 10:3–8). But offensive wars had been controversial for the colonies in the past. In 1653, when Connecticut Colony wanted to pursue an offensive war against the Dutch, Massachusetts balked, claiming that such a war was inconsistent with the Articles of Confederation, and asked: "Whether the commissioners of the united Collonies have power by articles of agreement to determine the Justice of an offecive or vindictive warr and to engage the Collonies therin." Finding a loophole in the original articles, the Massachusetts representatives argued that, while the commissioners could call for a defensive war and could decide the legitimacy of an offensive one, they lacked the authority to compel all the colonies to participate in an offensive war (*PCR* 10:26, 56, 74–88, 428–29; *Records of the Colony or Jurisdiction of New Haven, from May 1653, to the Union,* ed. Charles J. Houdly [Hartford, Conn.: Case, Lockwood & Co., 1858], 8).

50. Wheeler, *Thankefull Remembrance,* 239–40. Since Plymouth's initial involvement in the war had been subject to considerable criticism, Massachusetts and Connecticut always explained their involvement in the war as merely helping Plymouth. Increase Mather was quick to observe that "It is known to every one, that the Warr began not amongst us in Mat-

achusets Colony; nor do the Indians (so far as I am informed) pretend that we have done them wrong. And therefore the cause on our part is most clear, and unquestionable: For if we should have suffered our Confederates, and those that were ready to be slain, to be drawn to death, & not have endeavoured to deliver them, when they sent unto us for that end, the Lord would have been displeased; nor should we have acted like the Children of Abraham, Gen. 14. 14. Yea, all the world would justly have condemned us" (Mather, *Brief History*, 212–14). Samuel Nowell also cited Genesis 14:14 in reaching his conclusion that "To take up arms for the defence of friennds and Allies is lawfull. . . . Hence our late War was justifiable, though the Quarrel was firstly with our neighbours." In addition, Nowell argued, this story demonstrated that "it is lawfull by war to defend what we lawfully obtained and come by, as our possessions, lands, and inheritance here, to which we have as fair a title as any ever had, since Israels title to Canaan" (Nowell, *Abraham in Arms*, 276).

51. Such metaphors can be found in Joshua Moodey, *Souldiery Spiritualized: or the Christian Souldier* (Cambridge, 1674); Samuel Willard, *The Heart Garrisoned, or, the Wisdome, and Care of the Spiritual Souldier* (Cambridge, 1676); J. R., *The Necessity of a Well Experienced Souldiery* (Cambridge, 1679); Urian Oakes, *The Unconquerable All Conquering & more-then Conquering Souldier* (Cambridge, 1674).

52. J. R., *The Necessity of a Well Experienced Souldiery*, 7.

53. Walker, "Captan Perse," 91. Walker compared the Indian enemies to Cain, Nero, Diocletian, and Domitio, all "monsterus beasts" who "atend only an evil speritt suggested by satan" (84). Therefore, any means necessary could be used to subdue them: "Tis very Just to doea the best wee Can / to yous all mens by sword or poysned dram / to send such souls to ther own place mor fitt / If god sucksed & say amen to it" (83).

54. Quoted in Robert A. Williams, Jr., *The American Indian in Western Legal Thought: The Discourses of Conquest* (New York: Oxford University Press, 1990), 30. For further articulation of the distinction between secular and holy war see Frederick H. Russell, *The Just War in the Middle Ages* (Cambridge: Cambridge University Press, 1975); James Turner Johnson, *Ideology, Reason, and the Limitation of War: Religious and Secular Concepts, 1200–1740* (Princeton, N.J.: Princeton University Press, 1975). The distinction was not absolute. As Russell observed: "In the heat of combat and controversy belligerents forsook the more restrained just war for the holy war. At the moment a just war was deemed necessary, it easily became a holy war that pursued the supreme goal of the belligerents" (2).

55. Williams, *The American Indian in Western Legal Thought*, 13–15, 43–46.

56. *MCR* 5:49–50.

57. Quoted in Williams, *The American Indian in Western Legal Thought*, 194–98.

58. Michael Walzer, *Revolution of the Saints: A Study in the Origins of Radical Politics* (Cambridge, Mass.: Harvard University Press, 1965), 57–66; Stuart, " 'For the Lord Is a Man of Warr,' " 523, 526; George, "War and Peace in the Puritan Tradition"; and Roland Bainton, "Congregationalism and the Puritan Revolution from the Just War to the Crusade," *Andover Newton Bulletin* 35 (1943): 1–20. The most comprehensive treatment of this phenomenon can be found in Johnson, *Ideology*, ch. 3. Johnson identifies six characteristics of English holy war thought: "(1) religious purpose, (2) expansion of classic just war doctrine to include defensive war by the state as warranted for defense of religion, (3) introduction of a concept of offensive war for religion, usually enunciated as a concept of war 'comanded' by God, (4) assertion of the necessity that soldiers for the right be personally godly, usually accompanied with the assumption that those on the other side are personally sinful, (5) a change in the meaning of

the term 'just' war from 'justifiable' to 'justified' war, implying a thoroughly righteous cause and thoroughly righteous or godly ('justified') champions for it, (6) occasionally the requirement or suggestion that holy war must be prosecuted more scrupulously according to the dictates of charity, in tension with an equally occasional insistence that holy war be fought without restraint" (Johnson, *Ideology*, 132).

59. On Ames' influence in New England see Miller, *The New England Mind: The Seventeenth Century.*

60. Most ideas about war were based in the "law of nature" (or natural law), which, according to who was doing the philosophizing, was either innately known by all of humankind, commonly shared by all who know God, or easily deducible by all those capable of reason. If non-Christians did not even "know" natural law, what rules would dictate wars against them? Grotius' answer to this dilemma, however, was not very much of an answer at all. Initially he claimed that all people know the law of nature since, by definition, that law is universally known: "That is according to the law of nature which is believed to be such among all nations." But then again, maybe not. "Or," Grotius added, perhaps a consensus on natural law exists only among those nations "that are more advanced in civilization" (*De Jure Belli*, 1:42–43).

61. Johnson, *Ideology*, 155–58. For another useful summary of Vitoria's writings see Etienne Grisel, "The Beginnings of International Law and General Public Law Doctrine: Francisco de Vitoria's *De Indiis prior,*" in *First Images of America: The Impact of the New World on the Old*, ed. Fredi Chiapelli (Berkeley: University of California Press, 1976), 305–34.

62. Francisco de Vitoria, *Political Writings*, ed. Anthony Pagden and Jeremy Lawrence (Cambridge: Cambridge University Press, 1991), 239–44, 250, 263–72.

63. "Vitoria assumed the truth of Thomas Aquinas's belief that natural law could be known quite apart from revelation by the correct use of human reason. This meant for the Spanish theorist that the Indians inhabiting the New World could, even though they were not Christians and might never have heard of Christ, know the natural law. Thus the Spanish could treat with them and had a right to expect a certain sort of behavior from the Indians encountered" (James Turner Johnson, *Just War Tradition and the Restraint of War: A Moral and Historical Inquiry* [Princeton, N.J.: Princeton University Press, 1981], 76–77).

64. As Williams argues, "From this point of view, international law was conceived of as mutually binding on all nations still in a state of nature by virtue of their sovereignty, and was binding on them in exactly the same way as the prepolitical law of nature had been binding on individuals when they also lived in a state of nature" (Williams, *The American Indian in Western Legal Thought*, 97–107).

65. Ultimately, as Williams argues, "Vitoria's Law of Nations provided Western legal discourse with its first secularly oriented, systematized elaboration of the superior rights of civilized Europeans to invade and conquer normatively divergent peoples.... Only Christian Europeans could offer the Indians a rationalized existence, which the Indians by the Law of Nations were obliged to accept." Having thrown out the pope's mediating role, Williams argues, Vitoria replaced it with more acceptable Thomistic humanist foundations: "These foundations stressed the autonomy of human reason and the universal obligations of a Eurocentrically constructed natural law. The savage could be conquered and colonized by Christian European nations seeking to enforce or inculcate the rational norms binding on all humankind under a natural Law of Nations" (Williams, *The American Indian in Western Legal Thought*, 97–107).

66. Peter Hulme has argued that the "colonial discourse" describing the Virginia massacre of 1622 employed the same strategy: "it was quite clear under the Law of Nations that it was not lawful for Christians simply 'to usurpe the goods and lands of these Heathens.' Such usurpation could only be justified by infractions of Natural Law" (Peter Hulme, *Colonial Encounters: Europe and the Native Caribbean, 1492–1797* [London: Methuen, 1986], 159–61).

67. Grotius, *De Jure Belli*, 1:22–23.

68. Johnson writes that Grotius' "natural-law doctrine on war applies to all men since it is knowable by reason. Christians, by faith, possess some additional knowledge, which in part supplements and in part replaces that which natural reason provides. If warring nations are Christian, then, they are bound by limits that are unknown to other nations and therefore do not bind them. In wars between non-Christian nations natural law alone provides the rules by which war should be fought" (Johnson, *Ideology*, 210–11).

69. Hugo Grotius, *On the Origin of the Native Races of America* (1642; reprint, Edinburgh, 1884, ed. Edmund Goldsmid).

70. The European "discovery" of the New World exerted an incalculable influence on Western political philosophy. As Johnson has argued, "By thrusting Europeans into contact with people totally outside the traditions of European civilization," the encounter with the New World "stimulated the attempt to create a natural law/just war theory" (Johnson, *Just War Tradition*, 172–73). See also Arthur J. Savin, "The American Principle from More to Locke," in *First Images of America*, 139–64.

71. John Locke, *Two Treatises of Government* (1690), 34.

72. Thomas Hobbes, *Leviathan*, ed. Michael Oakeshott (Oxford: Basil Blackwell, 1947), 82–83.

73. Thomas Morton, *New English Canaan or New Canaan* (Amsterdam: Jacob Frederick Stam, 1637; reprint, Prince Society, Boston, 1883), 140.

74. Quoted in Robert F. Berkhofer, Jr., *The White Man's Indian: Images of the American Indian from Columbus to the Present* (New York: Vintage Books, 1979), 37. On Indians' actual religious worldview see Simmons, *Spirit of the New England Tribes*, 37–64.

75. Karen Kupperman, *Settling with the Indians: The Meeting of English and Indian Cultures in America, 1580–1640* (Totowa, N.J.: Rowman & Littlefield, 1980), 54–55.

76. Massachusetts Council to the Indian Sagamores, March 31, 1676, Mass. Arch. 68:193.

77. John Winthrop, Jr., to Major Savage, July 12, 1675, *MHSC*, 5th ser., 8 (1882): 172.

78. Francis Jennings, *The Invasion of America: Indians, Colonialism, and the Cant of Conquest* (New York: W. W. Norton & Company, 1975), ch. 9; Kupperman, *Settling with the Indians*, 55–56. On the French Jesuits' similar attitude toward the Iroquois see Richter, "War and Culture," 528. See also Thomas S. Abler, "Scalping, Torture, Cannibalism and Rape: An Ethnohistorical Analysis of Conflicting Cultural Values in War," *Anthropologica* 34 (1992): 3–20.

79. Barbara Donagan, "Atrocity, War Crime, and Treason in the English Civil War," *AHR* 99 (1994): 1139.

80. Roger Williams to Robert Williams, April 1, 1676, *The Correspondence of Roger Williams*, ed. Glenn W. LaFantasie (Providence: Brown University Press, 1988), 2:720. Emphasis mine.

81. Harris, *A Rhode Islander Reports,* 28. See Patrick M. Malone, *The Skulking Way of War: Technology and Tactics among the New England Indians* (Lanham, Md.: Madison Books, 1991).

82. John Freeman to Josiah Winslow, July 3, 1675.

83. Walker, "Captan Perse," 82.

84. The Indians "very suddaynely and violently fell upon our neighbouring people, first robing and burning their houses, and after in a sculking, unmanly way, destroying many of our people" (Josiah Winslow to John Winthrop, Jr., July 29, 1675).

85. Samuel Gorton to John Winthrop, Jr., September 11, 1675, *MHSC,* 4th ser., 7 (1865): 627.

86. Roger Williams to John Leverett, October 11, 1675, *PCR* 10:453–55.

87. Urian Oakes, *The Soveraign Efficacy of Divine Providence: . . . As Delivered in a Sermon Preached in Cambridge on Sept. 10. 1677* (Boston, 1682), 26. On Europeans' disdain for Indian strategies to limit their fatalities (strategies Europeans called cowardly) see also Richter, "War and Culture," 536; Abler, "Scalping, Torture, Cannibalism and Rape," 6–15; John E. Ferling, *A Wilderness of Miseries: War and Warriors in Early America* (Westport, Conn.: Greenwood Press, 1980), 34–36.

88. *At a Council Held in Boston August the thirtieth 1675* (Cambridge, 1675), brs.

89. Hubbard, *Narrative,* 1:15.

90. This is a question that Vitoria, writing about the Aztecs, had not even identified, since he failed to consider the possibility that Indians might have had their own "law of nations," different, but no less developed than that of Christian Europeans. As Johnson has observed, "Instead of using the new knowledge of Indian customs to modify European understanding of natural law, [Vitoria] tended to fall back upon European customs, vouchsafed by the belief that they had been ratified by revelation, to criticize certain of the Indians' cultural practices: these he declared to be the result of invincible ignorance" (Johnson, *Just War Tradition,* 76–77). It would seem that just as he argued that the Indians had a form of religion (however inferior to Christianity), Vitoria might have argued that they had their own form of international law. After all, the Aztecs had complicated diplomatic and military relations with other Mexican tribes. But this kind of cultural relativism would have been impossible for Vitoria and is in fact probably irreconcilable with the idea that there exists such a thing as natural law. As Tzvetan Todorov has shown, discovery-era Europeans were able to see Indians as either the same and equal or different and inferior; different and equal was not an option (*The Conquest of America,* trans. Richard Howard [New York: Harper & Row, 1987]).

91. While this argument has traditionally been made by scholars from the "innatist" school, who argue that people are born with an instinct to fight (e.g., Irenaus Eibl-Eibesfelt, *The Biology of Peace and War* [New York: Viking Press, 1979]), I am here using it to make a cultural rather than a biological argument.

92. Tompson, *New England's Crisis,* 218. John Leverett to "All People unto whome these prsente may come," September 12, 1676, Stewart Mitchell Papers, MHS.

93. Wheeler, *Thankefull Remembrance,* 255. Emphasis mine.

94. Samuel Gorton to John Winthrop, Jr., September 11, 1675, *MHSC,* 4th ser., 7 (1865): 627.

95. Benjamin Batten to Sir Thomas Allin, July 29, 1675.

96. Later, when an edited version of Batten's letter appeared as the lead story in *The London Gazette,* it was acknowledged that the trial "probably may have incensed him" (*The London Gazette,* August 16–August 19, 1675).

97. Josiah Winslow to John Winthrop, Jr., July 29, 1675, *MHSC,* 5th ser., 1 (1871): 428. Emphasis mine.

98. Roger Williams to John Winthrop, Jr., June 25, 1675, *Correspondence of Roger Williams* 2:693; Roger Williams to John Winthrop, Jr., June 27, 1675, *Correspondence of Roger Williams* 2:698.

99. Easton, "Relacion," 11.

100. Ibid., 9–12.

101. Peter, the son of the "squaw sachem" Awashonks, was seeking English protection (*PCR* 5:202). For a typical interrogation, in which the only information sought was about the location of enemy Indians, and testimony about who was involved in certain attacks, see the Connecticut Council's examination of Menowniett ("halfe a Moheag and halfe a Naragoncett"), August 1676 (*CCR* 2:471–72).

102. On the two cultures' different practices and ideologies of war see Adam J. Hirsch, "The Collision of Military Cultures in Seventeenth-Century New England," *JAH* 74 (1988): 1187–1212; as well as Francis Jennings, *The Invasion of America,* especially 146–70. For an interesting treatment of Iroquois warfare see Daniel K. Richter, "War and Culture: The Iroquois Experience," *WMQ* 40 (1983): 528–59. For a somewhat outdated but influential treatment of Indian warfare see M. W. Smith, "American Indian Warfare," *New York Academy of Sciences, Transactions,* 2nd ser., XIII (1951). Most of these works, however, emphasize the practice of war rather than the reasons and justifications for it. In this regard see especially Malone, *The Skulking Way of War.*

103. Richter, "War and Culture," 528–29.

104. John Underhill, *News from America; or, a New and Experimentall Discoverie of New England* (London, 1638); reprinted in *MHSC,* 3rd ser., 6 (1837): 27.

105. Alexander Young, ed., *Chronicles of the Pilgrim Fathers of the Colony of Plymouth, 1602–1625* (Boston, 1841), 221. Traditional Indian warfare also spared women and children (Hirsch, "The Collision of Military Cultures," 1191).

106. William and Joseph Wannuckkow and John Appamatogoon to the Massachusetts Council, September 5, 1676, Mass. Arch. 30:216–17. A warrant had been issued for their arrest on August 11, 1676 (Massachusetts Council to the Constable, August 11, 1676, Mass. Arch. 30:210a), and they had been apprehended on August 14 (Constable to the Massachusetts Council, August 14, 1676, Mass. Arch. 30:210b), whereupon they confessed (Joseph Indian and others to the Massachusetts Council, August 14, 1676, Mass. Arch. 30:211). Thomas Danforth wrote to Governor Leverett for advice on how to handle the case (Danforth to Leverett, August 14, 1676, Mass. Arch. 30:212a), which suggests that he might have intervened and suggested the argument by which the Indians subsequently defended themselves.

107. The defense employed by these seventeenth-century Indians is probably most familiar to us in its more modern, distorted form, used during the Nuremberg trials in an attempt to exonerate Nazi war criminals. This is a jarring familiarity, and an unlikely resonance between King Philip's War and World War II, but it serves to illustrate that the principal components of just war doctrine have an astonishingly long history, and, all told, have remained remarkably consistent.

108. M. W. Smith, "American Indian Warfare." On nonwar-related mourning rituals among New England Indians see Simmons, *Spirit of the New England Tribes*, 48–49.

109. Richter, "War and Culture," 536.

110. Hirsch, "The Collision of Military Cultures," 1190. Wendell S. Hadlock, "War among the Northeastern Woodland Indians," *American Anthropologist* 49 (1947): 204–21. Alden Vaughan: "The Indians, of course, had fought among themselves before Europeans arrived in America and continued to afterward. But Indian wars had seldom incurred heavy mortality; most tribes were too small to bear high losses without jeopardizing their survival, and the relative abundance of land and shortage of material goods virtually eliminated wars of conquest. Accordingly, Indian warfare, compared with European, required less destruction and more symbolic satisfactions—such as the torture of some captives, the assimilation of the rest, and occasional ritualistic cannibalism" (Vaughan, *New England Frontier*, xx). See also Salisbury, *Manitou and Providence*, 41–42, 46, 70–71, 229; and Jennings, *Invasion of America*, 155–59.

111. Jennings, *Invasion of America*, 158.

112. Quoted in Jennings, *Invasion of America*, 158–59.

113. What happens when a state society wars against a nonstate society? Usually we call that conquest. Anthropologists rarely study wars of conquest (R. Brian Ferguson with Leslie E. Farragher, *The Anthropology of War: A Bibliography* [New York: H. F. Guggenheim Foundation, 1988], iv), and historical studies of such wars are often terribly burdened with moral judgments (e.g., Jennings, *The Invasion of America*, 298). For another discussion of Algonquian and English ideologies of restraint in warfare see James Drake, "Severing the Ties That Bind Them: A Reconceptualization of King Philip's War" (Ph.D. diss., UCLA, 1995), 202–48.

114. The distinction was introduced by Henry Holbert Turney-High in 1949 (*Primitive War: Its Practice and Concepts* [Columbia, S.C., 1949]); in 1967 the American Anthropology Association officially changed "civilized" to "modern," and today "tribal" has replaced "primitive" (R. Brian Ferguson, ed., *Warfare, Culture, and Environment* [Orlando, Fla.: Academic Press, 1984], 26). For a summary and review of what has come to be called the "anthropology of war" see John Keegan, *A History of Warfare* (New York: Alfred A. Knopf, 1993), 84–94 and Jonathan Haas, ed., *The Anthropology of War* (Cambridge: Cambridge University Press, 1990).

115. Mason, "Brief History of the Pequot War," 41. Williams quoted in Hirsch, "Collision of Military Cultures," 1191.

116. Lawrence H. Keeley, *War before Civilization* (New York: Oxford University Press, 1996).

117. Walker, "Captan Perse," 91.

118. Unfortunately, evidence that would contribute to an understanding of Indian warfare rituals is extremely limited and, where available, difficult to interpret. Simmons, *Spirit of the New England Tribes*, 59–60.

119. Mary Douglas, *Natural Symbols: Explorations in Cosmology* (New York: Pantheon, 1970), 8.

120. *Farther Brief and True Narration*, 3–4.

121. Mary Douglas, *Purity and Danger: An Analysis of the Concepts of Pollution and Taboo* (New York: Praeger, 1966), 94.

122. William Ames, *Conscience, with the Power and Cases Thereof* (London, 1643), 184.

123. The colonists may have made some distinction between "grounds" and "provocation" for war. In a letter to the squaw sachem Weetamo, Josiah Winslow first wrote that Philip had begun war "upon no ground nor unfairness in the least from us," but later crossed out the word "ground" and substituted "provocation" (Josiah Winslow to Weetamo, June 15, 1675, Winslow Papers, MHS).

124. John Russell to the Massachusetts Council, October 6, 1675, Mass. Arch. 67:288.

125. Mather, *Exhortation*, 174.

126. Michael Puglisi has argued that the colonists' failure to attend to Indian motives made the experience of the war all the more traumatic. "Perhaps if New Englanders had been able to recognize the real issues which drove Metacom's Wampanoags to hostilities, the trauma of the Indian war might have affected them less seriously. They could have made 'a Business of the War,' defeated the natives, healed their own wounds, and put the whole affair behind them" (Puglisi, *Puritans Besieged*, 25–26).

127. Saltonstall, *Present State*, 44. Emphasis mine.

128. Easton, "Relacion," 17.

129. Roger Williams to Robert Williams, April 1, 1676. Emphasis mine. The attack on Providence is also related in Harris, *A Rhode Islander Reports*, 44–46. Christian Indians fighting with the English, however, insisted that God was on their side. When an English soldier said it was useless to shoot at a fleeing enemy Indian (he being too far away), William Nahauton told him to try "and God shall direct the bullet," whereupon he fired and shot the Indian down (*True Account*, 7).

130. Nowell, *Abraham in Arms*, 276. On the importance of the Artillery Election Sermon see Richard Slotkin and James K. Folsom, eds., *So Dreadfull a Judgment: Puritan Responses to King Philip's War, 1676–1677* (Middletown, Conn.: Wesleyan University Press, 1978), 259–60.

131. Moodey, *Souldiery Spiritualized*.

Chapter 5 · Come Go Along with Us

1. In April 1677 Mary and Joseph Rowlandson and their surviving children moved to Wethersfield, Connecticut, where Joseph had been appointed minister. Three days after preaching his final sermon, on November 21, 1678, Joseph Rowlandson died. By 1680 Mary had remarried; she outlived her second husband, Captain Samuel Talcott, and died in her early seventies in 1711 (David L. Greene, "New Light on Mary Rowlandson," *EAL* 20 [1986]: 24–38).

2. For the most persuasive speculation on when Rowlandson wrote her account see Kathryn Zabelle Derounian, "Puritan Orthodoxy and the 'Survivor Syndrome' in Mary Rowlandson's Captivity Narrative," *EAL* 22 (1987): 83–84. See also Robert D. Diebold, "Mary Rowlandson," in *American Writers before 1800*, ed. James A. Levernier and Douglas R. Wilmes (Westport, Conn.: Greenwood Press, 1983), 1246.

3. Numerous historians and literary scholars have marked Rowlandson's narrative as a "foundational" American text. See, for instance, Roy Harvey Pearce, "The Significance of the Captivity Narrative," *American Literature* 19 (March 1949): 1–20; Richard Slotkin, *Regeneration through Violence: The Mythology of the American Frontier, 1600–1860* (Middletown, Conn.: Wesleyan University Press, 1973), chs. 4–5, pp. 257–59, 326–30, 384–93, 440–59, 518–39. Richard

Slotkin and James K. Folsom argue that "Rowlandson's book is . . . to be taken not only as the creation of a Puritan myth, but as the starting point of a cultural myth affecting America as a whole" (*So Dreadfull a Judgment: Puritan Responses to King Philip's War, 1676–1677* [Middletown, Conn.: Wesleyan University Press, 1978], 302).

4. James Printer had joined the Natick church, was educated in Cambridge, and worked closely with Eliot in translating and, more importantly, in setting the print for the books that would form the "Indian Library." In 1659 Printer was apprenticed to Samuel Green, Sr., and probably worked with him at the Cambridge Press until sometime in 1675. Printer returned to Hassanamesit after the war, where he lived until his death in 1717. See Samuel Gardner Drake, *Book of the Indians* (Boston, 1841), 2:50–51; Hugh Amory, *First Impressions: Printing in Cambridge, 1639–1989* (Cambridge, Mass.: Harvard University Press, 1989), 41.

5. Rowlandson, *Soveraignty*, 325. Contemporary accounts of the attack on Lancaster can also be found in Mather, *Brief History*, 117–18; *News from New-England*, 3–4; *True Account*, 1; Saltonstall, *New and Further Narrative*, 83; Gookin, "Historical Account," 490; Hubbard, *Narrative*, 1:165–66. The devastation to the town is evaluated by Jacob Farrar in a letter to the Massachusetts Council, March 3, 1676, Mass. Arch. 68:156.

6. Rowlandson, *Soveraignty*, 365–66. Goodwife Thurston of Medfield echoed Rowlandson when she told her neighbors that "all her afflictions was swallowed up in the loss of her poore child gone into Captivity" (Noah Newman to John Cotton, March 14, 1676, Curwen Papers, AAS).

7. [Edward Cressy], *Captivity Improved to Spiritual Purposes, or Spiritual directions, Given to Prisoners of all sorts whether Debtors or malefactors, principally designed for the use of those who are Prisoners in those prisons which are under the Jurisdiction of the city of London, as Newgate, ludgate, the Counters, c. Though also applyable to others under the like circumstnces else where* (London, 1675).

8. Rowlandson, *Soveraignty*, 366. Emphasis in original.

9. For a related reading of Rowlandson see Charles E. Hambrick-Stowe, *The Practice of Piety: Puritan Devotional Disciplines in Seventeenth-Century New England* (Chapel Hill: University of North Carolina Press, 1982), 258–62.

10. Derounian argues that Rowlandson was affected by what clinical psychologists call "survivor syndrome" ("Puritan Orthodoxy," 82–93). A related argument is made by Mitchell Breitwieser in *American Puritanism and the Defense of Mourning: Religion, Grief, and Ethnology in Mary Rowlandson's Captivity Narrative* (Madison: University of Wisconsin Press, 1990), where he claims that Rowlandson's narrative was motivated by a need to commemorate the dead.

11. Yet even the vividness of her nightmares only caused her to give greater thanks to God for his mercies. "When all are fast about me, and no eye open, but His who ever waketh, my thoughts are upon things past, upon the awfull dispensation of the Lord towards us, upon His wonderful power and might, in carrying us through many difficulties, in returning us to safety, and suffering none to hurt us" (Rowlandson, *Soveraignty*, 365).

12. Ibid., 325.

13. Ibid., 324–25.

14. Ibid., 325.

15. Although there is little scholarship that focuses particularly on the Algonquian practice of adopting captives, useful comparisons can be drawn from other works, many of which

have focused on Iroquois cultures. See especially Daniel K. Richter, "War and Culture: The Iroquois Experience," *WMQ* 40 (1983): 530–34; Anthony F. C. Wallace, *Death and Rebirth of the Seneca* (New York: Vintage, 1979), 101–3; John E. Ferling, *A Wilderness of Miseries: War and Warriors in Early America* (Westport, Conn.: Greenwood Press, 1980), 50–51. See also James Axtell, *The Invasion Within: The Contest of Cultures in Colonial North America* (New York: Oxford University Press, 1985), 302–27; and John Demos, *The Unredeemed Captive: A Family Story from Early America* (New York: Alfred A. Knopf, 1995).

16. If any parallel exists to John Eliot's missionization program, the Algonquian practice of taking captives comes the closest. Both were strategies aimed at cultural conversion (although English captives were accepted by Algonquian communities in ways that Christian Indians were never accepted by the English).

17. Rowlandson, *Soveraignty*, 325.

18. Mather, *Exhortation*, 174–75.

19. Rowlandson, *Soveraignty*, 328, 333.

20. Rowlandson, *Soveraignty*, 335. Signs of English habitation could be not only intoxicating but also life-saving. Another returning captive, a young boy, claimed to have made his way back to the English by following an English plant: "Though the Boy knew not a step of the way to any English Town . . . yet God directed him aright and brought him to the sight of Plantane (the Herb which the Indians call English-foot, because it grows only amongst us, and is not found in the Indian Plantations) whereupon he concluded he was not far from us" (*True Account*, 3).

21. Rowlandson, *Soveraignty*, 342–43.

22. Rowlandson, *Soveraignty*, 360–61. There was, nonetheless, "a Report that they had forced Mrs. Rowlinson to marry the one eyed Sachem, but it was soon contradicted; for being a very pious Woman and of great Faith, the Lord wonderfully supported her under this Affliction, so that she appeared and behaved her self amongst them with so much Courage and majestick Gravity, that none durst offer any Violence to her" (Saltonstall, *New and Further Narrative*, 83). Still, Rowlandson's insistence on her freedom from sexual violation seems all the more frantic, since few colonists would have expected her to receive such treatment.

23. Rowlandson, *Soveraignty*, 360–61.

24. For a compelling argument attributing the preface to Mather see Kathryn Zabelle Derounian, "The Publication, Promotion, and Distribution of Mary Rowlandson's Indian Captivity Narrative in the Seventeenth Century," *EAL* 23 (1988): 240–43. Derounian bases her claims in part on work done earlier by David Minter, "By Dens of Lions: Notes on Stylization in Early Puritan Captivity Narratives," *American Literature* 45 (1973–74): 343; and David A. Richards, "The Memorable Preservations: Narratives of Indian Captivity in the Literature and Politics of Colonial New England, 1675–1725," unpublished Yale College thesis, 1967. Rowlandson may also have been first inspired to write her narrative by reading several other chronicles of the war or by speaking with their authors. During the year she lived in Boston, Rowlandson met with both Increase Mather and William Hubbard, and she may well have read one or more printed accounts of the war (several of which told the story of her captivity). On Rowlandson's encounters and relationships with Mather and Hubbard see Derounian, "The Publication, Promotion, and Distribution," 241–42, and Breitwieser, *American Puritanism and the Defense of Mourning*, 7.

25. Rowlandson, *Soveraignty*, 320.

26. This telling metaphor, between Indian captivity and publication, was also invoked by Samuel Nowell in the preface to his own account of the war, in which he wrote, "The Love I have for this Country . . . hath made me Run the Gauntlet by exposing this to the world" (Nowell, *Abraham in Arms,* 273).

27. Rowlandson, *Soveraignty,* 320.

28. Ibid., 321.

29. Roger Williams to John Leverett, January 14, 1676, *The Correspondence of Roger Williams,* ed. Glenn W. LaFantasie (Providence: Brown University Press, 1988), 2:711. Tift also apparently provided the English with important information; Major Treat reported to the Connecticut Council that Tift, before he was executed, had impeached the Narragansett sachem Ninigret for sending mats to enemy Indians after their wigwams were burned (Major Treat to the Connecticut Council, January 1676, *CCR* 2:401).

30. An elaborate story of Tift's betrayal was told by James Arnold in the late nineteenth century. Arnold (who spelled the name "Teftt") suggested that Tift, rather than Stonewall John, was behind the construction of the Narragansett fort at the Great Swamp. Arnold, however, provided no primary sources to document any of his claims (James N. Arnold, "Joshua Tefft," *Narragansett Historical Register* 3 [1884]: 164–69). More recently, Douglas Leach has suggested that "whether Tefft was actually as much of a traitor as he was thought to be may now be open to doubt. His argument that he had joined the Indians under duress may very well have been essentially correct" (*Flintlock and Tomahawk,* 139–40). Writing in 1984, Colin Calloway ("Rhode Island Renegade: The Enigma of Joshua Tift," *Rhode Island History* 43 [1984]: 137–45) suggested that Tift had been living as a "renegade" for fourteen years and had married a Wampanoag woman, but as I show here, that version of the story is contradicted by other seventeenth-century evidence.

31. "The Examination of Thomas Warner, that had been a Prisoner with the Indians," February 25, 1675, in *A Narrative of the Causes . . . with other Documents,* ed. Franklin B. Hough (Albany, N.Y.: J. Munsell, 1858), 144. See also "Narrative of the Captivity of Quentin Stockwell" in Samuel Gardner Drake, ed., *Tragedies of the Wilderness* (Boston, 1846), 60–68; Harris, *A Rhode Islander Reports,* 42, 66, 78–80.

32. Saltonstall, *Present State,* 39–40. More general accounts of the torture of captives can be found in Wharton, *New-England's Present Sufferings,* 1–2; Saltonstall, *New and Further Narrative,* 98–99; Harris, *A Rhode Islander Reports,* 66. As suggested in the Prologue, the colonists were not unlikely to participate in the infliction of torture, or to inflict it themselves. An important difference between Indian and English torture, however, is that the English most often inflicted torture to extract a confession, while the Indians inflicted torture to fulfill a social and cultural need, as discussed in the Prologue. In addition, the techniques employed by the two peoples differed considerably. The most detailed account of colonists' torture methods has Captain Samuel Moseley in the role of torturer, inflicting psychological as well as physical torments:

> Capt. Moseley took two Indians, a Father and his Son, and willing to examine them both apart, proceeded thus: Took the old Man and bound him to a Tree, after he was so bound, he sent away the Son by a File of Men out of Sight; the old Man there confessed he was a Praying Indian, and that he was only hunting for deer thereabouts, but said that his Son was one of those Men that wounded Capt. Hutchinson: So then, after they had pumped him as much as they could, they fired a Gunn with no Bullet in it over his Head, untied him, and sent him another

Way . . . ; then brought they his Son, bound in like Manner, they telling him that they had shot his Father, and would shoot him also, if he would not confess what he was, and what he knew: He fairly told them, that he was a Praying Indian, but his Father made him go with him to the Nipmog Indians, and that there they shot three or four Times a Piece, whereupon they then brought the old Man and tied him to his Son, and Examined them together, at Length they confest they were both among the Nipmoogs, and that the Son did wound Captain Hutchinson; after their Examination they were both shot to Death (Saltonstall, *Present State,* 39; see also Gookin, "Historical Account," 456–57).

33. Rowlandson did report the torture of a pregnant Englishwoman who had tried to escape her captors. To make an example of her the Indians "gathered a great company together about her, and stripped her naked, and set her in the midst of them; and when they had sung and danced about her (in their hellish manner) as long as they pleased, they knocked her on head, and the child in her arms with her: when they had done that, they made a fire and put them both into it, and told the other children that were with them, that if they attempted to go home, they would serve them in like manner" (*Soveraignty,* 332).

34. Roger Williams to John Leverett, January 14, 1676.

35. James Oliver to unknown, January 26, 1676, *NEHGR* 39 (1885): 380.

36. Mather, *Brief History,* 108. Saltonstall, *Continuation,* 67. Joseph Dudley to unknown, December 21, 1675, *NEHGR* 40 (1886): 89.

37. Major Treat to the Connecticut War Council, January 1676, *PCR* 2:401. James Oliver to unknown, January 26, 1676. Saltonstall, *Continuation,* 67.

38. Laurel Thatcher Ulrich, *Good Wives: Images and Reality in the Lives of Women in Northern New England, 1650–1750* (New York: Vintage Books, 1991), 6–10, 230–34. A developing literature on the "gender frontier" of early Indian-European relations is now emerging, which argues that emerging identities of race were complicated (and sometimes reinforced) by each culture's ideas about gender. Kathleen M. Brown, for instance, has recently discussed this in relation to Jamestown ("The Anglo-Algonquian Gender Frontier" in Nancy Shoemaker, ed., *Negotiators of Change: Historical Perspectives on Native American Women* [New York: Routledge, 1995], 26–48).

39. Rowlandson, *Soveraignty,* 360.

40. June Namias has recently explored the gendered meanings of captivity in *White Captives: Gender and Ethnicity on the American Frontier* (Chapel Hill: University of North Carolina Press, 1993). She points out, for instance, that male and female captives were treated differently (only men were required to run the gauntlet).

41. Daniel K. Richter, *The Ordeal of the Longhouse: The Peoples of the Iroquois League in the Era of European Colonization* (Chapel Hill: University of North Carolina Press, 1992), 71. For a contrary argument, proposing that what ethnohistorians have called the adoption context actually was a form of slavery, see William A. Starna and Ralph Watkins, "Northern Iroquoian Slavery," *Ethnohistory* 38 (1991): 34–57.

42. Mather, *Brief History,* 154.

43. Gookin, "Historical Account," 476. See also Leach, *Flintlock and Tomahawk,* 100.

44. Daniel Gookin sent orders dated November 2 for Captain Joseph Syll to take Indian spies from the praying town of Natick and meet up with Henchman and his soldiers to investigate the situation at Hassanemesit (Daniel Gookin to Captain Joseph Syll, November 2, 1675, *NEHGR* 41 [1887]: 403). Henchman sent scouts ahead on November 3 and arrived

there himself on November 5. On November 9 Henchman and twenty-two soldiers marched to Hassanemesit again, suspecting enemy Indians might now be occupying its wigwams; on their arrival, they were met with gunfire and eventually retreated (Henchman to Massachusetts Council, November 3, 1675, in *Annals of the Town of Mendon, 1659–1880*, comp. John George Metcalf [Providence, 1880], 71–72; Henchman to the Massachusetts Council, November 5, 1675, *Annals of Mendon*, 72–73; Henchman to the Massachusetts Council, November 10, 1675, *Annals of Mendon*, 73–74).

45. Daniel Henchman to the Massachusetts Council, November 5, 1675.

46. Massachusetts Council to Richard Smith, November 6, 1675, Mass. Arch. 68:46b; Massachusetts Council to Captain Appleton, November 11, 1675, Mass. Arch. 68:57, 58; magistrates and deputies of Boston to Richard Smith, November 21, 1675, Mass. Arch. 30:188–89. Emphasis mine.

47. Gookin, "Historical Account," 455–62. Hubbard, *Narrative*, 1:95–96. Moseley was later asked to account for his actions and supplied a halfhearted apology (Moseley to John Leverett, October 5, 1675, *NEHGR* 37 [1883]: 179). On Moseley's order to have an Algonquian woman torn to pieces by dogs see Samuel Moseley to John Leverett, October 16, 1675, Mass. Arch. 68:18; reprinted in *NEHGR* (1883) 37:180.

48. Gookin, "Historical Account," 455–61. Drake, *Book of the Indians*, 3:81.

49. William Harris reported that "one Mr Eliote & Some other Soe much standing up in favor of the said Indeans Supposed were in great danger of the mulltitude of Some outrageous English . . ." (Harris, *A Rhode Islander Reports*, 66). According to Nathaniel Saltonstall, James Oliver berated Daniel Gookin for his advocacy of the Indians, telling him "that he ought rather to be confined among his Indians, than to sit on the Bench; his taking the Indians Part so much hath made him a Byword both among Men and Boys" (Saltonstall, *Present State*, 40). On the lynching party see Saltonstall, *Present State*, 40–41. For a general discussion of these events and of the wartime fate of Christian Indians more broadly see Leach, *Flintlock and Tomahawk*, 147–54.

50. Gookin, "Historical Account," 450–52. This order stipulated that such Indians were not to "travel above one mile from the center of such of their dwellings unless in company of some English, or in their service . . . on penalty of being taken as our enemies or their abettors" (Order of the Massachusetts Council, August 30, 1675, Grafton, Massachusetts, Local Records, AAS). Some Christian Indians had in fact asked the Council for protection (Anthony and James to the Massachusetts Council, July 19, 1675, Mass. Arch. 67:220). Connecticut passed a similar resolution, making it lawful for Indians traveling alone to be shot at will, on August 31 (*CCR* 2:359).

51. *MCR* 5:46, 57. Gookin gives a lengthy report on the debate over whether to confine the Indians to Deer Island in his "Historical Account" (468–71). One author claims, against all the evidence, that the Indians themselves requested confinement on the island (*Farther Brief and True Narration*, 4). Similar measures were adopted in other colonies. In Rhode Island, Indians over age twelve living in English households were ordered "bound in the day time (if he goeth abroad from his house)" and "locked up in the night" in March 1676 (*RICR* 2:534). In Plymouth Colony orders were given on February 29, 1676, "that the Namassachesett Indians be speedily removed to Clarkes Iland, and ther to remaine, and not to depart from thence without lycence from authoritie upon paine of death" (*PCR* 5:187).

52. Reverend Emerson to the Massachusetts Council, September 17, 1675, in *Annals of Mendon*, 65, but see also 69–70 and 71–72.

53. Gookin, "Historical Account," 436.

54. John Lyne and Numphow to Thomas Henchman, c. November 15, 1675; reprinted in Gookin, "Historical Account," 483.

55. Gookin, "Historical Account," 473–74.

56. *MCR* 5:64.

57. Order of the Massachusetts Council, November 26, 1675, Mass. Arch. 30:185b.

58. Gookin, "Historical Account," 485. At some point during the winter a Christian Indian called "Old Ahaton" (the father of William Nahauton) sent a petition to the Massachusetts Council asking for "liberty to goe too som place wheare I might get som clames som wood and som corne." He claimed the English owed him a favor since he "hath long been a friend unto the Inglish and hath gone forth with them at all tymes as hee hath been called and would have been willing to suffer with them" (Old Ahaton to the Massachusetts Council, undated, Mass. Arch. 30:200a).

59. Mary Pray to James Oliver, October 20, 1675, *MHSC*, 5th ser., 1 [Gookin] (1871): 105. Pray also claimed that "it is report by the Indians them selves that Cap. Gucking helps them to powder, and they sel it to those that are imployed by Philip to bye for him."

60. Roger Williams to John Leverett, January 14, 1676.

61. Saltonstall, *Present State*, 49. See also Richard Waldron to John Winsley, February 10, 1676, Gay Transcripts, MHS. Significantly, Increase Mather later preached against the persecution of praying Indians (*Exhortation*, 186–87).

62. Gookin, "Historical Account," 494. In late February Thomas Shepard (with whom Rowlandson and her husband would live after her redemption in May) testified before the Court that a man from Malden had approached him and "asked him if he would goo with him to Dere Island. His words were these. will you go with us to Deere island to destroy the Indians" (Deposition of Thomas Shepard given before the Massachusetts Council, February 15, 1676, Mass. Arch. 68:136b). After hearing Shepard's testimony the Council warned the plotters against the project (Gookin, "Historical Account," 494).

63. Deposition of Edward Page before the Massachusetts Council, February 15, 1676, Mass. Arch. 68:136.

64. Ambrose Dawes and others to the Massachusetts Council, February 22, 1676, Mass. Arch. 68:140 and 141. There are several other letters in the Massachusetts Archives advocating the use of stronger measures against the Indians, including one proposing the use of dogs (unknown to the Massachusetts Council, April 21, 1676, Mass. Arch. 68:214, 215).

65. Gookin, "Historical Account," 497–500.

66. Deposition of Elizabeth Belcher, Martha Romington, and Mary Mitchell before the Massachusetts Council, March 4, 1676, Mass. Arch. 30:192. Scott later delivered a petition claiming he did not "remember Ever I uttered Such Expressions" but that he did remember being drunk (Richard Scott to the Massachusetts Council, March 26, 1676, Mass. Arch. 30:196).

67. "By the Society A.B.C.D.," February 28, 1676, Mass. Arch. 30:193, 193a.

68. Order of the Massachusetts Council, February 29, 1676, Mass. Arch. 30:194a.

69. Order of the Massachusetts Council, March 14, 1676, Mass. Arch. 30:197.

70. *MCR* 5:84.

71. Gookin, "Historical Account," 517–18.

72. Tukapewillin's name is also rendered as Tuckapewillin and Tachuppouillan.

73. On February 21 the Massachusetts authorities had ordered John Curtis of Roxbury "to take sixe Indians from the island for his assistance, with their armes, some of which Indians may be improved for spies" (*MCR* 5:74). Among the six selected were Job Kattenanit, James Quanapaug, and William Nahauton (Gookin, "Historical Account," 500–501).

74. Thomas Hinckley to his wife, February 10, 1676, *MHSC,* 4th ser., 5 (1861): 1.

75. Job Kattenanit to the Massachusetts Council, February 14, 1676, Mass. Arch. 30:190a. James Quanapaug, who spied with Kattenanit, also reported that "Marlborough Indians are with them; they say, they were fetched away by the other Indians; some of them are very willing to come back" (deposition of James Quanapaug before the Massachusetts Council, January 24, 1676, *MHSC,* 1st ser., 6 [1799]: 208). Meanwhile, Jonathan Fairbanks, who had traveled with Kattenanit on his search for his family, later petitioned the Council to release from Deer Island a ten- or twelve-year-old Indian girl whom he had found with Kattenanit's family and wished to keep for himself (Jonathan Fairbanks to the Massachusetts Council, April 19, 1676, Mass. Arch. 30:200). Like Kattenanit, Awaukun, another Christian Indian who had fought with the English, also petitioned the Massachusetts Council for help in freeing his son, captive among the Nipmucks (Awaukun to the Massachusetts Council, undated, Mass. Arch. 30:191a).

76. Gookin, "Historical Account," 490–91.

77. Order of the Massachusetts Council, August 30, 1675, Grafton, Massachusetts, Local Records, AAS (the note about Tukapewillin's visit is written at the end of the order, and undated, though it must date from the following spring); see also Gookin, "Historical Account," 504–5, in which it is claimed that Eliot visited Tukapewillin at Captain Page's house.

78. Gookin, "Historical Account," 489.

79. "Rev. John Eliot's Records of the First Church at Roxbury, Mass.," *NEHGR* 33 (1879): 299. Captain Tom is occasionally referred to by an Algonquian name, Wattasacompanum.

80. Massachusetts Council to the Constables of Dorchester and Milton, June 19, 1676, Mass. Arch. 30:204a.

81. James Quanapaug's name is also rendered as Quannupokkis or Quannapohit, and he is sometimes referred to as Rummy Marsh and by an entirely different name, James Wiser (deposition of James Quanapaug [here spelled Quannupokkis] Alias Rummy Marsh before the Massachusetts Council, undated, Mass. Arch. 30:172). On James Quanapaug's journey among the Nipmucks see the full testimony he provided upon his return, dated January 24, 1676, and transcribed in *MHSC,* 1st ser., 6 (1799): 205–8.

82. Depositions of Edmond Rice and Abraham Gale before the Massachusetts Council, June 19, 1676, Mass. Arch. 30:204b.

83. Deposition of John Partridge before the Massachusetts Council, June 19, 1676, Mass. Arch. 30:205b. Edmund Randolph's account is also revealing here: "With many such reasons, but whatever be the cause, the English have contributed much to their misfortunes, for they first taught the Indians the use of armes, and admitted them to be present at all their musters and trainings, and shewed them how to handle, mend and fix their muskets, and have been furnished with al sorts of armes by permission of the government, so that the Indians are become excellent firemen. And at Natick there was a gathered church of praying Indians,

who were exercised as trained bands, under officers of their owne; these have been the most barbarous and cruel enemies to the English of any others. Capt. Tom, their leader, being lately taken and hanged at Boston, with one other of their chiefs" (Randolph, "Short Narrative").

84. Gookin, "Historical Account," 476–77.

85. William Nahauton to the Massachusetts Council, September 22, 1675, Mass. Arch. 30:176. In addition to serving as a missionary and later testifying at John Sassamon's trial, Nahauton had served with the English as a soldier in the war (Massachusetts Council to Josiah Winslow, April 21, 1676, *NEHGR* 41 [1887]: 400–401).

86. Daniel Gookin to the Prison Keeper in Boston, September 22, 1675, Mass. Arch. 30:176a.

87. Eliot accompanied Tom to his execution ("Rev. John Eliot's Records," 413, emphasis mine). Five Christian Indians also petitioned for the release of Captain Tom, his wife and two children, and another family in prison. The Massachusetts Council refused to release Captain Tom, insisting on his guilt, but agreed to spare his wife and children (Gookin, "Historical Account," 527–29).

88. *The Diary of Samuel Sewall, 1674–1729*, ed. M. Halsey Thomas (New York: Farrar, Straus, & Giroux, 1973), 1:18. Mary Rowlandson also recorded Captain Tom's fate, noting, "Another Praying Indian was at Sudbury fight, though, as he deserved, he was afterwards hanged for it" (*Sovereignty*, 353). The author of *True Account* was more sympathetic, writing, "On the 22d of June, was Executed at Boston Captain Tom, alias Watasocamponum, and another with him. This Captain Tom was taken by our Indian Scouts, having been with the Enemy this last Winter; they both dyed (as is to be hoped) penitent, praying to God not like the manner of the Heathen" (5).

89. Mather, *Historical Discourse*, 9.

90. Massachusetts Council to the Indian Sagamores, March 31, 1676, Mass. Arch. 68:193. Probably during this same mission, Dublett succeeded in bringing Joseph Tukapewillin's wife back, at which time she, too, was presumably sent to Deer Island. Their son, however, had died (Gookin, "Historical Account," 502–3). Tom Dublett is also known as Tom Nepanitt or Neppanit.

91. *True Account*, 2.

92. Sam Quanohit and Kutquen with Peter Jethro as scribe to the Massachusetts Council, April 12, 1676, in Gookin, "Historical Account," 508.

93. Ibid.

94. Rowlandson, *Sovereignty*, 352. Conway was also known as Tatatiquinea.

95. James Printer to the Massachusetts Council, April 27, 1676, Mass. Arch., *Hutchinson Papers*, 2:282; and transcribed in Henry S. Norse, *Early Records of Lancaster, Massachusetts, 1643–1725* (Lancaster, 1884), 111–12.

96. Massachusetts Council to Indian Sachems, April 28, 1676, Mass. Arch. 30:201a.

97. Rowlandson, *Sovereignty*, 354–58.

98. Of Printer's return, the author of *True Account* wrote, "A Revo'ter he was, and a fellow that had done much mischief, and staid out as long as he could, till the last day but one of a Proclamation set forth" (5). See also *Diary of Samuel Sewall*, 1:18.

99. Mather, *Brief History*, 172–73; see also Hubbard, *Narrative*, 1:249.

100. Hutchinson, *Warr in New-England Visibly Ended*, 105. James Printer to the Massachusetts Council, April 27, 1676.

101. Thomas Whalley to John Cotton, July 18, 1676, Davis Papers, MHS. Harris, *A Rhode Islander Reports,* 74.

102. Massachusetts Council to Daniel Gookin, July 3, 1676, Mass. Arch. 30:207.

103. Though the English used the word "head" to refer to scalps as well as actual heads, it is usually clear from the context that a "head" carried off is a scalp, but a "head" erected on a pole is an actual head. Saltonstall, writing of a man who brought home "two Indian Heads," added, in parentheses, "(i.e., the Skin with the hair on it)" (Saltonstall, *Present State,* 30). As William Harris explained, "some of the men of Swansy wear kild, And theyr heads (to Say) the Sculpes (that is) the skin & hayre of the top or crowne of the head flead of, as they use of all they kill (if they have time) to cut it rounde: & tear it of: & carry away." Such scalps were "Sure signes of whome they have kild of both cects [sexes]; as formerlly foreskins of males" (Harris, *A Rhode Islander Reports,* 28). On the other hand, when Roger Williams wrote that Indians "are much delighted after battell to hang up the hands and heads of their enemies," he was referring to actual heads (Roger Williams, *A Key into the Language of America* [Detroit: Wayne State University Press, 1973], 132).

104. Derounian, "Publication, Promotion, and Distribution," 245. Printer continued working at the press into the eighteenth century. In 1683 John Eliot, working on a new edition of the Indian Bible, lamented that "we have but one man, viz. the Indian Printer, that is able to compose the sheets, and correct the press with understanding" (quoted in Drake, *Book of the Indians,* 2:51). In 1682 and 1685 his name appears on land deeds (James Printer et al. to the Massachusetts Council, February 2, 1682, Mass. Arch. 30:265; James Printer et al. to the Massachusetts Council, May 27, 1685, Mass. Arch. 30:300). And Printer's name appears for the last time on an imprint of a work from 1709. See also *Diary of Samuel Sewall,* 2:625.

105. Rowlandson, *Soveraignty,* 322.

106. Frank Mott, *Golden Multitudes: The Story of Best Sellers in the United States* (New York: Macmillan, 1960), 303. See also Derounian, "Publication, Promotion, and Distribution," 239–61.

Chapter 6 • A DANGEROUS MERCHANDISE

1. "Wootonekanuske" has been commonly accepted as the name of Philip's wife, but it was only first asserted in 1841 by Samuel Gardner Drake (*Book of the Indians* [Boston, 1841], 3:13). I have not found any contemporary evidence to support Drake, though his data regarding seventeenth-century names are usually reliable. George Howe claimed Philip's wife was named "Nanuskooke" (*Mount Hope: A New England Chronicle* [New York: The Viking Press, 1959], 58). Current-day Wampanoag tradition asserts that Philip's son was named "Metom" (Ann McMullen, personal communication, August 17, 1992), though I have found no seventeenth-century evidence to that effect. It may be a corruption of the nineteenth-century romantic term for "Metacom," "Metamora" (see Chapter 8).

2. Mather, *Brief History,* 189.

3. John Leverett to All People, September 12, 1676, mss. bound, MHS. Josiah Winslow to all Christian People, August 9, 1676, Stewart Mitchell Papers, MHS.

4. Josiah Winslow to all Christian People, August 9, 1676.

5. Samuel Arnold and John Cotton, September 7, 1676, *MHSC,* 4th ser., 8 (1868): 689.

6. Increase Mather to John Cotton, October 20, 1676, *MHSC,* 4th ser., 8 (1868): 689.

7. James Keith to John Cotton, October 30, 1676, Davis Papers, MHS.

8. John Cotton to Increase Mather, March 9, 1677, *MHSC,* 4th ser., 8 (1868): 232.

9. See Douglas Leach, *Flintlock and Tomahawk: New England in King Philip's War* (New York: The Macmillan Company, 1958; reprint, East Orleans, Mass.: Parnassus Imprints, 1992), 224–28. In July 1677 the wife and children of at least one other notorious Indian, Popanooie, were also sold into slavery, though it seems that only Popanooie himself was sent out of the country (*PCR* 5:243–44).

10. Almon Wheeler Lauber, *Indian Slavery in Colonial Times within the Present Limits of the United States* (New York: Columbia University Press, 1913), 138–43. Observations of Indians being sold into slavery early in the war include Saltonstall, *Present State,* 30.

11. *CCR* 2:297.

12. *PCR* 10:401.

13. *MCR* 5:72. *The Diary of Samuel Sewall, 1674–1729,* ed. M. Halsey Thomas (New York: Farrar, Straus, & Giroux, 1973), 1:18. James Oliver to unknown, January 26, 1676, *NEHGR* 39 (1885): 379.

14. When Josiah Winslow sent Benjamin Church on an Indian-hunting mission on August 28, 1676, he empowered him to "demand and receive of the Governor and Authority of Rhode island, all such of our Indian Enemys, whether Men, Women, or Children, as whilst our fforces were abroad ranging, the adjacent Parts of our Collony, in Pursute of the said Enemyes, were received by, and are entertained upon the said Island. And having received them, he is ordered to guard and conduct them to Plymouth aforesaid and alsoe impowered to sell and dispose of such of them" (Josiah Winslow to the Governor of Rhode Island, August 28, 1676, transcribed in "Record of a Court Martial Held at Newport, R.I. in August, 1676, for the Trial of Indians charged with being engaged in Philip's Designs," in *A Narrative of the Causes . . . with other Documents,* 15–16).

15. Samuel Shrimpton to Elizabeth Shrimpton, July 8, 1676, photostats, MHS.

16. Daniel Gookin to the Massachusetts Council, January 18, 1677, Mass. Arch. 30:235.

17. Paine declared that "the Indians Conceive that I betrayed & Sould them" (John Paine to the commissioners of the United Colonies, undated, *Further Letters on King Philip's War* [Providence: Society of Colonial Wars, 1923]). For another deposition related to Paine's petition see James Sweet (and other Narragansett Indians) to the Massachusetts Council, October 10, 1675, Mass. Arch. 30:180.

18. William Waldron to the Massachusetts Council, August 24, 1676, Mass. Arch. 30:213a. Waldron claimed he was innocent and petitioned for his release, but at least as of August 24, 1676, the Council refused to grant his request. See also George H. Moore, *Notes on the History of Slavery in Massachusetts* (New York: D. Appleton, 1866), 47–48.

19. Church, *Entertaining History,* 119.

20. For references to the trial of captured Indians see *Farther Brief and True Narration,* 4. In meting out punishment, a stay of execution, at least a temporary one, might be gained if the captured Indian had information to offer (see, e.g., John Lake to the Massachusetts Council, September 15, 1676, Mass. Arch. 30:221b).

21. John Easton served as one of the judges in Quinnapin's trial ("Record of a Court Martial Held at Newport," 176). On Weetamoo's fate see Richard LeBaron Bowen, *Early Rehoboth* (Rehoboth, Mass.: privately printed, 1945–50), 3:79–80.

22. Order of the Massachusetts Council, August 7, 1676, Mass. Arch. 30:209. On surrenders in the summer of 1676 see also Harris, *A Rhode Islander Reports,* 60–62.

23. *MCR* 4:115.

24. *CCR* 2:297.

25. *PCR* 5:204–5. Wotuchpo's name is also rendered as Tuchpo.

26. On the sale of surrendering and Christian Indians see Gookin, "Historical Account," 449; Moore, *Notes on the History of Slavery*, 38–42; Lauber, *Indian Slavery in Colonial Times*, 143–44.

27. William Nahauton to the Massachusetts Council, July 3, 1676, Mass. Arch. 30:207a. Nahauton and others made a similar request regarding a young Indian boy named Peter (Natick and Punkapoag Indians to the Massachusetts Council, c. 1676, Mass. Arch. 30:222).

28. Anthony and James to the Massachusetts Council, July 19, 1675, Mass. Arch. 67:220.

29. Massachusetts Council to Daniel Gookin, August 28, 1676, Mass. Arch. 30:214.

30. Richard Waldron to Daniel Gookin, November 2, 1676, *NEHGR* 43 (1889): 290.

31. Order of the Massachusetts Council, November 23, 1676, Mass. Arch. 30: 228a. Richard Waldron to Daniel Gookin, November 2, 1676.

32. Saltonstall, *Present State*, 33. See also *Farther Brief and True Narration*, 4.

33. John Eliot to the Massachusetts governor and Council, August 13, 1675, *PCR* 10:451–52. Benjamin Church, too, later claimed to have opposed slavery (*Entertaining History*, 52).

34. William Leete to John Winthrop, Jr., September 23, 1675, *MHSC*, 4th ser., 7 (1865): 578–80.

35. News of the practice of selling Indians into foreign slavery must have traveled fast in the native community. In September 1677 English captive Quentin Stockwell observed Nipmuck Indians from Wachusett spreading news of the sale of Uncas' men ("Narrative of the Captivity of Quentin Stockwell" in Samuel Gardner Drake, ed., *Tragedies of the Wilderness* [Boston, 1846], 63).

36. John Eliot to the Massachusetts governor and Council, August 13, 1675.

37. Roger Williams to the commissioners of the United Colonies [?], October 5, 1654, *PCR* 10:438–42.

38. John Eliot to the Massachusetts governor and Council, August 13, 1675.

39. Ibid.

40. My discussion of the debate at Valladolid relies on Lewis Hanke, *Aristotle and the American Indians: A Study in Race Prejudice in the Modern World* (Bloomington: Indiana University Press, 1959), especially Chapters 4 and 5.

41. See Aristotle, *Nichomaen Ethics*.

42. Quoted in Hanke, *Aristotle on the American Indians*, 47.

43. Bartolomé de Las Casas, *In Defense of the Indians*, trans., ed., and annotated by Stafford Poole (DeKalb: Northern Illinois University Press, 1974).

44. Las Casas, *In Defense of the Indians*, 26, 40.

45. John Eliot to the Massachusetts governor and Council, August 13, 1675.

46. Moore, *Notes on the History of Slavery*, 36–37.

47. On the lack of principled objection to the enslavement of Indians in New England see David Brion Davis, *The Problem of Slavery in Western Culture* (New York: Oxford University Press, 1966), 176–77. The colony of Rhode Island did declare, on March 13, 1676, that

"no Indian in this Collony [shall] be a slave" (*RICR* 2:535), but Yasuhide Kawashima has rightly pointed out that Rhode Island's antislavery legislation was not effective (Yasuhide Kawashima, "Indian Servitude in the Northeast," *HNAI* 4:404–6); and, in August 1676, Rhode Island's Council oversaw the sale of "slaves" for terms of nine years (*RICR* 2:549).

48. Elizabeth Donnan, ed., *Documents Illustrative of the History of the Slave Trade to America* (Washington, D.C.: Carnegie Institute of Washington, 1935), 3:4. The Body of Liberties also allowed for "such strangers as willingly sell themselves or are sold to us, and such shall have the Liberties and christian usage which the Law of God established in Israel concerning such persons doth morally require" to be enslaved. In 1670 the word "strangers" was dropped, but if that measure was taken so the order would more fully include Indians, it need not have been. As it stood, the Body of Liberties also included a catchall phrase: "Provided this exempts none from servitude who shall be judged thereto by Authority." See also Jordan, "The Influence of the West Indies on the Origins of New England Slavery," 243–50. The Body of Liberties only retroactively legalized a practice that had already begun: In 1638 Indians captured during the Pequot War had been shipped to the Caribbean and exchanged for African slaves. See Lauber, *Indian Slavery in Colonial Times*, 109–11, 123–25; Moore, *Notes on the History of Slavery*, 4. See also George Francis Dow, *Slave Ships and Shipping* (Salem, Mass.: Marine Research Society, 1927), 267. Another kind of precedent existed as well: Indians convicted of heinous crimes might also be sold into foreign slavery. In 1674, for example, an Indian convicted of rape and sentenced to life was instead "subjected to 10 years slavery" in the West Indies (*MCR* 5:25).

49. Donnan, *Documents Illustrative of the History of the Slave Trade*, 3:8 (emphasis mine). Winthrop no doubt did know "verie well" how advantageous it might be to exchange troublesome, rebellious Indians for African slaves. The next year, the commissioners of the United Colonies declared that "because it will be chargeable keeping Indians in prisone, and if they should escape they are like to prove more insolent and dangerous after, that upon such seazure, the delinquent or satisfaction be againe demanded . . . or if it be denyed, that then the magistrates of the Jurisdiccon deliver up the Indians seased to the party or parties indamaged, either to serve, or to be shipped out and exchanged for the Negroes as the cause will justly bear" (quoted in Moore, *Notes on the History of Slavery in Massachusetts*, 31–32).

50. In citing a "solemn League and Covenant," Leverett and Winslow were not alone. This covenant—a treaty signed by Philip's father, Massasoit, in 1621 and renewed by Philip himself in 1662 and 1671—assumed a prominent place in the colonists' public writings about the war; several published narratives summarized or reproduced these treaties within their pages (e.g., Saltonstall, *Continuation*, 68–71). Their self-consciousness in doing so is well represented in a passage from *A Farther Brief and True Narration:*

> It may be of some remark to let the World know that in the year 1621 on the 21 of March Massasoit (alias Woosamequen) acknowledged himself voluntarily in open Court at Plymouth to be a Subject to King James. . . . And August sixth 1662, this very Philip, our most turbulent and implacable Enemy, again renewed the acknowledgement of himself as a Subject to our King that now is, and his Heirs and Successors Kings of England. . . . The Original Instruments Signed with their own Hands, and the chief of their Men, still remain on Record in the Register of the Court of New-Plymouth (12).

51. Hubbard, *Narrative*, 1:54–55.

52. Similarly, William Harris maintained that "Phillip did openly Rob & kill the Kings Subjects," thereby committing "high treason" (*A Rhode Islander Reports*, 20).

53. And a rebellion, according to Hugo Grotius, was not only against the laws of war but also against the law of nature (*De Jure Belli Et Pacis,* trans. Francis W. Kelsey [Oxford: Clarendon Press, 1925], 139).

54. *The Cherokee Nation v. The State of Georgia,* 30 U.S. 1 (1831).

55. Francisco de Vitoria, *Political Writings,* ed. Anthony Pagden and Jeremy Lawrence (Cambridge: Cambridge University Press, 1991), 239–44.

56. When the colonists wanted to establish the legitimacy of their own land ownership, they nonetheless "bought" property from the Indians. Indians, then, could be considered "proprietors" when they signed a deed documenting the purchase or transfer of lands, but at no other time. For a fuller discussion of English ideas about Indian possession see Chapter 3.

57. Francis Higginson, *New-England's Plantation* (London, 1630; reprinted in Alexander Young, ed., *Chronicles of the First Planters of the Colony of Massachusetts Bay* [Boston, 1846]), 256.

58. Christopher Levett, *A Voyage into New England, begun in 1623, and ended in 1624* (London, 1628; reprinted in *Collections of the Maine Historical Society* 2 [1847]), 96.

59. Commissioners of the United Colonies to unknown, November 12, 1675, Mass. Arch. 68:55. Alden Vaughan has argued that rumors of Indian conspiracy date from the end of the Pequot War in 1637 and in fact encouraged the establishment of the confederation of New England colonies in 1645 (*New England Frontier: Puritans and Indians, 1620–1675* [New York: W. W. Norton & Company, 1965; revised ed., 1979], 157). At the start of King Philip's War, colonists, fearful that the "adjacent pettie Kings or sachems" were "too prone" to join with Philip, sent representatives to negotiate alliances (Josiah Winslow to Weetamo and her husband, July 15, 1675, Winslow Papers, MHS). See also Massachusetts Council to Ninigret and Squaw Sachem, undated, Mass. Arch. 67:201. Benjamin Batten to Sir Thomas Allin, July 29, 1675, Gay Transcripts, MHS; also printed in *The London Gazette,* August 19, 1675.

60. Daniel Witherell to John Winthrop, Jr., July 30, 1675, *MHSC,* 3rd ser., 10 (1849): 119; Massachusetts Council to John Winthrop, Jr., July 28, 1675, Mass. Arch. 67:209. See also Easton, "Relacion," 14; Benjamin Batten to Sir Thomas Allin, July 29, 1675; and Richard Wharton to John Winsley, February 10, 1676, Gay Transcripts, MHS.

61. Samuel Gorton to John Winthrop, Jr., September 11, 1675, *MHSC,* 4th ser., 7 (1865): 627.

62. Roger Williams to John Winthrop, Jr., June 25, 1675, *The Correspondence of Roger Williams,* ed. Glenn LaFantasie (Providence: Brown University Press, 1988), 2:693.

63. Easton, "Relacion," 10.

64. As Easton wrote, "the English wear jelous that ther was a genarall plot of all indians against English and the indieans wear in like maner jelous of the english" ("Relacion," 14).

65. Anon., *Great News from the Barbadoes. Or, a True and Faithful Account of the Grand Conspiracy of the Negroes against the English. And the Happy Discovery of the same with the number of those that were burned alive, Beheaded, and otherwise Executed for their Horrid Crimes* (London, for L. Curtis, 1676), 10. Samuel Green, ed., *Diary of Increase Mather, March, 1675–December, 1676* (Cambridge, Mass.: John Wilson & Son, 1900), 18.

66. Saltonstall, *Continuation,* 71–74 (emphasis mine). Saltonstall also recounted the recent violent storms in Boston (and implicitly compared the damage of such storms to the damage of the war), noting that "such another Blow will bring Barbadoes near the Horizon" (ibid., 74).

67. Governor Sir William Berkeley to [Thomas Luddwell?], February 16, 1676, quoted in Washburn, "Governor Berkeley and King Philip's War," *NEQ* 30 (1957): 366. In a letter to Williamson, Berkeley conveyed news both of New England and Virginia's troubles, hoping "it wil not be impertinent to give you the relation of our Neighbours as wel as of our selves and the more because their Troubles were the cause and beginning of ours" (Governor Sir William Berkeley to Secretary Sir Joseph Williamson, April 1, 1676, quoted in Washburn, "Governor Berkeley and King Philip's War," 374).

68. Governor Sir Jonathan Atkins to Secretary Sir Joseph Williamson, November 4, 1675, *CSP* 9:301. Peter Beckford of Jamaica received similar news from ships arriving from New England (Peter Beckford to Secretary Sir Joseph Williamson, *CSP* 9:411).

69. Quoted in Jerome S. Handler, "The Amerindian Slave Population of Barbados in the Seventeenth and Early Eighteenth Centuries," *Caribbean Studies* 8 (1969): 57. Handler also notes that some Barbadian Indian slaves may have been shipped out to New England (including Tituba, of Salem witch trial fame). By 1688 a law was passed again that "all Persons whatsoever are prohibited to bring, sell and dispose of any Indians to this Island, upon pain of forfeiting the same unto his Majesty" (William Rawlin, *The Laws of Barbados Collected in One Volume* [London, for William Rawlin, 1699], 171). See Richard Hall, *Acts Passed in the Island of Barbados from 1643 to 1762* (London, for Richard Hall, 1764), appendix. Winthrop Jordan has argued that the practice of chattel slavery emigrated from the West Indies to New England, making it ironic that New England's slaves were subsequently turned away from the West Indies ("The Influence of the West Indies on the Origins of New England Slavery," *WMQ* 18 [1961]: 243–50).

70. Donnan, *Documents on the Slave Trade*, 1:415. Ann C. Van Devanter, *American Self-Portraits, 1670–1973* (Washington, D.C.: International Exhibitions Foundation, 1974), 16; Jonathan Fairbanks, ed., *New England Begins: The Seventeenth Century* (Boston: Museum of Fine Arts, 1982), 3:474.

71. See Leach, *Flintlock and Tomahawk,* 226. On the possible destinations of Indian slaves see John Hull to Philip French, September 2, 1675, John Hull's Letterbook, AAS; Lauber, *Indian Slavery,* 125–31; and Handler, "The Amerindian Slave Population of Barbados," 38–64.

72. John Eliot to Robert Boyle, 1683, *MHSC,* 1st ser., 3 (1794): 183.

73. C. Mather, *Magnalia.*

74. A family of contemporary Wampanoag Indians, calling themselves the Royal House of Pokanoket, claim that Philip's son was shipped to Bermuda but that his own son, a man named Simon Simeons, made his way back to New England around the time of the Revolutionary War and became an aide to George Washington (Everett Weedon [Tall Oak], personal communication, February 22, 1995).

Chapter 7 · THAT BLASPHEMOUS LEVIATHAN

1. Church, *Entertaining History,* 125–26. See also Hutchinson, *Warr in New-England Visibly Ended,* 104–5; William Jones to Governor Leete, July 5, 1676, *PCR* 2:470; and John Leverett to the king of England, September 6, 1676, *MCR* 5:106.

2. Mather, *Brief History,* 195.

3. Church, *Entertaining History,* 125–26. The bucket-of-rum story comes from George Howe, *Mount Hope: A New England Chronicle* (New York: The Viking Press, 1959), 55. One

colonist, giving news of Philip's death to William Leete, regretted that his informant, James Shore, had not been able to see the decapitated head: "They cut off Philip's head and hands and brought them away; the said Shore saith that he might have seene the head could he have staid one hour longer there, but was forced to com away" (William Jones to William Leete, September 5, 1676, *CCR* 2:470).

4. A Dutch soldier named Cornelius captured Philip's hat early in the war (Saltonstall, *Present State*, 29). Philip's belt and bow are owned by the Peabody Museum, Harvard University; bowl, Massachusetts Historical Society; and war club, The Fruitlands Museums. (The war club, which was stolen from the museum in the 1970s, has recently been returned.) Very little direct evidence connects any of these museum objects to Philip.

5. Josiah Winslow to the king of England, June 26, 1677, *MHSP* 7 (1864): 481–82.

6. W. DeLoss Love, *The Fast and Thanksgiving Days of New England* (Boston, 1895), 68–77.

7. Church, *Entertaining History*, 125–26. An early bounty of twenty coats had been offered for Philip's head, ten times the normal rate for an Indian scalp or head (Saltonstall, *Present State*, 34). On Church's pursuit and the removal of Philip's head to Plymouth see the account in Douglas Leach, *Flintlock and Tomahawk*, 233–36. Philip's head had been long sought after. In a letter from July 1675 John Freeman reported to Josiah Winslow that he had engaged several Narragansett Indians to attempt to bring in Philip's "men," but then crossed out "men" and wrote instead "head and his men" (John Freeman to Josiah Winslow, July 18, 1675, Winslow Papers, MHS).

8. The day of thanksgiving had been appointed before Philip's death, and, while John Cotton, minister at Plymouth, wrote in his church records that Philip's head arrived in Plymouth the same day he was killed (and that the day of thanksgiving was observed that day), Mather and Hubbard report that both transpired on August 17. Mather, *Brief History*, 197; Hubbard, *Narrative*, 1:267–68; Love, *Fast and Thanksgiving Days*, 201–3. John Cotton's Plymouth Church Records, in *Publications of the Colonial Society of Massachusetts* 222 (1920): 152–53. News of Philip's death spread quickly, reaching Newport, Rhode Island, by three o'clock on August 12 (Harris, *A Rhode Islander Reports*, 84).

9. C. Mather, *Magnalia*, 563, 576 (emphasis mine). C. Mather, *The Life and Death of the Renown'd Mr. John Eliot* (London, 1691), 95.

10. John Foster, *An Almanack of coelestial motions for . . . 1676* (Boston, 1676), Watkinson Library copy. John Hull also noted Philip's death in his diary on August 12: "Sagamore Philip, that began the war, was slain" ("Diary of John Hull," *Transactions and Collections of the American Antiquarian Society* 3 [1857]: 242).

11. Mather, *Brief History*, 195. Earlier in the war, writers had made a clear connection between the war continuing and Philip still living. As the author of *Farther Brief and True Narration* wrote, "the Rod of Gods Anger is still upon us; For the Pocanaket Sachem Metacom, alias Philip, still lives!" (3).

12. On fatalities due to disease see Mather, *Brief History*, 205.

13. See Mather, *Brief History*, 207–8; Church, *Entertaining History*, 67–68; Saltonstall, *New and Further Narrative*, 88–89, 97; Leach, *Flintlock and Tomahawk*, 142; Francis Jennings, *The Invasion of America: Indians, Colonialism, and the Cant of Conquest* (New York: W. W. Norton & Company, 1975), 314–24. (Jennings also offers an important perspective on New York's interest in the conflict.) On New England Algonquian traditional enmity with (and

fear of) the Mohawks see Daniel Gookin, "Historical Collections of the Indians in New England [1674]," *MHSC,* 1st ser., 1 [1792]: 162–68; "Narrative of the Captivity of Quentin Stockwell" in Samuel Gardner Drake, ed., *Tragedies of the Wilderness* (Boston, 1846), 62. More broadly see Gordon M. Day, "The Ouragie War: A Case History in Iroquois–New England Indian Relations," in Michael K. Foster et al., eds., *Extending the Rafters: Interdisciplinary Approaches to Iroquoian Studies* (Albany: SUNY Press, 1984), 35–50.

14. Harris, *A Rhode Islander Reports,* 18. Francis Jennings has argued that "the Indians never for a moment aspired to drive out all the English or hoped for mastery over them. Their purpose was to salvage some measure of self-government in secure territory. Nor did any of the colonists worry about being driven into the sea" (Jennings, *Invasion of America,* 300). My reading of the evidence, however, leads me to disagree on both points. Like Harris, many colonists did fear that the war might force them to abandon their settlements in New England, and many Englishmen and -women outside of New England held similar fears (Governor Berkeley, for instance, wrote that "the New-England men are ingaged in a warr with their Indians which in al reasonable conjectures wil end in their utter ruine" [Governor Sir William Berkely to Thomas Ludwell, April 1, 1676, quoted in Washburn, "Governor Berkeley and King Philip's War," 371]). And the Indians' taunts, as well as their actions, suggest that they may have had broader goals in mind in waging war against the colonists. It does not seem unreasonable to suppose that the Wampanoags, at least, wished to regain territory they had sold or otherwise lost to the English.

15. Mather, *Brief History,* 206.

16. *Diary of Samuel Sewall,* 25–26.

17. Russell Bourne, *The Red King's Rebellion: Racial Politics in New England, 1675–1678* (New York: Oxford University Press, 1990); Michael J. Puglisi, *Puritans Besieged: The Legacies of King Philip's War in the Massachusetts Bay Colony* (Lanham, Md.: University Press of America, 1991); Richard Melvoin has followed the fate of one New England town, Deerfield, throughout this period (*New England Outpost*).

18. Richard Slotkin, *Regeneration through Violence: The Mythology of the American Frontier, 1600–1860* (Middletown, Conn.: Wesleyan University Press, 1973), 68, 79.

19. "The English go many of them now to their Old Habitations and Mow down their Ground, and make Hay, and do other Occasions necessary for their resettling" (Hutchinson, *Warr in New-England Visibly Ended,* 105). When Quentin Stockwell was taken captive in September 1677 he struggled on his march into captivity, made lame by wounds sustained during King Philip's War ("Narrative of the Captivity of Quentin Stockwell," 61).

20. The economic repercussions of the war are best detailed in Puglisi, *Puritans Besieged;* and Stephen Saunders Webb, *1676: The End of American Independence* (New York: Alfred A. Knopf, 1984), especially 221–44, 411–12. The memory of the war no doubt contributed to what Jon Butler has called the "sacrilization of the landscape" (*Awash in a Sea of Faith: Christianizing the American People* [Cambridge, Mass.: Harvard University Press, 1990]).

21. Mather, *Historical Discourse,* 1.

22. *Diary of Samuel Sewall,* 1:23.

23. In the first month of the war a Dutch soldier named Cornellis "pursued Philip so hard, that he got his Cap off his Head, and now weareth it" (Saltonstall, *Present State,* 29). Nathaniel Knowles, "The Torture of Captives by the Indians of Eastern North America," *American Philosophical Society Proceedings* 82 (1940): 152–53; and Jennings, *The Invasion of America,* 152.

24. Edward Rawson to Josiah Winslow, August 20, 1676, Winslow Papers, MHS.

25. Saltonstall, *New and Further Narrative,* 90–91. See also Mather, *Brief History,* 133–34; Hubbard, *Narrative,* 1:182–83; Walker, "Captan Perse," 92; Harris, *A Rhode Islander Reports,* 47; *True Account,* 2.

26. *CCR* 2:262.

27. *Diary of Samuel Sewall,* 1:18. Hubbard, *Narrative,* 1:240–41.

28. Wheeler, *Thankefull Remembrance,* 247.

29. Saltonstall, *New and Further Narrative,* 99.

30. Hubbard, *Narrative,* 1:110–11.

31. Mather, *Brief History,* 180.

32. *Brief and True Narration,* 5.

33. Geoffrey Abbot, *Lords of the Scaffold: A History of the Executioner* (London: Robert Hale, 1991), 17.

34. For example, see Fitz-John Winthrop to unknown, July 26, 1675, *MHSC,* 6th ser., 3 (1889): 44; John Pynchon to the Connecticut War Council, August 8, 1675, *CCR* 2:348; Mather, *Brief History,* 191–92. On the English practice of decapitation and display see Puglisi, *Puritans Besieged,* 43; Jennings, *Invasion of America,* 166–68; Thomas S. Abler, "Scalping, Torture, Cannibalism and Rape: An Ethnohistorical Analysis of Conflicting Cultural Values in War," *Anthropologica* 34 (1992): 6–9.

35. William Scranton Simmons, *Cautantowwit's House: An Indian Burial Ground on the Island of Conanicut in Narragansett Bay* (Providence: Brown University Press, 1970), 54.

36. John Sherman, *An Almanac* (Cambridge, 1677).

37. Previous to King Philip's War, anniversaries were not commonly celebrated in almanacs. The Puritans, on the whole, were not enthusiastic celebrators of anniversaries. And when John Foster began recording anniversaries of the war, he didn't then also include anniversaries of other events. From the 1679 almanac, for instance, only two non–King Philip's War anniversaries are noted, and both of these are great calamities: from July 10, 1677: "The Vessel arrives at Nantasket which brought that contagious Distemper the Small Pox . . ." and November 27, 1676: "Bostons greatest fire."

38. John Foster, *An Almanack . . . 1679* (Boston, 1679).

39. In John Danforth's 1679 almanac he includes "A Brief Memorial of some few Remarkable Occurrences in the Six Preceding Yeares in N-E." Of forty-two such "Remarkable Occurrences" from 1673 to 1679, nineteen are from King Philip's War (the remainder consist mostly of the deaths of eminent colonists). John Danforth, *An Almanack* (Cambridge, 1679). John Foster's "Chronology of very memorable things to 1679" lists "The Creation of the World," "Noah's Flood," "The Nativity of Jesus Christ," "The Most Rare Invention of Printing," and, not least among these, "The War with the Indians" (Foster, *An Almanack . . . 1679*).

40. Foster, *An Almanack . . . 1679*; John Foster, *An Almanack . . . 1681* (Boston, 1681).

41. See Samuel Clough, *The New-England Almanack, for the year 1701* (Boston, [1700]).

42. Elaine Scarry, *The Body in Pain: The Making and Unmaking of the World* (New York: Oxford University Press, 1985), 113–14.

43. Mather, *Exhortation,* 168.

44. Urian Oakes, *The Soveraign Efficacy of Divine Providence; . . . As Delivered in a Sermonn Preached in Cambridge on Sept. 10, 1677. Being the Day of artillery Election there* (Boston in New-England: Printed for Samuel Sewall, 1682), 26.1.

45. Increase Mather, *The Danger of Apostacy* (Cambridge, 1679). Emphasis mine.

46. John Canup, *Out of the Wilderness: The Emergence of an American Identity in Colonial New England* (Middletown, Conn.: Wesleyan University Press, 1990), 43–44.

47. Quoted in Ronald Takaki, "The *Tempest* in the Wilderness: The Racialization of Savagery," *JAH* 79 (1992): 909. On the colonists' less metaphorical fears, fears of real renewed warfare, see Peter N. Carroll, *Puritanism and the Wilderness: The Intellectual Significance of the New England Frontier, 1629–1700* (New York: Columbia University Press, 1969), 213–14.

48. An Act to Prevent Outrages against the Indians, May 4, 1681, Ms. Amer., JCB.

49. *At a Council Held in Boston August the thirtieth 1675* (Cambridge, 1675), brs.

50. An Act to Prevent Outrages against the Indians, May 4, 1681.

51. James Axtell, "The Vengeful Women of Marblehead: Robert Roules's Deposition of 1677," *WMQ* 31 (1974): 647–52.

52. John Leverett to the king of England, September 6, 1676. See also Ezra Stiles, who claims that "All the Indian Malecontents retreated from N. Eng. to Skotacook [N.Y.] after 1676" (Stiles, *Extracts from the Itineraries and Other Miscellanies of Ezra Stiles, 1755–1794* [New Haven, Conn.: Yale University Press, 1916], 136).

53. See Daniel R. Mandell, *Behind the Frontier: Indians in Eighteenth-Century Eastern Massachusetts* (Lincoln: University of Nebraska Press, 1996); Laurie Weinstein, " 'We're Still Living on Our Traditional Homeland': The Wampanoag Legacy in New England," in *Strategies for Survival: American Indians in the Eastern United States,* ed. Frank W. Porter III (Westport, Conn.: Greenwood Press, 1986), 85–112; Laura E. Conkey, Ethel Boissevain, and Ives Goddard, "Indians of Southern New England and Long Island: Late Period," in *HNAI* 15: 177–89; Frank Speck, "Mythology of the Wampanoags," *El Palacio* 25 (1928): 83–86; Donna Keith Baron, J. Edward Hood, and Holly V. Izard, "They Were Here All Along: The Native Presence in Lower-Central New England in the Eighteenth and Nineteenth Centuries," *WMQ* 53 (July 1996): 561–86; and Ann McMullen, "What's Wrong with This Picture? Context, Conversion, Survival, and the Development of Regional Native Cultures and Pan-Indianism in Southeastern New England," in *Enduring Traditions: The Native Peoples of New England,* ed. Laurie Weinstein (Westport, Conn.: Bergin & Garvey, 1994), 123–50; Colin G. Calloway, ed., *After King Philip's War: Presence and Persistance in Indian New England* (Hanover, NH: University Press of New England, 1997); Jean O'Brien, *Dispossession by Degrees: Indian Land and Identity in Natick, Massachusetts* (Cambridge, Mass.: Cambridge University Press, 1997).

54. In 1696 Betty deeded her land to her own daughter Mercy (*PCR* 12: 235). See also Weinstein, " 'We're Still Living on Our Traditional Homeland,' " 96.

55. On the Mashpees' limited involvement in the war see Gookin, "Historical Account," 434.

56. *Extracts from the Itineraries . . . of Ezra Stiles,* 115. On Narragansetts in the eighteenth century see William S. Simmons and Cheryl L. Simmons, eds., *Old Light on Separate Ways: The Narragansett Diary of Joseph Fish, 1765–1776* (Hanover, N.H.: University Press of New England, 1982), xxx–xxxvii. On Narragansett survival see Paul R. Campbell and Glenn W. LaFantasie, "Scattered to the Winds of Heaven—Narragansett Indians 1676–1880," *Rhode Island History* 37 (1978): 67–83.

57. Mandell, *Behind the Frontier,* 2–6. O'Brien, *Dispossession by Degrees,* 9–10.

58. Mandell, *Behind the Frontier,* 9–14; on early Natick house styles see also Elise Brenner, "Strategies for Autonomy: An Analysis of Ethnic Mobilization in Seventeenth-Century Southern New England" (Ph.D. diss., University of Massachusetts, Amherst, 1984), 127–34. Mandell has argued that "Natick's postwar material culture was clearly far more aboriginal than English" (38).

59. Kathleen J. Bragdon, "The Material Culture of the Christian Indians in New England, 1650–1775," in Mary C. Beaudry, ed., *Documentary Archaeology in the New World* (Cambridge, Mass.: Cambridge University Press, 1988), 130.

60. Kathleen Bragdon, "Probate Records as a Source for Algonquian Ethnohistory," in William Cowan, ed., *Papers of the Tenth Algonquian Conference* (Ottawa: Carleton University, 1979), 136–41; and Bragdon, "Material Culture," 126–31.

61. Quoted in Bragdon, "Material Culture," 131.

62. Ann McMullen, "Native Basketry, Basketry Styles, and Changing Group Identity in Southern New England," in *Algonkians of New England: Past and Present,* ed. Peter Benes (Boston: Boston University, 1993): 76–88.

63. Bragdon, "Material Culture," 130.

64. Stiles, *Extracts,* 203.

65. Baron et al., "They Were Here All Along," 564–67.

66. Anthropologist Ann McMullen has argued that New England Algonquian culture became covert (McMullen, "What's Wrong with This Picture?" 123–50).

67. Nathan Fiske, *Remarkable Providences to be gratefully recollected, religious improved, and carefully transmitted to Posterity. A Sermon Preached at Brookfield On the last Day of the Year 1775* (Boston, New-England: Printed by Thomas and John Fleet, 1776), 25–28.

68. See also Robert Breck, *Past Dispensations of Providence called to Mind. In a Sermon, Delivered in the first Parish in Springfield, on the 16th of October 1775. Just one hundred Years from the burning of the Town by the Indians* (Hartford, Conn.: Barlow & Babcock, 1784). The war was apparently not so well remembered by redcoats: a soldier's guide printed by the British War Office during the Revolution said of Bristol that it was famous for "King Philip of Spain having a palace nearby and being killed in it" (quoted in Howe, *Mount Hope,* 61).

69. These connections have been observed and documented by Captain Greg Sieminski in "The Puritan Captivity Narrative and the Politics of the American Revolution," *AQ* 42 (1990): 35–56. Church's history of King Philip's War was printed many times in Forrest's lifetime—in 1825, 1827, 1829, 1834, and 1842—but it probably sold in greatest numbers during the 1830s and 1840s, at the height of *Metamora*'s popularity.

70. For evidence of Boyle's support for the patriot cause see "Boyle's Journal of Occurrences in Boston, 1759–1778," *NEHGR* 84–85 (1930–31): 142–71, 248–72, 357–82.

71. William Hubbard, *A narrative of the Indian wars in New-England . . .* (Boston: Printed and sold by John Boyle, 1775), viii.

72. Mary Rowlandson's captivity narrative continued to be reprinted all through the 1780s, 1790s, and well into the nineteenth century. Hubbard, too, remained popular, and most early nineteenth-century editions of his history included the 1775 Boston preface. A "memory book," printed in Philadelphia in 1795, included fights from King Philip's War among its lists of important events that form the national heritage (James Hardie, *The American*

Remembrancer, and Universal Tablet of Memory [Philadelphia: Thomas Dobson, 1795], 146, 149). By 1804 one of those fights, at least, had been recast; a schoolbook history of New England that told the story of the Great Swamp fight told it as a tragedy, and expressed sympathy for the Indians who died there (Jedidiah Morse, *A Compendious History of New England, designed for Schools and Private Families* [Charlestown, Mass.: Samuel Etheridge, 1804], 249–64).

73. Quoted in Colin G. Calloway, *The American Revolution in Indian Country: Crisis and Diversity in Native American Communities* (Cambridge: Cambridge University Press, 1995), 285–87. See also Calloway, "New England Algonkians in the American Revolution," in *Algonkians of New England*, 51–62; Gregory Evans Dowd, *A Spirited Resistance: The North American Indian Struggle for Unity, 1745–1815* (Baltimore: The Johns Hopkins University Press, 1992); Paul Brodeur, *Restitution: The Land Claims of the Mashpee, Passamaquoddy, and Penobscot Indians of New England* (Boston: Northeastern University Press, 1985), 15–16, 76.

74. J. Hector St. John Crèvecoeur, *Letters from an American Farmer* (London, 1782; reprint, New York: Duffield & Company, 1908), 54, 148–55. Crèvecoeur was not the first to celebrate the Indian Bible as an American monument. In 1691, in his eulogy for John Eliot, Cotton Mather had written, "Behold ye Americans, the greatest honour that ever you were partakers of! This Bible was printed here at our Cambridge; and it is the only Bible that ever was printed in all America, from the very foundation of the World" (*The Life and Death of . . . Eliot*, 87–88).

75. *Old Light on Separate Ways*, 61–62, 88–89, 91. Fish recorded, for instance: "Octr. 2d. 1769 . . . The School kept, but poorly attended, by Children—but *one* Schollar to day, and but About ½ Dozn. a Day last Week. The Indians Seem Stupidly to Neglect and Despise the Privilege" (61).

76. For an important and useful discussion of commemoration and public memory see John Bodnar, *Remaking America: Public Memory, Commemoration, and Patriotism in the Twentieth Century* (Princeton, N.J.: Princeton University Press, 1992), especially the prologue, for its discussion of the debate over the Vietnam Veterans Memorial in Washington, D.C. As Bodnar argues, "The shaping of a past worthy of public commemoration in the present is contested and involves a struggle for supremacy between advocates of various political ideas and sentiments" (13).

77. Quoted in William Simmons, *Spirit of the New England Tribes: Indian History and Folklore, 1620–1984* (Hanover, N.H.: University Press of New England, 1986), 141–42.

Chapter 8 · THE CURSE OF METAMORA

1. John Augustus Stone, "Metamora; or, the Last of the Wampanoags: An Indian Tragedy in Five Acts as played by Edwin Forrest," in *Metamora and Other Plays*, ed. Eugene R. Page (Princeton, N.J.: Princeton University Press, 1941), 40. *Mourning Courier* and *New York Enquirer*, December 16, 1829. The opening performance was filled to capacity—even standing room was filled. For other reviews of this performance see *New York Evening Journal*, December 16, 1829, and the *New-York Mirror* and *Ladies' Literary Gazette*, December 29, 1829.

2. Stone, "Metamora," 22, 20, 21, 30.

3. Gabriel Harrison, *Edwin Forrest: The Actor and the Man* (Brooklyn, N.Y., 1889), 39.

4. For the text of Jackson's address see Andrew Jackson to the Speaker of the House, December 15, 1829, in James D. Richardson, ed., *A Compilation of the Messages and Papers of*

the Presidents (New York: Bureau of National Literature, Inc., 1897), 3:1026. On Indian removal see Ronald N. Satz, *American Indian Policy in the Jacksonian Era* (Lincoln: University of Nebraska Press, 1975); William McLoughlin, *Cherokee Renascence in the New Republic* (Princeton, N.J.: Princeton University Press, 1986); Michael Paul Rogin, *Fathers and Children: Andrew Jackson and the Subjugation of the American Indian* (New York: Alfred A. Knopf, 1975); Francis Paul Prucha, *American Indian Policy in the Formative Years* (Cambridge, Mass.: Harvard University Press, 1970); and Reginald Horsman, *The Origins of Indian Removal: 1815–1824* (East Lansing: Michigan State University Press, 1970).

5. Other scholars have noticed the coincidence of *Metamora*'s debut and Jackson's endorsement of Indian removal, most importantly B. Donald Grose, "Edwin Forrest, *Metamora*, and the Indian Removal Act of 1830," *Theater Journal* 37 (1985): 181–91; and Jeffrey D. Mason, "The Politics of *Metamora*," in *The Performance of Power: Theatrical Discourse and Politics*, ed. Sue-Ellen Chase and Janelle Reinelt (Iowa City: University of Iowa Press, 1991).

6. Werner Sollors has argued that the "curses" of dying Indians such as Metamora were ultimately blessings, exonerating white Americans for their treatment of the Indians and urging them forth into a new nation. See Werner Sollors, *Beyond Ethnicity: Consent and Descent in American Culture* (New York: Oxford University Press, 1986), 119–25. As Sollors writes, "Whether it appears as a curse, a blessing, or a projection of pure Christian conduct, the Indian speech functions as the departing chieftain's last will and testament to his paleface successors and resembles a parent's last wish for his child" (123). While Sollors' explanation is suggestive, it fails to adequately consider the complexity of Americans' attitudes toward Indian removal.

7. Church, *Entertaining History,* 125–26. Mather, *Brief History,* 195.

8. Biographies of Forrest include Harrison, *Edwin Forrest*; Montrose Moses, *The Fabulous Forrest: The Record of an American Actor* (Boston: Little, Brown, & Company, 1929); William Alger, *The Life of Edwin Forrest, the American Tragedian* (Philadelphia: J. B. Lippincott, 1877); and, more recently, Richard Moody, *Edwin Forrest: First Star of the American Stage* (New York: Alfred A. Knopf, 1960). Forrest's scandalous divorce is chronicled in *The Forrest Divorce Case* (Boston, 1852).

9. Advertised in the *Critic,* November 28, 1828. On the "search of a national drama" see David Grimsted, *Melodrama Unveiled: American Theater and Culture, 1800–1850* (Chicago: University of Chicago Press, 1968), ch. 7. Forrest's prize may have been inspired in part by George Custis's 1827 *Indian Prophecy.* See Murray H. Nelligan, "American Nationalism on the Stage: The Plays of George Washington Parke Custis (1781–1857)," *Virginia Magazine of History and Biography* 58 (July 1950): 299–324.

10. Beyond the initial prize money, Stone benefited little from the success of his play. He killed himself five years after its debut. Forrest paid for a monument at his graveside that reads, "In memory of the Author of 'Metamora,' by His Friend, E. Forrest" (James Rees, *Life of Edwin Forrest* [Philadelphia, 1874], 98). Stone's passing was wryly noted by Charles Congdon, who found his chief work uninspired, to say the least: "Mr. Stone did what he could to atone for the injury he inflicted upon the world by the production of this play . . . he drowned himself on 1 June 1834, in the Schuylkill River. We will accept his presumptive apology" (quoted in Dennis P. Walsh, "Many Metamoras: An Indian Drama in the Old Northwest," *Old Northwest* 12 [1986]: 466).

11. On Forrest's success with *Metamora* see Richard Moody, *America Takes the Stage: Romanticism in American Drama and Theater, 1750–1900* (Bloomington: Indiana University

Press, 1955), 93, 96; Moody, *Edwin Forrest,* 99. A twelve-day schedule in St. Louis, for example, brought a record profit of $2,157.00. Receipts for Forrest's opening night in Mobile performing *Othello* were $528.50. Subsequent performances were as follows: *Macbeth,* $330.50; *King Lear,* $324.50; *Metamora,* $656.00; *Damon,* $319.75; and *Richard III,* $448.00. (Noah Miller Ludlow, *Dramatic Life as I Found It* [St. Louis: G. I. Jones, 1880], 559). On the popularity of Shakespeare in America see Lawrence Levine, *Highbrow, Lowbrow: The Emergence of Cultural Hierarchy in America* (Cambridge, Mass.: Harvard University Press, 1988), 11–82. Some scholars have argued that Forrest's success in Shakespearean roles was largely because they were "extensions of his stage Indian, Metamora transplanted to another time and place, but still the proud, doomed individual" (Grose, "Edwin Forrest," 185). Finally, see Eugene R. Page, "Introduction," *Metamora,* 4.

12. Indian plays had been written and performed in America since the late seventeenth century but only became widely popular in the 1830s and 1840s. *Metamora* is often considered the catalyst for this development, since it led to copycat plays "from which," as Laurence Hutton put it, "theatergoers throughout the country suffered between the years 1830 and 1840" (Laurence Hutton, *Curiosities of the American Stage* [New York: Harper & Brothers, 1891], 13). On Indian drama see Rosemarie K. Bank, "Staging the 'Native': Making History in American Theater Culture, 1828, 1838," *Theater Journal* 45 (1993): 461–86; Marilyn J. Anderson, "The Image of the Indian in American Drama During the Jacksonian Era, 1829–1845," *Journal of American Culture* 1 (1978): 800–810; Don B. Wilmeth, "Noble or Ruthless Savage?: The American Indian on Stage and in the Drama," *Journal of American Drama and Theater* 1 (1989): 39–78; Richard E. Amacher, "Behind the Curtain with the Noble Savage: Stage Management of Indian Plays, 1825–1860," *Theater Survey* 7 (1966): 101–14; Moody, *America Takes the Stage,* 78–109; Eugene H. Jones, *Native Americans as Shown on the Stage, 1753–1916* (Metuchen, N.J.: The Scarecrow Press, 1988). For a review of this scholarship see Flynn, "Academics on the Trail of the Stage Indian," *Studies in American Literature* 2 (1987): 1–16. On *Metamora*'s place in early nineteenth-century melodrama see, for instance, Grimsted, *Melodrama Unveiled,* 216–18. On *Metamora* and romanticism see Paul Ronald Cox, "The Characterization of the American Indian in American Indian Plays, 1800–1860 as a Reflection of the American Romantic Movement" (Ph.D. diss., New York University, 1970).

13. Quoted in Hutton, *Curiosities of the American Stage,* 18.

14. Walsh, "Many Metamoras," 459. See Frank R. Abate, ed., *Omni Gazetteer of the United States of America,* 11 vols. (Detroit: Omnigraphics, 1991).

15. My thanks to Joanne Chaison of the American Antiquarian Society for pointing me to the King Philip nursery rhyme.

16. Quoted in Sherry Sullivan, "Indians in American Fiction, 1820–1850: An Ethnohistorical Perspective," *Clio* 15 (1986): 244–45.

17. Joseph Sabin, comp., *Catalogue of the Library of Edwin Forrest* (Philadelphia, 1863). "Metamora Wardrobe and Properties" is Item #72.

18. Sabin, *Catalogue,* 52. James Fenimore Cooper, *The Wept of Wish-ton-Wish* (Philadelphia, 1829). As Cooper wrote in a letter to Rufus Wilmot Griswold in 1844, "Wish-ton-Wish appeared in 1829. It did not succeed" (James Franklin Beard, ed., *The Letters and Journals of James Fenimore Cooper* [Cambridge, Mass.: Harvard University Press, 1960–68], 4:461). Nonetheless, the dramatic version of the novel, which bears little relation to it (see *The Wept of the Wish-ton-Wish. A Drama in Two Acts. From J. Fennimore [sic] Cooper's Celebrated Novel of the Same Name. As performed at all the Principal Theatres in the United States* [New York:

Samuel French, n.d.]), was widely performed (e.g., see playbills in the Crawford Theatre Collection, Yale University, Box 12, Folder 70, Box 27, Folder 206). See also Constance Rourke, *American Humor: A Study of the National Character* (New York: Harcourt, Brace, & Company, 1931), 114.

19. Forrest owned Irving's essay in a multivolume edition of his *Sketchbook* (Sabin, *Catalogue*, 54).

20. Metamora Clippings File, Harvard Theatre Collection, Harvard University; Edwin Forrest Poster Box, Harvard Theatre Collection, Harvard University.

21. Washington Irving, "Philip of Pokanoket," in *The Works of Washington Irving. v. 2. The Sketchbook* (New York: George Putnam, 1851), 364, 372. Irving's Philip was "a patriot attached to his native soil—a prince true to his subjects, and indignant of their wrongs—a soldier, daring in battle, firm in adversity, patient of fatigue, of hunger, of every variety of bodily suffering, and ready to perish in the cause he had espoused" (382–83).

22. William Hubbard, *A narrative of the Indian wars in New-England . . .* (Boston: Printed and sold by John Boyle, 1775), viii.

23. Richard Slotkin, however, has argued that "the emergence of the Indian as a model for an American heroism and the tendency of writers to set this American-model hero against the British model" has its roots in the French and Indian War (*Regeneration through Violence: The Mythology of the American Frontier, 1600–1860* [Middletown, Conn.: Wesleyan University Press, 1973], 223).

24. Stone, "Metamora," 36.

25. *North American Review* 33 (1831): 407–49.

26. Sabin, *Catalogue*, 42, 48. See the unfinished poem "Oliver Newman, A New-England Tale" in Robert Southey, *The Poetical Works of Robert Southey*, vol. 5 (Boston: Houghton, Osgood, 1880), 263–358. See also Albert Keiser, *The Indian in American Literature* (New York: Oxford University Press, 1933), 38–44. It is possible that Southey never finished his King Philip's War poem because of the bad advance reaction in the States. When rumors spread that the famed British poet laureat was planning to write an epic poem about Philip, at least one American was outraged at the prospect of an Englishman writing on this very American subject. "It would be strange, indeed," an irate reader wrote to the *New York Literary Magazine*, "when the people of Great Britain, even those who are the best informed on other important subjects, are so extremely ignorant of this country, of its character, manners, and government, and in many instances even of its geographical divisions, if they should understand the Indian character. We know of no subject that could occupy the attention and talents of a literary stranger, in which he would be less likely to succeed, than that which Mr. Southey is said to have chosen" (Dr. Robert Jarvis, "Southey's New Poem," *New York Literary Magazine* 3 [May 15, 1820]: 54; see also pp. 55–56).

27. James Eastburn [and Robert Charles Sands], *Yamoyden, A Tale of the Wars of King Philip: In Six Cantos* (New York: Clayton & Kingsland, Printers, 1820), 1.

28. Sabin, *Catalogue*, 80. Forrest later obtained an 1855 edition of Cotton Mather's *Magnalia Christi Americana* (ibid., 87).

29. Branford Swan, *An Indian's an Indian, or the Several Sources of Paul Revere's Engraved Portrait of King Philip* (Providence: Rhode Island Society of Colonial Wars, 1959).

30. The text of the epilogue is reprinted in the *New-York Mirror,* and *Ladies' Literary Gazette,* December 29, 1829.

31. Quoted in Jeffrey D. Mason, "The Politics of *Metamora*," 99. Forrest's political rhetoric was not always limited to the cultural sphere; in 1838 he considered running for Congress, after an enthusiastic reception to his Independence Day address. See Edwin Forrest, *Oration Delivered at the Democratic Republican Convention . . . Fourth July 1838* (New York: 1838).

32. Ralph Waldo Emerson, *The American Scholar, an Address Delivered . . . 1837* (New York: The Laurentian Press, 1901).

33. *Albion*, September 2, 1848, quoted in Barnard Hewitt, *Theater USA* (New York: McGraw-Hill, 1959), 109. Emphasis mine.

34. Moody, *Edwin Forrest*, 220.

35. See *Account of the Terrific and Fatal Riot at the New-York Astor Place Opera House* (New York: 1849) and Richard Moody, *The Astor Place Riot* (Bloomington: Indiana University Press, 1958). On Forrest vs. Macready, American vs. European, see Grimsted, *Melodrama Unveiled*, 68–75; Levine, *Highbrow, Lowbrow*, 63–68.

36. Quoted in Levine, *Highbrow, Lowbrow*, 66.

37. Richard Moody writes, "In physical proportions Metamora was the model for all later Indians in painting and sculpture. He was the embodiment of all those qualities that today are immediately brought to mind by the mention of the 'noble red man' " (Moody, *America Takes the Stage*, 94). Richard Slotkin and James Folsom briefly allude to this transformation in *So Dreadfull a Judgment: Puritan Responses to King Philip's War, 1676–1677* (Middletown, Conn.: Wesleyan University Press, 1978), 42–43. Curiously, Forrest was, according to Moody, "the only actor who ever gained much distinction from acting the noble red man" (Moody, *America Takes the Stage*, 96). On the broader phenomenon of "playing Indian" see Philip Deloria's brilliant and important "Playing Indian: Otherness and Authenticity in the Assumption of American Indian Identity" (Ph.D. diss., Yale University, 1994).

38. As Brian Dippie has remarked, "The Indian, as the First American, was necessary to any such attempt at self-definition. He *was* the American past" (Dippie, *The Vanishing American: White Attitudes and U.S. Indian Policy* [Middletown, Conn.: Wesleyan University Press, 1972], 16).

39. *Albion*, September 2, 1848. The *New-York Mirror*, December 14, 1833.

40. *New York Morning Herald*, December 28, 1837, quoted in Mason, "Politics of *Metamora*," 104–05.

41. Alger, *Life of Edwin Forrest*, 238–40.

42. Ibid.

43. Harrison, *Edwin Forrest*, 37.

44. Moody, *Edwin Forrest*, 342.

45. Alger, *Life of Edwin Forrest*, 126–27, 137–39. Forrest also considered Metamora his finest character (untitled Philadelphia newspaper clipping, 1867, Edwin Forrest Clippings File, Scrapbook, Harvard Theatre Collection, Harvard University).

46. Ibid.

47. A rich literature on American masculinity has recently emerged, much of it a departure from earlier, important work by Ann Douglas, *The Feminization of American Culture* (New York: Alfred A. Knopf, 1977). See E. Anthony Rotundo, *American Manhood: Transformations in Masculinity from the Revolution to the Modern Era* (New York: Basic Books, 1993);

Michael Kimmel, *Manhood in America: A Cultural History* (New York: The Free Press, 1996); and Gail Bederman, *Manliness and Civilization: A Cultural History of Gender and Race in the United States, 1880–1917* (Chicago: The University of Chicago Press, 1995).

48. Irving, "Philip of Pokanoket," 363–64.

49. Others have argued that Forrest's performance as Metamora was specifically enacting a Jacksonian ideal of individualism (Eric Ray Marshall, "Playwriting Contests and Jacksonian Democracy, 1829–1841" [Ph.D. diss., University of Southern California, 1983], 188–96; see also 137–38, 141, 145–49).

50. See Sullivan on "Americanization" of the Indian ("Indians in American Fiction," 239–57). David Grimsted points out that early nineteenth-century critics looking for a distinctive American literature argued that in drama "the first essential" was "nationality" (*Melodrama Unveiled*, 138).

51. Increase Mather, *The Necessity of Reformation* (Boston, 1679), 5.

52. *American Quarterly Review* 8 (1830): 145.

53. John Gorham Palfrey. "Review of Yamoyden," *North American Review* 12 (1821): 480–88. Palfrey wrote,

> in this particular instance, where the contest was equally on both sides for existence, it strikes us as no better than sentimentality to represent [the English colonists] as remorseless oppressors, and the other party as cruelly wronged. . . . Politically speaking, Philip had perhaps a right to attempt to rid the country of his English neighbors; but, politically speaking, they had an equal right to keep their ground, if they could.

Palfrey cited Josiah Winslow (who had claimed, "I think I can clearly say, that before these present troubles broke out, the English did not possess. . . . but what was fairly obtained by honest purchase . . .") approvingly and argued that Western ideas of just war cannot be used to evaluate King Philip's War. "It was a conflict in which the existence of one party depended on the destruction of the other. The Indians, had they known how to use it, had an overwhelming superiority of force; and though there are sentiments of humanity which under all circumstances generous minds respect, yet in the contest with such an enemy,—so wanton and so impracticable,—Grotius and Vattel lose their authority."

Palfrey's lament about the historical inaccuracy of representing Philip as a hero did not go entirely unheeded. In 1834 a writer for the *Western Monthly Magazine* prefaced an article about Philip by declaring, "It is not my intention to inflict upon the reader a fictitious tale of Indian cruelties. I am aware that for a few years past the press has been prolific, in publications illustrative of Indian life and character; that the public taste has become in a degree satiated with this kind of reading." Instead, this writer offered mixed praise. Philip, he argued,

> was brave, artful and ambitious; his savage nature by the treachery and encroachments of the whites, had been wrought up to the highest pitch of relentless ferocity; and he engaged in this christian war of extermination, with the unalterable purpose of driving the intruders from his dominions, or of dying in the effort. And though he proved unsuccessful, yet the talents, the prowess and the address displayed by him in this bloody war, entitle him to a place among the first captains of past time (R. H., "King Philip, Or the Tradition of Manardan's Rock," *The Western Monthly Magazine* II [March 1834]: 140–44).

54. Alger, *Life of Edwin Forrest*, 240.

55. *New York Morning Herald,* December 28, 1837, quoted in Mason, "Politics of *Metamora,*" 105.

56. James Murdock, *The Stage, or Recollections of Actors and Acting from an Experience of Fifty Years* (Philadelphia: J. M. Stoddard & Company, 1880), 298–300.

57. Quoted in Moses, *The Fabulous Forrest,* 332–33.

58. Murdock, *The Stage,* 298–300.

59. George E. Foster, *Se-Quo-Yah, The American Cadmus and Modern Moses* (Philadelphia, 1885); and Willard Walker, "Early History of the Cherokee Syllabary," *Ethnohistory* 40 (1993): 70–94.

60. [Jeremiah Evarts], *Essays on the Present Crisis in the Condition of the American Indians* (Boston: Perkins & Marvin, 1829), 6.

61. *Cherokee Nation v. Georgia,* 30 U.S. 1. For review and analysis of this case see G. Edward White, *The Marshall Court and Cultural Change, 1815–35* (New York: Macmillan Publishing Company, 1988), 703–40; and Priscilla Wald, "Terms of Assimilation: Legislating Subjectivity in the Emerging Nation," in *Cultures of United States Imperialism,* ed. Amy Kaplan and Donald E. Pease (Durham, N.C.: Duke University Press, 1993), 59–84.

62. Child had written an Indian novel, *Hobomok,* in 1824, after reading Palfrey's review of *Yamoyden.* On the origins of Hobomok see Carolyn L. Karcher's Introduction to Lydia Maria Child, *Hobomok and Other Writings on Indians* (New Brunswick, N.J.: Rutgers University Press, 1986). Child went on to do much more Indian reform work. See, for example, her *An Appeal for the Indians* (New York, 1868). On Child's place in the larger reform movement see Robert Winston Mardock, *The Reformers and the American Indians* (Columbia: University of Missouri Press, 1971).

63. Lydia Maria Child, *The First Settlers of New England or Conquest of the Pequods, Narragansets, and Pokanokets* (Boston, for the author by Monroe and Francis, 1829), 131, 155–56, 170.

64. Sarah Savage, *Life of Philip the Indian Chief* (Salem, Mass., 1827), 39, 58.

65. Edward Everett, *An address delivered at Bloody Brook, in South Deerfield, September 30, 1835, in Commemoration of the fall of the 'Flower of Essex,' at that spot, in King Philip's War* (Boston: Russell, Shattuck, & Williams, 1835), 8, 10–11. Everett's opposition to Indian removal is best summarized in his essay "The Cherokee Case," *North American Review* 33 (1831): 136–53.

66. *The Massachusetts Spy,* October 12, 1831. My thanks to Kenneth Moynihan for pointing me to this event.

67. Quoted in Dippie, *Vanishing American,* 16–17.

68. Leslie J. Cappon, ed., *The Adams-Jefferson Letters* (Chapel Hill: University of North Carolina Press, 1959), 2:310–11. Or, as Charles Sprague proclaimed from Boston in 1825, "Here they warred; the echoing whoop, the bloody grapple, the defying death-song, all were here" (quoted in Dippie, *Vanishing American,* 14–15).

69. Joseph Story, *The Miscellaneous Writings, Literary, Critical, Juridical, and Political, of Joseph Story* (Boston: James Munroe & Company, 1835), 78–79. Emphasis mine.

70. John Marshall to Joseph Story, October 29, 1828, cited in White, *The Marshall Court,* 713–14.

71. John Marshall, *A History of the Colonies Planted by the English on the Continent of North America* (Philadelphia, 1824), 166–67.

72. [Evarts], *Essays,* 101.

73. Andrew Jackson, Second Annual Address, December 6, 1830, in *Papers of the Presidents* 3:1084.

74. Quoted in Satz, *American Indian Policy in the Jacksonian Era,* 19.

75. *Papers of the Presidents* 3:1020.

76. McLoughlin, *Cherokee Renascence,* 436–37.

77. Andrew Jackson, Second Annual Address, December 6, 1830.

78. Everett, *An address delivered at Bloody Brook,* 8, 10–11.

79. Stone, "Metamora," 38–40.

80. *American Quarterly Review* 8 (1830): 145.

81. Robert F. Berkhofer, Jr., *The White Man's Indian: Images of the American Indian from Columbus to the Present* (New York: Vintage Books, 1979), 88.

82. Eastburn and Sands, *Yamoyden,* 4.

83. John Greenleaf Whittier, "Metacom," *Ladies Magazine* 3 (1830): 58.

84. Sollors, *Beyond Ethnicity,* 126.

85. Quoted in Moses, *The Fabulous Forrest,* 332–33.

86. Dippie, *Vanishing Indian,* 71. Or, as Robert Berkhofer has argued, "No matter how inapplicable in this case, traditional Indian imagery rationalized the needs of the United States in the continued push of Native Americans from lands desired by White" (Berkhofer, *White Man's Indian,* 160).

87. *Boston Morning Post,* November 8, 1833. This account is briefly discussed in Bank, "Staging the 'Native,' " 481.

88. *Boston Morning Post,* November 8, 1833.

89. Alger, *Life of Edwin Forrest,* 240.

90. Ibid. Indian attendance was an enhancement of the performance; in a sense, they were a part of it, and could be a tremendous draw, helping fill the house with curious onlookers. In 1834, the Sauk chief Black Hawk even attended a one-night-only performance of a play about himself, *Black Hawk,* at the Bowery Theater in New York. But, just two years after his capture by Jackson's forces, *Black Hawk,* the play, wasn't the performance; Black Hawk, the man, was (Jones, *Native Americans as Shown on the Stage,* 86).

91. *Boston Morning Post,* November 8, 1833.

92. Story, *Miscellaneous Writings,* 79.

93. Quoted in Hewitt, *Theater USA,* 107–8.

94. Rourke, *American Humor,* 123.

95. Quoted in Alger, *Life of Edwin Forrest,* 476–77.

96. *Papers of the Presidents* 3:1020.

97. On the Penobscot claims and controversies of 1833 see Paul Brodeur, *Restitution: The Land Claims of the Mashpee, Passamaquoddy, and Penobscot Indians of New England* (Boston: Northeastern University Press, 1985), 78. On the Mashpee see Brodeur, *Restitution,* 16–19; Donald M. Nielsen, "The Mashpee Indian Revolt of 1833," *NEQ* 58 (1985): 400–420; Francis G. Hutchins, *Mashpee: The Story of Cape Cod's Indian Town* (West Franklin, N.H.: Amarta Press, 1979), 95–112; Jack Campisi, *The Mashpee Indians: Tribe on Trial* (Syracuse, N.Y.: Syra-

cuse University Press, 1991), 101–6; Barry O'Connell, ed., *On Our Own Ground: The Writings of William Apess, A Pequot* (Amherst: University of Massachusetts Press, 1992).

98. Massachusetts Senate Document 1833, Doc. 14:5; quoted in Laurie Weinstein, "We're Still Living on Our Traditional Homeland: The Wampanoag Legacy in New England," in *Strategies for Survival: American Indians in the Eastern United States,* ed. Frank W. Porter III (New York: Greenwood Press, 1986), 93.

99. *Boston Advocate,* September 11, 1833, quoted in Apess, *On Our Own Ground,* 202. Hallett employed this rhetorical device on several other occasions as well: "We have had an overflow of sensibility in this quarter toward the Cherokees, and there is now an opportunity of showing to the world whether the people of Massachusetts can exercise more justice and less cupidity toward their own Indians than the Georgians have toward the Cherokees" (August 5, 1833, quoted in Apess, *On Our Own Ground,* 196).

100. Apess, *On Our Own Ground,* 167.

101. Quoted in Brodeur, *Restitution,* 18.

102. Apess, *On Our Own Ground,* 177, 205.

103. Nielsen, "The Mashpee Indian Revolt," 416.

104. Forrest performed *Metamora* at the Tremont on November 3, 1837 (Metamora Clippings File, Harvard Theatre Collection, Houghton Library, Harvard University), and a poster from the Boston Academy of Music in 1861 noted that Forrest was then giving "his 22nd Appearance in Boston in five years," suggesting that he visited the city with great frequency (Edwin Forrest Poster Collection, Harvard Theatre Collection, Harvard University).

105. Apess, *Eulogy on King Philip* (Boston, 1836), 6, 47. Karin M. Tiro has argued that Apess's lecturing and publishing were intricately related to his Methodism ("Denominated 'SAVAGE': Methodism, Writing, and Identity in the Works of William Apess, A Pequot," *AQ* 48 [1996]: 653–79).

106. Apess, *On Our Own Ground,* 51.

107. Apess, *Eulogy,* 6, 47, 14. Apess had also read Mary Rowlandson and Daniel Gookin (Tiro, "Denominated 'SAVAGE,' " 664).

108. Ibid.

109. Whittier, "Metacom."

110. Stone, "Metamora," 25.

111. Tompson, *New-England's Crisis,* 218.

112. Apess, *Eulogy,* 27–28. See also Philip's speeches in *Yamoyden,* 28–36, 39–44. A speech attributed to Philip by some historians (Bourne, *Red King's Rebellion,* 107), is also fictitious. This speech, which ends with the oft-quoted line, "I will not die until I have no country," is actually a rather liberal Revolutionary-era updating of John Easton's conversation with Philip and his counselors in June 1675. The Eastern dialogue was first modernized (and embellished) by Theodore Foster (c. 1770) and later taken as literal fact by Samuel Greene Arnold (*History of the State of Rhode Island* [NY; 1859–60], 1:394–5).

113. Apess, *Eulogy,* 48.

114. *Boston Daily Evening Transcript,* January 6, 1836.

115. John Brougham, *Metamora; or, the Last of the Pollywogs* (New York: Samuel French, n.d.), 17–18. See Moody, *America Takes the Stage,* 106–7, and Sollors, *Beyond Ethnicity,* 133–41.

116. Brougham, *Metamora,* 7, 15–16. In one telling scene, Metamora's wife (here called "Tapiokee") sings to her infant,

O, slumber, my pappose! thy sire is not white;
And that injures your prospects a very dear sight;
For the hills, and the dales, and the valleys you see,
They all were purloined, my dear pappoose, from thee.

117. George S. Boutwell, *Address of Governor Boutwell at the dedication of the monument to the memory of Capt. Wadsworth, at Sudbury Mass., Nov. 23, 1852* (Boston?: s.n., 1852?), 1–2, 8.

118. Nonetheless, interest in King Philip's War continued, albeit diminished. Several novels about the war were published in the latter half of the century, including Albert W. Aiken, *Metamora, the Forest King* (New York, 1870, 1885); Daniel Pierce Thompson, *The Doomed Chief; or, Two Hundred Years Ago* (Philadelphia, 1860) and G. H. Hollister, *Mount Hope; or Philip, King of the Wampanoags, an Historical Romance* (New York, 1851). Robert B. Caverly ("Poet and Historian") also published a play about the war in 1884: *King Philip (N.E.) An Historical Drama* (Boston, 1884), which was followed a decade later by Alfred Antoline Furmar's five-act *Philip of Pokanoket* (New York, 1894).

119. Undated Washington, D.C., news clipping (c. 1867), Scrapbook, Edwin Forrest Clippings File, Harvard Theatre Collection, Harvard University.

120. *New York Times,* October 31, 1877.

121. Buffalo Bill himself even showed up at one performance (*New York Times,* January 4, 1887). On the decline of Indian plays more broadly see Kathleen A. Mulvey, "The Growth, Development, and Decline of the Popularity of American Indian Plays before the Civil War" (Ph.D. diss., New York University, 1978).

122. My thanks to Ed Gray for his assistance on this subject. See also Edward Gray, "Indian Language in Anglo-American Thought, 1550–1820" (Ph.D. diss., Brown University, 1996).

123. Robert Caverly, *King Philip. An Historical Drama* (Boston: published by the author, 1884), Act I, Scene I; Act II, Scene III.

124. For accounts of the capture of the "distinguished brave of the Seminole tribe" who was called "King Philip" during the Seminole wars see *Niles National Register,* August 4, 1838, and *Army and Navy Chronicle,* July 6, 1837.

125. Ann McMullen (Ph.D. diss., Brown University, forthcoming).

126. *Narragansett Dawn* 1 (November 1935): 172.

Epilogue • The Rock

1. Edmund B. Delabarre, "The Inscribed Rocks of Narragansett Bay," *Rhode Island Historical Society Collections* 13 (1920): 1–28. I thank Reinhard Battcher of the Bristol Historical Society for giving me flawless directions for finding the rock.

2. Ibid., 9–21. There is considerable evidence that Algonquians in New England traditionally used rocks as sacred and memorial cites, sometimes called "Sacrifice Rocks" (Constance Crosby, "The Algonkian Spiritual Landscape," in *Algonkians of New England: Past and Present,* ed. Peter Benes [Boston: Boston University, 1993], 38–41).

3. On the Cherokee syllabary see Willard Walker and James Sarbaugh, "The Early History of the Cherokee Syllabary," *Ethnohistory* 40 (1993): 70–94.

4. Willard Walker, personal communication, December 4, 1994.

5. Cotton Mather, *The Life and Death of the Renown'd Mr. John Eliot* (London, 1691), 73. The history of the rock is best detailed in Edmund Delabarre, "Early Interest in Dighton Rock," *Publications of the Colonial Society of Massachusetts* 18 (1916): 235–99.

6. H. R. Schoolcraft, *Archives of Aboriginal Knowledge: Information Respecting the History, Condition, and Prospects of the Indian Tribes of the U.S.* (Philadelphia: Lippincott, Grang, & Company, 1854), 4:108–20.

7. Willard Walker, personal communication, December 4, 1994; Ann McMullen, personal communication, July 22, 1992.

8. Delabarre, "Inscribed Rocks," 22–24.

9. Eugene Vetromile claimed in 1866 that the Abenakis (also known as Penobscots) had their own hieroglyphic writing system, which they used to make carvings in rocks and on tree bark. Vetromile was clearly among those antiquarians obsessed with the search for Indian writing, and his claims are thus deeply suspect, but it is possible that they are based at least in part on fact and that there is some precedent in Penobscot culture for carving inscriptions on rocks (Vetromile, *The Abenakis and their History* [New York: J. B. Kirkner, 1866], 40–43).

10. Barry O'Connell, ed., *On Our Own Ground: The Writings of William Apess, A Pequot* (Amherst: University of Massachusetts Press, 1992), 177, 205. I would like to thank Ann Fabian for first suggesting that William Apess and the Mashpee Wampanoags might have been involved in carving the Mount Hope Rock inscription.

11. Delabarre, "Inscribed Rocks," 21–22.

12. William J. Miller, *Notes concerning the Wampanoag Tribe of Indians* (Providence: Signey S. Rider, 1880), 123.

13. Ebenezer W. Peirce, *Indian History, Biography, and Genealogy: Pertaining to the Good Sachem Massasoit of the Wampanoag Tribe, and His Descendants* (North Abington, Mass.: Zerviah Gould Mitchell, 1878), iii.

14. Josiah Winslow to Increase Mather, May 1, 1676, in Mather, *Brief History*, 2–3.

15. Peirce, *Indian History*, iii.

16. Ibid., 210–19.

17. On the anniversary see Robert A. Trennert, "The Indian Role in the 1876 Centennial Celebration," *AICRJ* 1 (1976): 7–13.

18. "King Philip's Day," *RIHSP* 6 (1875–76): 61, 62. Finally a member of the Committee of Arrangements read aloud a passage from a speech given by Lucis Barber in Simsbury, just a few months before, commemorating the bicentennial anniversary of the destruction of that town. Of Philip, Barber insisted, "*We* can afford to be just to his memory." See Lucis Barber, *The Burning of Simsbury: A Bi-Centennial Address* (Hartford, 1876). Other bicentennial addresses include Henry Morris, *Early History of Springfield. An Address delivered October 16, 1875, on the Two Hundredth Anniversary of the Burning of the Town by the Indians* (Springfield, Mass.: F. W. Morris, 1876).

19. "King Philip's Day," 54.

20. Paul R. Campbell and Glenn W. LaFantasie, "Scattered to the Winds of Heaven— Narragansett Indians 1676–1880," *Rhode Island History* 37 (1978): 67–83. See also Paul A. Robinson, "A Narragansett History from 1000 B.P. to the Present," in *Enduring Tradition*, 79–89.

21. Quoted in Robinson, "A Narragansett History," 87.

22. *Narragansett Dawn* 1 (September 1935): 109–11. *Narragansett Dawn* also printed Justice Joseph Story's Salem vanished-Indians speech ("there is something in their hearts which passes speech") almost word for word but retitled it "Fate of the Narragansetts" and claimed as its author "Eagle Eye" (Ernest Hazard). *Narragansett Dawn* 1 (September 1935): 107–8.

23. Everett Weeden (Tall Oak), personal communication, February 23, 1995. Weeden is a grandson of Red Wing. See also *Narragansett Dawn* 1 (September 1935): 109–11.

24. Ann McMullen, personal communication, August 17, 1992.

25. Ann McMullen, "What's Wrong with This Picture? Context, Conversion, Survival, and the Development of Regional Native Cultures and Pan-Indianism in Southeastern New England," in *Enduring Traditions: The Native Peoples of New England,* ed. Laurie Weinstein (Westport, Conn.: Bergin & Garvey, 1994), 138–44. On a Nipmuck community's efforts to maintain traditions see Diane Fisk Bray, "Change and Continuity of Spiritual Practice among the Chaubunagungamaug Nipmuck Indians of Webster, Massachusetts," in *Algonkians in New England,* 114–20. An intriguing consideration of an indigenous peoples' interest in documenting their past can be found in Joanne Rappaport, *The Politics of Memory: Native Historical Interpretation in the Colombian Andes* (Cambridge: Cambridge University Press, 1990).

26. Colman McCarthy, "The Narragansetts' Trail of Tears," *Washington Post,* September 15, 1985; Judith Gaines, "New England's Indians Strive to Rebuild Tribes; Goal Is to Reclaim Identity, Pride, Power," *Boston Globe,* April 16, 1989.

27. Nanepashemet, personal communication, February 20, 1995.

28. The SCW's mission was "to perpetuate the names, memory or deeds of those brave and courageous men, who, in military, naval or civil service, by their acts or counsel assisted in the establishment and continuance of the American colonies," but King Philip's War had always been the chief interest of the New England chapters of the society, and since about the turn of the century they had celebrated two holidays, commemorating the colonists' two greatest victories: August 12, Philip's death, and December 30, the Great Swamp fight. See The Society of Colonial Wars in the State of Rhode Island and Providence Plantations, *The First Record Book of the Society of Colonial Wars in the State of Rhode Island and Providence Plantations, 1897–1902* (Providence: Snow & Farnham, 1902); The Society of Colonial Wars in the State of Rhode Island and Providence Plantations, *The Second Record Book of the Society of Colonial Wars of Rhode Island and Providence Plantations, 1902–1914* (Providence: Standard Printing Co., 1914); The Society of Colonial Wars in the State of Rhode Island and Providence Plantations, *The Third Record Book of the Society* (Providence: E. L. Freeman Company, 1925). A sister organization, the Society of the Daughters of Colonial Wars in the Commonwealth of Massachusetts, was incorporated in 1921 (*Year Book and History. Society of the Daughters of Colonial Wars in the Commonwealth of Massachusetts, Inc.,* Publication 5 [1932]).

29. The best surveys of King Philip's War historical sites can be found in a multi-issue series in *Traveler's Record* 38 (1902–1903), nos. 8–14, and 39 (1903), nos. 1–6; and in Eric Schultz, *Discovering King Philip's War: A Traveler's Guide to the War that Shook New England,* unpublished manuscript.

30. David Arnold, "Native Americans Ponder Past, Future; Deer Island Deaths Marked in Ceremony," *Boston Globe,* October 31, 1991. See also Scott Allen, "Search for Indian Graves to Proceed on Deer Island," *Boston Globe,* October 1, 1993; Keith Regan, "Harbor Project Opposed; Indian Group Says Deer Island Sacred," *Boston Globe,* February 22, 1993; Michael Kenney, "An Island of Sad Memory for Indians," *Boston Globe,* February 19, 1993; "Indian

Group Retraces March," *Boston Globe,* August 31, 1992; Peter J. Howe, "MWRA Disturbing Graves, Say Indians," *Boston Globe,* June 17, 1992; Alan Lupo, "Deer Island Left to Its Ghosts," *Boston Globe,* January 1, 1992. As a result of the protests, the Massachusetts Water Resource Authority, which refuses to cancel construction, plans to build a public memorial site on the island (Len Cawley, Massachusetts Water Resource Authority, personal communication, February 21, 1995).

31. The Society of Colonial Wars in the State of Rhode Island and Providence Plantations, *A Record of the Ceremony and Oration on the Occasion of the Unveiling of the Monument Commemorating the Great Swamp Fight, December 19, 1675, in the Narragansett Country, Rhode Island* (Boston: Societies of Colonial Wars, 1906). The ceremonies resumed later in the day, under the cover of nearby Memorial Hall, where several additional speeches and addresses were delivered.

32. Delabarre, "Inscribed Rocks," 2.

33. John Christian Hopkins, "Tracing the Narragansett Legacy," *Norwich Bulletin,* October 7, 1993.

Acknowledgments

It must be said that I have spent long hours babbling about King Philip's War to more than a few weary listeners. Friends have listened patiently, colleagues have offered advice, and librarians have handed me wonderful, dusty books. To all I am deeply grateful.

I would like to thank, first of all, the friends whose care has sustained me: Benjamin Filene, Jane Levey, Rachel Seidman, and Wendy Weitzner. I have thanked them before, and surely I will thank them again. They have helped me to see sense where it is to be seen and to know nonsense for what it is. I'd have been blind without them. I thank them for each and every insight, right down to the last, furtive E-mail message, and for regularly luring me out of my study for road trips, gingersnaps, bad movies, and woodswalking with dogs. And, for wisdom and friendship and much, much more, I thank also Adrianna Alty, Heidi Ardizzone, Lee Busch, Andrea Clark, Elizabeth DeSombre, Charlotte Gill, Jennifer Hall, Jane Kamensky, Mary Renda, Nancy Rome, Kelly West Schlosser, Erik Seeman, and Rebecca Tannenbaum.

For teaching me the craft of history I thank John Demos, whose keen advice and kind words have contributed to this work beyond measure. I could have asked for no better mentor. Others, friends and colleagues alike, have read parts of this manuscript, in this and earlier forms, and their criticism has helped me immensely. For poring over these pages and telling it to me straight I thank Jean-Christophe Agnew, Jon Butler, Andrew Cayton, Duane Champagne, Nancy Cott, William Cronon, Michael Denning, John Farragher, Richard Fox, Karen Kupperman, Ken Lockridge, Daniel Mandell, E. Anthony Rotundo, Neal Salisbury, Bruce Schulman, Erik Seeman, Harry Stout, Fredrika Teute, Laurel Thatcher Ulrich, and Richard White, as well as the anonymous readers and seminar participants and brown-baggers who commented on parts of this work on earlier occasions, and the Americanist writing group at Harvard: Elizabeth Abrams, Steven Biel, James Cullen, Hildegard Hoeller, Kristin Hoganson, Allison Pingree, and Laura Saltz. Ann Fabian, Jane Levey, and James Merrell each gave the entire manuscript an especially close and perceptive reading. Colleagues at the University of California, San Diego, especially Michael Meranze and Rachel Klein, helped me to think about this project in the context of early American cultural history. And Jane Garrett at Knopf encouraged me to push on.

Several people have graciously shared their ideas with me regarding topics close to my own, including Hugh Amory, Rosemarie K. Bank, Cathy Corman, Philip Deloria, James Drake, Edward Gray, B. Donald Grose, J. Edward Hood, Jeffrey Mason, Ann McMullen, Jennifer Pulsipher, Eric Schultz, David Waldstreicher, and Willard Walker. In addition, I am extremely grateful to the late Nanepashemet at Plimouth Plantation, and to Everett Weeden (Tall Oak) and John Brown of Charlestown, Rhode Island, for beginning to educate me about contemporary views of King Philip's War within the New England Native American community.

I completed much of the work of this project during a year-long fellowship at the Charles Warren Center at Harvard University, where I learned a great deal from fellow fellows David Blight, Kathleen Dalton, Kristin Hoganson, Bruce Schulman, and Nina Silber. I thank them for all the wonderful talks over coffee and lunch and for putting up with my intrepid dog, Cooper, who poked around the halls. During those final months of writing, Cooper trudged into Harvard with me nearly every day, and, as a fixture in my office, served as my muse in her own irrepressible, tail-wagging way.

I am extremely grateful both to the Warren Center for the fellowship, and to my dean and department at Boston University for allowing me to accept it. I would never have been able to write this book without the generous support not only of the Warren Center but also of several archives, institutions, and foundations who funded my research at earlier stages: the American Antiquarian Society, the John Carter Brown Library, the Massachusetts Historical Society, the Pew Charitable Trusts, the Whitney Humanities Center at Yale University, and the Woodrow Wilson Foundation. Nor would the research have been as pleasurable without the wonderful staffs at the archives and libraries where I conducted research, including those at both Yale and Harvard.

I also thank my parents, Marjorie and Frank Lepore, to whom this book is dedicated. My father taught me to love words, my mother to love pictures. Together they have taught me to look wide at the world, and I only wish I could thank them better. Finally, I thank Timothy Robert Leek, for all those things that matter most.

Index

Page numbers in *italics* indicate illustrations.

A NOTE ABOUT THE AUTHOR

Jill Lepore was born in Worcester, Massachusetts, in 1966. She received her B.A. from Tufts University, M.A. from the University of Michigan, and Ph.D. from Yale University. She was Assistant Professor of History at the University of California, San Diego, 1995–96; a fellow at the Charles Warren Center, Harvard University, 1996–97; and Assistant Professor of History, Boston University, 1996–present. Her Ph.D. dissertation won the Ralph Henry Gabriel Dissertation Prize of the American Studies Association and the Charlotte W. Newcombe Dissertation Fellowship.

A NOTE ON THE TYPE

This book was set in a modern adaptation of a type designed by the first William Caslon (1692–1766). The Caslon face, an artistic, easily read type, has enjoyed more than two centuries of popularity in our own country. It is of interest to note that the first copies of the Declaration of Independence and the first paper currency distributed to the citizens of the newborn nation were printed in this typeface.

Composed by North Market Street Graphics,
Lancaster, Pennsylvania

Printed and bound by Quebecor Printing,
Martinsburg, West Virginia

Designed by Cassandra J. Pappas